JUDO TRAINING METHODS:

a sourcebook

PLATE 1. The Kodokan, Tokyo, Japan—World Mecca of Judo.

JUDO TRAINING METHODS:

a sourcebook

by
TAKAHIKO
ISHIKAWA
and
DONN F.
DRAEGER

*"following the principle of physical education
we will observe the rule that a moderate
exercise should come before a strenuous
exercise, as well as a symmetrical exercise
before an irregular exercise."*

Jigoro Kano

TUTTLE PUBLISHING
Boston • Rutland, Vermont • Tokyo

PLEASE NOTE THAT THE AUTHOR AND PUBLISHER OF THIS BOOK ARE **NOT RESPONSIBLE** IN ANY MANNER WHATSOEVER FOR ANY INJURY THAT MAY RESULT FROM PRACTICING THE TECHNIQUES AND/OR FOLLOWING THE INSTRUCTIONS GIVEN WITHIN. SINCE THE PHYSICAL ACTIVITIES DESCRIBED HEREIN MAY BE TOO STRENUOUS IN NATURE FOR SOME READERS TO ENGAGE IN SAFELY, IT IS ESSENTIAL THAT A PHYSICIAN BE CONSULTED PRIOR TO TRAINING.

First paperback edition published in 1999 by Tuttle Publishing, an imprint of Periplus Editions (HK) Ltd., with editorial offices at 153 Milk Street, Boston, Massachusetts, 02109.

ISBN 0-8048-3210-2
Library of Congress Card No. 61-5059

Distributed by:

USA
Tuttle Publishing
Distribution Center
Airport Industrial Park
364 Innovation Drive
North Clarendon, VT 05759-9436
Tel: (802) 773-8930
Tel: (800) 526-2778

Japan
Tuttle Shokai Ltd
1-21-13, Seki
Tama-ku, Kawasaki-shi
Kanagawa-ken 214-0022, Japan
Tel: (044) 833-0225
Fax: (044) 822-0413

Canada
Raincoast Books
8680 Cambie Street
Vancouver, British Columbia V6P 6M9
Tel: (604) 323-7100
Fax: (604) 323-2600

Southeast Asia
Berkeley Books Pte Ltd
5 Little Road #08-01
Singapore 536983
Tel: (65) 280-1330
Fax: (65) 280-6290

05 04 03 02 01 00 99 10 9 8 7 6 5 4 3 2 1

Printed in the United States of America

To
Henry A. Stone,
American pioneer in
kinesiology and
Kodokan Judo

Table of Contents

List of Plates

How To Use
This Book

*Knowledge is an excellent drug, but no drug is sufficiently
strong to preserve itself without alteration or corruption.*
Montaigne

THIS IS a book on general and specialized training methods for the Judo trainee and
instructor alike. It is intended to serve the major needs of the Judo exponent. As
a textbook, it is intended to be a suggestive guide for trainees, and does not replace the
necessity of a teacher, nor does it obviate the need of study and continued research on
the part of each instructor. However, it would hardly be fair to expect all that is known
about Judo training to be found between the covers of this text; yet that which is described
can be utilized in different ways.

You will notice that the book has been divided into two parts, Part I—Principles—and,
Part II—Practice. This division allows for two ways of reading the book. You can pick it
up and begin reading from cover to cover as you do most books. This method is indispensable for all Judo instructors, athletic coaches, trainers, etc. Or, you may ignore Part I
and concern yourself with the essentials of Part II. This method may be used by the
trainee, but sooner or later he will realize the necessity of reading Part I, which will
enhance his general understanding of training and provide guidance in applying the proven
methods of training.

When you come to utilize the contents of this book, there are four fundamental approaches. First, decide what training problems exist for you as a trainee or as an instructor. Then look for ways of solving these personal stumbling blocks by consulting the Table
of Contents and the Index. You perhaps will find a direct answer, or a lead to corrective
measures. Second, look up and check interesting practices that you have been employing
or are familiar with. Carefully check the performance as described and compare it to what
you understand to be the correct method. Evaluate any differences in performance and
judge what this new method can accomplish for your purposes. Third, decide what you
would like to improve in your learning or teaching. Begin this course to improvement by

finding new tools to accomplish this. This book lists various proven methods leading to training efficiency. Finally, as an instructor, improve your Dojo by offering a well-balanced, integrated training program which is progressive. A good Dojo is not just a hodgepodge of methods as described in this book, but represents intelligent planning and application.

This book is not offered as a "bible" of training, although to many it will be defended as such. Those who use this book and its methods will merely be supporting age-old traditional methods proven effective in making Judo excellence, but beyond that, they will also be pioneers; pioneers in the field of new scientific approaches to Judo training. You may not agree with every practice described herein, but whatever becomes useful to you may be good. It is urged that no one adopt any new practice blindly without having tried it for himself, simply because it is in this text. True, each method has been found to work, but many improvements can be made. The detail of each practice listed is not necessarily inflexible. Some readers may find adaptation to his particular circumstances will bring a more satisfactory result. Each user will be breathing new life into these methods, and thus bring about an important contribution of his own. The resourceful and alert trainee or instructor may be able to devise new practices which are better than anything described here. Judo is in need of better practice in the training vein...and the foundation for progress in any field of endeavor is research. Let this book be a challenge to you to improve not only your Judo, but the Judo training methods of the world.

Authors' Foreword

Custom is no small matter.
Plato

THE PHYSICAL and mental benefits provided by constant Judo exercise are many and varied. Within these dimensions, countless books describe the performance of the techniques of Judo, but none specifically are devoted to the general principles of training. Yet, it is necessary to distinguish training methods from actual technique. The dual object of this book is to categorically compile and describe some of the traditional Judo exercises and training methods which have produced outstanding Judo exponents and champions, and to sensibly combine other exercises, outside the normal Judo realm, with these traditional movements with a view toward perfecting the anatomy of training and increasing Judo efficiency by scientific methods.

Heretofore, all Judo exercises have been considered a more or less "dry" and uninteresting subject, having been empirical and casually recorded on the premise that Judo, idealistically, is a complete exercise in itself. The plain and simple facts are that neither excellence in Judo nor vibrant health can be nurtured without subsidiary exercise. The exercises described within these pages represent the product of a combined research period totaling about thirty years. The methods depicted are not exhaustive within their scope, but have been specially selected as those methods most adaptable to all persons practicing Judo and those non-Judo exponents interested in beneficial exercise to tone and maintain body health. All exercises are in concert with, and coterminous with Kodokan doctrine and are patterned under the well-known Judo slogan, "Maximum Efficiency" or "Best Use of Energy."

We are here concerned with the elements of physical Judo, especially the phases referred to as "contest" Judo preparation. This text includes a discussion of the value, compatibility, and necessity for weight training exercises in developing and maintaining body health in serious Judo study. The exercises were carefully selected, based on re-

13

search, and are clearly described to enhance correct performance. They have been somewhat scientifically arranged to provide necessary balance from a kinesiological standpoint.

No system is as good as it could be...this is a truism. In Judo, veneration for the past and conservatism, of which it is a product, has had its progress inhibited by sole adherence to traditional training methods. If current "old fashioned" methods are held to, with no variance, there is little chance for advancement in knowledge or ability. We do not suggest that this attenuated progress reflects discredit on the basic values of Judo, but rather that a more dynamic and imaginative approach to the methodology of Judo training be instituted. Training is improved, not by changing everything a Judo exponent does, but by changing very specific and relatively small details that may consume only a part of his time. In the main, the time-consuming tasks of training will remain.

Each practice described in this book is a tool...a tool for training. All trainees and instructors have various tools in their bag of tricks; some have more than others, and almost all could use a few more good substantial ones. The reliance upon bland generalities to mask ignorance of correct training methods is inexcusable. Likewise, the heavy utilization of tools that have become superseded has little or no merit. Perhaps no trainee or instructor is applying in every facet of his learning and teaching the optimum procedural level which is available. To improve upon this situation, it is not necessary to turn everything "topsy-turvy," or to discard. If we can just add one more method of direct value, this makes for improvement and progress.

All methods described in this text have been thoroughly studied, developed, and tested in serious Judo training. They have been discussed, compared, and used by the authors throughout the Orient, North, South, and Central America, and Europe. It is our firm conviction that these methods have contributed manifestly toward the general body excellence which produces championship caliber Judo, and the continued optimum level of physical and mental health of the advocates of these exercises.

Should this book contribute to general good health and physical fitness of Judo and non-Judo exponents alike, it will have served its intended purpose. It should be especially helpful to all Judo instructors, particularly those of Western Dojo, physical educators, and various athletic coaches in the furtherance of their teachings. These exercises have been extensively used as conditioning exercises for football, basketball, track, swimming, wrestling, boxing, tennis, baseball, and other sports with effective results.

Special acknowledgments are due for the technical assistance given so generously by Y. Matsumoto, Nobuo Nishimori, the instructors and members of The Kodokan Kenshusei, and Allen Clifford; to the Kodokan Judo Institute and Korakuen Gymnasium, Tokyo, Japan, the Judo Institute of Maryland and Lipsky's Gymnasium, Baltimore, Maryland, for the use of those facilities; to Isao Inokuma, 1959 All-Japan Judo Champion, who has supported and utilized weight training methods; and to Lanny Miyamoto of Baltimore, Maryland, Robert S. Nishi of Honolulu, Hawaii, and Fred Marianni of Geneva, Switzerland, for their invaluable photographic assistance, all without which this book would not have been possible.

TAKAHIKO ISHIKAWA
DONN F. DRAEGER

Tokyo, Japan
January, 1962

JUDO TRAINING METHODS:

a sourcebook

PART I

Principles

THIS *Part of the book brings a re-evaluation of physical Judo theory and technique which has been much blurred throughout past time. For many, Judo technique has been devalued into a synonym for thoughtless routine in which understanding of method of training was isolated from academic considerations. Herein, the physiological principles tantamount to Judo are discussed, exploding the many misunderstandings concerning strength. Further, functional methodology in regard to Judo training methods is presented in traditional fashion and at the same time, offers the new concept of weight training a positive place in modern Judo. Systematized, proven training routines are outlined in detail for direct use by instructors and trainees. Finally, a statistical analysis of the great Japanese Judo champions is presented which clearly reveals support of the book's thesis.*

PLATE 2. *Upper:* Jigoro Kano, founder of Kodokan Judo. *Lower:* Risei Kano, son of J. Kano, the present President of Kodokan and The International Judo Federation.

CHAPTER 1

Physical Judo
Re-examined

The men of fact wait in grim silence to make a throw and claim a point.

Holmes

KODOKAN JUDO today is actively practiced as an international sport in more than 40 countries. In the U.S.A. it is a nationally recognized competitive event growing in popularity in private organizations, public schools, community activities, and the military armed services under the sanction of the Amateur Athletic Union (AAU) of the U.S.A., and the administrative guidance of the only official national Judo body, the Judo Black Belt Federation of the U.S.A. (J.B.B.F.). As a competitive event, more and more emphasis is being placed on sporting excellence, and volumes have been penned concerning the actual detailed execution of the various Judo techniques of throwing, counter-throwing, combination throwing, and all the phases of grappling. This preoccupation with the "meat" of Judo technique is of course understandable, but the unassailable fact of the matter is that without an understanding of the basic preparation of the body and training methods to obtain Judo excellence, one is forever doomed to mediocrity. This book specializes in bringing to the reader for the first time, the basic preparations and training methods of traditional Judo which have developed past champions. It also introduces an entirely new concept of Judo training which is relatively unexplored, but growing in popularity; the application of weight training methods to Judo.

Kodokan Judo, founded in precept by the late Dr. Jigoro Kano, in 1882, is a system of training mind and body for the most efficient use of mental and physical energies. It is likewise an art of contention, of personal control, reflecting purposeful movement. Judo exponents are vitally interested in this purposeful movement, giving undivided attention to obtaining, improving, and maintaining it. As a logical prerequisite to excellence of technique, methods of body preparation and training must be thoroughly studied, understood, and applied. Training in any competitive entity is not static, and must undergo constant revision to improve performance that "one inch"—that "one second" —or increase personal efficiency so that purposeful movements will be more efficient. Judo is not exempt from these considerations.

Success in competitive Judo lies in coupling efficient Judo technique with a strong and healthier body. All Judo exponents agree that efficient technique is mandatory, although unfortunately, many do not agree that strength is necessary. This is due in part to what appears to be a well-established "myth" that in Judo, *strength is unnecessary*. The bases of this Judo "myth" are far reaching, and lie in, (1) a misinterpretation of the meaning of Judo, (2) a misunderstanding of the dynamics of Judo, and, (3) a misunderstanding of what strength really is.

The Judo "myth" has been brought about by a misinterpretation of what physical Judo is, via the age-old translation of the meaning of the Japanese *kanji* (characters) JU and DO of JUDO. It is difficult, without waxing philosophical, to give a distinct mechanical interpretation to the word *Judo,* and for this reason, only the character *Ju* will be attempted. *Ju* has been translated as "gentle," "soft," or "gentleness," and "softness." With all due respect to these translations, it is apparent that the implied meanings, in English, have given rise to misinterpretations and misconceptions of the basic physical principles of Judo. These misconceptions have even reached into the actual preparation and training given students by instructors. Many Western instructors have seriously limited the competitive Judo value of their students, insisting that Judo is performed "gently," sometimes in an almost "prissy" manner, and that all movements are to be executed as such. Unfortunately, but unavoidably, such advocates have not had the opportunity to physically witness Judo or practice it in Japan. It is certain that one short trip to any *Dojo* (Judo exercise hall) would erase erroneous ideas about the "gentleness" of Judo and provide new insight as to its correct performance.

Dr. Kano defined the purpose of Judo as the development of physical strength by training one's mind and body in the techniques of combat. His teachings show emphasis on the building of strength of both body and spirit through prescribed exercises, but always along the course of effective utilization of such strengths. So as not to be accused of venting a polemical attack in a sacrilegious manner against the Kodokan tradition, or polluting Kanoian doctrine, the authors refer directly to Master Kano's own words (italics ours):

"A main feature of the art is the application of the principles of *nonresistance* and taking advantage of the opponent's loss of equilibrium; hence the name Jujutsu (literally soft or gentle art), or Judo (doctrine of softness or gentleness). Now let me explain this principle by actual example...

"Suppose my opponent tries to lift my body, intending to make me fall. If I resist him, I shall be thrown down, *because my strength to resist is not sufficient to overcome his.* If, on the other hand, I leave him unresisted and, while so doing, pull him this way (illustrating), throwing my body voluntarily on the ground, I can throw him very easily.

"I could multiply these examples, but probably those I have given will suffice to enable you to understand how one may beat an opponent by *not resisting him.* But *there are cases in which this principle does not apply.* Suppose, for instance, my opponent takes hold of my right wrist and I resist him; there is no means of releasing it from his hold. The best way would be to move my arm so that my *whole strength* is used to counteract his hand grip, the strength which is of course far inferior to my concentrated strength and therefore gives way to it. *In such a case I used my strength against his, contrary to the principle of nonresistance...* These examples serve to show that *the principle of non- resistance is not applicable in all cases.*

"Is there then, any principle which never fails of application? Yes, there is! And that is the principle of the Maximum Efficiency in Use of Mind and Body. *Nonresistance is only ONE instance of the application of this fundamental principle."*

The basic principle of physical Judo lies then within "Maximum Efficiency in Use of Mind and Body." This principle has been shown to have *two* divergent factors, *nonresis- tance* and *resistance.* Each is, in its appropriate application, patterned after *maximum efficiency,* equally compatible with the ideals of Kodokan Judo. We find here then, no condemnation of strength, but merely the regulatory measures necessary for efficient func- tioning. Dr. Kano was not opposed to strength, but rather the *unnecessary expenditure* of strength. His "best use of energy" slogan implies economic considerations in regard to body powers. Those who insist that Judo is based entirely upon nonresistance are quite obviously ignoring the factor of resistance described appropriately by Dr. Kano.

Returning to our discussion of "gentle" Judo, what is, by any stretch of the most fertile imagination, "gentle" about two bodies crashing together at full speed, each bent upon the overthrow of the other? Does the action of the actual Judo competition shown in Figure 1 appear as a "gentle" movement? Here two opponents are locked together, one literally *smashing* his opponent to the mat *by a proper Judo throwing technique* executed against his unfortunate opponent's momentary weakness in balance. Or does the top-level championship action shown in Figure 2 demonstrate any "gentleness" or "softness" in the preparation for either use of body strength to execute or resist the throw? Further, does the scene shown in Figure 3 suggest a "soft" attack? Here, one opponent is on his way to the mat and inevitable defeat by the very *powerful rushing* attack of a well-executed throwing technique. These are but a few of countless examples which are found in Judo competition which exemplify the need for revision of our mechanical ideas of Judo princi- ple. Contest rules of the Kodokan Judo in Article 29—Judgment of "Ippon"— state: Judgment of "Ippon" (one point) shall be made on the basis of the following conditions: A. Nage-Waza (throwing technique):

(1) When a contestant applying a technique or countering his opponent's attacking technique, throws down his opponent on to his back *with sufficient force;* (italics ours).

This requires the opponent to be deposited on the mat with anything but a "gentle"

placement and seasoned Judo competitors often recall their failures to throw their opponents powerfully enough, meriting the cry only of *mo sukoshi* (a little more) from the stoic referee in lieu of victory.

Dr. Kano's keen and all-observing mind saw no conflict in choosing the terms "gentle" and "soft" to describe the *Ju* of Judo, but these words to the Western mind, have different connotations than intended by the Japanese interpretation. Perhaps the most accurate and satisfyingly synonymous with the founders ideas is the adaptation by French Judo exponents of the term "supple" or "flexible." This term has sometimes been used by the Japanese. Here we can easily visualize the "giving way" to superior forces with the idea of *nonresistance* at the proper moment to utilize the opponent's loss of equilibrium *or* the clever application of our body power with the idea of *resistance* at the proper moment to misdirect the opponent's actions to his disadvantage.

Equally culpable in spreading the Judo "myth" that strength is unnecessary in the performance of Judo, is the misunderstanding of the dynamics of Judo. In this sense, Judo is a functional neuro-muscular skill, a technique facilitated by highly organized developments of flexibility, agility, speed, and *strength.* Purist Judo exponents will balk at the acceptance of the strength factor as a prerequisite to effective Judo technique, and discredit the "muscle-men" as "muscle-bound clods." Insisting that Judo effectiveness is purely the result of technique, they proceed to build their vehement non-recognition of strength upon a false premise...*the premise that muscle and existent strength is synonymous with the improper use of strength.* The possession of muscle and strength as its concomitant does not necessarily imply that such qualities will be misused. True, that if a force of 75 pounds is used to defeat an opponent *via Judo tactics,* when only a force of 35 pounds is needed to do the job, then such resort to wasteful use of energy does *not* constitute true Judo technique, however effective. But the ability to execute the 75 pounds of force may serve its possessor in good stead under different conditions, whereas the non-possessor will be unable to execute any decisive action, regardless of his theoretical understanding of the mechanics of the Judo techniques, or his well established technique which is effective only under less demanding circumstances. Certainly it takes more body strength to unbalance and throw a 225 pound opponent than it does a 145 pound opponent, even if the technique is correctly applied. This is most graphically demonstrated by the skilled performances of young women or male oldsters who are unable to generate sufficient strength in the performance of their Judo, but whose technique is skillful, and who fail to actually throw their stronger-bodied opponents.

British Judo exponents lampoon the advocates of "no strength" Judo. They tell of a purist instructor teaching his beginning Judo class the principles of Judo by explaining the manner of gripping the *Judogi* (Judo costume), and the technique of *Kuzushi* (unbalancing) thus,..."and you grasp the jacket lightly, gently, ever so softly with three fingers of each hand, then,...*you pull with the strength of King Kong!"*

This leads us to our final consideration, the understanding of what strength really is. Strength will be discussed in Chapter 3 in some detail, but the reader must bear in mind that it is a relative term connoting the ideas of overcoming resistance *and* the capacity for sustained exertion without undue fatigue—an endurance aspect. In its former context, it is spoken of as "mere muscle," while in the latter it means the physical fitness of an organism.

The human body is a wonderfully complex machine of many intricate variables. Devices found naturally, or products of man's ingenuity cannot begin to match the precisions of the human body. Machines have been constructed that are proportionately larger, stronger, and capable of producing greater work, power, and speed, but these considerations are limited. No machine exists or is likely to be produced which can perform acts of walking, climbing, throwing, lifting, striking, twisting, or bending, as the situation demands, except the human body. Yet, the feelings of the average person are so aptly summarized by the late Wilbur Pardon Bowen, Professor of Physical Education, Michigan State Normal, Ypsilanti, Michigan:

"Civilized man is inclined to show a certain amount of scorn for what he is in the habit of calling 'mere muscle,' but the fact remains that everything he does depends ultimately on the action of muscles. The muscle fiber is, in the last analysis, the sole instrument by which the human will can act upon the outside world. No matter how great the refinements of civilization, no matter how much machinery may be devised to do our work for us, man can never get away from the necessity for muscular work."[1]

The strength factor in the performance of contest Judo is a vital "must" if the Judo exponent is to utilize his full potentialities. This strength, however, must be used wisely in accordance with the principles of Judo. What has been dubbed *Godo* (strength way) by the Japanese and the wanton display of body strength without technique is certainly to be discouraged. In the West the term "power Judo" has been used to signify, somewhat inappropriately perhaps, the type of contest Judo which makes use of excessive strength. Judo is *power*...we must not mistake that, but we must be aware that certain vital elements of application such as timing, direction, and technique are vital in this meaning. Under no circumstances may we assign the quality of sheer brute strength as a synonym for the basis of Judo performance. However, *used properly, strength directly affects the establishment of Judo contest proficiency.* The winning performance in competitive Judo, all other considerations being equal or *nearly equal,* will fall to the *stronger* opponent.

One need only to look to the past records of Japanese Judo Champions to verify this statement. Such champions as Matsumoto, Kimura, Ishikawa, Yoshimatsu, Daigo and other notables such as Hirose, Hatori, Hosokawa, Ito, of former years, are all examples on an efficiently coupled Judo technique and a strong physique. More recent champions such as Natsui, Sone, Inokuma and the current Kaminaga and such notables as Shigematsu, Koga, Watanabe, Kawano, Yamashiki, Oda, Takahashi, and Ito, are further examples of body power and skillful Judo. *There never has been a small Japanese Judo champion.* All of them have been 175 pounds or more (a big man) and extremely powerful in the execution of lightning-fast Judo technique. This reference is made within the framework of contemporary Judo *(List 1, page 140),* since in earlier times, statures were for the most part considerably smaller than today, and the "big" Judo exponent was almost unknown.

The authors well recall the past efforts of the brilliant Osawa, considered by many as the all-time technician of Japanese Judo. Possessing dazzling speed, clever strategy, and tiger-like ferocity in contests, Osawa tore through every and all opponents to establish

1   Wilbur P. Bowen & Henry A. Stone, *Applied Anatomy and Kinesiology,* Philadelphia: Lea & Febiger, 7th ed., 1953, p. 93.

himself as a serious threat to the All-Japan title. This championship level was never reached, due to, he himself believes, his mere 145 pounds. Matched against the gigantic Yoshimatsu who weighed about 240 pounds, the authors can still see the powerful osoto-gari (major outer reaping) executed by Yoshimatsu as it turned the game little Osawa almost fully around in mid-air. Against equally or near equally skilled heavier opponents, he could not surmount his disadvantage of inferior weight. It is interesting to note that Osawa himself is a strong supporter of the weight class idea for competitive Judo as well as the use of weight-training exercises in Judo training.

In today's competitive scene, small Judo exponents such as Iwata, Yoneda, and Shinohara are all reminiscent of Osawa, but their climb to championship levels is seriously handicapped by their Lilliputian proportions. It is true that these smaller Judo exponents possess powerful bodies, far beyond the average *untrained* man, *be he large or small*, but their small bodies cannot house the strength and body power potential found in larger body structures. Gradual recognition of this factor is being seen today in Japan, notably among the college and university teams. During the recent university championship team matches, Meiji University, the almost perennial winner, was matched against highly rated and inspired Nihon University. Meiji, captained by the small Shinohara all season, announced a substitute captain who weighed in the neighborhood of 200 pounds. This was done because the captain of the Nihon team was a burly and dangerous *heavy* opponent. Meiji was unwilling to risk its title chances by pitting the admittedly more skillful Shinohara against a substantially heavier opponent.

In the Western World, DeHerdt, Geesink, and Pariset of Europe; Lebell, Harris, Imamura, and Williams of North America, all demonstrate the superiority of the powerful and skillful body. Two former North American champions, Hunt and Osako, also possessed powerful bodies, but to a lesser degree than their successors. European notables such as Bourgoin, Collonges, Palmer, Grabher, Bloss, Dazzi, Young, Dupre, Gruel, Collard, Grossain, Legay, Rabut, Reymond, Ryan, Maynard, Petherbridge, Tempesta, Guldemont, Vallauri, and Bluming give further evidence of the necessity of a powerful body. It is interesting to note that as Courtine and Outelet increased their physiques, coupling more body power with an already excellent Judo technique, they joined the above ranks of European notables and became more formidable opponents. North American notables include Leszczynski, V. Tamura, Kato, Campbell, Alseika, Nishi, and Colgan who are anything but weak-bodied. In South America, Kawakami reigns supreme and appears to be, at first glance, an exception to the need for a powerful body. Kawakami who weighs but 150 pounds is an extremely fast and powerful Judo exponent, but against near equally or equally skilled stronger opponents, his chances have proven slim. His successes in Latin America have been largely due to his superior Judo technique which stands far above any other in South America, where contest Judo is relatively new and highly skilled technicians do not exist in the true sense of the word. But, as the technique of heavier and more powerful Latin American Judo exponents improves, Kawakami and others like him will find it increasingly difficult to remain champions.

That the skilled Judoka of olden days did possess powerful bodies and did apply strength in contest is clearly illustrated by the following story told personally to the co-author by the now famous master, Y. Kanemitsu, 9 Dan. As a young competitor of 5 Dan skill, Kanemitsu faced a veteran opponent of equal grade in S. Hashimoto. After a one hour struggle of little or no advantage to either Judoka, a grappling opportunity was taken by Kanemitsu, who in his enthusiasm, applied a body holding so tightly that he cracked Hashimoto's ribs! Victory was thus assured to Kanemitsu who to this day emphasizes the study of very powerfully applied, but skillful grappling techniques.

If the reader is yet unconvinced of the importance of strength in Judo, let him find exception to the words of the immortal Judo master of the Kodokan, Sakujiro Yokoyama, renowned for his combinations of resistance exercises and skillful, powerful Judo: "It is a tradition handed down from old times that in Taijutsu or in Jujutsu, the more strength one has, the more liable one is to be beaten on account of the strength, and it does one more harm than good. But this is a great mistake. Other things being equal, the stronger man is bound to win. It is quite true however, that one with less strength sometimes is the superior, on account of his greater skill, to one with more strength. Again one who has much strength is apt to rely on it, often applying his strength against the principles of Judo. He may beat those with very much less strength than himself, but he can never win over one who is very skillful in his tricks or another who has equal strength, much less over a person who has more strength. Besides, he will get into a bad habit of doing his tricks against Judo principles and in a slovenly way, which habit he will find a great obstacle in his progress. This fact seems to have been the cause of that mistaken tradition. But this never comes of the fact that a man has much strength, but of the fact that he lacks coaching and he has his own way in training himself; that is, trusting entirely on his strength. If a strong man, however, trains himself thoroughly, paying careful attention to the principles of Judo, there will be no fear for his being taken advantage of by his own strength; he will never fall into the mistake of applying his tricks in a wrong way; his progress in the art will have no obstacle, and he will be able to make the most proper use of his strength. There is no doubt that his strength together with his skill will make him a formidable exponent. *If the great masters of Judo in former days had had more strength, they would have been still more proficient* (italics ours). Briefly speaking, strength is very necessary to enable one to keep one's own proper posture, to break one's opponent's posture, and apply one's tricks upon him. Judo pupils should cultivate their strength in order to use it properly whenever necessary."

Lest it appear that we have in this chapter anathematized the "little man," we hasten to add this closing note. It is hard to dispel the truth of the old adage, "A good big man is better than a good little man," but all who enter into competitive Judo should constantly bear the "good" in mind. It is the responsibility of all who do compete to make the most of their potentialities. By preparation of their body through better training methods, they will come to realize that responsibility. The "big man" too carries an observer-pinned anathema in that he is more often than not accused of that dread Japanese word, *Chikara* (strength), in his performance of Judo. However, in the final analysis, Judo is open to all sizes and statures, and requires proof by contest preformance to determine among "believer" and "non-believer" alike, just who is superior.

PLATE 3. Co-author explaining weight training fundamentals to Kodokan Kenshusei (special research students).

CHAPTER 2

Classification of Exercises and Muscle Groups

The names that can be named are not unvarying names.
Lao Tzu

HENCEFORTH, the reader will be confronted with various terms which must, for clarity, be standardized. The terms *Preparatory, Supplementary, Compound,* and *Auxiliary* have been chosen to categorize the various exercise movements. The following definitions apply:

Preparatory Exercises: Those introductory exercises which provide suitable stimulation to all parts of the body in order to prepare the body for more severe exertion without the risk of injury and/or malfunction. Considered the *Junbi Undo* ("warm-up" exercises) or *Taiso* (calisthenics) of Judo. When used at the termination of a severe exercise period to "cool" the body down, they are referred to as *Shumatsu Undo* (closing exercises).

Supplementary Exercises: Those exercises which embody special features to supply a need or want in the development of body coordination for Judo. The "pattern" establishing exercises. Performed as both *Tandoku Renshu* (solo practice) and *Sotai Renshu* (partner practice), the traditional *Uchikomi* or *Butsukari* ("fitting" movement) of Judo falls within this classification.

Compound Exercises: Those exercises which are representative of efficient functioning combining several elements united as a whole toward increased performance of a movement. The special "situation" exercises necessary for *Katame Waza* (grappling techniques).

Auxiliary Exercises: Those exercises which are performed by use of special equipment so as to rapidly induce the desired result in support of the non-equipment exercises. The "aid to strength" exercises of which resistance movements are the major type.

To aid the selection of Preparatory and Auxiliary Exercises, and to more systematically present them to the reader, certain arbitrary divisions have been made. These divisions concerning the major muscle groups of the body, are based on an anatomical consideration, and while essentially scientific, they are not precise nor are they intended to be more than a convenience for the trainee and instructor. At times they will overlap, but for the most part they will be self-explanatory. These divisions are:

Leg Group: Contains the muscles of the legs and feet.

Abdominal Belt Group: Contains muscles of the abdominal and lower-back region of the trunk.

Upper Back-Neck Group: Contains the muscles of the upper-back and neck.

Chest Group: Contains the muscles of the chest.

Arm-Shoulder Group: Contains the muscles of the arms and shoulders.

Finally, the translations of Japanese terminology is not, in all cases, a direct or literal one. What has been done, is to give meaningful equivalents for the various Japanese words rather than the sometimes picturesque, but rather obscure direct translations. For the critical reader, the Japanese words and their common Kanji are listed in the Glossary.

The use of Japanese terminology in the study of Judo is mandatory in most Dojo of the West. This terminology is largely concentrated on the names of the various techniques, and trainees are expected to learn the specific movements by their Japanese names. At the outset, the beginning trainee may imagine this an almost impossible task, but with repeated practice of the technique and use of the name, an association develops which in short order becomes a familiar bit of knowledge. As Judo experience increases, the Japanese terminology can be fluently used without a conscious translation to English in order to be meaningful. The use of traditional Japanese terminology is considered as an integral part of the study of Judo, and actually facilitates understanding.

For the experienced Judo exponent, many of the translations in this book may seem elementary, but in order that all may benefit, Japanese terminology is used throughout this book. Such terms will be shown with an appropriate English equivalent when first encountered, but subsequent usage may omit the equivalents. Terminology forgotten may easily be found in the Glossary. The trainee who has mastered the terminology found in this book will have a broad basis for a better understanding of Judo.

PLATE 4. Isao Inokuma, 5 Dan, demonstrating principles of concentric contraction during a weight training session at Kodokan.

CHAPTER 3

Kinesiological Principles About Muscle

If we could first know where we are, and whither we are tending, we could better judge what to do and how to do it.
Lincoln

Biological Design: Every single muscle or groups of muscles will exhibit both qualitatively and quantitatively all the necessary properties of design required for their functioning. These properties, within a wide range of limits, must effect a compromise between the various needs. To take a concrete example in Judo, speed of movement is a highly desirable quality, but so is economy of energy in maintaining force or posture. Fast muscles are more wasteful in postural effort, so a balance must be provided between the two requirements. We shall see that the intrinsic speed of muscles is inherent in the muscles themselves and also somewhat dependent upon physico-chemical factors in the muscle construction and operating mechanisms, not merely in control by the nervous system, though that too is adjusted to the needs of the organism. For a given weight of muscle, greater force can be generated if more and shorter fibers are arranged in a parallel fashion, but since this design places limits on the range of potential contraction, a compromise must be made here too, according to the position and function in the body.

Muscle Fiber and Strength: Skillful movement, such as Judo performance, requires the use of muscle to guide and direct employment of energy. The use of muscles, whether as prime movers, fixation, neutralizing, or antagonist actions, requires adequate strength. Bodily movement cannot exist without strength. Strength, for our purpose, is a highly relative term, meaning the ability to overcome resistance *and* the capacity for sustained exertion without undue fatigue. It may be considered in this sense, as the endurance of the body. It can only exist by muscular action. Muscle fiber was made to do just one thing—contract, and it is made to do this when it receives the signal to do so from its nerve fiber which responds to adequate stimuli. We know that as a muscle contracts it exerts tension which can be utilized in the production of useful and purposeful movement. The immediate sources of energy which makes this contraction possible are the various foodstuffs stored within the muscle and those which are carried to the muscle by the blood. It follows that an insufficient supply or inadequate distribution of food will adversely effect proper muscular action, possibly causing injury to the muscle fiber which in turn would necessitate a period of rest so that necessary repairs could be made by the body. Muscle is a machine which converts chemically stored energy into mechanical work.

Muscle being as contractile as it is, is of several types. We are primarily interested in voluntary muscle, and will therefore limit ourselves to an explanation of its functions. There are about 200 pairs of voluntary muscles in the human body, but only about 75 pairs are used in posture and movement. The wide range of Judo movements and other exercises described in this book will provide adequate exercise to develop and healthfully maintain these muscles. We first must understand the workings of muscle fibers.

Muscle is an organic structure whose working parts are made largely from two proteins...*Actin* and *Myosin*. These two structural proteins seem to be organized into separate filaments. Neither type of filament extends continuously along the muscle length, although there is a continuous backbone structure of unknown composition and very low density. The filaments are arranged into a succession of separate patterns, each pattern containing filaments of one type arranged in line with and overlapping the next pattern of filaments of the other type. Because of this construction, muscle gives a banded appearance. When the muscle contracts or is stretched, the two patterns of filaments slide past each other.

Muscles are composed of small fibers which vary in dimensions from 1/25 to 1½ inches in length and from 1/250 to 1/2500 inch in thickness. These fibers, grouped together in bundles, are wrapped in a sheath-like tissue. The bundles in turn are also wrapped in the sheath-like tissue. The sheath-like tissues are connected and anchored on tendons at the ends of the muscles, which are attached by insertion to the bones.

Resting muscle is quite soft and freely extendible. This state demonstrates great economy of energy. However, it is not to be supposed that muscle in the state of rest is completely relaxed. A state of very weak contracture existing independent of voluntary innervation, is exerted by resting muscle. This imparts a feeling of firmness to the muscle and is considered a normal condition. This state is called *Tonus* and keeps the muscles in condition for free and easy movement. Tonus is influenced by muscle-stretching exercise. Another term, "muscle tone" refers to the changes in the tension of muscles when they are not in ordinary contraction. Different degrees of relaxation are effected by sendentary habits, certain illnesses, heat, certain mental conditions, and sleep, all which tend to lower muscle tone. An active life, cold, fear, and excitement tend to raise muscle tone. The fact that tonus and muscle tone can be increased by suitable exercises will give us a basis for various training movements. Over-exercise and improper training can cause excessive muscle tone and be detrimental to the performance of Judo.

On stimulation, muscle transforms into a new physical state—it becomes hard, develops tension, resists stretching, and acts against resistance. Under this tension, muscle produces heat which has a direct bearing on the fatigue of muscle and is the basis of the argument that good posture must be maintained to avoid prolonged resistance to an opponent's movements. A resting muscle shortens when warmed, lengthens when cooled. During shortening, a muscle does mechanical work according to the resistance it must overcome. This is in addition to the heat it releases. Under ideal mechanical conditions the work may amount to about 40% of the whole initial energy. Muscle has the property of recovery from fatigue, which is about 50% of the initial energy expended. A rapid muscle produces a large amount of heat in contraction; a slow muscle produces a small amount. Raising the temperature of a muscle makes it quicker, but produces more heat in a maintained contraction and thus fatigues sooner. Thus in the application of the Preparatory Exercises, used to "warm up" the body prior to strenuous efforts, we use this information, taking care not to induce fatigue of any intensity.

Two important factors concerning working muscles are to be noted. First, the force a muscle can exert depends upon the number and size of its fibers. Second, the extent through which it can contract and exert strength depends upon the length of its fibers. The amount of work done by a muscle depends upon the amount of force used, and the distance or extent of movement. Kinesiologists have proven that the ability of a muscle to perform useful work varies greatly with the resistance applied. Their conclusions bear out the principle that if a muscle is intended to perform with *Maximum Efficiency*, then that muscle should operate against about one-half of its maximum contraction force. To increase muscle strength, we must exercise at about 60–85% of our maximum ability. The constant use of muscles contracting at higher than 85% of their maximum ability will also increase muscle strength, to be sure, but many additional undesirable side effects are suffered, prominent among which is the over toning effect. Knowledge of the above information will be applied later in Auxiliary Exercises.

Muscle fiber has been indentified in two distinct classes by physiologists. The Red Fiber, and the Pale Fiber. The Red Fiber is formed by doing tasks of extremely slow, heavy, or vastly prolonged exertion, while the Pale Fibers are developed by fast contractions and quick actions. The body adapts a balance of both fibers necessary to normal existence, but it is possible by exercise to develop one or the other in the majority. The Judo exponent must develop the proper balance of these fibers.

Muscle Contraction: A muscle properly stimulated develops tension, but whether it shortens or not, and thus produces work, depends upon the resistance it operates against. Kinesiologists have categorized the types of muscular contraction as follows:

Concentric Contraction: The tension movement of muscle fiber through a range of normal contraction and relaxation under conditions of imposed resistance in which actual shortening of the muscle and movement of the bone to which it is attached, occurs. This type of contraction does positive work, accelerates movements, and works through a *full range* of motion. The contraction of the muscle group in the drawing so that the weight is moved from A to B and returned to A *without* controlled raising or lowering. (Sometimes referred to as isotonic or phasic contraction).

Isometric Contraction: The tension nonmovement of muscle fiber under conditions of imposed resistance in which muscle is unable to shorten and retains its original fixed length. This type of contraction does no work, but imposes fixation on the surrounding bones. An example of this would be an *unsuccessful* attempt of the muscle group in the drawing to move the heavy weight from A to B. (Sometimes referred to as static contraction).

Eccentric Contraction: The tension movement of muscle fiber under conditions of imposed resistance in which muscle is actually lengthened instead of shortened. This type of contraction does negative work, and controls lowering movements. This is demonstrated in the drawing by *controlled* lowering of a weight, *very slowly,* from B to A. During a long continued contraction, a muscle becomes progressively slower and more economical. The slowest muscles can maintain contractions for a long time with little expenditure of energy, while the fastest ones fatigue rapidly.

To many, the use of Auxiliary Exercises, especially those using weight training methods, is just a simple matter of "picking up a weight" and doing an exercise. Unfortunately, it is not so simple, and direct application of kinesiological principles about muscle must be thoroughly understood. The success of weight training methods applied to Judo depends upon the utilization of proper contraction movements. Judo efficiency will develop and not be retarded if sensible training is applied. (See Chapter 10, page 205.)

How Muscles Grow: Comprehensive studies of muscular hypertrophy have been made and it is generally established that hypertrophy is a function of the amount of work performed per unit of time. A muscle exercising under proper conditions, will increase in size, each muscle fiber increasing individually in proportion. Additionally, the sheath-like tissues covering the muscle fibers and muscle bundles increase their bulk. There is no change in fiber length or number of fibers. Increased activity of the muscle brings about an increase in blood supply which acts as a means of transportation for nutrients required in an additional amount by the muscles. As the nutritive foodstuffs are stored, the muscle gains in size. The muscle, acting as a storehouse, lays away nutrients for future use in preparation for the anticipated demands. The system of weight training described in the Chapter on Auxiliary Exercises makes use of this flooding of tissue spaces, termed "storage by innundation" by some physiologists, and produces muscular hypertrophy effectively.

Growth of muscles depends largely upon the type of training utilized and the individual qualities of the trainee. The latter quality is constant and cannot be changed by human efforts, so we must concentrate on our training methods to effect increased muscle growth and resultant strength. This will be discussed in a later chapter.

Muscle Speed and Reaction Time: Every muscle has two optimum speeds; one for maximum efficiency—work done, energy used; one for maximum power output—work done per minute. In the human body, these two speeds are about the same, though whatever the differential, the Judo exponent is directly concerned. At very high and very low extremes of speed, efficiency and power output become small. The optimum speed of a muscle is somewhat less than 30% of the maximum speed at which it can shorten under zero load (no resistance). This is called the intrinsic speed. Intrinsic speeds vary widely from one muscle to another within the human body, making possible the complexity of movements characteristic of man.

The Judo exponent in his training must utilize every and all means to increase his reaction time. Neuromuscular speed cannot appreciably be increased, but a trainee can fully develop his speed potentiality by performing over and over again the actions required for a particular movement. In this manner, muscle resistance can be reduced, power increased, joints loosened, and economy of motion realized. Methods of decreasing obstacles to speed are extensively explained in the following chapters. (See Chapter 8—Supplementary Exercises.)

Muscle fiber is quantitatively categorized in terms of speed by such terms as *Latent Period, Contraction Period, Relaxation Period,* and *Refractory Period.* All these conditions directly effecting muscle fiber speed are interesting to the Judo exponent. The Latent Period is the time interval between the application of an adequate stimulus and the muscle's first indicated response to that stimulus. Contraction Period is the time during which the muscle performs its response of contraction, thus producing useful work. The Relaxation Period is the time during which the muscle returns to its normal state. This normal state is not one of perfect relaxation, but rather of Tonus, or weak contracture, referred to earlier in this chapter. The Refractory Period is the interval during which the muscle does not respond to additional stimuli and is unable to further produce contraction.

Times vary appreciably between trained and untrained persons. The actual tested speeds of muscle for the trained athlete may be:

Latent Period	.001 seconds
Contraction Period	.04 seconds
Relaxation Period	.05 seconds
Refractory Period	.001 seconds
Total Time of Muscle Speed	.092 seconds

A physical factor briefly discussed earlier under Muscle Fiber and Strength, greatly influences the speed of muscles. This is the factor of temperature. The speed of a muscle is reduced two or three times by a drop in temperature of only 10°C. Still another limiting factor plays a dominant role in the speed of muscles. This is the mechanical strength of the structural material with and on which muscle functions. Injuries in sports such as tearing of tendons and muscles indicate that the safety margin is not large. The human body might have been designed to grow quicker muscles, sacrificing economy of effort in maintaining load or posture, and suffering from greater susceptibleness to fatigue, but it is probable that if this new design had been inherited, the greater accelerations so available would have brought with them stresses and strains to our anatomical structure that could not hold up, and frequent damage would be the concomitant. Experimentation has shown that muscles can be quickened about 20% by raising the body temperature 2°C. This has been accomplished by powerful diathermy. However, diathermy can upset the nervous control of our body, and, as was pointed out before, improved performance would cause serious mechanical damage.

We must be content, at least for the present, to accept methods of training which do "heat" the body, such as the Preparatory Exercises, prior to engaging in heavy exercise. Correct application of these exercises will enhance our Judo performance.

Muscular Activity During Movement: A complete understanding of muscular activity of the human body in motion would involve a very scientific knowledge of the changes in tension and length of a very large number of muscles. This is impossible and impractical within the limits of this text, but nevertheless, the Judo exponent should have an idea of what occurs.

In Judo, your ability to exert a push, a pull, or whatever force is appropriate, depends on your power to operate your bones as levers. This can only be done by muscular action. A muscle cannot exert tension against a bone without, at the same time, exerting an equal but opposite force against the bone to which the other end of the muscle is fixed. A muscle cannot exert tension against either of these bones without applying a related amount of compression between the two joint surfaces across which it exerts. In more mechanistic parlance, the effect of an exerting muscle is the application of equal but nevertheless opposite couples to the two bones, the moment of these couples being dependent on the tension of the muscle and its distance from the center of rotation of the joint.

Judo performance gives great emphasis to the stability of the body. Such stability relies on the fact that the resultant of the forces exerted by the limbs against the shoulders and hips is exactly equal, but opposite to the weight of the body acting through its center of gravity. Possession of powerful fixation muscles obviously affects our stability.

Functions of Muscles: It is not generally possible or desirable to arrange the muscles so that all of them that need to be used in a cooperative fashion with each other can be geographically joined. While muscles usually work together in groups to effect the desired motion, and while our nervous system is patterned in terms of total movement rather than isolated or piecemeal actions, different muscles in the execution of any specific action, have different functions. Each may function primarily, while at the same time, complement in a subsidiary role. In Judo training, we are especially interested in understanding the roles of these various muscle groups in order to apply our methods of increasing Judo performance and efficiency. To assist in this, kinesiologists have classified muscle functions as follows:

Prime Movers: Those muscles which act directly to effect the desired motion. Different postural attitudes may bring gravity into the role of a prime mover.

Antagonists: Those muscles which during contraction in a desired motion, have reverse movement compared to their primary action.

Fixation: Those muscles which by their action, stabilize other parts or hold those parts in proper position so that the desired movement can be made.

Neutralizing: Prime movers require ensurance against subsidiary muscle action which may detract from skillful and coordinated movements. Those muscles which aid in the elimination of this undesirable effect.

The Auxiliary Exercises to be described will make use of the above functions by patterning the proper exercise for Judo. A thorough knowledge of the functions of muscles is necessary in order that we choose the correct movements to increase our Judo performance. Special attention must be paid to the amount of development of the muscles antagonistic to Judo movements and a corresponding interest must be placed in the proper development, along the lines of sensible training, of all muscle functions required by efficient Judo technique.

Muscular Fatigue: When we perform a severe exercise such as contest Judo, our strength will eventually begin to fail and our technique will suffer. This is especially true in the *Kohaku* (red & white) events in which the winner remains on the mat, taking on all opponents until he is defeated. Fatigue has been shown to lie in the muscles and is due to the failure of the muscle to contract when motor impulses reach it. Muscular fatigue makes little difference to performance, however, until muscles are too weak to make the necessary motion. If we continue to perform near the limits of our endurance, we will soon experience a sudden "breakdown" of performance.

During relatively short performances of muscular exertion the accumulation of chemical breakdown products, "metabolites," and oxygen uptake are relatively unimportant as the circulatory and respiratory adjustments are only required when the products of oxidation are oxidized under a sustained exertion. The physiology of muscular fatigue is very complex, and it is not necessary to attempt a complete description of it here, but the Judo exponent will do well to practice conservation of both mental and physical energies to avoid premature fatigue. Experiments by the famed runner from Great Britain, Dr. Roger B. Bannister, show that while muscular fatigue is induced and performance is limited by two main factors, (1) contractile activity of muscle and (2) rate of supply of oxygen with corresponding removal of the products of muscular contraction, there is a third factor which has a great bearing on performance and fatigue. This is the capacity for mental excitement which brings about an ability to overcome or ignore discomfort and pain in the muscles. Thus, while physiology posits respiratory and circulatory limits to muscular effort, psychological and other factors may upset the delicate balance of the scales which determine defeat or victory and just how closely the Judo exponent can near the limits of maximum performance.

Fatigue of muscles is manifested in another common way, which can be the plague of all athletes including Judo exponents. Under maximal stimulation, as fatigue sets in the muscle, the force and amplitude of contracture decreases and the muscle is unable to completely relax between the oncoming stimuli. This inability to completely rest between stimuli causes muscles to "tie up" or cramp. This is termed *Contracture* and is induced in a healthy body by factors of fatigue, alkalosis, dehydration, and cold. The athlete should consider it normal and to be expected when maximum exertion is prolonged.

Contracture or cramping cannot be completely avoided. However, the Judoka is able to minimize such unpleasantries. Little can be done about muscle fatigue as a result of prolonged exertion whereby there is an accumulation of waste products of exertion and in spite of increased circulation, the blood is unable to drain off the metabolites. Proper use of Preparatory Exercises to warm-up the body will somewhat reduce the chances of premature fatigue.

Another aid to muscle cramping is a condition referred to as "alkalosis." Normally, the human body has a specific acid-alkaline balance. When this balance is thrown out of kilter due to reduction of the acid sources of the body—loss of fluids, sodium chloride (salt), and carbon dioxide— cramping can occur. Heavy exertion will promote excessive perspiration which in turn depletes fluid and salt quantities of the body. Heavy exertion also will place heavy demands upon the respiratory system which in its accelerated search for oxygen, puts the carbon dioxide at a low level. During training and contests, the Judoka will experience difficulty in keeping body fluids at the proper level *(see Chapter 4, page 71)*. What is important, is that the post-training or post-contest liquid intake must be sufficient to replace what has been lost, so that the next session, whether training or serious contest, begins with the body at normal or near normal fluid level. Salt is easily replaced by the consumption of salt tablets. This is particularly necessary during the hot weather training sessions or contests, though it is in order at any time that excessive perspiring is experienced. The carbon dioxide level may be aided by breathing into a paper bag and rebreathing the same air for a few minutes.

The subject of dehydration is directly linked to the condition of alkalosis, for with the excessive loss of perspiration, body fluid and salt levels are reduced. Loss of fluid is more pronounced when the body's salts are at a low level, with the loss of fluid coming from the cells and in the tissue spaces surrounding the cells. This dehydration tends to make the muscles less "plastic," making them more susceptible to injury as well as areas of concentrated waste products of exercise. The muscle area is literally "poisoned" by these waste products and rebels in the form of cramping. Water taken prior to training or contest sessions is not a good practice. There is inconclusive physiological evidence that drinking water just before or during exercise produces harmful effects, though, depending on the quantity, a bloating and "sloshing" effect will not make for unhampered exertion. Perhaps more important is the fact that the body's fluid level should be at par prior to training or contest (see Chapter 4, page 71). If liquids must be taken, the quantity should be strictly limited—sometimes several rinsings of the mouth and throat is sufficient—and the temperature of the water used should not be cold.

Cold conditions will aid cramping in that the body has its blood circulation attenuated and the muscles with sub-par oxygen and accumulating wastes, refuse to function under conditions of prolonged exertion. The need for staying warm is evident, and judicious use of Preparatory, Supplementary, or Compound Exercises and the sweatsuit (see Chapter 4, page 93) will generally satisfy this need.

Coordination and Skill: No spectacle can produce such self-satisfaction or draw such great spectator interest and enthusiasm as exhibitions of human skill. Judo is such a skill. How we develop such pleasing movements and bodily processes of response to complex physical and mental problems involving balance, movement, coordination, speed, and strength, are of concern to the Judo exponent.

We have seen that nervous, chemical, and physical factors resulting from muscular exertion and resultant contraction, play a dominant role in the integration of muscular effort. Further, the physical capacity of an individual is directly limited by the speed of contraction of the muscles and the force of contraction of those muscles. As a muscle nears its maximum force, the velocity of contraction lessens. This velocity is believed to be limited by chemical reactions which produce muscular energy and are in turn limited or controlled by the force acting on the muscle.

The function of muscle membrane is to receive the stimulus from the nerve and transmit it to the contractile substance of the muscle. Just how this is accomplished is not completely known, but when a certain movement is made, the motor centers have to call into action the necessary muscles in correct sequence, and to ensure that, at each instant, the strength of contraction in each muscle is accurately graded to its intended task. The nervous system controls the grading of muscular action according to the "All or None" principle, which demonstrates that each muscle fiber and its related motor unit contracts with all its force or not at all.

We are able to vary the strength of our muscular contraction and exertions because the motor units will respond to slight stimuli, while others will necessitate more. The number of motor units called into play also affects the strength of our contraction. By some motor units working and some remaining idle, a graded effect can be secured depending upon the circumstances. Under exertion, muscle cells are broken down, only to be replaced by new ones in greater abundance. If we use a muscle constantly and progressively increase its exertion, but not to the point of destroying cells, more and more cells will grow. We shall make use of this fact in designing weight training methods for Judo.

Common everyday bodily movements such as walking, eating, sitting, etc., consist of continuous repetitions of simple reflex acts. Complex bodily movements found in various athletic skills, or technical skills, require advanced motor learning, but follow the same general principles and patterns as common daily movements. The incoming stimuli from the muscles, joints, and skin must be present continually to keep reacting muscles informed and under control. The ear and the eye augment these stimuli involving poise and balance such as is paramount to Judo movements. The cortical reflexes which involve muscular response to conscious stimuli are usually conditional or learned reflexes and are not inherent in the central nervous system. Such a motor response is impossible without the image of the object on the visual cortex. Eyes, inner ear, and proprioceptive sources act as information centers and inform us of unbalance and we mechanically adjust to more stable postures.

The learning of a Judo skill can be greatly facilitated if certain basic steps are followed. First we should obtain a full understanding of the skill desired, intended purpose, when it is to be employed, the mechanics of its execution, and results of its application. Judo instructors should insist on this first step in the presentation of a Judo technique. Next, we must watch a skilled performer demonstrate the action, perhaps on a reduced speed basis so that the construction of the technique is presented. At this time, we must attempt to mentally picture what to do as we follow the demonstration. This demonstration phase should be repeated several times to clearly present to the student the pattern of the technique and the movements required. Thirdly, we must individually begin the movement from a crude state of akward imitation with failures and varying degrees of success to the final state of a polished and correctly executed reflex action. It is at this point that the instructor is vital, for he must correct, adjust, and advise the performer so that mistakes are gradually eliminated. Through constant repetition, the desired movement is developed, and at last we no longer concern ourselves with minute details of the execution. We pass on from mechanical imitation to reflex action via a nervous circuit which has been developing in response to adequate stimuli. Such a circuit will improve with use. *There can be no muscular sense of a movement we have never made.* Such a sense has to be developed by constant repetition of a movement utilizing the *Uchikomi* style of training. Students and instructors of Judo alike, must understand and utilize this training method (see Chapter 8).

Spoken of in terms of reflex action, we use the highly complimentary word "skillful" to describe correct performances. Skillful movement wastes little muscular exertion. It is patterned after the fundamental principle of Kodokan Judo—*Maximum Efficiency*—or—*Best Use of Energy.* Skillful movement is graceful, pleasing to the eye, and void of lumbering, unsightly, and wasteful motion. Three factors are essential to skillful movement:

Use of Right Muscles: Utilizing those muscles in the performance of an action which can accomplish the desired result most effectively and efficiently. Judo movement can be developed only by adequate practice. New movements require coordination by constant repetition while old movements remain in the reflex category by continued practice of the already learned coordination (see Chapter 8).

Right Amount of Force: Control, or accuracy of our muscle forces is essentially the product of practical experience and in Judo this quality has a bearing on our technique. It is referred to among Judo experts as the "blow of a sledge hammer" or the "blow of a keen-edged sword," contrasting the forces executed to bring about a *Waza* (technique).

Timing: Even though our Judo movement meets the required use of the right muscles and proper force, we would have nothing resembling Judo technique if the moment of application was ill-chosen. Unquestionably this factor is essential to an economical application of force, and its disregard results in awkwardness and possible injury.

Skillful movement requires the use of muscle and strength in various capacities of function described elsewhere in this chapter. The use of prime movers, antagonists, fixation, and neutralizing muscles cannot be ignored. Speed is also essential to Judo performance, but it depends upon the muscle's reaction to stimuli and the ability for that muscle to contract forcibly. Skill in the final analysis depends entirely on muscular control. Skill connotes precision and accuracy of movement, choosing the proper movement in response to an intended purpose, as well as economy in the force applied, which requires the utilization of the right muscles at the right time with the right amount of force. In order to accomplish this performance in totality, *strength* is necessary. This then is the principle of Kodokan Judo applied synergistically to our bodily musculature.

Coordination is the "teamwork" of muscles associated with *strength, speed,* and *skill.* Grace and ease of motion are the products of coordination. The economic use of muscles with accurate interplay again follows the principle of *Maximum Efficiency,* the fundamental basis of all Kodokan Judo.

Kiai: The somewhat mysterious entity and esoteric values attached to the phenomena called *Kiai* ("spirit meeting") in Judo, has given rise to speculation about the value of this "stomach shouting" commonly used in contest and various Kata demonstrations. We will not attempt a complete discussion of the psychological aspects of Kiai, but will impart a distinctly mechanical flavor to it by a physiological explanation.

The nervous system mechanism which controls the breathing muscles, works automatically and is not subject to normal voluntary control. This inherent action governs the amount of movement necessary in rest and exercise, without conscious effort. Yet, through training, it is possible to modify these muscular movements in relation to rate, depth, and form of breathing. By training we are able to vary our habitual coordination through different styles of breathing. An excellent example is seen in the manner of breathing of voice experts and singers, who first by conscious effort and later by habit, acquire through training, inhalation and exhalation that holds the chest high. Inspiration is performed before the chest is fully depressed, giving the chest the part of a "resonance cavity" making the quality of the sound better. Other variations exist in which the abdominal muscles are contracted during inspiration so that the diaphragm is unable to function normally, and costal breathing is effected, or the diaphragm is permitted full-range action by an expanded chest. The variety in manners of breathing is larger than normally thought, but all methods are directed to the harmonization of breathing and the muscular movement being made so that the greatest economy of nervous and muscular force is achieved. This then, reverts to the basic principle of Kodokan Judo—*Maximum Efficiency*.

In the Kiai of Judo, we have a form of suppression of breathing to allow movements of the greatest force possible. Both the muscles of the upper body and those of the lower body are strong, but unless the mid-section can unite them in a concerted function, they will act as uncoordinated units. In the various movements of Judo, the upper and lower body muscles require so much force that the trunk must be made a solid base or whole in order to permit the moving muscles to act on it with all their ability. To do this, we take a deep breath, close the glottis, and trap air in the lungs, forcing the chest to retain the air. By a contraction of the abdominal muscles, the solidarity of the trunk is achieved and both upper body and lower body function uniformly. What we experience is a feeling of "breathing into our stomach," much like the normal breathing pattern when we lie down to rest. In this position, our chest appears to expand little and the stomach swells and deflates with our breathing. Judo breathing must limit "chest" breathing, which only serves as a firm support for the arms to function, and seek to achieve "stomach" breathing, which serves to unite the entire body.

The Kiai shout used by many of the younger contestants is merely a way of releasing imprisoned air to strengthen the body to a maximum degree. This release must be timed with the effort of the technique. It is a physiological fact that breathing of any type is more efficient when the abdominal walls are strong and well-muscled. The use of proper training methods will bring effective breathing and coordinated body movement.

Application: The contents of this chapter is of direct concern to Judo instructors and athletic coaches rather than students. However, understanding of the physiology and kinesiology of the body will bring increased Judo performance. Scientific training methods described in this book are based upon sound principles discussed in this chapter. We have seen the physiological bases of muscular action and have determined the necessity of strength in Judo. Strength has taken on new meanings beyond the ability to resist force. The compatibility of strength with Judo technique has been clearly demonstrated and we are able to design training appropriate to Judo study.

The training exercises and actual applications involved in developing championship Judo ability are outlined fully in Part II. The trainee who seeks continual active Judo participation supplementing such study with the exercises recommended in this book, will be rewarded by an improved physical condition and a more skillful performance of Judo beyond his first expectations. The reader is asked to remember that there will always be inequalities in the degree of neuro-muscular skill between individuals in spite of the excellence of instruction and the trainees devotion to training. The so-called "natural athlete" is given by hereditary factors and physical composition a variety of neuro-muscular experiences from which he draws and performs in a superior manner.

Within the limits of this text, no effort is made to design a bodybuilding program for the physique trainees, nor is an attempt made to teach the rudiments of the Olympic lifting techniques. The authors are rather interested in bringing proper, sensible training techniques to the Judo exponents who are interested in improving their Judo performance. Non-Judo exponents will find a sensible pattern of prescribed exercise which will positively lead to improvement in health and better functioning of bodily processes.

PLATE 5. Heavy training for M. Kato, (top) 4 Dan, pays off in All-Japan Judo Championship matches, 1960, as he scores by Uchimata makikomi.

CHAPTER 4

Judo Training
Advice

There is no end to training. Once you begin to feel that you are masters, you are no longer getting on the way you are to follow.

Hagakure Bushido

General: The various levels of proficiency in Judo performance make it difficult to describe in the short space of one chapter, all the necessary information regarding Judo training. However, in training for the championship levels of Judo performance, we can find an alliance between the proper method of exercise, diet, and sleep requirements which will give us the basis for our discussion. This triad holds the secret to physical fitness and the efficient performance of our body. We must pay strict attention to these requirements, for by so doing, we will give to our body a great advantage in allowing it to pursue our training efforts. To avoid any one of these items, is to penalize our body and subject it to energy-sapping and wasteful practices. Too often training becomes nothing more than "smoking a big, black cigar and a fast walk around the block."

Objectives and Purposes of Training: A well-known Judo instructor once remarked when asked the best way to obtain success in Judo; "There are just three rules. First,—*practice*. Second,—*practice*. Third,—*practice*." Besides being an over-simplification, this is of course not the whole picture. While generally sound advice, it must be expanded if it is to satisfy the conditions of today's contest Judo performances. The ultimate objective of Judo training today remains the same as intended by its founder, Dr. Kano, and may be summarized as:

Physical development
Contest proficiency
Mental development

Modern concepts lay stress on the second quality, which most advocates support as the fundamental axis of Judo. Translated in more direct terms, Judo today, even in Japan, has become equated with contest or sporting efficiency. This is the very thing that Dr. Kano warned against. Competitive Judo should only be a *means* to the end of skill and principles for higher self-development, and any "drift" toward "contest" Judo as the *sole* interpretation of Judo should be carefully regulated. This "drift" has set in, in major proportions, and in the minds of many experts, technique has suffered and Judo has become nothing more than a sport in which "win at all costs" is the underlying philosophy.

The emphasis placed on competitive excellence is perhaps somewhat out of proportion to what was intended by Master Kano, and this is evidenced nowhere more clearly than in Japan where the victorious are extolled in terms of rapid advancement in rank far beyond their ability to understand Judo except in terms of physically scoring a point. Indeed, this emphasis has reached into the ranks of Western Judo exponents who can be heard to ask daily, "How many points have you got?" as they query other Judo exponents at Kodokan and other Dojo in Japan. The "point" has become all-important as it is the underlying factor for advancement in rank. There are of course other considerations which enter promotion, but aside from serious character weaknesses, and sometimes "time-in-grade" deficiencies, the "fighting machine" will almost always realize a more rapid advancement than the longer-experienced, possibly less physically gifted exponent, who nevertheless has a deep understanding of intrinsic Judo. Apparently, the means intended by Master Kano are being mistaken for the ends. Contest Judo is vital to the health of Judo as an entity, but the objectives of Judo as originally defined are mutually supplementary and will best be continued by proper training methods which are suited for physical development *and* the regard for the growth of technique on a balanced foundation which regards each individual Judo exponent.

It is via proper Judo training that we learn skillful execution of technical theory. Initial individual response to Judo training will be increased physical development and improved physical fitness. Mental development will respond along lines of self-confidence, increased ability to be decisive, spirit of sportsmanship, and improved reflex-action. In considering Judo as a program of physical training, it is well to note that the prescribed exercises of the traditional Judo pattern and those complementing Judo, will specifically develop, increase, and maintain:

Strength: muscle development and capacity for endurance.
Coordination: integration of all body units into efficient purposeful movement.
Speed and agility: changing of body direction and position in a quick, efficient manner.
Balance: sense of stability in all positions.
Endurance: efficiency of heart, lungs, and vascular system.

An understanding of our purpose in Judo training will help both instructor and trainee understand what part complementary means of exercise play in increasing Judo performance. The purpose of Judo training is simply to prepare the body for efficiency and skill in this given activity. Under proper training methods, our efficiency and skill will rise. Note that this implies no divergence from the founder's intended purpose of all Judo objectives being met. Conversely, if we utilize improper training methods, we can never hope to attain the intended objectives, let alone the championship proficiency desired. To more adequately understand proper training methods, it is well to realize that training should be directed toward four areas: *building technique, building strength, building endurance,* and *building speed.*

Technique is the correct and efficient performance of Judo movement in accord with the principles of Judo. It is never a mechanical process in its true aspect, but rather a reflex action developed by intelligent practice. It is further, specific actions effected without conscious effort. The elements that go into developing Judo skill have already been discussed in Chapter 3. Further elaboration will be made in this chapter.

Strength is the ability to overcome resistance and the capacity for endurance. It is effected through the muscles of the body. Muscles have but one primary function... to work. As a muscle is made to work, nature causes the muscle to grow to meet the demands placed upon it, and appropriately adds just a little more than is necessary in anticipation of heavier work to come. A weak muscle which is subjected to a systematic program of progressively harder work, thickens and increases in size. With increase in size, comes added weight and strength. The more a muscle exercises, within limits, the more it becomes able to exercise.

Endurance then, is a direct outgrowth of progressive training. It is the ability to resist fatigue. We have seen that muscular fatigue is caused by waste products of muscular contraction and that it limits performance. Endurance must be built by developing the circulatory and respiratory systems as well as muscles, so that waste products can be more efficiently carried away and thus reduce the onset of fatigue. This must be done according to a systematic plan of progressive training intensity. Best results are obtained by *daily* training.

Speed is the ability of our muscles to contract forcibly in minimum time, causing our body to move in a desired manner. Greater strength in contraction will bring about greater speed. When all obstacles to muscle contraction have been reduced or removed, speed is a natural development. Obstacles such as antagonistic muscle action, selection of right muscles in a particular movement, and the right use of force all bear directly on speed.

The *totality* of the four areas described above must be regarded in designing an effective training program for the Judo exponent.

Separation of the qualities is virtually impossible, and our methods must reach into all areas if they are to be at all efficient. We must seek to develop technique, strength, endurance, and speed by all and every means possible. Skillful Judo will be the result of such sensible training.

Principles of Learning: An understanding of the term "learning" is often taken for granted as an elementary subject not worthy of consideration. However, instructors will do well to have a well-grounded understanding of the processes involved, since Judo is an educational entity.

Definitions vary depending upon one's philosophical basis, but for our purpose, a feature of learning is the acquisition and improvement of abilities in Judo. It is a process by which we are able to do something which we previously could not. We know that it is impossible to learn anything without trying or without repetition, yet use and repetition alone are not enough. There are certain well-established facts which though not rigid, are applicable. Such are the Principles of Learning.

The first of these principles is referred to as the *Principle of Exercise* which is a logical implication that practice or repetition and usage tends to keep learning at an optimum while lack of practice or repetition causes learning to weaken. Human minds retain what they use. Retention is based on use, but it is not proven that learning is directly proportional to the amount of exercise or practice. Repetition alone however, is not sufficient to guarantee proper learning and this introduces a second principle.

Such is the *Principle of Readiness* which means that the individual will respond with success and satisfaction to a situation only when the response is within his capacity and when the response meets some felt need. This can be thought of as "mental set," "desire" or "motivation."

Next, the *Principle of Effect* tells us that learning accompanied by a pleasant of satisfying sensation is strengthened, but that learning associated with an unpleasant or unsatisfying feeling is weakened. Here we can interpolate an emotional zone of activity which influences learning.

Finally, the *Principle of Self-Activity* shows that learning takes place *only* during activity. It is never a passive process of absorption, but an active process with a distinct personal tone. We must "do" to learn.

The significance of these psychological implications transposed to Judo training is obvious and the core of efficient teaching and learning. They are not separate and independent of each other, but are actually inter-related. All four are operative all the time, though at any one point in the learning process, one may be primary. We must think of the learning process as a "whole" to avoid failures.

Sincerity in Training: Sincerity of purpose in the study of and training for Judo is essential to successfully build a creditable technique. In the words of a committee of high grade Judo masters of the Kodokan: "The masters of Judo, celebrated alike for their Judo science, their efficiency, and their personal social value, are all Judo exponents who have worked enormously. At Judo, one cannot arrive at even medium results without serious and perseverant training. One may obtain brilliant effects by use of pure force, but one rapidly falls victim to this practice.

"Experience teaches that the more training one has the better will be the result, provided one does not overdo physically. No matter what his age, the youth and happiness of a man depend upon the energy or the lassitude that he feels—his way of thinking, his hopes, his actions, also his physical appearance. All these points rest upon two factors; —a vigorous and active body, and, an enquiring and enterprising mind.

"Judo contributes to the development of these two major factors, but an enterprising and inquiring mind can only remain so in a healthy and active body."

Regularity of Training: The serious Judo exponent trains *every day,* with an occasional rest day. It is this devotion to Judo exercise that has brought the Japanese into Judo dominance. Daily training is expected and carried out by all serious students *(see Chapter 6).* Students will do well to recall the classic reply of Pablo Casals, world's foremost cellist who at 84, when asked why he practiced daily, said, "Because I think I am making progress."

Modern living however, makes it imperative that daily training be foregone under most circumstances. Yet, whether the trainee partakes in daily exercise or occasional exercise, such training must be consistent and well organized. This is especially true if reduced training is undertaken. You must get the "most" for your efforts. It is well to establish a minimum for Judo training. If championship caliber of Judo is desired, no less than daily training 6 days a week should be established. For less serious levels of Judo, two or three sessions per week will prove adequate. Sufficient time must be set aside for a sensible program which involves the use of Preparatory, Supplementary, and Compound Exercises in addition to actual *Randori* (free Judo exercise), and *Kata* (prearranged form exercise). Trainees complementing their training with Auxiliary Exercises must further insist on a schedule of regularity. Time must be set aside for the desired program to be completed.

The famous masters of old Japan required intense and long hours of Judo training. It was thought that if the trainees did not perspire blood and water, the training was inadequate. It is often told that the famous master of the Kito Ryu, Kishimoto, trained himself daily for six consecutive hours beginning at 5:00AM and required the same dedication to training of his students. S. Kotani, 8 Dan, recalls that during his student days there was never a chance to rest. The drinking of water was forbidden. After one and one-half hours of steady exertion, perspiration would cease to flow, and that around two hours, salt would form on the lips and tongue. While modern training methods would advisably question this practice, nevertheless the records show that it was the combination of the teachers driving their students and the resolve of the subject students to carry on in spite of fatigue, that produced the remarkable Judoka of Japan. This "Spartan" system is still used by all major Judo activities in Japan, but is often modified due to increased demands of modern life.

The actual amount of time that should be devoted to each training session will vary with individual requirements, differences, and facilities. A little time is better than none at all, but to really obtain beneficial results, each training session should not be less than 50 minutes or an hour in length, while maximum limits should be placed no higher than 3 hours. Exceptions to this may be made from time to time in the form of a special clinic or instructional class which meets on an "all day" basis. This form is seen in Japan during student and teacher courses offered by the Kodokan. For those who are physically able and energetically inclined, a form generally popular with university Judo students in Japan can be instituted. These university students will train two or three times each day, each session being broken by at least an hour's rest. Needless to say, time is the greatest obstacle to this method of training, and only a very few dedicated trainees ever attempt this in the Western World. The design of training programs must consider the time factor. Normal men cannot within normal time limits exercise in extreme fashion. Only, as has been indicated, the favored few can hope to devote themselves to training extremes. Yet, the serious athlete must strive for a *balanced, sensible* program. The factor of time is not the only consideration, as energy too must be given attention. The average man may, however, be somewhat relieved to find that careful exercise not to the point of heavy fatigue can be beneficial. The training program must regard the problem of fatigue. Undue fatigue by exercise is not physiologically condoned, yet there are tendencies to push a trainee until he literally "drops." Such is an excess and is to be avoided if it becomes the "rule" rather than the "exception." This is not to infer that protracted exercise is completely unwise, and never has utility. The prime requisite for addition of strength is short-lived but intense exertion, while protracted exercise builds endurance. This information will be utilized in design of the Auxiliary Exercises to be discussed in future chapters.

Over Training: Each workout session should be entered into with energy and enthusiasm. Merely going through the motions may result in injury to you or to your partner, and most certainly will not bring good results. It is possible, and common, to train to extremes and to produce an overtrained condition known in the athletic world jargon as "stale." Physiologically, this condition is undesirable, and should be avoided. Here are some of the symptoms of over-training: A generally tired and unenergetic feeling. A decrease in power when applying usual movements. Continued muscle soreness from work-out to workout, which makes each workout uncomfortable. Normal muscle soreness is to be expected when training, but it should not be continual. Loss of weight. Loss of interest in training. Nervousness and inability to sleep comfortably. Loss of appetite.

If any of the above symptoms appear and continue...you are probably over-trained and should spend a few days of *complete* rest, particularly in the physical sense, and a complete lay-off from training should be taken. A minimum of one week is essential, though additional time may bring increased benefits. After this, a return to sensible training, starting with less than your limit for at least two weeks, will bring new energy and better results.

Under Training: Generally this condition consists of a lazy and sluggish mental outlook. When we do not fully apply ourselves to sensible training, and when each workout merely becomes "something to do" and we avoid real exercise which produces perspiration, we are under-training. Signs of under-training are: Initially there is no goal in mind and we merely make the motions. All motions are applied haphazardly. Muscle soreness is never experienced. Lack of seriousness in training. Workouts are a "breeze."

The remedy is simple...set a purpose or goal to your training and then train regularly.

Instructor Advice: For those who are philosophically minded, the term "instructor" may not be idealistically suitable, and the term "teacher" deemed more appropriate. In Eastern parlance, the *instructor* is the passer on of information, the producer of a technician, while the *teacher* does this and additionally builds the character of his subject trainees. Such an implication extends beyond mere technique giving and regards that realm of Judo beyond the physical, and brings Judo within the sphere of educational values. Here in the Western world, there is an obvious shortage of true Judo teachers. To those who aspire to become teachers, let their *practice* of Judo become a true *study*.

Recalling the Principles of Learning discussed earlier in this chapter, we have come to understand that we cannot really "teach" anyone anything—all we can do as instructors is to provide situations to which the student may react in some way, and by so reacting, learn. Our purpose as an instructor is to lend him assistance in this effort. If the situations we present are too meaningless to arouse the student to reaction, then our efforts at teaching are failing for there can be no learning without reaction. We must, therefore, promote activities which are intrinsically interesting to the student. We must provide a pattern for the student and carefully explain its intricacies while arousing stronger motivation.

Modern psychology has confirmed that we do not possess isolated mental faculties. This means that observation, attention, memory, etc., do not work in isolation. Our minds work as a whole and mental efficiency in any given situation depends upon a large number of factors. *Interest* and *motivation* are probably the most important. If we want the effects of our teaching to produce results, we must arouse intense interest, avoid rule-of-thumb instruction, and help the student to see the relation between all the single items we teach. We must teach intelligently and not mechanically. We cannot afford to isolate ourselves from the student. Avoid complete reliance on the crutch of routine.

Instructors divide into conservatives and progressives. Some adopt changes more readily than others. Some are steeped in tradition and will not change. However, there is hardly ever an instructor who will not alter his methods to some extent if he is *convinced* that an addition or change is a more effective teaching procedure than the one it replaces. The art of teaching can be regarded as the sum total learned from theory and practice. This holds true for both the conservatives and progressives, and all of the instructors' efforts must be supported by purpose. Yet, purpose is meaningless without a method of achievement, and improvement of students can only come from the instructor making judicious choice of training methodology. Effective teaching is the responsibility of each instructor who should endeavor to become a better instructor.

First interest in Judo is usually based upon student curiosity and a misunderstanding of the abilities of exponents skilled in this art. From this seemingly shallow motivation, true interest may be developed by varied instructional procedures. These procedures will depend upon the experience of the instructor. Application of such procedures should be conducted along the lines of established methods. The following outline has proven functional, though it should not be considered codified as absolute, but rather flexible:

Class Orientation:

Discuss scope and objectives of training program

Discuss history, development, and rationale of Judo

Discuss class procedures, methods of practice, evaluations, ranks and awards

Use films appropriate to the instruction

Class Sessions:

Length of instructional periods should not exceed 2 hours except in highly specialized training programs.

Classes should use the standard *Go Kyo no Waza* (Five Principles of Technique) of Kodokan as a guide (see Appendix, page 299). Stress basic Waza selected primarily from the first three Kyo in the Go Kyo no Waza. Tendencies to attempt too fancy a technique will result in slow learning. The various Kata may also be used.

Individual skills to be recorded periodically. Ability tested by examinations and contests. Prospective instructors may be found among highly skilled, exceptional students.

Competition:

Each session should include controlled competitive play whereby the trainee is able to exercise the skills he is attempting to master. This is best done by means of *Randori*.

Actual contests should be held within the Dojo proper to afford competitive training. These are termed *Tsukinami Shiai* (monthly contests). They offer the instructor a basis of individual student evaluation for future promotional considerations.

Contests with outside Dojo are desirable in order to fully develop the student. Competition confined only to the home Dojo will not bring the students to a high level of skill.

Continued contest performance too early in a beginning trainees' experience can easily attenuate or cancel proper progress. The core of this is both physical and psychological. Beginners have not yet established Judo fundamentals and will perform with stiff bodies and primarily arm and shoulder power. Then too, personal attachment to success and

reputation and the desire to "win" is strong. Both elements are positive impediments to Judo development. Instructors must be sure that beginners are ready for contest. Those advanced trainees should receive every opportunity to enter contests. The *Shinkyu Shiai* (promotional tournament for Kyu) is especially valuable.

All competitive Judo will conform to the standard rules of Kodokan Judo.

Instructional Procedure: (see above pictures)

Large groups must be handled by dividing the class into smaller groups. Mass teaching is bad, except initially, during the study of basic fundamentals. Divide students according to the level of skill and give them appropriate Judo techniques commensurate with their abilities. Do not "over" or "under" teach them.

Limited mat space requires that groups work in "shifts" in order to safely apply physical actions. The resting group can learn also by attentively watching the performance of their fellow trainees. Rotate partners. Levels of basic—intermediate—advanced Judo must further give consideration to differences in age and physical fitness. Instructional procedure must be flexible enough to allow for individual differences.

Preparation of Instruction:

An extensive study of Judo training programs reveals that they fall within one of two categories. Either they are pre-structured or they are not. Generally, the pre-structured training programs radiate the competence of highly imaginative and aggressive instructors with a resultant progress of commendable excellence, while the non-pre-structured training programs exhibit lesser degrees of attainment and are led by instructors who are either incompetent, indifferent, or at best, not convinced that other methods are better.

Considering, for a moment, the non-pre-structured programs, it is self-evident that they can cast a reflection upon the quality of the Judo training presented. Sometimes they are supported under the guise of psychological methodology which does not pay attention to logical or systematic organization of subject matter. In this type of program, the trainee studies according to his needs and interests. Instructors monitor the instruction only to the extent that material studied should be consistent with the capacity of the trainee.

Pre-structured training programs are logical learning patterns which are organized on the basis of "first things first," and from the simple to the complex. Subject matter is taken up in a prescribed order which leads progressively to predicted levels of skill. Under this system, instructors have increased responsibilities and must be well qualified. Experiments have proven that students can learn by the seemingly orderless psychological method as well as by the rigid logical procedure. The authors experience favors the logical program, the pre-structured plan (see programs pages 126–130 and 144).

Analyze the situation by considering the objective, reason, and purpose of the training. Time available is also an important consideration, both from the aspect of individual session and total program duration. The methods to be used must depend on the training area and facilities that can be utilized.

Selection of subject matter is a vital consideration. Important in this consideration are the limitations, capabilities, and the training objectives of students. A thorough understanding of the techniques and key points of each technique is necessary.

Planning the lesson requires that we know what must be taught. A definite sequence of instruction should be considered. No sequence of meaningful experience can be planned in absentia for any given group of trainees. To be meaningful, these experiences must be planned with complete understanding and regard of the individuals to be taught.

Proper facilities must be available. Training is strictly limited by facilities. Safety measures are a paramount consideration when setting up a physical location for training.

An instructor, foremost, must know the subject he teaches. One cannot understand the rudiments of an important subject without knowing it at higher levels—at least not well enough to teach it. The instructor must continue to learn his subject and not withdraw behind a shield of complacent smugness. Refresh or petrify!

Technique of Instruction:

Explanation will arouse attention and interest. Create a "learning attitude" by clarified discussion of the purpose of the training. This is partly clarification of subject, partly of terms. Connect the ideas into a "whole."

Introduce the material by a logical step-by-step presentation. Stress *Yoten* (key points). Do not present too many techniques at any one session. Use examples, comparisons, and contrasts. Remember that the composition, experience, and needs of each class differs.

Demonstration is a vital phase. Emphasize the key points by clarified positions. Emphasize a high standard of skill based on technique. Use training aids frequently. This should include the use of charts, blackboard, film, slides, pictures, dummies, and miscellaneous apparatus appropriate to the subject.

Application of the material presented must be required of all trainees. Maintain constant supervision so that improper movements are corrected promptly. Because of the many implications in technical issues, instructor will always have to help students recognize and deal with the important points which are not always explicit in a general demonstration. In Chapter 3 we learned that there can be no muscular sense of a movement we have never made. This means that new movements cannot be "felt" with any accuracy. Judo instructors must get trainees to move hands, feet, head, and abdominal-belt region, as applicable to the technique being studied, for these parts of the body are most easily felt. It may be necessary to break the instruction down into unit parts, but too much stress on isolated skills is apt to block rather than encourage progress.

Examination is the final phase to determine understanding and ability of trainees as well as to determine the success of the instructors teaching. Subject matter of all examinations should be in accord with national standards. *(See Appendix, pages 301–306.)*

Measuring Individual Achievement:

Organized progressive training must produce results. The alert instructor is aware of the importance of the objectives he outlines in relation to the type of group he will instruct. Training problems vary, and it is frequently necessary for the instructor to adapt accordingly, emphasizing only instruction which will obtain positive results.

Individual achievement will only develop with individual enthusiasm. Enthusiasm is a product of the leadership ability of the instructor and his qualified presentation of Judo technique.

The following check list will serve to aid instructors in analyzing individual progress:

Is the trainee developing a directional sense, coordination, and flexibility in both *Tachi* (standing) and *Ne* (reclining) positions?

Is the trainee's physical fitness improving?

Is the trainee developing proper waist action necessary for effective application of basic *Naga Waza* (throwing techniques)?

Is the trainee becoming proficient in the fundamentals of Judo such as *Shisei* (posture), *Shintai* (body movement), *Taisabaki* (body turning movement), *Kumikata* (forms of grasping), *Kuzushi* (unbalancing), and *Ukemi* (falling)?

Is the trainee establishing proper form in the basic techniques?

Is the trainee proficient in the basic Judo terminology?

Does the trainee adhere to the rules of the local Dojo, and the rules of Kodokan Judo?

Is the trainee maintaining cleanliness of self and costume?

Does the trainee observe common sense and safety precautions necessary to sensible training?

Does the trainee have a basic knowledge and appreciation of the ideals of Kodokan Judo?

Methods of Evaluation:

The objectives of individual evaluation include the determination as to whether or not the following factors are present: the instruction is accomplishing the desired results; the stimulus to motivate the participant toward a higher level of competitive skill; the screening for qualified future instructors; and the source to improve instruction techniques.

Actual evaluations should conform to the accepted standards of Kodokan Judo which are enforced by the national Judo body, *The Judo Black Belt Federation of the U.S.A.* (JBBF). This national body sets the standards and conduct of Judo, both technically and administratively, via its officially recognized *Yudanshakai* (Black Belt Associations). These standards are available from the various local Yudanshakai, and periodically examinations are offered by these organizations. A schedule of the various contests and examinations can be obtained by contacting any nationally recognized Yudanshakai (see Appendix, pages 288–89).

Miscellaneous:

Keep in mind your limitations and capabilities as an instructor. This is your obligation to your students. Bear in mind that no one instructor knows all the answers regardless of his skill or repute. No one instructor can give all the necessary ingredients for a polished Judo technique. Encourage and welcome "outside" instructors to come to your training sessions. It will not lower your prestige, but more likely improve it and greatly benefit the Judo performance of you and your students.

Each Dojo should be administratively organized just as it has technical organization. The Dojo may be an independent body, or an "exercise area," one of several, of a larger organization called a "Judo Club."

Regardless, the independent body, whether the Dojo or the Club, must be organized administratively and technically. The technical training and progress of the Judo trainees will depend upon a good administrative setup. The Dojo or Club should be established under a written constitution and by-laws. (See Appendix). Officers should be elected to serve in the usual capacities of President, Vice-President, Secretary, Treasurer, or their counterparts. Records should be kept on each student, listing full name, address, possible phone number, and specific information as to age, and other vital statistics. Each individual trainee record should contain information as to the students date of entry into Judo study, and a complete record of his progress, listing ranks obtained, and the dates such ranks were awarded. Each Judo exponent should be, if eligible, registered with the local office of the Amateur Athletic Union of the U.S.A. (AAU) to ensure his amateur status. Dojo or Club officials should be conversant with AAU policy in regard to amateurism, sporting events, and the like. Qualified Judo exponents should seek office as AAU Judo Committeemen, via their local Yudanshakai. Miscellaneous records and files may be kept by the Dojo or Club and may include training information, rules of contest, books, and Judo supplies. Technical Judo cannot grow without suitable administrative support. Such administrative procedures as are appropriate to the body in question must be established, and once established, must be exercised just as body muscle, if they are to remain healthy and functional. Purchase Judo supplies from your local Yudanshakai.

Watch for weaknesses in your students. These may be mirror-images of your own deficiencies. Make every effort to improve yourself. Study your students systematically and prepare a training program which has a long-range effect. Do not enter the Dojo with little or no idea of what is to be taught. If you have assistants aiding you, insist on co-ordination between what each is and has been teaching. You will thus avoid needless duplication and omission. But, remember that a good Judo school is not a conglomeration of the practices such as described in this text. It should represent not a hodge-podge of methodology, but rather, a well integrated effort. As an instructor you must be patient.

Insist on all safety precautions. The following check list will aid you:

Mat and training area conditions must be free from hazards which might directly or indirectly cause injury.

Cleanliness of mats and area must be maintained.

Stress individual personal cleanliness and physical fitness.

Emphasize the importance of basic skills to be performed in accordance with correct Judo principles.

Stress rules of the Dojo and Kodokan Judo.

Adhere to good sensible training and make use of Preparatory Exercises for both warming up and cooling off.

Supervise all sessions and minimize distraction to sideline activity.

Keep first aid material available in the Dojo.

All doubtful health conditions should be referred to the appropriate medical authorities.

Do not take unknown Judoka at face value, particularly Kyu ranks. Check out their abilities before assigning them contact work.

Insist on proper Dojo etiquette at all Judo sessions. The mark of a good Judo exponent extends beyond his ability to perform physical techniques on the mat, and his demeanor is a direct reflection on the standards of his instructor.

Register yourself individually with the national Judo body via your local Yudanshakai. Information regarding this procedure can be obtained by contacting your parent Yudanshakai *(see Appendix, pages 288–89)*. Be an active member of your local Yudanshakai by taking part in its functions and serving in various capacities as an official of that organization. Remember that you have specific responsibilities as an instructor and that all you do for Judo should be properly in accord with national standards. Specific regard must be held for promotional authority and the standards required for each rank to be awarded trainees *(see Appendix, pages· 289–90)*.

Affiliate your Dojo with the appropriate local Yudanshakai *(see Appendix, pages 288–89)*, having administrative supervision over the area in which you reside. This affiliation will bring your Dojo national recognition and support. The benefits of the technical assistance, training advice, and administrative support which will be supplied by your local Yudanshakai will add to your prestige and will enhance your position as an instructor. By being a Dojo affiliate of a recognized Yudanshakai, your Dojo can take part in the many contests, promotional examinations, social events, and teaching clinics offered periodically by the Yudanshakai. For information, contact the local Yudanshakai. Become national-effort conscious. Contribute to this effort by being an active instructor in an active Dojo which is affiliated with a nationally recognized Yudanshakai.

Student Advice: It is not always possible to select our Judo instructor; nevertheless, care taken in the initial selection is vital to our future success. Ensure that the instructor is a nationally recognized Judo exponent. This may be done by contacting the local Yudanshakai *(see Appendix, pages 288–89)* having administrative supervision over the area in which you reside. It is also possible that your instructor will have some credentials from the local Yudanshakai supporting him as a qualified instructor commensurate with his rank. Additionally, the Dojo you join may have a certificate of affiliation with a parent Yudanshakai, which serves to establish its reputation and reliability. Credit for your Judo study and subsequent gradings can only be awarded by nationally recognized instructors and their organizations. While it is best to find a *Yudansha* (Black Belt) instructor, many parts of the country preclude this because there are no residents of this degree of skill, and a *Mudansha* (ungraded) instructor of *kyu* rank (class) may be your teacher. Regardless, if the instructor is nationally recognized through the local Yudanshakai, your chances of obtaining good instruction are higher than if you study under an instructor of no national standing. By joining a nationally recognized Dojo with an accredited instructor, your rank and future promotions will be officially recorded both with the local Yudanshakai and the national Judo body. "Let the buyer beware" applies here... Select your instructor carefully.

As soon as possible after admission to a Dojo or Judo Club, learn the rules of that organization and adhere to them to the letter. A good Judo exponent is always recognized by his demeanor as well as by his technique. Various Dojo have "ground" rules in addition to the traditional patterns of etiquette which must always be observed. Learn the rules of Kodokan Judo, as they will aid you to become more proficient. Take an active part in all the Dojo affairs and do not become just an "exercise-shower-go home" student.

Attend all classes promptly. Do the required work with spirit and develop sincerity in your training. Regularity will bring results. Excuses, insincerity, and general laziness will not bring your Judo to a skillful level. You must do Judo to learn Judo! Remember that careless practice is disrespectful to the spirit of Judo and is a loss of valuable time. The technique you are attempting to learn is but a means to an end. Learn it and forget it . . . that is, let the initially mechanical movements become conditioned reflex action. The use of complementary training such as Preparatory, Supplementary, Compound, and Auxiliary Exercises are all important to be sure, but alone, they will not build a complete Judo technique. You must take an active part in Randori, Kata, and *Shiai* (contest) sessions. Don't "wallflower." Ask for practices. S. Kotani, 8 Dan, is a fine example for each and every Judo trainee to emulate. During his student days, he would practice with every powerful and skillful Judoka he could lay his hands on, rather than avoid the "beating" he knew would be coming. To be thrown, immobilized, or strangled, was nothing but delight for him. The thing that really counted was *practice!*

The demeanor of the Judo exponent is of vital importance. Dojo etiquette is always to be observed. The Judo student will note that conduct does not begin and end at the mat's edge, but continues throughout daily life. He will be expected to abide by the standards of Kodokan Judo at all times. Judo in the idealistic sense, trains the mind as well as the body, and all students should maintain a high level of decorum. Juniors must always request practice of seniors.

The *Judogi* (Judo costume) should always be clean and in good repair *(see page 56, #1–3).* Judogi specifications must adhere to the Kodokan regulations *(see Appendix)* in the interests of safety and practicability. The use of old, torn, or dirty Judogi is not only dangerous, but undignified and improper. Stripping off the jacket while in the Dojo is never correct unless specifically directed by the instructor for purposes of some training objective. Laxity in wearing the Judogi is inexcusable *(page 57, #1–9).* Close and adjust the obi prior to all salutations for practice, contest, or meeting of other Judoka. It is well to own more than two Judogi in order to allow rotation between use and the laundry. The mark of a good Judo exponent is also seen in his Judogi—one that is clean and in good repair. It is interesting to note that in Japan, Judo team members of *Kyoiku Daigaku* (Tokyo Teachers College) always compete in brilliantly clean, new or almost new Judogi. This is the traditional school of Jigoro Kano and emphasizes his thinking in connection with costume cleanliness. The use of indiscriminate markings, emblems, etc. on the Judogi is to be avoided. One's name can be embroidered or lettered on the *Obi* (belt) at one end, and on the Judogi at the bottom end of the lapel on the outside surface, so that the name may be seen by the instructor. Dojo emblems or monograms may be used, but they should conform to the instructions and standards of the particular organization they represent. *(For folding Judogi, see page 57, #10–16.)*

After all exercise sessions, a shower or bath must be taken to cleanse the body. It is good practice to allow a well-heated body, so heated from strenuous exercise, to "cool" down a bit prior to taking a shower. A 5 or 10 minute wait will be ample. Taking too hot a shower after exercise will tend to relax the body muscles it is true, but in many cases, will also undo much of the stimulation exercise has produced. Unless a specific relaxation is desired, it is well to limit the use of too hot water and to finish the hot water shower with a cold one regardless of the season. This is the advice of the great Judoka, T. Hirano, 6 Dan, who used a warm shower in hot weather, and a cold shower during the cold season. All-Japan Judo Champion, I. Inokuma finishes his post-workout warm shower with a series of cold water rinses.

Remember that learning Judo skills is a process of self-activity. The instructor is not present to "give" you the movements or thoughts and ideas, but to "convey the spirit" so that you may rediscover them for yourself. This is the only way of obtaining a lasting and worthwhile personal benefit. Do not plague the instructor with questions about your "readiness" for a Judo rank. Qualified instructors will know best when you are ready for promotion, and will appropriately promote you within their limits of authority, or recommend you to the parent Yudanshakai for examination.

The wearing of rings, medals, wrist chains, bracelets, neck chains, etc., is a direct violation of the rules of Kodokan Judo, if worn during practice or contest sessions. These items must be removed prior to each practice session. Likewise, fingernails and toenails which are too long are dangerous to you and to your partner. Keep them well-trimmed.

Dojo Facilities: A Dojo is always to be considered a place for serious study. Quietness, simplicity, and cleanliness must be maintained. It is obviously better if all Judo training is done in a suitable Dojo. However, under certain conditions of limitations in time, money, and accommodations, this requirement can be disregarded. Certainly, the various Preparatory, Supplementary, Compound, and Auxiliary Exercises described herein, can for the most part be performed almost anywhere. Actual Judo Randori and Shiai must be confined to a suitably prepared mat area which is always constructed on the basis of common sense principles.

Select an area which has adequate ventilation and general sanitary conditions. Ensure that the area is sufficiently large enough for Judo practice. Judo practice with little or no movement will never develop high-levels of skill. Western Dojo are prone to disregard the space factor. The size of the area depends on many factors among which consideration must be given to the size of the group training, age levels, and economic factors. No actual dimensions can be set as a standard, but Dojo areas of less than 15 by 15 feet are usually considered undesirable. This is of course a minimum dimension, and a great variety of sizes exist up to the newly constructed Dojo of Kodokan which is the largest in existence for the practice of Judo. It consists of a mat area about 100 feet

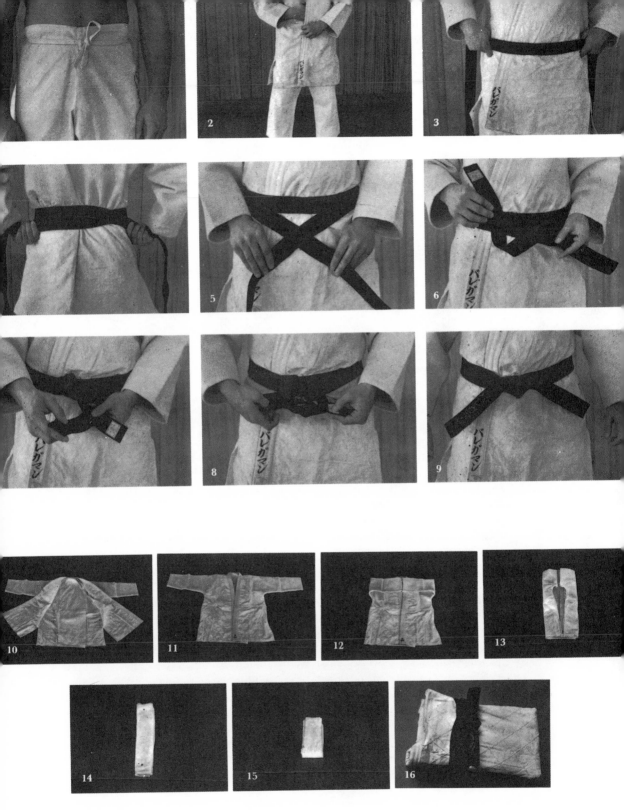

by 80 feet, providing ample room for hundreds of persons at one time *(see #1 to #3)*. Other noteworthy Japanese Dojo of considerable size include the Tokyo Keishicho Taikan (Tokyo Metropolitan Police Judo Instructor School), *(#4 and #5),* and the Kyoto Budokuden (Kyoto Military Virtues Palace), *(#6 and #7).*

Smaller Dojo areas follow the same general pattern of architectural organization of a reduced basis. *(See #8 to #10.)* Important is the selection of an area for training which regards safety measures highly. There should be no sharp corners or hard surfaces near the actual mat area which might lead to injury of the trainees. Here, too, lighting and ventilation are basic considerations after floor space. *See #11 and #12* which show ideal areas for training.

Ceiling heights vary, but a minimum of 9 feet is considered standard. Higher ceilings result in better air circulation and regulation of temperatures in addition to safety and every effort should be made to locate a Dojo with a high ceiling.

A prominent physical feature of most Dojo is the *Kamiza* (Upper Seat) which is the side of the Dojo reserved for instructors. *#13 to #18,* show some typical arrangements. If physical identity of the Kamiza is impossible by using the raised dias, it is always recognizable by the traditional picture of Dr. Kano or an appropriate personal photograph or *Gaku* (framed calligraphy) of philosophical connotation, which hangs centered in this area. *#19.*

Among the traditional fixtures of any Japanese Dojo is the *Nafudakake* (name board) as shown in *#20–#21.* Here the membership of the Dojo is displayed in appropriate order of seniority. This feature is not utilized by many American Dojo, but is quite common in European Dojo. It is a valuable aid to the instructor in many ways, but must be kept up-to-date if it is to be useful.

Judogi left in the Dojo should not be rolled up or otherwise left in a condition that precludes proper airing and drying. Many systems suggest themselves, among which is found the overhead drying racks of the Japanese Dojo *(#22 and #23)*.

The features discussed above all require some degree of permanence of the Dojo. Obviously if we are able to equip an area to serve as a Dojo, it is desirable that such equipments be more-or-less left in their proper places rather than having to pick them up and store them after each training session. If we are able, we must choose permanent sites.

The mat area proper presents additional problems to the Western Judo world. In the Orient, the use of the traditional *Tatami* (rice mat) in its various forms *(#24 and Appendix, page 298)* ranging from uncovered rice straw to canvas-covered rice straw and finally to the newly-developed Plasmat cover, the mat surface is no problem. In the West, Dojo are not so fortunate as to have this proven best type of mat surface for the practice of Judo. Only a few can afford this luxury and by and large, Western Dojo must be content with the usual canvas wrestling mats, improvised sawdust and canvas covered mats, or foam rubber, Ensolite, etc. padding, covered with canvas. Examples of well organized Dojo in the U.S.A. include the Detroit Judo Club *(#25 to #27, page 60)*.

Various important factors present themselves in the selection of a suitable mat surface. The primary consideration is of course that the mat be a smooth, continuous surface. The use of smaller piece mats is not conducive to good technique, and may induce injuries, but if unavoidable, then the piece mats should be covered with a one-piece canvas to give it the properties of a one-piece mat. The individual mats should be tied together or otherwise kept from separating. The mat surface must be level and firm. With Tatami this is an automatic condition, but with other expedients, this is not always the case. The surface must not be abrasive to the body, and yet it must be durable. Various brands of canvas are too rough while rubber coverings often offer a "stick-slip" surface and thereby increase the danger of injuries. New experimentation with rough surfaced plastic covers are proving satisfactory, although it is interesting to note that in all major contests in Japan, old style, uncovered tatami is used to provide the fastest and safest Judo.

A second consideration is the ensurance of enough padding to provide a safe, shock-

absorbent surface when falling. Placing thin mats on a hard, non-yielding wooden or concrete surface is not considered appropriate in that it places undue trauma in the body after a fall and may lead to undesirable physical conditions. While this is often said to "harden up" trainees, such thinking is questionable from the standpoint of health and is to be discouraged. The opposite extreme of a soft, loosely covered mat is equally undesirable, often causing foot injuries, sluggish Judo techniques and general bad Judo performance. Some sawdust mats are unhealthy in that they stir up a fine dust during the force of the fall which can be injurious to the health.

The undersurface which supports the mat should be of a flexible, yielding, yet resilient type. It must be able to absorb the punishment imposed by falling bodies. In the Orient, most all Dojo are equipped with spring-suspended floors beneath the Tatami. It is obvious that shock and trauma are thus reduced. Those Dojo unable to enjoy spring-suspended floors can obtain a similar effect by building flexible wooden platforms underneath the mat surface.

Provision should be made in the Dojo for a walking surface so that the mat areas are never touched by anything but the bare feet of the participants. Dirty mats are dangerous to health and must not be tolerated. The choice of an appropriate mat surface facilitates cleaning. This cleaning must be periodically done to insure sanitary conditions.

Training devices can be used in the Dojo, but such equipment as wall pulleys, mirrors, padded posts, etc., must be located so as not to interfere with actual Judo performance on the mat.

Oriental Dojo are known for their utter disregard of climatic conditions. In winter, there is no heat in the Dojo proper, except those Dojo in areas of extreme cold. The authors can well recall their practice sessions in the Dojo of Manchuria, North China, and Korea where in spite of the heating provided, the temperature was constantly in the vicinity of 32°F! One Dojo in the interior of mountainous Korea is an outdoor area, so hot in summer that water has to be sprinkled on the mats frequently to keep feet from burning. This practice has proven functional in the Orient but Western Dojo need not necessarily abide by the lack of heat in winter, and there is some evidence to point to the fact that a cold Dojo can induce more injuries than a slightly warmed one, especially when the Preparatory Exercises are not used. A heated Dojo may be used, but the heat must be kept below 65°F.

During the hot months in Japan, no provision is made to cool the Dojo in any way except by natural air circulation and ventilation. Experiments with air conditioning have proven discouraging. During heavy exercise, there have been disagreeable results which could lead to health complications.

The average Dojo is a victim of its geographical location, but every effort should be made to make the usual Spartan conditions fall within sensible limits and tolerances of healthful conditions. The degree of Dojo permanence mentioned earlier, directly affects the controls we are able to establish toward this end. It is interesting to note that in the West, European Dojo are almost always permanent as are those of Africa, Oceania, Canada, South and Central America, while those in the U.S.A. are largely situated in sites which are part of larger private and public organizations which afford little or no permanency. Exceptions exist primarily in major cities such as Honolulu, San Diego, Los Angeles, San Francisco, Seattle, Chicago, Detroit, Washington D.C., Baltimore, New York, and U.S. Air Force bases throughout the country. But these exceptions are not in proportion to the country's size when compared to foreign countries in which permanent Dojo are to be found in the smallest communities. One of the most delightful Dojo is located adjacent to the warm, sun-drenched, palm-fringed shores of Havana's Biltmore Yacht Club.

Adequate locker room facilities and showers are more a necessity than a luxury and should be considered when organizing a Dojo (#28). Additional area for an office where Dojo files and records can be maintained is advisable, though these can be kept elsewhere with less efficiency (#29). While spectator areas are a secondary consideration, some provision should be made.

A prominent feature of the Dojo should be a bulletin board which is easily seen by all members. All Dojo activities should be posted on this board, and a more orderly and efficient administration will result with regular use of a bulletin board. The board must not be allowed to become a useless decoration by leaving non-applicable and old information posted. A regular posting of information which is current must be maintained.

Dojo Etiquette: Important in Judo training is the emphasis laid on what is referred to as *Reigisaho* (etiquette or "mat manners"). The Western Judo exponent often fails to see the traditional Dojo etiquette as anything more than a hierarchal system of respect to seniors. This is true, in part, but there is much more to the formality of etiquette. Through very specific customs, an orderly, functional, and efficient method of conduct has been laid down for use in the Dojo. This facilitates the ceremonial and contest events as well as normal training sessions. Instructor and student alike are able to perform their intended functions in an efficient manner. The Westerner need not suffer embarassment in the performance of the specified Dojo etiquette, but neither should he seek to "Westernize" or neglect it. It is a positive part of the Judo realm and as such, takes a prominent place in the development of true Judo exponents. Physical location and facilities make modifications necessary in Western Dojo as well as in Oriental Dojo, but for the most part, basic patterns should be adhered to by all Judo exponents.

One of the first items of etiquette which the student must learn in order to participate in training sessions is the ability to sit correctly in *Seiza* position (Kneeling-Seated). Sitting in this manner is not easy for the Western Judo student. Stiffness of body, especially in the knees, weak backs and inflexible hip and ankle joints make this posture somewhat painful. However, constant attention to utilizing the Seiza position will increase the period of sitting time from an original few minutes to perhaps fifteen or twenty minutes. This will be done slowly over a period of time without undue discomfort and will be accompanied by physical benefits helpful to Judo performance.

The following mistakes should be avoided when assuming the Seiza position.

Standing with the feet wide apart when beginning the kneeling action or after returning to the standing position after sitting. Heels should be together. *#1, page 63.*

Kneeling onto the wrong knee. Always kneel onto the left knee first (knee on line with right ankle) when lowering the body, moving the left foot straight back. In arising, bring the right leg up first. *#2.*

Flattening out the feet, resting the top of the arches (heels vertically upward) on the mat when the left leg is back or when both legs are alongside each other during the action of kneeling or rising. The arches must rest on the mat only while sitting. At all other times the feet must be placed with the heels up and standing on the toes. *#2–4.*

Resting the feet directly on the arches when sitting (heels vertically upward). Rather turn the heels outward and rest along the outer edge of the soles and ankle bones with the big toes just touching or slightly overlapped. For long periods of sitting, the arches may be overlapped. *#5–6.*

Holding the knees too close together or too wide apart. The distance between the knees should be about the width of two fists. *#7.*

Supporting the body with the arms resting or pressing hard against the thighs or knees while sitting. Hold the body erect without support from the arms. *#8.*

Careless posture during kneeling and standing or sitting actions. Hold the body erect with eyes to the front during all movement and while sitting. *#9.*

Generally Judo exponents sit in the Dojo when instructed to do so, when assembling for class or when closing a practice session, when listening to instruction, when watching demonstrations or others practice, when during exercise or contest it becomes necessary to adjust the Judo costume, while on the mat and not practicing but needing a rest, or when it becomes necessary to perform the formal salutation *(see pages 66–69).*

Every training session will require at least one form of salutation to be used. Whether the *Ritsurei* (Standing Bow) or *Zarei* (Seated Bow) is performed, dignity must be the keynote. Continued practice and use of these salutations will polish existing technique and bring physical benefits helpful to Judo practice.

The following mistakes should be avoided when assuming the salutations.

In performing the Ritsurei: Standing with the feet wide apart when beginning or finishing the bowing action. Heels should be together. *#10.*

Curving or bending the back causing the head to drop too low. The neck must never be shown to the opponent. Inclining the body forward from the hips to about 30° is adequate. *#11–12.*

Bowing too quickly so that the motion is like a "Jack-in-the-box" movement. The motion should be slow and deliberate with the lowest position held for about one second before returning to the standing position.

Improper holding of the arms and hands. When bowing, let the hands and arms slide from their starting position along the sides to a point on the front thighs with the finger tips just touching the knee caps. *#11–13.*

In performing Zarei: Always begin from Seiza position. *#14.*

Improper movement of the arms and hands when beginning the bowing action. Slide the hands down the thighs onto the mat. *#15.*

Placing the hands too far from the knees during the bowing action. Place the hands so that the heels of the hands are about one hand width from the knees. *#16.*

Placing the hands too wide during the bowing action. Always place your hands equal to or slightly less than the width of your knees. *#16.*

Placing the hands with the fingers spread and pointing straight ahead. The hands must be placed slightly "toed-in" with the fingers held together. *#16.*

Raising the buttocks from the legs during the bowing action. The buttocks must continue to touch the legs. *#17.*

Bending or curving the back causing the head to drop too low. Keep the head and back straight. *#17.*

Bowing too quickly so that the motion is like a "Jack-in-the-box" movement. The motion should be slow and deliberate with the lowest position held for about one second before returning to the sitting position of Seiza.

All properly trained Judo exponents use the salutations as a sign of mutual recognition and respect *(see pages 66–69).* Inexperienced Judo students sometimes feel strange and suffer embarassment when performing the salutations which are generally thought of as a distinctive Oriental mannerism. This is usually due to a misunderstanding about the intended idea of the salutations. All sporting events and social activities have particular manners of etiquette. The student should be made to see that like fencing, the salute of the opponents, or like wrestling, the handshake and circling of opponents, or like the toast given before drinking a beverage, Judo makes use of the bow. There is nothing anti-Western about bowing, no more than the examples just mentioned which all came from foreign soils. It is factual that the bow has been used as the standard of greeting in the office of various presidents of the U.S.A., and is seen today in diplomatic circles. Judo students must come to understand the bow as a display of respect and courtesy for an opponent, an instructor, or honored official. It should also be noted that the bow is not a "one-way" affair, being returned and thus making it a mutual sign of respect.

During intermediate and advanced levels of skill, Judo students will have need to study *Katame no Kata* (Forms of Grappling) in which a position known as *Kyoshi no Kamae* (Kneeling Posture) is necessary. This posture is also useful in practicing various other grappling techniques aside from those listed in the Kata.

The following mistakes should be avoided when assuming Kyoshi no Kamae.

Standing improperly when beginning the kneeling action. Kneeling may begin either from a heels together position or from *Shizenhontai* (Natural Posture). *#18.*

Kneeling onto the wrong knee. Always kneel onto the left knee first (knee on line with right ankle) when lowering the body, moving the left foot straight back *#19.*

Flattening out the left foot, resting the arch on the mat when the left knee is down. The left arch never rests on the mat, but the foot must be held standing on its toes with the heel vertically upward. *#19–23.*

Improper placement of the arms and hands. When lowering the body, the left arm hangs loosely at the left side while the right arm bends permitting the right hand to rest on the top of the big muscle inside the thigh and just above the knee. Cup the hand with the fingers together. *#19–23.*

Improper movement of the right leg. Slide the right foot directly to the right side, using the pulling or opening of the right arm to achieve this. *#20.*

Improper placement of the right leg and foot. The right leg must stop at a position which allows the big toe of the right foot to be on line with the left knee. The right lower leg makes an angle slightly greater than 90° with the mat. *#20–21.*

Careless posture during kneeling and standing actions. Hold the body erect with eyes to the front during all movement and while kneeling. The left side makes a right angle with the mat. *#19–22.*

Improper forward and backward movement. The right leg is slid from the extended position to a point where the toes of the right foot are next to and in line with the left knee. *#19.* From this point, the right leg is advanced by sliding the foot directly forward (this complete motion is a 90° movement and forms the letter "L"). The right leg is advanced far enough to permit the right foot to rest fully on the sole and provide a firm base of support for movement of the left leg. *#23.* The left leg is slid, foot on the toes *#24,* to a relative similar position it possessed before the forward movement was begun. Backward movement is achieved by reversing the above essentials.

The Kyoshi no Kamae is a valuable exercise but a severe one. Trainees should be drilled in this posture and posture with movement until the performance is efficient. Five or ten minutes of this exercise will bring adequate stimulation to the body. Of course, for the sake of an exercise, the positions may be reversed by performing the Kyoshi no Kamae on the other knee.

Students will find the use of a training partner or a training mirror a great advantage in getting the feel of the Seiza, the Ritsurei, the Zarei, and the Kyoshi no Kamae. Training partners can make corrections in position while the mirror will show inefficient actions glaringly.

Certain geographical aspects must be understood about the Dojo proper. Each of the four sides have traditional relationships which set the foundations for positional etiquette in Judo. The senior side of the Dojo is termed the *Kamiza* (Upper Seat). Because of involved philosophical aspects, this term is sometimes referred to as *Joza* (Upper Seat). However, this introduces linguistic problems. This is the side which houses the customary dais for instructors and officials in Oriental Dojo, and often, the picture of Dr. Kano. It should be considered the seating area for all instructors and the place for all honored guests. Sometimes along its wall area will be found special entranceways for instructors only, leading to the dressing and locker rooms. *(See diagrams, page 66.)*

Directly opposite the Kamiza is the side termed the *Shimoza* (Lower Seat). This side usually provides an entrance for all students and lesser ranked instructors to the Dojo, and is the axis along which all students gather for formal class openings, closings, and various ceremonies. *(See diagrams, page 66.)*

Looking from the Kamiza, and located on the left, is the side of the Dojo which may be referred to as the *Joseki* (Upper Side or Place). The use of this side in Dojo formalities will be discussed later. *(See diagram, page 66.)*

The final side of the Dojo, as seen from the Kamiza and on the right, directly opposite to the Joseki, is the *Shimoseki* (Lower Side or Place). The use of this in Dojo formalities will also be discussed later. *(See diagram, page 66.)*

Students entering the Dojo should enter at the Shimoza side and prior to stepping into the Dojo area, should execute either the *Zarei* (Seated Bow) or the *Ritsurei* (Standing Bow) toward the Kamiza. Today in Japan, the latter salutation is preferred. Instructors will enter the Dojo from the Kamiza side entrance if provided, but regardless,

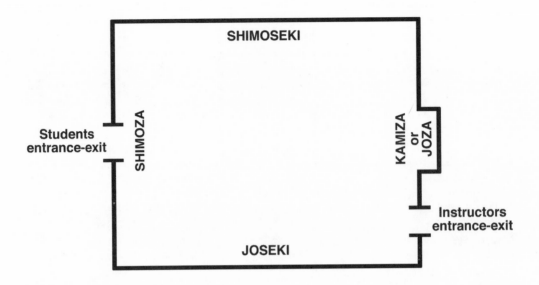

will also execute one of the salutations similarly. Students and instructors leaving the Dojo must turn and face the Kamiza and execute either salutation prior to departure.

Every Judo session should begin formally with the students seated in *Seiza* position (Kneeling-Seated Posture) along the axis of the Shimoza, with the senior student in the first rank, on the left as seen from the Kamiza. *#1 page 67.* Order of student seniority runs as shown by the arrows. The instructors line up as indicated with the head instructor on the right as seen from the Kamiza. An alternate method sometimes used, puts the head instructor in the center of the rank, #6, but this is optional, as is usually used for formations of instructors or honored guests who are posing for a picture. (In the latter case, the assembly of students is absent, and only the line of instructors is present.) Both instructors and students are in Seiza, a kneeling-sitting posture with the legs folded under the body, and face each other. The senior student gives the verbal command of, *Kamiza Ni,* which is a preparatory command and as the line of instructors turn around toward the Kamiza, the senior student utters the command of execution, *Rei,* on which signal, both students and instructors simultaneously make the bowing salutation to the Kamiza. Upon completion of this, the instructors turn and face the line of kneeling students and the senior student verbally commands, *Sensei Ni,* a preparatory command followed by the command of execution, *Rei,* and students and instructors exchange bowing salutations. All salutations at this point have been in the form of Zarei. At the close of each Judo session, the reverse procedure is used, *#1,* with students and instructors exchanging salutations and then both students and instructors bowing toward the Kamiza. All salutations are again performed in Zarei.

Ceremonies of all kinds, such as the introduction of honored Judo exponents and distinguished guests, awarding of ranks, trophies, etc., are effected from the positions shown

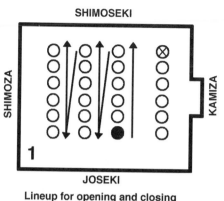

SHIMOSEKI

SHIMOZA

KAMIZA

JOSEKI

Lineup for opening and closing of a class: ceremonies, or conducting a class.

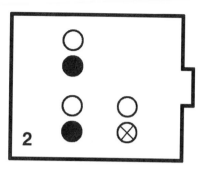

Lineup for beginning and ending a workout between pairs.

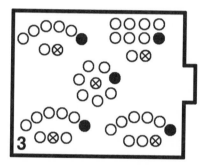

Lineup for class instruction in semi-circular and circular forms.

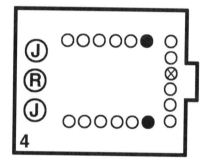

Lineup for contest judo.

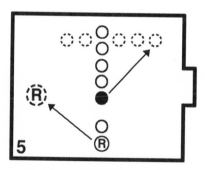

Lineup for performance against multiple consecutive opponents.

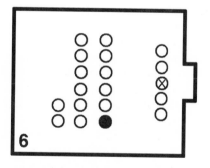

Lineup for instructors more than two in number (alternate manner).

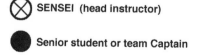 SENSEI (head instructor)

 Referee

Performer

Senior student or team Captain

 Judge

in #1. One modification may be made, if the ceremony is short, and that is that all present will take a standing position during the proceedings, executing the Ritsurei. Such is the practice during the pre-shiai ceremony and awarding of trophies, post-shiai. The alternate position of the head instructor shown in #6 may also be used. (*See page 67.*)

Individual practice sessions follow a definite pattern of etiquette as shown in #2. The senior student or instructor positions himself in Seiza position on the Joseki side of the Dojo and the junior student stations himself on the Shimoseki axis of the Dojo, facing his opponent, a few feet in front of his partner. They exchange salutations simultaneously. After practice, this procedure is repeated. If Dojo space does not permit the Zarei salutation, the Ritsurei may be used, but Zarei is preferred, especially when working with a very senior instructor. All exchanges of salutations should be performed on the sidelines rather than in the center of the mat.

Distance between partners performing salutations will vary according to Dojo limitations, but should range between four to twelve feet. For training practice sessions, it is well to conserve space when performing salutations and the minimum spacing is adequate. However, for competitive bouts and Kata, distances should more nearly approach the maximum footage.

Class instruction may be arranged in a variety of positions as shown in #1 or #3. In the latter case, it is assumed that the formal opening of the class has been accomplished. Dojo with extreme physical limitations in the form of narrowness and with arrangement similar to that shown in #3, may often use the formation in the upper right hand corner of that illustration to open and close a formal class, rather than the method shown in #1.

Contests should be conducted with the lineup shown in #4. Note the teams are labeled Red and White, for use in refereeing procedures to facilitate recognition and recording of results. All are in standing positions, except possibly the line of high ranked instructors or guests seated in front of the Kamiza. The Red competitors always take their positions on the left as seen from the Kamiza. All face the Kamiza and execute Ritsurei, then turning to face each other, execute Ritsurei, all upon the verbal command of the Referee. The teams then sit down on their respective sides of the Shiaijo (Contest mat area), the officials take their places and the contest begins. The procedure is reversed at the end of the matches, with the Red and White teams facing each other, the officials in position as shown in #4. The Referee again verbally commands the exchange of salutations, first team to team, then all competitors turn to face the Kamiza, and upon another verbal command, all simultaneously execute the standing salutation.

Students not actually exercising should be seated in orderly fashion at the perimeter of the mat in Seiza position or the easier method of "flat sitting" *(Anza)* on the buttocks with the legs folded in front. #1, page 69. At no time should the legs be stretched out as this position may cause serious injuries. #2–3. Students should not sit with their back to the mat, but should at all times pay attention to the mat area, not only to learn, but to avoid injury. #4. Running in the Dojo is forbidden unless it is a part of the organized training program. Either running or walking across the mat while the trainees are practicing is also out of order. Walking in the center of the mat should be reserved for instructors who are aiding the trainees.

The lineup and formalities for one man performing against multiple opponents in consecutive fashion is shown in #5, p. 67. The performer takes his position on the Joseki side of the rank (on the left as seen from the Kamiza), while his potential opponents take their positions on his immediate left with the senior opponent next to the performer. All face the Kamiza in a standing posture. At the verbal command of the Referee, all execute Ritsurei to the Kamiza. The senior opponent then takes his place on the Shimoseki side of the Dojo about 10–12 feet from the performer and the other opponents form a rank along the axis of the Shimoseki with the senior opponent closest to the Kamiza. The performer and the opponents face each other and at the command of the Referee, execute the Ritsurei simultaneously to each other. The performance then begins. After its completion, the above procedure is reversed.

The position of Uke (Receiver) and Tori (Performer) in relation to the Kamiza and the form of salutation used depends upon the specific Kata being demonstrated. Nage, Katame, Kime no Kata require that Tori position himself on the right as seen from the Kamiza. Ritsurei is performed by Uke and Tori in the direction of the Kamiza after which they turn and perform Zarei to each other. In Ju no Kata, Tori positions himself on the left as seen from the Kamiza and the Ritsurei is performed by Uke and Tori to the Kamiza and after turning, to each other. In the Itsutsu no Kata, Tori positions himself on the right as seen from the Kamiza and the Ritsurei is performed by Uke and Tori to the Kamiza and after turning, to each other. Koshiki no Kata requires Tori to station himself on the left as seen from the Kamiza. Uke and Tori perform the Ritsurei to the Kamiza and Zarei to each other. In all the Kata demonstrations, after the performance of the Kata, Uke and Tori take their original starting positions and execute the appropriate salutation (the one they performed to each other at the start) and then turn and execute the Ritsurei to the Kamiza.

Presentation and Receiving of Awards Etiquette: Termination of the tournament may require the presentation and receiving of appropriate awards in the various forms of medals, plaques, trophies, etc. It is well to make any presentation in a somewhat ceremonial manner. Competitors and officials should take their places as shown in #5-6 *(see below)*. The official or guest of honor making the presentations should be aided by an announcer who will call the individual to a position in front of the awarding official.

The individual receiving the award should position himself, when called, about nine feet in front of the presenting official, pause and execute a standing salutation. He then moves directly to the presenting official and executes another standing salutation as he receives his award. Then, without hesitation, he moves a few paces backwards arriving at his original position and executes another standing salutation. After completing this final salutation, he moves to his position in the ranks of competitors. *#7-8 below. (Also see #1 and #6, page 67.)*

It is probable that Dojo physical dimensions and other geographical and physical limitations may force some modifications in the described procedures, but every effort made to preserve these traditional forms produces well-disciplined Judo exponents. Every well-trained class exhibits traditional etiquette of Judo. The disintegration of Judo eti-

quette, whether premeditated or produced by careless neglect, will lead to the disappearance of the true values of Judo. Etiquette is intrinsic to Judo and it is the responsibility of each exponent to preserve the traditional forms.

Food and Sleep: We have determined that physical fitness is essential to championship performance in Judo. To a large extent, hereditary aspects control our height and final size, but with proper methods of training, using Auxiliary Exercises, we are able to become bigger and stronger. Stronger muscles mean larger muscles and the larger the muscles, the heavier they are. However, it is not possible to build body muscle to gain weight and strength unless we have adequate nutrition and rest. Failing to supply the body with what it needs for the construction of muscle, it fails to repair, construct, and maintain our body.

No special diet need be maintained for the practice of Judo. However, the body must be given an adequate source of energy foodstuffs. Most people do not really know what constitutes a good diet, or at least, if they do know, they do not practice what they understand. Common sense eating of wholesome, nutritious foods giving an appropriate balance of proteins, carbohydrates, and fats together with the needed minerals and vitamins, will keep the body above par and enable it to function in your favor. Merely "eating like a horse," filling your stomach with bulk, does not necessarily mean that you are getting adequate nutrition. Food is not beneficial because it is food, but because it is digested. Then too, it is the *quality* not the quantity of the food that is important. Eat generously, but sensibly, of fresh fruits, vegetables, lean meats, milk, fish, eggs, whole grain cereals, nuts, unsulphered dried fruits, cheeses, etc. In the preparation of the food, avoid overcooked foods which have been robbed of vitamins and minerals. Wheat germ oil, high protein supplements, various kinds of sugars, gelatine, and vitamin B1 have received serious study as applied to improving the performance of athletes who make a regular inclusion of them individually or in combination in their diets. The results are varied and inconclusive, but it can be said that sensible use of any of them will not injure you and may be important in your performance. Mr. Inokuma, 1959 All-Japan Judo Champion, is a constant user of high protein food supplements and attributes much of his energy content to his diet. Remember—*you will be no better than what you eat.*

It is not physiologically sound to exercise on a full stomach, nor is it wise to go to the other extreme and exercise on a completely empty stomach. Traditionally, Judo custom speaks of the "rule of 3 and 8." This means that no heavy exercise must be performed until approximately 3 hours after the meal. This allows time for digestive and assimilation processes to complete their work. Also, this rule implies that any energy desired from a meal must not be counted on being available for Judo performance until about 8 hours after eating. This of course depends on the nature of the food. Fast-burning simple sugars and energy foods designed for special training diets, considerably reduces this time.

Proper exercise and food intake *must* be supplemented by proper rest. A sound sleep allows the body to repair tissue, make body growths, and replenish general body reserves. Rest is not just a simple matter of doing nothing. It is a matter of repair. The exact amount of sleep required, varies with each individual, but generally 8 hours should be considered a minimum. Resting before a contest is essential and must be a regular part of the training schedule. Avoid unnecessary expenditure of strength and energies.

Food and sleep, like exercise, must be taken regularly if a beneficial effect is to be expected. They act, under proper conditions of proportion, on an accumulative basis. Mere trial for a day, or a week, or even one month will not bring optimum results. These factors are able to produce accumulative beneficial results if *regularity* in their use is established. Waiting to repair a rapidly breaking down machine may result in little or no real repair. Maintain long efficient functioning of your body by frequent rest periods, adequate sleep. Repair as you go!

The drinking of water or any liquid beverages prior to exercise is unwise. The body should "dry out" a few hours before severe exercise for best performance. A lemon, tangerine, lime, or orange may be used at contest time to ease thirst. Drinking water or liquid beverages immediately after severe exercise is also unwise. It is best to allow the body to cool down somewhat before drinking any cool liquids. A 30 minute period is ample to return the body to normal. If liquid must be taken, warm water or liquid beverages will reduce the chances of disagreeable results. A topic often avoided, but nevertheless important in training, is the matter of elimination of waste material from the body. Proper daily habits are essential to good health and should be obvious matters of personal attention.

Tobacco and Liquor: The extremely personal matters of smoking and drinking habits are those of individual choice. In so far as Judo training is concerned, the use of tobacco will certainly not improve the physical condition of the individual and is therefore generally considered as something to be avoided by serious trainees. Aside from this, smoking should be prohibited within the Dojo mat area, both from the standpoint of trainees who should be otherwise occupied and spectators who must respect the trainees need for pure air during exercise sessions. In extremely large Dojo, smoking is permitted in specially designated areas. Such is the case within the Kodokan Dojo mat area for the convenience of officials.

The personal use of alcoholic beverages is likewise an extremely undesirable habit for serious trainees. The use of liquor will not in any way enhance the performance of the Judo exponent and is therefore to be avoided. Under no circumstances should a Judo exponent who has been drinking, be allowed to perform on the mat. Aside from possible undignified conduct, it is probable that injury will result either to the drinker or his partner.

Age and Judo Practice: Assuming organic soundness or otherwise wholesome conditions of the human body, Judo may be begun and practiced at any age. Sensible training however must be utilized in harmony with the trainees physical condition. The flexibility of Judo training makes easy adaptation on an individual basis possible and should not produce the mistaken idea that Judo is for the young only. Cases exist which demonstrate that trainees as young as one year old and as old as octogenarians, have practiced Judo. The late E. J. Harrison, 4 Dan, reportedly found time for practice, redolent of his youth, in his 88th year.

Inasmuch as contest Judo is an activity which requires superior physical and mental conditioning, there are certain age limits which appear to be guides for adjusting a trainees performance in competitive matches. Speaking of top level international competition, it would appear that no matter the training devotion possessed by a Judoka, his contest days beyond 35 years of age are over. Indeed, long before this time, Judoka find it increasingly difficult to achieve championship stature. Hard and fast limits cannot be set, but long experience has proven that sometime between the ages of 30 and 35 a Judoka will decline in top-level contest ability. There is a tendency for this maximum age limit to be reduced as the current youthful crop of Judoka demonstrate their physical prowess. See Chapter 6, page 139.

In recognition of this, some areas in Japan have passed regulations which exempt Judo exponents over 30 years of age from serious, top-level competitive events. This does not entirely eliminate competition as a variety of events of lesser physical demands have been designed.

Use of the Kodokan Emblem: The standard emblem of the Kodokan is an 8 petaled flower of the cherry tree. *(See below.)* It was adopted by feudal Samurai because the flower is detached from the branch at the apogee of its beauty in order to die. It symbolizes a degree of maturity within the individual which is summarized by the expression, "Strong within, but gentle without." The fire red color of the center of the emblem indicates the "fire" or "ardor" of the individual. The spirit of the Kodokan combines the strength of iron forged to red heat inside the silk, supple and white flower. This is symbolic of the union of body strength and the resistant suppleness and flexibility of the pure spirit developed by the Judo exponent of Black Belt grade. It is a sign of personal attainment.

In the U.S.A., the Kodokan emblem is issued by Yudanshakai only to Kodokan Yudansha. Its use by other than Yudansha is not authorized. Judo exponents of Mudansha ranks are issued a lapel pin of slightly different design. Both the Yudansha and Mudansha pin representing Yudanshakai and national Judo organizational affiliation are issued to members in good standing. Information concerning this membership can be had upon application to any of the nationally recognized Yudanshakai listed in the Appendix.

The use of the traditional Kodokan emblem on organizational stationery and various forms is encouraged, but use on individual membership cards should be restricted to Yudansha members. Judo Dojo, Clubs, Institutes, etc., should clearly understand and adhere to national requirements in this matter as published by the appropriate local Yudanshakai. See the Appendix, pages 288–89.

Organizational Spirit: Undeniably, there are many factors which go into the development of organizational spirit, just as there are a variety of methods to obtain this desirable quality. The team, the Dojo, the Club or any level of organization which exhibits superior organizational spirit will contribute more to the cause of Judo than those groups of lesser organization.

The organization which is composed of well-trained individuals, each at the optimum level of physical and mental condition, has the basic ingredients necessary in the cultivation of organizational spirit. It must now add, consciously or unconsciously, a ment-

al set which permeates its entire structure. Organizational spirit is gained by skillful and dynamic leadership, inspirational guidance from a source within itself. It is manifested in the spirit of fair-play, cooperative training, and organizational worth. All these items should be directed toward the national organizational effort.

Individuals working and training together under competent guidance aimed at a mutually acceptable goal gives the best chance to those aspiring to organizational spirit. Instructors and organizational officials should endeavor to impart the spirit of organizational unity by training the potential members as a unit.

Teams develop spirit by a degree of successes. Successes are not limited to competitive interpretations, but if such is the intended goal, training sessions—warmup, uchikomi, randori, etc.,—should be performed as a unit and led by an appointed leader. Specific methodology is the prerogative of each leader or instructor.

Cutting Weight: Traditionally, Judo has never regarded weight as a problem for the trainee who has been free to enter competition regardless of his avoirdupois, with strikingly lesser bodied opponents. It is not uncommon to see differences of 75 to 100 pounds between contestants, and in one case the heaviest Judoka in Japan, a young 4 Dan from a local Tokyo university who weighs in the vicinity of 300 pounds, competed against a slight lad of about 140 pounds, much to the amusement of the audience.

With the internationalization of contest Judo, it is slowly coming to be evident that weight categories must be established. It is not the purpose of this discussion to weigh the merits or shortcomings of the weight system, but rather the calling of attention to the fact that should weight systems be established, such as the A.A.U. competition in the U.S.A. requires, on an international basis, then Judo training will be beset with the problems of "cutting weight." Other combative sports such as wrestling and boxing afford a base of knowledge that will be applicable.

"Cutting weight" to "make weight" categories can be physiologically safe if done within specific limits. Trainees should limit themselves to less than 5% (of their starting body weight) body losses. Beyond that, body strength and physiological processes may be adversely affected. This is particularly true if the trainee is a well-trained and muscled athlete without surplus tissue or an adolescent unhampered by adipose tissue. Methods of losing weight include diet, exercise, heat and steam, and "drying out" the body by reducing water intake. Prolonged expectoration makes it possible to "spit off" 3 or 4 pounds in a relatively short period of time. *(See page 219.)*

Injuries: There is no substitute for safety measures and careful, intelligent, sensible training, but unavoidably, there will be injuries in the practice of Judo. Statistics, however, show that injuries are far fewer than sustained in other forms of athletics. Qualified medical attention promptly after such injuries are incurred, has no substitute. The "self-doctoring" and Judo instructor first aid should only be applied to very minor injuries.

Of the more serious injuries in Judo, sprains top the list, followed in order by dislocations, teeth and mouth injuries, contusions, and fractures. When considering the frequency of occurrence of the anatomical localities, the order is led by ankle joint sprains, knee joint sprains, shoulder joint sprains, wrist sprains, shoulder joint dislocations, and finally teeth and mouth injuries, in that progression. Fractures are led by fractures of the ribs, followed closely by fractures of the clavicle. Though based on Japanese injuries, these statistics are closely borne out in foreign countries.

An interesting fact noted in Japan is that Judo exponents who are able to execute both right and left hand techniques are most frequently injured. The cause of injuries in Judo are varied, and may be attributed to lack of Judo experience through which the performer, with disregard for the proper application of technique, applies a movement by overstraining himself. He may also apply his concept of the technique in a crude fashion, thus injuring his partner. Lack of physical fitness contributes greatly to injury statistics. Almost equally culpable is the lack of seriousness during training and the resultant careless application of technique or counter-technique. Lack of preliminary exercise to warm up the body with Preparatory Exercises before strenuous exercise such as Randori or Shiai, is also a major cause of injury. Occasionally Dojo facilities are inadequate and safety measures are thereby reduced, resulting in injuries which could have been avoided. Sometimes, unavoidably, through hard and powerful movements, injury is sustained by the tremendous speed and forces generated by skillful Judo exponents as they perform, but this is a minimum source of injury. Finally, the deliberate use of foul tactics, resulting from personal differences, also enter the statistics, and the instructor is faced with the responsibility of stopping such potential injury sources before they develop.

Minor injuries should not be used as an excuse for loafing or otherwise cutting training sessions. The Japanese Judo exponents are examples of complete disregard for injury, and often they will be observed competing and most certainly practicing with injuries which would keep the Westerner on the sidelines. It is told how the late Master Iizuka, 10 Dan, while a young man, fought victoriously through five opponents with a *broken rib*, without a visible sign of his pain. This practice is well and good, if it is confined to *minor* injuries. However, injuries of a more serious nature, such as sprained or dislocated joints, must be given ample time to rest and thus heal. The authors cannot agree completely with the traditional Japanese outlook which ignores injuries, makes practice mandatory. I. Inokuma, 1959 All-Japan Judo Champion, tells of a tournament in his high school days which he was forced to enter by his instructor. He had previous to this tournament, severely injured his knee by tearing some muscle tissue which prevented him from standing fully on the knee or using it in normal fashion. He nevertheless, threw three 3 Dan opponents! Mr. Inokuma also entered the 1960 All-Japan Championships shortly after undergoing surgery on an abcess (sub-cutaneous) in his leg. There are too many "crippled" and "broken" Judo exponents to be seen about Oriental Dojo who at their now advanced age, find it hard to walk, sit, or demonstrate expected flexibility which to some degree could have been eliminated by more intelligent training.

No extensive statistical study has been made in the U.S.A. on the nature and causes of injuries, but as mentioned earlier in this section, for the most, the patterns displayed by the Japanese statistical studies are similar. Every Dojo has its share of injuries sustained, and in most cases, it should not be a reflection upon the instruction and supervision qualities, but rather considered as operational normality. Of course, with too many injuries, one each session or one each week as an example, perhaps the training methods should be re-examined, or the facilities checked to see what basic cause is producing the undesirable effect. This reference to injury is made in a strict interpretation implying those of a serious nature. Minor bumps and bruises are excluded.

A training application of unknown origin but doubtlessly of questionable merit, is the practice of anesthetizing an injured muscle area with certain medical preparations so that the trainee or competitor may enter or continue his contest. This practice is seen in other sporting fields, but places regard for the individual below some other objective, usually confined to "winning." The anesthetized muscle area can be used with a minimum of pain of course, but may undergo further injury leading to serious complications. Intelligent coaching should regard the physical condition of the trainees above any objective and discard this practice. Nature provides pain as a signal of warning. If we disregard this warning, we are inviting trouble.

It is not the purpose of this section to discuss the various treatments applied to Judo injuries, but there are certain aspects of self-applied aids and protection methods, which are commonly used in Japan, which may find useful application. One particularly effective method is the use of rubber elastic bands to support injured areas; particularly weakened joints of the ankle, knee, and shoulder. The rubber is usually selected from bicycle inner tubing which is cut into appropriate widths and lengths depending upon the area to be supported. Usually, each experienced Judoka keeps two or three rubber supports among his personal Dojo gear, two of which are about 4 or 5 inches wide and 3 or 4 feet long for use on larger areas, and the third about half those dimensions for the smaller areas. Bicycle inner tubes prove to be long-wearing, strong, and very flexible. They are more popular than manufactured elastic supporters which, though functional, do not keep their elasticity with wear, and prove annoying by constant slipping. The bicycle tube type support is wound around the part concerned, with tension to suit the wearer. The end is tucked under the existing bands. It may be applied directly to the skin, or on top of a padded surface. #1–4 show typical applications.

Professionally prepared elastic bands of varying sizes are also useful to support injured areas and may be used under the above bicycle tube type of support. If used alone, experience has shown that the usually provided metal clips which hold the elastic bandage in place, are quite sharp and can inflict serious cuts during exercise. These clips are unnecessary as the end can be tucked under the existing bands to provide suitable fixation.

Toes which are frequently stubbed or even sprained can be taped to an adjacent member which provides "splint" action and greatly supports the injured toe. Toe injuries can be quite painful and most serious cases require that the trainee refrain from exercise for at least a few days. Certain Judo exponents suffer "cracks" at the area where the big toe joins the ball of the foot. Sometimes these will reach a depth which could hold a thin pencil; an open wound which is very susceptible to infection. Cleansing the wound and applying some germicide is necessary, adding just a bit of vaseline gauze and covering with a thin strip of adhesive tape (½ inch×5″) for protection, has proven completely adequate. Care must be taken to ensure that the tape is applied so that it will remain as a protective cover for the opening. A loop of thick twine around the big toe is also effective. Practice may be resumed without discomfort. #5, p. 76.

Injuries of a bump and bruise or strain and sprain nature should promptly receive *cold* compresses as soon after occurrence as possible. This treatment should be continued periodically during a 24–30 hour period, after which the normal heat applications may be used. Injuries which have prolonged healing, such as joint areas, have been helped by the technique of alternate hot and cold immersion directly on the area concerned.

1

2

3

4

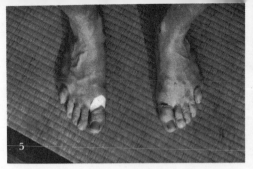

This can be done in a shower, allowing the injured part to receive a stream of hot water for several minutes, then suddenly switching to cold water for an equal period of time, and so on alternately for 5 or 10 changes. Post-injury exercise, at the proper time, in the form of Auxiliary Exercises is beneficial. Special use of the Leg Curl Machine (*page 227*) is valuable. Hematoma of the ear lobe (Othematoma) should be properly treated by medical experts and a self-made "ring" of cloth can be used to protect the ear during practice until healing is complete. #6. It is easily made by winding lengths of guaze around a ring made of cotton, paper, or soft cloth. Fastening over the ear can be accomplished by elastic strings or bands. Heavy contact work should be avoided.

Training Applications: The development of Judo technique is often thought to lie within the specific movements of throwing or grappling motions, and the beginner is apt to give little or no study to the fundamentals which are absolute prerequisites to an effective technique. His mind is concerned largely with the final stage of the execution —the actual throw or grappling effect— and as a result, inferior technique is developed. No attempt is made herein to describe the actual techniques of Judo, but rather to stress the aspects of *Kihon Renshu* (fundamental practice) which go into building creditable technique, and to show training methods by which these fundamental qualities may be developed. A qualified instructor is indispensable to the development of championship performance, but trainees who must practice Judo somewhat on their own, will find a reliable text on the techniques of Judo their "instructor."

One of the greatest weaknesses in Western Judo is the inability to execute a proper *Ukemi* (falling method). Too often the Ukemi is considered merely a form of protection and nothing more, being executed only to get the trainee falling, "down safely." True, Ukemi is a form of protection, but in its full meaning, it mirrors the Judo abilities of the performer. A Judo master is able to determine the potential Judo ability or Judo ability of a Judo exponent merely by watching the performance of Ukemi. The confidence, flexibility, and spirit of a student is reflected in his performance of Ukemi. His ability to execute throwing techniques is in part limited by his performance of Ukemi. Should he be unable to fall properly, he will lack confidence in the movement of his body, and when attacking his opponent, part of his concentration is diverted, namely, to a concern over what will happen to him if he should fail in his movement to execute a throwing attempt. As a result, his movement will be uncertain, probably stiff, and most likely awkward. On the other hand, having confidence in his Ukemi, he will not be distracted by a fear of being thrown, and he will attack with confidence. It is a very pleasing sight to see Japanese Judo exponents in action, attacking and defending, without any regard for consequences which involve execution of Ukemi. Ukemi is an automatic reaction, not a mechanical process for the Japanese Judo exponents. The avoidance of Ukemi is not desirable except in highly skilled levels of performance. Instructors must insist on the proper Ukemi form in all students. There is a direct relationship between progress in Judo and mastery of Ukemi. All forms of Ukemi must be practiced *at each training session* and constant correction and attention to details must be applied.

Another primary source of sub-par Judo is *Shisei* (posture). Judo is based on efficient use of energy, and only through good posture will an economical expenditure of energy be possible. Adherence to upright forms of posture will ensure the best Judo. Exceptional circumstances permit the use of more defensive postures, but these must be minimized to allow best use of energy and give mobility to the body. Instructors must drill students thoroughly in the various stances of Judo based on the *Shizenhontai* (natural posture) in the *Migi Shizentai* (Right Natural Posture) and the *Hidari Shizentai* (Left Natural Posture) forms. Use of the *Jigohontai* (Defensive Posture) in its *Migi Jigotai* (Right Defensive Posture) and *Hidari Jigotai* (Left Defensive Posture) should be applied only in special situations and not as basic Judo posture.

Coupled to Shisei is *Shintai* (body movement). Static Judo can never be fully efficient. Motion in Judo is desirable, and all students should be versed in the principles of *Ayumi Ashi* (normal Judo movement) and *Tsugi Ashi* (follow-foot movement). Individual or partner practice of movements, utilizing these forms should be conducted for all beginning students, giving constant attention to fundamental considerations of Shisei. The great Japanese Judo Champion, M. Kimura, 7 Dan, continually practiced walking posture so balanced that a thin sheet of paper could be slid under his heels at all times. This method is also advocated by Y. Kanemitsu, 9 Dan, who practiced similarly in his competitive days.

Taisabaki (body turning movement) is related to Shintai and Shisei as a basic exercise, and holds the key to effective Judo attack and defense. Its various forms should be practiced individually or by a partner method by all beginning students. There can be no effective Judo without correct Taisabaki. The use of Taisabaki has advanced defensive connotations, being applied at the moment of the opponent's Tsurikomi and entry for throwing action to "cut" away the outside arm, thus rendering the attack ineffective. See figures #1–5, below.

The only effective way Judo technique may be applied against the opponent and thus in competition defeat the opponent, is for the body of the attacker to make contact with the opponent. The major manner in which this is accomplished is through the arms. *Kumikata* (forms of grasping) are essential and championship performance depends upon proper grasping of the opponent. Trainees should train themselves to become effective from more than one "pet" grasp. If a Judo exponent's technique is limited to one grasp, he will be easily stopped by a smart opponent who does not allow this one grasp to be applied. A variety of gripping should be practiced, both right and left sides, both from the standpoint of attack and defense grips. The manner of taking hold is also very important. If you clutch with great strength, the rigidity of your arms will make you capable of nothing more than defense. Remember that your opponent is mastered only through *attack*. To be able to attack with efficiency, you must hold the opponent's Judogi primarily with the lower fingers—the little finger, the ring finger, and the middle finger.

This is your point of strength. The forefinger and the thumb are closed on the Judogi, firmly, but not with "clutching" strength. After unbalancing and entry are obtained, the hands may clasp the opponent's Judogi equally with all fingers as the throw is executed. Beginners are apt to discard this type of gripping as weak or impossible to perform, but with subsequent practice, it will be proven that this method allows the quickness of movement, fullest flexibility of the wrists, and best control of the opponent essential to sound technique. See #1–8, above.

Perhaps 75% or more of the completed Judo technique of throwing is in the Kuzushi (unbalancing) of the opponent. Without Kuzushi, Judo cannot be effected. A thorough study of the principles of Kuzushi must be made by *all* Judo exponents regardless of level of proficiency. This study is not a "one-time" affair, but rather a constant study and reappraisal to improve and apply methods of unbalancing the opponent. It is usually performed along one of two lines. The first of these is a direct method in which the opponent is brought into unbalance by you the attacker applying a form of *Happo no Kuzushi* (eight forms of Kuzushi), imparting it by action of your body forces against his weak line of balance. The second case is termed *Hando no Kuzushi* (reaction forms of Kuzushi), and is an unbalance that the opponent imposes on himself by his body reactions to your diversionary attack. Study each individual technique in an effort to determine the most efficient manner of obtaining the unbalance of the opponent. Make use of both types of Kuzushi, Happo no Kuzushi and Hando no Kuzushi at every training session, and your Judo technique will improve.

If the Judo exponent has met the requirements of posture, movement, body turning, grasping, and unbalancing of the opponent, he has yet to effect the Tsukuri (blending action). This implies the blending of the attacker's body to that of the opponent *while* the opponent is in the state of unbalance. The use of *Tsurikomi* (lift-pull) is a force applied to the opponent's body, using the entire body forces in unison to effect a state of unbalance. Beginners are apt to apply the Tsurikomi with the arms alone, neglecting the major source of body power which lies in the trunk proper. True Tsurikomi makes use of the entire body, with the arms acting as a connecting link to bring the body

forces against the opponent. Tsukuri cannot be effected properly without good Tsurikomi. Trainees should strive for effective Tsurikomi during the practice of Tsukuri. The actual Tsukuri varies somewhat with the technique being applied. This entry is termed *Hairi-kata* (method of entry), and can only be learned by competent instruction and constant practice. The proper use of the body is essential, and the mere use of strength is to be discouraged. However, strength applied properly will bring more effective Judo. Develop patterns of entry based upon the basic movements of the technique being applied.

The final stage of a Judo technique, *Kake* (execution) is an automatic condition of the proper application of Judo fundamentals already discussed. The true Judo *Waza* (technique) shows no distinct separation of Kuzushi, Tsukuri, and Kake, but rather a blend of these stages into a smooth motion which is faster than the eye. *See above picture.*

Speed of Judo technique is of paramount importance and training methods must give emphasis to its development. The speed of Japanese Judo and Western Judo compared, shows a distinct difference. Western Judo exponents upon their first contact with the Japanese experts, are baffled by the blend of speedy movements applied. In the West, there is a tendency toward lumbering body action, due primarily to the lack of polish of the Judo fundamentals more than a misunderstanding of the technique. Speed will come from many sources, among the most important being a reduction of antagonistic muscle action by proper training methods. A further source of speed comes from an understanding of the technique being applied and the economical use of the body in its performance. Search for speed—but respect technique. Speed is partly a mental aspect, reflecting confidence in your bodily movement. Speed is also physical in that the force of muscle contraction determines speed. During the practice of *Uchikomi* (fitting practice), speed will become a natural concomitant as the proper technique develops.

Training methodology: We so far in our discussion, merely pointed out the key fundamentals which go into building Judo technique. Training methodology must now be discussed in order that the trainee has the best opportunity to improve the performance of those fundamentals. Japanese Judo gives little emphasis in thought to describing these methods, for the great number of high-grade Judo masters with their wealth of training knowledge makes it more-or-less simply obvious that these methods exist. In the West, however, where qualified Judo instructors are relatively few, training methods are not sufficiently developed. The small Dojo without a high-grade instructor suffers for the lack of know-how and as a result, Judo efficiency is limited. The following methods of training will be welcomed by these Dojo and are proven methods of training which have in the past, produced champions.

Practice of Shisei, Shintai, and Taisabaki can be combined into one method of practice which produces valuable results and is interesting to students. It must be assumed that the trainees are fully grounded on the basic forms involved in these separate entities and that they are fully ready to put them to use.

Two partners face each other in any posture (Uke shown in Migi Shizentai—Tori in Shizenhontai). #1 below. Uke moves forward selecting either Ayumi or Tsugi Ashi movement and aims his finger tip thrust directly at Tori's face (Migi Tsugi Ashi shown). #2. Tori evades the thrust by performing any Taisabaki or Tsugi Ashi which will bring his body away from Uke's hand thrust (forward and 90° left turn shown). #3. The partners repeat this performance, changing Uke and Tori parts frequently.

The combinations of movement by Uke to thrust and Tori to evade are many and can be left to the imagination of the student or the instructor. It is possible to have Tori receive repeated thrust attacks with a minimum of time between them from training partners who are moving in follow-the-leader fashion, or by utilizing training partners attacking from different directions. It is important however that the timing of this evasion by Tori be correct and executed at the very last moment before Uke's thrust is scheduled to collide with Tori's face. Movement to evade which is premature allows Uke to follow the evasion and counter attack before Tori can defend.

Advanced trainees may often shirk practice of Ukemi, rejecting such practice as "old stuff" and unimportant to the furtherance of their Judo progress. This is erroneous, and it is noted that in Japan, one *never* outgrows the practice of Ukemi. Top university team Judoka of 4 Dan are required to practice Ukemi daily. Two methods of Zenpo Kaiten Ukemi (forward somersault falling) are noted. In the first, trainees try for distance, that is, a contest develops in which the amount of distance covered between take-off and first touch point becomes the object. In the second method, the class is broken into two groups placed at opposite or diagonal ends of the mat area. One trainee from each side runs full speed at each other, and just prior to collision, one trainee drops to the mat and the other executes an Ukemi over his outstretched body. The person to execute the Ukemi is assigned *prior* to the exercise (one side being performers of Ukemi and the other side being the hurdle to dive over). After execution of Ukemi, both trainees hastily get off the mat and take their places at the end of their respective lines. The second man in each line then repeats this practice, and so on in "follow the leader" fashion until the line is exhausted. This becomes also an exercise in mental alertness, and full attention to practice must be maintained.

Japanese instructors will often assign a series of Ukemi to a trainee who has just finished his daily training in Randori. In this method, the selected trainee is required to take fifteen or twenty Ukemi from fast throwing techniques performed by a training partner or the instructor himself. This is a favorite method of Y. Osawa, 7 Dan, who applies it to his university trainees.

British Judoka, T. P. Leggett, 6 Dan, advocates the use of basic Ne Waza (reclining techniques) to bring beginning Judo trainees into familiarity with mat contact as they are learning Ukemi, especially if a fear of falling is exhibited.

Kodokan instructors, S. Kotani, T. Otaki, Y. Matsumoto, all 8 Dan, and K. Hosokawa, 7 Dan, all utilize methods of teaching Ukemi which maintain student interest. One of these methods requires trainees to form a column and execute either the Koho Ukemi or Zenpo Kaiten Ukemi from the standing position by having the training partner be-

hind, shove the man in front who will execute the Ukemi. (number 2 shoves number 1; number 3 shoves number 2; etc.) Attention must be paid to safety, with only one trainee executing Ukemi at a time. This method is particularly good in small Dojo.

Ukemi training methods include a great variety of ideas, but underlying them all must be the emphasis on safety. Beginning trainees must be given careful attention and supervision. Correct spacing between individuals or training couples must be maintained. See all figures. Advanced levels of skill do not preclude safety precautions, but less supervision will be required. Various devices by which organized practice of Ukemi is fully profitable are available to the alert instructor who will utilize many training methods to develop and maintain student interest in Ukemi. These methods will vary with the size of the Dojo used, and the level of the trainees.

Practice of the *Koho* Ukemi (Rear Falling), *Zenpo* Ukemi (Forward Falling), and the *Sokuho* Ukemi (Side Falling), requires no great linear displacement and the class may be arranged in ranks and columns with about 8 feet distance between students (side to side, and back to breast). See #1–3 above.

In the practice of *Zenpo Kaiten* Ukemi (Forward Somersault Falling), provision must be made for linear displacement. Basic practice may be done on a "follow the leader" type of movement in a single or multiple columns across the mat, or it may be circular around the mat perimeter. It is best to keep about 8 feet between each trainee during this performance. See #1–6 below.

After a period of fundamental self-practice, beginners may be encouraged to fall correctly from a reasonable height without fear of injury by using the method shown in #1–4, top page 82. The trainee kneels and grasps the instructor as shown. The instructor then applies a throwing action much in the form of *Sasaetsurikomiashi* (Propping-drawing ankle) against the trainee's *knee* which is resting on the mat. This action can easily be guided to give the trainee varying degrees of speed in falling.

A useful method to encourage proper Ukemi is a partner method in which one trainee executes Ukemi while the other acts as a guide and support. Starting from the position shown in #5, top page 82, the guiding partner grasps his falling partner's sleeve. The

falling partner then executes the Ukemi as shown in #6–8, shown above. The guiding partner must not tug or pull too hard on his partners sleeve. Gradually the supporting partner may remove his assistance. Such self-ukemi is the evidence of mastery of self-control and confidence as well as mastery of fundamentals. All Judo trainees must be able to execute this type of Ukemi eventually. *#1–6, below.*

Uchikomi or Butsukari will be discussed in Chapter 8. It is undeniably the key method for the development of technique when it complements contact Judo in Randori. However, some information concerning this method of training is applicable at this point. Common errors or ommissions in observance of sound Judo principles will relegate even the most spirited practice of Uchikomi to a position of little value. These points are:

Disregard for the fundamentals of posture, body turning, grasping, movement, applying Kuzushi, Tsukuri, and the technique proper.

Warning the opponent that the attack is about to develop by "cocking" a rear leg in order to gain momentum for entry is certainly a case of "telegraphing" the oncoming technique, and gives the opponent time to prepare a defense. #1, page 83.

Performing on the basis of a controlled count method—"one-two-three," etc., must become a continuous motion once the basic movement is understood. It must become automatic, not mechanical. Discontinue counting as soon as trainees have a minimum familiarity with the particular movement being used.

Disengaging an arm prior to entry warns the opponent of your attack. #2, page 83.

Insufficient depth of the entry robs the attacker of necessary contact with the opponent. Cast your legs in under the opponent, inside or equal to his foot spacing.

After entry, the buttocks should not be behind the heels. A straight line drawn vertically from buttocks to the ground should fall in front of the heels. #3, page 83.

Insufficient repetitions will never fix a technique as an automatic action. A minimum of 25 repetitions of a movement daily or during each training session should be your goal. If you have time, increase that into the hundreds.

Vary your speed of entry, gradually gathering speed as your repetitions progress. Make the movement light and fast.

Too much "pulled punch" Uchikomi, that is stopping short of the actual throw or *Kake* (execution), may be detrimental for some trainees. Utilize periodic "throwaway" Uchikomi as described on pages 179 and 180.

Engage your body properly in accordance with the technique you are applying. Lack of contact will cause failure.

Hip action must be correct for such movement brings rapid acceleration to the body and incorrect movement...subpar Waza.

The position of your head during the movement must be studied and harmonized with the basic fundamentals of the technique applied.

Your Tsurikomi must be strong. Pull hard, using your entire body force.

Since Uchikomi is a repetitive process, it is essential that a sufficient amount of correctly executed repetitions be performed so as to set the pattern for the technique intended and that these repetitions be executed against a variety of different opponents. Confining Uchikomi movements to one opponent will greatly reduce effectiveness when our opponent in contest does not conform to the general stature and characteristics we are accustomed to in practice. Instructors must insist on a *variety* of partners during Uchikomi practice.

A basic method of providing a variety of partners for Uchikomi is utilized by Japanese university instructors. The class is divided into two groups of equal number. Trainees are then paired off, facing each other in two ranks, though in smaller area Dojo, more ranks will be formed. See #1–2, page 84. Uchikomi is commenced on signal. Trainees select whatever Waza they wish to employ, but it is generally confined to an *Owaza* (major technique). One rank acts as *Tori* (performer), while the other rank acts as *Uke* (receiver). Ten repetitions are performed and then Tori becomes Uke, and Uke becomes Tori, and ten repetitions are also performed. This process of ten repetitions done alternately with one's partner is repeated as many times as possible within a 3 to 5 minute time limit. At the expiration of this time limit, partners are exchanged by having one rank stand fast and the other moving up (man at head of line moves of end of line). This process of Uchikomi usually is continued until a minimum of ten opponents have been engaged by each trainee.

An alternate method requires a rank of Dojo senior trainees to face the remainder of the Dojo students. Dojo students will pair off with the senior trainees, while surplus students stand by, waiting their chance. Twenty-five repetitions of an assigned or selected Waza are performed by the students, at the completion of which, new students take their places and practice their Waza in Uchikomi form. By this method senior trainees can guide the practice of junior students and also increase their stance efficiency against various attacks. See #3. By reversing the above situation, senior trainees are made to perform Uchikomi against consecutive junior opponents for hundreds of repetitions.

The precise method or variation of these methods can be left to the instructor to devise appropriately. All practice should bear in mind the fundamentals of Uchikomi described in this section and in Chapter 8.

Uchikomi is usually performed against no movement of the opponent. This alone will not be sufficient to develop effective Judo. To surmount this, a form of practice known as *Yakusokugeiko* (prearranged practice) is utilized. This is a form of Randori or free practice which is performed without resistance and in a supple manner. The attacker performs his techniques of attack with the prearrangement with his opponent that there should be no resistance. Both performers benefit; the attacker learns to develop his attack while the opponent gets Ukemi practice and learns to develop a "feel" for defense against the various throwing techniques.

Another form of practice in training is the *Sutegeiko* (throw away practice). In this method, generally the more skillful performer acts without undue resistance and accepts the throwing techniques of his attacker, offering corrective advice from time to time as to fundamentals. The idea here is that the "point" is thrown away, that the throwing technique is not a true technique, but allowed in order to train the one throwing. Instructors can utilize this method by pairing more skilled students with beginners and thus train prospective instructors.

A *resistance* exercise frequently used by university Judo trainees is the charging and pushing exercise much in the fashion of *Sumo* wrestling. This method pits one opponent against the other and requires a fast start, hard charging but careful regulation of balance. It is certain to overcome shyness in hard body contact. See #1–2 below.

Randori must not develop into a contest type of Judo. True Randori is a hard-practiced event it is true, but it is a period of training and not a deterimination as to who is a winner or loser. There should be many throws and consequent falls during the course of a Randori. Attitudes of "losing" must be dispelled if Randori is to fulfill its purpose. Resistance is made in response to the throwing and grappling efforts of the opponent, but always with the idea of learning in mind, not winning or losing. Combination throwing, evasion, and counter attacking should be practiced freely. Westerners are more apt to fail to understand that it is a period of "study" and for fear of losing their reputation, will turn the session into a "fight" that often brings little value to either partner.

84

Randori should not be permitted to become a static affair. Movement is to be encouraged. Such is the practice termed "supple Randori" in Europe.

In Japan, special Judo training in groups takes place annually whereby teams "camp out" or "board out" together in a secluded area for the purpose of serious Judo study. This is termed *Gasshuku* and brings great advancement to the individuals and at the same time, team spirit and efficiency. There is nothing comparable in the U.S.A. to this practice, but notable in Western Judo is the practice of various European countries such as the well-organized Judo administration of Great Britain, which sponsors coaching courses and clinic sessions on a "board out" basis. These events are eagerly awaited and attendance is usually full-house. The sincerity and devotion to Judo of the European Judo exponents can be begun to be measured by this response. While primarily for Judo exponents of Great Britian, male and female Judoists travel from countries as far as Sweden, Italy, and Switzerland to attend. See Gasshuku program, pages 129–30.

A severe training method used frequently in Japan to sharpen top performers is the *Go Nin Gake* (Five Man Take-down) or *Ju Nin Gake* (Ten Man Take-down) sometimes referred to as "one against five" or "one against ten." In this practice one competitor will face either 5 or 10 opponents and attempt to defeat them all consecutively within a period of time. Depending upon the level of skill of the performer, the lineups are chosen to include Judo exponents one or more grades inferior to the Judoka being tested. By way of example, trainees may see this process in action in a 16mm film prepared by Tai Guchi Productions in Tokyo in 1950, in which the then All-Japan Judo Champion, T. Ishikawa, 7 Dan, neatly disposes of his five opponents of fourth and fifth grade skills. This film is available at Kodokan on request. In the current training of I. Inokuma, 5 Dan, he is frequently called upon to demonstrate his abilities against a 10 man line of 3 Dan competitors. A very interesting application of this method is sometimes seen in which the performer will announce to his competitors just what throw he will confine himself to when he faces them. Of course, he fails to tell them on which side he will execute it—being proficient on both sides! Instructors may well employ this method to bring a particularly promising competitor to contest sharpness by requiring him to take on a 5 man line *each* training session. Brown Belts may face White Belts while Black Belts should face other Black Belts or combinations of Black, Brown and White Belts. *(See #5, page 67.)*

The Go Nin Gake or Ju Nin Gake training method may be further utilized to develop tremendous contest efficiency when the performer is required to dispose of his opponents in consecutive fashion as quickly as he possibly can. This requires a very skillful and rapid start by the performer, taking full advantage of every opportunity. It is a severe test of efficient technique. It is generally applied as an exhibition or public display, where it never fails to draw spectator approval. It should not become limited to exhibitionary usage. Employed within the Dojo as a training measure, it will develop "quick start" Judo performance. As far as is known, no official records are kept on how fast the 5 or 10 man lineups have been defeated. It is inaccurate to compare such performances since the quality of the lineups varies greatly. However, 5 man lineups have been defeated in a total of less than one minute running time, and 10 man lineups in approximately double the time. Average time against skilled opponents is one minute.

Endurance training is necessary for all trainees. One of the best methods, consists of

requiring the performer to "take on" in consecutive fashion, as many Judo exponents as he can within a set time limit. A limit of 30 minutes is usually sufficient to thoroughly exercise the performer. Whether each opponent facing the performer is assigned an amount of time to remain on the mat, or whether he is to retire after being once defeated, he must be aggressive and not confine himself to defensive Judo. Performers must be given a chance to apply attack, defense, counter-attack, combination attack, and general tactics of normal Shiai. This is the method of *Kakarigeiko* (repetition). K. Ito, 9 Dan, advocates a period of "no rest" training. He personally considers every training period a time which *must* produce a soaking wet Judogi, and trainees who remain "dry" are not easily found when he is in charge of a class. He himself at his advanced age of over sixty years follows this method each time he trains.

Taking on a line need not be confined to Nage Waza; that is, the method may be employed to develop the skill and endurance of trainees in grappling by requiring the performer to engage his five or ten men only in Katame Waza. Since the performer is presumably of higher skill than the opponents chosen for the lineup, it is customary to allow the performer to begin in a reclining position while his opponents attack from a standing or crouching position. However, this is not mandatory, and if the purpose of the exercise is to develop attack skill, from a standing-to-entry position, then the performer may take on consecutive opponents who are placed in the reclining position on the defense. This is a method which will guarantee the development of endurance, and instructors should use it frequently. #1 above shows alternate start position.

Another training method requires that the performer take on a five man line in Go Nin Gake style, starting as is usual, with the lowest ranked man and progressing to the highest rank using only Nage Waza. He is then required to take on the rank in reverse order (highest rank to lowest) in Katame Waza. This method may be reversed, Katame Waza to Nage Waza.

Vigorous training is augmented in Japan and a few Dojo of the West, along the lines of the traditional Kodokan *Kangeiko* (winter practice) and *Shochugeiko* (summer practice). These are annual events which are staged on the basis of as much as 30 days practice during the coldest and hottest times of the year respectively. Further spartan conditions are imposed by choosing the hours of the day at which the local climate is at its very worst. In winter, the early morning hours 4–7 A.M. are utilized, while in summer, 1–4 P.M. are scheduled. Modern life, however, has seen a modification, and even in Japan, the hours are more in keeping with daily living. Nevertheless, the purpose of this training is to test the sincerity of the Judo exponent and to give him severe training on an accelerated basis. Randori is the chief element of these practices, but special *Renshu* (practice) is offered in the form of lecture-demonstration. Such practices are only for the most spirited and physically fit Judo exponents. The young high school and college boys enjoy a special ten day period during the Kangeiko which requires a 2 mile run, barefooted, through the city streets and areas immediately surrounding the school, *prior* to the actual Judo session on the mat! This run is made regardless of snow, ice, or other winter conditions. It is not unusual for a well-bundled foreigner to be passed by a herd of running, panting Japanese Judo exponents, attired only in their Judogi, on the coldest days of the winter season.

During the course of a training session Randori, seek opponents of different size, weight, and style. Only through meeting all Judo exponents will you build a strong technique. Your Randori should include at least 4–5 opponents at each session. Serious champions vary their Randori from a minimum of 10 to a maximum of 30 opponents daily. A few minutes of serious Randori is worth more than an hour of puttering about the mat. Jigoro Kano advised his top Judoka not to waste a more or less "perfected" Waza against inferiors, but to seek to keep practice alive by intelligent use of new ideas and the development of new Waza. Your chance to perfect new techniques will be best with inferior opponents. Use this chance! Another good chance to develop new techniques is afforded by working occasionally with young boys. Reduce your strength to that of theirs and it requires excellent technique to throw them. Their shorter, very rapid movements will improve your timing, but only if you insist on keeping your superior strength from entering the practice.

Randori alone makes it difficult for trainees to develop a wide variety of techniques due to the heavy resistance of the opponent. Generally, attacks must be confined to a "pet" side and there is little chance for other development. To eliminate this, include *Uchikomi* and Kata in all training schedules.

A point of emphasis in training which often becomes forgotten in Western Dojo, is the method of Kata. Traditionally, Kata study should be scheduled before attempting Randori, as practice of the various techniques under its imposed ideal conditions will bring a better understanding of Judo and efficiency in technique than can be had from Randori. A persevering study of Kata will provide a stable basis for free-style Judo. However, confining study only to Kata will never produce complete Judo ability. The fundamentals learned during Kata practice must be put to use in Randori.

A tendency in Kata practice today seems to be the meaningless application of the various Kata, being studied and applied only as a prerequisite to the various Dan. Trainees enter into Kata quite reluctantly, and the average approach brings little material benefit. Instructors and trainees must employ Kata in their training sessions, and should understand that the prearranged exercises are to be practiced with meaning in accordance with the principles of attack and defense. Every action describes the fundamental aspects of attack and defense and should convey such spirit. Movements made with careless motion or those with no mental alertness become useless. In pure Kata application, Tori and Uke follow prearranged movements. Yet, the spirit of their attacks and defenses must clearly indicate meaningful practice. Uke attacks with vigor and spirit, while Tori applies the appropriate technique and conducts his whole actions as if under serious hand-to-hand combat conditions. This is particularly true in the performance of the Nage no Kata, Kime no Kata, and the Goshinjitsu, and is termed *Zanshin* (alertness).

Training methodology utilizes the Kata to improve the contest abilities of trainees. Generally, practice is best limited to the Nage no Kata and the Katame no Kata, which are often referred to as the forms of Randori. These Kata deal with the theory and practice of throwing and grappling respectively, commonly used in free exercise. Two methods have proven useful in training.

The first of these requires the true adherence to Kata procedure, in which Tori and Uke follow the prearranged order of techniques. As mentioned earlier in this discussion, the true spirit of attack and defense must prevail. In the Nage no Kata, Tori is best able to concentrate on the fundamentals of each throwing technique, such as Kuzushi, Tsukuri, and Kake, and giving priority to correct form. Uke, on the other hand, learns to perfect his Ukemi and the general handling of his body. In the Katame no Kata, Tori likewise can devote full energy to the form of each grappling technique and is able to perfect the fundamentals necessary to grappling. Uke should make strong efforts, using body power, to escape from the techniques applied by Tori. Weak or feeble escape actions will nullify the meaning of the Kata for Uke and Tori.

The second method of utilization of Kata for training permits Tori to apply any technique of his own free will, not announced or prearranged, while Uke adapts to the situation by accepting the situation imposed without undue resistance. The techniques applied by Tori may be chosen from within the Nage and Katame no Kata, or may be taken from the general repertoire. If desired, the technique can be announced by Tori, who repeats it for a number of times under perfect conditions. Tori's actions may be applied against a motionless or moving opponent according to what is required. This practice approximates the method of Yakusokugeiko *(see page 84)*.

The development of *Renraku Henka Waza* (Connection-Variation Technique) is essential to all championship aspirations. This type of technique is sometimes referred to as "combination technique" which implies the successive attacks by different methods against the opponent, but all techniques connected in that each one is more or less preparatory for the succeeding one. Renraku Waza makes full use of the principle of Hando no Kuzushi *(see page 78)*, taking advantage of the opponent's reaction to finally effect a technique. The direct attacking of a skilled opponent is almost certain to be doomed to failure. It is via a diversionary attack, followed by a strong attack where the opponent least expects it, that successes are scored. A useful example of Renraku Waza is the use of the combination of Kouchigari—Ouchigari —Taiotoshi. Beginning an attack with Kouchigari, the opponent's reaction to escape will bring him into position for Ouchigari. When attacked in Ouchigari, the opponent will set his body balance to avoid it, and thus fall victim to the intended Taiotoshi. Trainees must study Renraku Waza only when they have familiarity with basic techniques. Speed and efficient deception are essential in the performance of Renraku Waza. The terminal Waza of a combination is often the trainees pet throw, which is efficient and strong. *(see Tokui Waza, page 89)*. Renraku Waza applies both to Nage and Katame techniques, the result of Tori's initiative. Renraku for Nage Waza can be practiced in Uchikomi form until the movement is smooth, thereafter in Randori with Yakusokugeiko or Sutegeiko applications. By this method, the trainee will develop effective Renraku Waza.

Often, it will be necessary to continuously attack the opponent with one particular technique in order to effect it. Continued application of one technique, each technique connected together by proper timing, is referred to as *Renzoku Waza* (continuous technique). A trainee who attacks with Seoinage for five consecutive times against his opponent, is practicing Renzoku Waza. This is also the product of Tori's initiative. Renzoku Waza is easily practiced in Uchikomi form until smoothness is obtained, after which application in Randori via Yakusokugeiko or Sutegeiko is beneficial.

Opportunities to score in contest often are limited to *Kaeshi Waza* (counter technique). An opponent failing in his attack can sometimes be defeated by a well-placed counter. A full study of this phase will serve in good stead. Kaeshi Waza are the result of the opponent's initiative. Kaeshi Waza is ideally practiced in Uchikomi form whereby the original attacker becomes the "victim" of the counter movement. Here too, after smoothness is obtained in the technique, Randori under Yakusokugeiko and Sutegeiko conditions will bring Kaeshi ability to the trainee.

Judo exponents must not be limited to one stance, either right or left, but should train to develop techniques on both sides. A Judo exponent who throws or grapples on both sides with more or less equal facility is extremely formidable and will obtain success not open to the "one-sided" exponent. This is the teaching method of K. Sone, 8 Dan.

The practice of Renraku Waza, Renzoku Waza, Kaeshi Waza and various stances, should be carried out under the conditions of Yakusokugeiko and Sutegeiko, where they can be fully developed before attempting them in actual contest.

The development of a *Tokui Waza* (pet or favorite technique) is advisable, and trainees who specialize in the development of a movement will be able to effect it under most any circumstances imposed by the opponent. However, disregard for other techniques is not wise, and the exponent with a Tokui Waza and nothing else, will never realize top performance. It is well to strongly develop an *Owaza* (major technique) such as *Uchimata* (Inner Thigh), *Osotogari* (Major Outer Reaping), *Hanegoshi* (Spring Hip), *Haraigoshi* (Sweeping Loin), *Seoinage* (Shoulder Throw), *Taiotoshi* (Body Drop), and the like, but the ignoring of *Kowaza* (Minor Technique) such as *Deashiharai* (Advanced Foot Sweep), *Okuriashiharai* (Sweeping Ankle), *Kouchigari* (Minor Inner Reaping), *Kosotogari* (Minor Outer Reaping), *Kosotogake* (Minor Outer Hooking), etc., greatly limits the effectiveness of the exponent. Generally, timing in the execution of Kowaza, is more critical than with Owaza, and Uchikomi repetitions should be set considerably higher than with Owaza. Kowaza are essential, and their absence is detrimental to a polished technique. As a Judo exponent grows older, the Owaza become more difficult to effect due to changes in the body flexibility, but the Kowaza are lifetime friends which will always be effective. Study all variations of your Tokui Waza.

Many experts will point out that the true essence of Judo lies in the Ashi Waza, where precise timing is essential to success in contrast to some of the other categories which can, though incorrectly, be applied by pure power. Instructors should encourage the development of Ashi Waza to include the useful evasive counter action of *Tsubamegaeshi* (Swallow-like (bird) counter). Trainees who exhibit a tendency for *Ashiharai* action will usually do so by favoring one leg. This ability can be channeled to provide the basis for other Ashi Waza such as *Kouchigari* (Minor Inner Reaping), *Kosotogari* (Minor Outer Reaping), *Sasaetsurikomiashi* (Propping Drawing Ankle), *Haraitsurikomiashi* (Sweeping Drawing Ankle), etc., executed with the same leg.

Timing an attack is an important consideration in training *(Chapter 3, page 40)*. Success in contest is dependent upon the best application of our technical skill and strength and mental power. Mental power in the form of what is referred to as *Sen*

(Initiative), serves as the nexus between our physical abilities and the contest result. If we fail to secure some form of initiative, victory is impossible. Initiative is classified in several ways such as Go no Sen (Defensive Initiative) the lowest form in which the opponent who *is applying* an attack is countered by our appropriate action. A middle form of initiative is Sen itself which enables us to apply an attack against the moving opponent who is *just beginning* to place his attack. The highest form of initiative is manifested in the *Sen-sen no sen* (superior initiative) which allows us to master the opponent *before* he can attack. The various forms of initiative are strictly matters of timing. The following guide will suggest some appropriate moments at which to attack:

From a controlled opponent, attack directly.

Use the opponent's momentary weakness as he fails in an attack and as he moves out of the failed Tsukuri but *before* he can return to a stable posture.

Use the opponent's momentary weakness as he begins an attack, but *before* it is well on the way to completion.

From an evasion of the opponent's attack, utilizing his momentum.

Countering the opponent's attack directly with the same attack.

Follow up on the ground as your opponent falls to the mat as a result of his failure in attacking you.

Follow up on the ground after your attack brings the opponent to the mat, but fails to score a full point.

It is evident that we must be proficient at the basic skills in throwing and grappling before we can bring about an application of our mental power in some form of Sen. Through the constant practice afforded by intelligent Randori, it is possible to build creditable technique which will function favorably in contest application.

The importance of carrying out an "all out" attack cannot be overemphasized. The Japanese Judo exponents excel in this kind of attack, and foreigners are often amazed at the tenacity and ferocity with which they are attacked. To the Japanese, once the attack is started, there is no "in between," but rather complete success or complete failure. This fundamental attack philosophy usually culminates in the *Makikomi* (winding) application, whereby a resisting opponent is hurled to the ground by the attacker who "winds" his opponent around his body and hurls himself to the ground. The opponent has little chance of escaping this forced action, and suffers a hard fall. #1-6. Makikomi is almost essential in high-level Judo competition as merely throwing an opponent without following him to the ground, allows him to escape the point, by turning his body "in" or "out," twisting his body quickly or actually bridging his body off the mat as he strikes the mat, thus keeping his back from touching and a point from being scored. #7-10. The use of Makikomi must follow proper application of technique or serious injury can result. The Makikomi is correctly used to *polish* an already existing Waza, *not to force* a badly executed one, or a Waza not yet fully learned. Instruc-

tors should insist on basic employment of techniques before adding the finesse of Maki-komi. In the West notable examples of well-executed Makikomi are seen in the U.S.A.'s Nozaki and Osako, both 5 Dan, with Uchimata, and France's Pariset, 4 Dan, whose Seoi-nage pull continues until *his* head touches the mat!

With the idea of an all-out attack in mind, trainees will do well to practice with the idea of two points in mind. After scoring a throwing technique, for one point, continue *without hesitation* into Katame Waza by applying *Osaekomi* or *Kansetsu Waza* (holding or joint locking techniques). This is the advice of the famous teacher, S. Shirai, 8 Dan, a disciple of the legendary Professor Mifune, 10 Dan. Many times in contest, even after the attacker obtains a throw, and *thinks* it is a full point, he loses the opportunity so created by the stunned opponent, to follow up the advantage with grappling. This is necessary in the case of the Referee not calling a full point, or awarding anything. A chance created by a throwing technique is thus lost, and perhaps there will be no other chance. Never assume that your throw will produce a point...but follow up, continue your attack until you *feel* the Referee stopping you. There must be a definite ability to connect Nage Waza and Katame Waza. Mere proficiency in each department is not sufficient. Connect them! Honor only the Referee's physical signal that you have been successful in defeating your opponent, or your opponent's submission by the usual tapping or patting, or voice command of *Maitta* ("I'm beaten"). Listening for verbal commands of the Referee is not always possible, nor advisable. It is the Referee's job to tend to the conduct of the match. Let him worry about stopping the match, not you. Of course your methods of Judo performance must always be in full accord with the rules and regulations of Judo. Engaging in Katame Waza is strictly controlled by the contest rules of Kodokan Judo. All Judo exponents who hope for full Judo contest efficiency must be thoroughly grounded in these rules and must be able to take advantage of situations which permit grappling. The following guide will suggest some appropriate chances for engaging in Katame Waza:

Throwing your opponent imperfectly and attacking directly on the ground (discussed on page 90).

Being thrown imperfectly and attacking directly on the ground.

Attack with Shime or Kansetsu Waza in the standing position, bringing your opponent to the ground after some effect is achieved.

Drawing your opponent to the ground (either you or your opponent loses balance in attack or evasion and falls).

Conduct your performance as to invite attack on the ground.

Specific engagement in Katame Waza from the above methods, individually or in combination, can be brought into effect with the attacker either in the top or bottom position. It is well to consider the risks of entering into grappling by bearing in mind the following:

If opponents of equal strength engage in grappling, the uppermost will have the advantage and will usually win, while the undermost has every chance of losing.

If the opponent is more skillful, one has a chance of winning while in the upper position, but every chance of losing in the bottom position.

If the opponent is less skillful, one will have every chance of winning while in the upper position, and some chances to win in the bottom position.

Serious training methods in Japanese Dojo require trainees never to signal defeat when caught in either Osaekomi or Shime Waza (choking technique). Only when Kansetsu Waza is applied effectively, should trainees so caught, surrender. In the case of Osaekomi Waza, there is no imminent danger and the victim is encouraged to continue his struggle until escape is effected, or the instructor or person so holding releases the technique. Giving up in Osaekomi is unforgiveable to serious trainees. In the case of Shime Waza, the same policy is used, and trainees in predicaments caused by choking attacks must either be neutralized, escaped from, or proven effective by the victim being "blacked out." This practice is not free from physiological dangers and must be carefully supervised by trained instructors.

The use of Shime and Kansetsu Waza is generally limited to those trainees who are advanced enough to realize the dangerous potentials of these categories of grappling. There is no set rule by which to abide, and each instructor will have to evaluate trainees individually in this regard. It is recommended that Shime Waza be studied and practiced only by trainees over twelve years of age, and that all such study and practice be under the supervision of a competent Black Belt instructor. The use of Shime Waza in contest must be confined to matches supervised by well-qualified referees. Kansetsu Waza follows the same usage pattern as for Shime Waza, but use in contest is best reserved for trainees of Ikkyu skill and higher.

In the study of Katame Waza, the basic consideration must be the Osaekomi Waza. It is the fundamental category of all grappling movements, for without a correct use of immobilization of the opponent's body, Shime and Kansetsu will be ineffective. The trainee is prone to neglect the study of the somewhat laborious Osaekomi in favor of the more attractive Shime and Kansetsu. S. Kotani, 8 Dan, known for his skillful Katame Waza, often points to his three year *exclusive* study of Osaekomi as the key to his grappling fame.

The proper application of breathing is essential to good Judo performance. First, from the standpoint of proper use of energy, breathing through the nose will eliminate the discomforts usually associated with mouth breathing. Secondly, breathing directly affects one's stability and the ability to utilize body power. We have already discussed breathing in connection with Kiai (Chapter 3). Applied directly to attack and defense, it has been noted in research studies conducted by Kodokan, that an opponent is weakest and most susceptible to attack during his process of inhalation, and strongest and least susceptible to attack during his process of exhalation. Timing the attack so that it coincides with inhalation of the opponent is likely to offer more chance of success than if the attack coincides with his exhalation. This applies equally to Nage or Katame Waza.

One subject which receives interest and attention in growing proportion each year among Western Judo exponents is the use of or influence of *Zen* (a form of Oriental philosophy) on Judo. It would be beyond the scope of this book to do more than mention the physical use of various postures assumed for purposes of self-discipline and meditation which have Zen roots and are today seen in well-disciplined Judo classes. The kneeling posture required in Oriental Dojo, the Seiza, is frequently used at the close of a formal class, as a position in which to sit and remain motionless, without special thought, for a few minutes prior to the closing salutation to the instructor and the Kamiza. In this way, the trainee is allowed to properly compose his mental attitude, resting with a relaxed mind. The figures below demonstrate the Zen posture.

Training Potpourri: A subject of immediate debate among Western physical educators, athletic coaches, and trainees themselves is the controversy as to whether or not some form of athletic supporter be worn during the practice of Judo. By customary Japanese methods, no special device such as the elastic strap or cup is worn. Occasionally, a pair of normal underwear of the "shorts" variety is worn, or a loin cloth of similar nature. Many trainees use nothing, dressing directly into the *Zubon* (trousers) of the Judogi. Most Western athletes would consider this practice as foolish and quite dangerous. However, the record will bear out the fact that injuries to the groin area and private parts are far less than would be expected, and compare favorably with other contact sports which utilize supporter protection. It is largely a matter of getting accustomed to this idea. Scores of years of constant adherence to this policy attest to its effectiveness, but nevertheless it remains largely a matter of preference. In theory, the Oriental idea points out that the relative freedom of the private parts without athletic supporter will most easily absorb shock that may be directed into this region, whereas the more confined and thus tightly restricted area created by athletic supporter action, will be subject to undesirable rigidity and thus be a direct, relatively immovable target for applied forces.

A training device used frequently in the West, but almost unknown in the Orient in so far as Judo is concerned, is the use of the training suit, or sweatsuit. The wearing of a sweatsuit under the Judogi during periods of waiting for contest is basically sound and should be encouraged. The warmth provided the body will reduce the chances of injury caused by prolonged waiting and little chance to warm up for the match. Teams such as the European Champions from Great Britain and the powerful French team use the sweatsuit. In contrast, the Oriental teams will stoically endure the rigors of cold weather clad only in their Judogi.

The proper wearing of the Judogi is essential to the dignity of Judo. Certain mannerisms in the wearing of the costume and additive "gimmicks" have found their way into modern Judo. We have already discussed the proper wearing of the Judogi and the wearing of organizational or rank emblems on the Judogi. (See page 55.) Several other points are now offered.

The first is wearing under garments such as T-shirts, sweat shirts, etc., under the Judo

Uwagi (Jacket). This practice is, for men and boys, considered improper and should be discouraged. Judo trainees will sometimes complain of cold Dojo conditions which necessitate this practice, but during actual training sessions, this should be unnecessary. However, it is customary for men or boys to wear some appropriate undergarment when practicing with women or girls. Chafing at the neck, caused by new or stiff Judogi, may be eliminated by wearing a short bit of cloth or toweling around the neck. The Japanese hand towel is excellent for this use.

The habit of wearing the Obi loosely and pulled down onto the buttocks is likewise considered improper whether in training or contest. Contestants will often do this to put the opponent at a disadvantage. A loose belt will cause a loose Judogi which may be a source of danger. The custom of opening the Judogi and pulling it loose from the Obi prior to engagement with the opponent is likewise a modern innovation which should be discouraged. This is not Judo!

It is well to have a small towel or rag handy for use in wiping excessive perspiration during training sessions in hot weather. Continued wiping of body parts on the outer surface of the Judogi is not particularly hygienic.

Because Judo is practiced and contested in a regulated or controlled manner, it is necessary to establish a common signal of defeat which is to be respected by all Judo exponents alike. It is a signal to be used by the defeated who wishes to acknowledge begin beaten and wants the attacker to stop all offensive action. This signal may be verbal or physical, or a combination of both. Generally the signal is made by tapping vigorously twice in rapid succession with either the hand or the foot. This tapping action must be made with distinct, rapid action and with some unmistakable force. It should be made on the person who is attacking, striking him with the palm or the fingers of the open hand, on the mat, or on the body of the one defeated who is signalling. (See Contest Rules, Appendix.)

Timing devices with bell signal to determine specific desired times are valuable in the Dojo. Darkroom clocks or those made for sporting events can be used. In large Japanese Dojo, the *Taiko* (drum) is used to call all sessions to order and to conclude them. See below picture.

Judo is traditionally performed in bare feet. Under special circumstances of injury or foot fungus, a protective covering in the form of a bandage or stocking may be worn, though its use should be discontinued just as soon as possible. The use of stockings for normal Judo practice is not recommended since the slippery surface provided will most certainly lead to serious injury in the performance of the fast movements required in certain Waza. While the use of stockings for Judo is not normal, and in fact dangerous, nevertheless, certain educational institutions in the U.S.A. require their use. The authors recall a certain large institution in the Eastern U.S.A. which has this requirement, and resultant Judo of its students has been seriously handicapped by this regulation. The use of stockings as a preventive measure against foot fungus is a very weak argument and unnecessary if normal precautions are taken with individual trainee hygiene and Dojo cleanliness. As a case in point, attention is focused on the Dojo in the Orient where many more feet tread on the mat surfaces under usually less hygienic conditions, and rarely, if ever is foot fungus found. With the use of the new plastic mat surfaces, Dojo cleanliness becomes a simpler matter than in past years of canvas covered mats.

The use of rope climbing as a conditioning exercise is a valuable training method, almost totally absent in Oriental and Western Judo Dojo. As a developer of the upper body, from the large muscles of the back to the small finger muscles, rope climbing in its various forms, will bring new power to Judoka. Facilities which maintain rope or pole climbing equipment should employ it in all training programs.

The use of the Ashiharai movement in pre-contest training does not receive the emphasis it deserves. Its performance is discussed in Chapter 8, page 183, and trainees and instructors will do well to develop correct form in this movement. It is performed best on the basis of Tandoku Renshu and can be used either as a Preparatory or a Supplementary Exercise. Its correct performance brings a basic form of Taisabaki and general body management which is highly beneficial to Judo efficiency. Advanced trainees may well copy Japanese Judoka who sometimes will specialize on this movement, executing thousands of repetitions daily for a period of from two to four weeks prior to a major contest. There have been some champions who restricted their heavy contact work some weeks prior to a contest in order to avoid possible injury and inability to compete. The Ashiharai movement and Uchikomi was performed in lieu of the heavy contact work, and with excellent results. This method is not recommended for any trainees other than already skilled Judo exponents. Lesser skilled exponents must engage in heavy contact work to perfect their technique.

Post-workout massage is a valuable training adjunct. If the schedule permits, trainees may administer massage to one another. Otherwise, it must be done privately, perhaps periodically with a regular professional service skilled in massage. Dojo massage is a common post-workout practice at Japanese university Dojo. Two methods are most easily used. One requires the trainees to form a large circle, stripping the Uwagi from the body. Each trainee commences to rub and massage the trainee in front of him, finishing with a rapid slapping action with the open hand over the entire back surface. The other method requires that trainees pair-off. After several minutes, partners reverse so that all can receive the benefit of massage. See above pictures.

Some mention should be made of severe disciplinary measures, voluntarily imposed by Japanese Judo champions in their training routines. Outstanding here is the system of arising at midnight, for a period of a week or two, and performing one hour of Ukemi on a hardwood floor. Others have purposely engaged in training sessions at midnight or the very early morning hours and topped off the workout with buckets of cold water poured liberally over the body. The very famous S. Kotani, 8 Dan, of Kodokan, during his younger competitive days in Manchuria, made liberal use of cold water by pouring buckets full over his body after heavy training. This was done regardless of the seasonal temperature! (see page 56). The Westerner will scoff, perhaps not without reason, and rule these methods as ridiculous and unnecessary. However, the underlying idea is to develop a mental attitude which can endure all rigors imposed upon the body.

Training aids are almost purely a Western innovation, except for a few items. Dojo instructors should make full use of all available training aids, in all levels of instruction *(page 51)*. Most fundamental is perhaps the blackboard. This device is found in almost every Dojo and is useful to explain by diagrammatic sketching, the intricacies of the various techniques, terminology of Judo, and sometimes, the daily training schedule. A portable blackboard is more effective than one that is permanently mounted. (Picture above.)

The frequent use of motion pictures, film strips and slides to describe relevant study is a most valuable "second instructor" and Dojo which invest in the necessary equipment will find measurable rewards for their financial outlay by way of increased understanding and interest of the trainees. A useful arrangement exists in a small Dojo in France where the projector is housed in a cubicle in the Dojo office on a movable turntable which revolves to come into the Dojo by merely pressing on the right spot in the wall. The projector which is normally in the office, is thus reversed and brought into the Dojo and operated from the Dojo for trainees seated on the mat before the projector. A roll-away screen pulls down from the ceiling to complete the theatre arrangements. The projector is pre-loaded, prior to class, to use when the appropriate moment in the normal instruction at hand arrives. The projector may also be used within the office by revolving the turntable, leaving a flat wall surface in the Dojo.

Many instructors will endorse the use of training mirrors, large enough to full-view the body, as indispensible in Judo training. Watching the execution of basic fundamentals such as Shisei, Shintai, Taisabaki, etc., will bring defects and improper positional attitudes into glaring prominence. Further use of the training mirror to view the execution of various Waza in either Tandoku or Sotai styles, often exposes the weaknesses of movement. Mirrors of course must be so located so as not to present potential sources of danger.

Training devices can be invented to aid the development of technique and power. Such devices are left to the imagination of students and instructors, but may be patterned after the device used in the Detroit Judo Club for the practice of Uchimata (picture below). Professor Otami, 8 Dan, tells of his use of a post on which he had painted a small mark to indicate the height of an opponent's knee. By attaching cords to the post, he was able to add perfection to his Taiotoshi; the mark being the precise

place he would place his extended leg, and the cords the means by which he practiced pulling power. Other equipment is shown in pictures above.

"Roadwork" or running, common to other combative sports, does not receive the emphasis it deserves. There can be no doubt that running in its various forms is a rapid way to increase endurance and as such, it can bring additional aid to the Judo exponent in his serious quest for excellence. Distance running, at a slow jog, is fundamental. Trainees should begin with a slow mile and gradually, within a period of a week or so, bring this distance up to two miles. This distance has proven adequate for Judo purposes. Running can be performed on the basis of normal methods, or running "backwards." Springing off of the feet alternately also produces a very effective exercise. Normal running combined with short distances of "backward" running within a two mile limit can be augmented by an exaggerated "spring step," in which the trainee leaps high into the air as he runs. Some young Japanese Judo trainees run to or from school daily, making gripping motions with their hands to strengthen grasping power as well as legs and hips. K. Sato, 9 Dan, recalls his student days when he took long walks, punctuated by running over difficult terrain in order to strengthen his legs and hips and also strongly recommends the use of *Geta* (a form of wooden shoe, picture below), which strongly influence the calf muscles of the legs. Today in modern Japan, many serious Judo trainees continue to wear Geta for several hours each day. The trainee is left to his own imagination to devise methods of running. Some use of "wind sprints," short, full-speed efforts over short distances, will also aid endurance.

The *Kokoro-e* (spirit of appreciation) of Judo requires hard work and constant training. There can be no substitute. Your proficiency in contest will depend upon the amount of dedication to training. Even the most skillful instructor can only hope to show you the movement. You must practice constantly until your technique shows the improvement desired. Sincerity in practice is the ruling necessity in all Judo endeavor. Your understanding of Judo will be the product of sincere practice.

The Judo Contest: It is virtually impossible to arbitrarily assign rules, strategy, and tips on more than a very general basis. If the trainee will develop his technique, bring his physical fitness to peak performance, and obtain contest experience, it is assured that contest successes will follow. What this boils down to is *preparation* by *sensible training*. There can be no substitute. Only hard work will bring about this result. There are no shortcuts. You may read, see, and talk about Judo, but in order to become proficient, you must *do* Judo.

If pre-contest training has followed the lines specified in this book, with emphasis on physical conditioning and Judo technique, and such training has been made under the guidance of a well-qualified instructor or in his absence, well-principled self-study, the trainee can approach the contest with a full measure of confidence. The contest is but a means to the intended end of Kodokan Judo, but any temporal focus tuned on the

contest can be brought into balance by proper regard for the whole of Judo training.

Contest time brings, in addition to physical factors, intense psychological factors into play. It is not yet proven that contest proficiency depends entirely on technique and physical fitness, and there is some suggestion that the difference between an expert contestant and an indifferent one, lies in the ability of consciously or unconsciously being able to use muscular energy to its best physical advantage while at the same time, releasing a tremendous amount of mental energy. Needless worry over the outcome will rob you of energy. Nervousness is not the sign of inexperience for even experts display the usual pre-contest "nerves." This is a normal and good sign which will act as a stimulus to quicken our reactions. However, too much is detrimental, and a certain amount of "coolness" must be developed by experience as a calculated control of our mental energy. It is well to be present at the tournament site well in advance so that check-in, possible weigh-in, and usual pre-contest matters may be attended to with a minimum of rush. Keep nearby so that when your time comes, you need not suffer being "scratched." Observe the competition only when it brings you information about potential opponents. Merely watching in spectator fashion can be very exhausting. If you can, get off your feet, resting as much as possible. *Keep warm*. Warmup with Preparatory, Supplementary, and Compound Exercises about 15 minutes prior to your contest if possible. If this is impossible, and you have been waiting seated for prolonged periods, be sure to establish circulation by utilization of Preparatory or Supplementary Exercises about one contest in advance. Do not go in "cold."

Each contestant should bear in mind the sound advice of I. Kudo, 9 Dan, who insists that it is absolutely necessary to train one's mental stability, physical forces, and technical perfection. Competition is often decided on a very small detail. If the opponents are on an equal footing in technique, the state of mind will dominate and decide the victor; if they are technically and mentally on a par, the physical forces will decide the victor. Pursuit of technique only will not make the complete competitive Judoka. Mental stability and physical forces must be improved. This is accomplished in the Orient by severe self-discipline, such methods as described in this text. For the Oriental Judoka, the spirit of training is as natural as water flowing downhill.

Have confidence in your ability regardless of the reputation of your opponent. However, do not underestimate the opponent, and enter the spirit of the competition with the idea of not losing. Try for the *Ippon* (point), but do not set your mind on obtaining one specific technique. Rather let circumstances determine what attack will be effective. Sometimes if you execute good Judo Waza, you will return to the sidelines not knowing just what you applied to defeat the opponent. This is true Waza! It is possible to win a contest in the opening *seconds*. This is termed *"Deru-pon"* in Judo slang, that is, as the opponent comes forward to engage you...Pon (Ippon)! This type of victory requires that you win with your very first attempt. The theory under which this becomes practical is that early in each contest, the opponent is under tension and may be overly stiff. Adjustment in balance and the general "feel" of the contest has not yet been established. Deru-pon must be done quickly and with an "all out" attitude. It is a method by which weaker Judo exponents may defeat stronger. Naturally there is risk, but when up against a tough opponent, it often is successful. A brilliant example of this was seen during the 1958 International Goodwill Matches at Kodokan when

Brazil's Kawakami, 4 Dan, scored instantaneously against the Kodokan's Tokuyama, 4 Dan. Do not be content with obtaining a *Hikewake* (draw), but if a decisive victory is not possible, perform your Judo so that you may obtain the *Yuseigachi* (decision by superiority). Posture, spirit, and adherence to proper Judo will make this possible. Above all, do your best, regardless of the outcome. If your preparation is good and your technique and physical fitness at a maximum, you will perform at *your* best.

Types of Judo Contest and Usage: The emphasis on Judo competition which in many instances has reached proportions of overemphasis, does not in any way change the fact that competitions are valuable and judicious use of them adds interest and enthusiasm, both participant and spectator, to the Judo programs of organizations. Competitions are truly forms of tests and measurements, and as such are useful only if they aid the trainees and instructor to improve. Competitive events are best limited to those events which have a definite educational purpose. Tournament antics tending toward intense competitive schedules for the "win" as an end in itself, with the scores of such tournaments and the resultant records to be filed away without even so much as a cursory glance, are wasteful procedures which do not respect the educational values intended by Dr. Kano.

Contest results form a valuable source of information about trainee abilities and progress as well as the teaching abilities of the instructor. An analysis of contest records will often lay the basis for future training, and the foresighted instructor will make good use of them. Contest records are an important factor in determining advancement in rank, but such evaluations can only be made by qualified Yudansha who are nationally authorized to award Judo rank within certain limits. Higher ranks must be awarded by boards of examination within each Kodokan Yudanshakai *(see Appendix, pages 288–89)* which convene periodically to consider promotional aspects within their jurisdictions. Usually, contest records are required by such boards and accurate recording of all relevant contest data is required on designated forms for this purpose.

Judo competition has situations and circumstances peculiar to it. Because of this regard for traditional values, Judo competitions of various types have been designed. All types presented in this text have strong and weak points. Some serve one purpose well, while at the same time, fail to satisfy other requirements. None are all-around, one-shot answers to any one particular goal, though they may be quite efficient in any one application. A balanced variety of competitions should be instituted and maintained by each Dojo or Club and should be in concert with local Yudanshakai requirements. Yudanshakai patterns must in turn be directed toward national efforts and requirements.

The present international controversy over weight categories for Judo competition indicates that a majority of the world's national Judo bodies do not favor the adoption of weight categories. It is not the purpose of this text to discuss the merits and shortcomings of the weight category issue, but regardless of the stand taken, it is perfectly feasible and desirable for Judo organizations to conduct Judo competition both on weight and non-weight category bases without any conflict. Outstanding examples of this utilization in the U.S.A. are Hokka (Northern California) and Shufu (Capital Area) Judo Yudanshakai *(see Appendix, pages, 288–89),* who annually conduct both types of competition with high degrees of cooperation and success. There are certain types of Judo competitions which cannot make use of weight categories, while other events, in the opinions of the authors, are better suited to the use of weight categories. Yudanshakai and local affiliated Dojo and Clubs should schedule both traditional and AAU weight category events regularly.

Judo organizations sponsoring weight category competition may find it helpful to develop the conduct of the tournament along the lines suggested in the AAU handbook for Judo obtainable from any local AAU office or the national headquarters. Scoring and other pertinent details are discussed therein.

Those organizations which utilize weight categories and tend toward their exclusive use in lieu of traditional competition, should bear one very important fact in mind. The mental attitude, and therefore to some extent the physical ability of trainees, developed under the *exclusive or excessive use* of weight category competition which is currently in vogue in the U.S.A., will not properly train championship aspirants for meeting the caliber of international Judo presently sanctioned under the auspices of the International Judo Federation (IJF). Under the weight category system of the AAU which makes use of the penalty point system, Judo exponents of the U.S.A. enter into competition full knowing that the system provides a "second chance" should a defeat be suffered. In fact, under certain circumstances, a "third" or even more "chances" to win in spite of not winning by a complete point victory, exist. In contrast, the international opponent, the Judoka of the Orient or Europe (and other areas as well), has been trained on the basis of, "I get one chance—there is not a second chance—I win, or I lose. I must win." Trainees under this system will develop, and have developed a superior contest ability to that of the Judoka from the U.S.A. International contests have proven this and personal observation by many qualified Judoka clearly place the U.S.A. in an "also-ran" status.

International opponents developed under this "one chance" philosophy are extremely able Judoka who execute a relentless form of contest strategy designed to exploit any weakness in Judo attitude. Organizations which train solely on the penalty point system will never be able to completely challenge the superiority of traditionally trained Judoka. Should weight categories become internationally accepted, this gap will still be in evidence during the early days of this acceptance, in that the "one chance" trained Judoka will enter this new form of lesser demanding Judo with his original philosophy firmly imbedded in his physical contest technique. Until such time as the penalty point system is fully utilized by all countries, traditional Judo competition must be continued and should be given a prominent place in the training schedule.

The term "Kohaku Shiai" has traditional significance for the contest phase of Judo. Its historical genesis is outside the discussion of this chapter. Modern usage assigns a mechanical meaning to the Kohaku as a device for the convenience of refereeing and judging procedures. The Japanese ideograph, "Kohaku" may be translated directly to mean, "Red and White." Kohaku Shiai is then a "Red and White Tournament" in which two colors are used to identify the competitors. Whether established on an individual or team basis, the Kohaku Shiai merely uses two colors as a device for rapid and positive recognition of opponents. It is not necessarily synonymous with a "type" of tournament or particular method of match conduct, though common usage implies this. Generally, all types of competition, whether team or individual, and regardless of purpose (eliminations, championships, promotional, evaluations) utilize the Red and White colors to aid officiating. One opponent will wear a red ribbon around his midsection, while the other opponent will wear white or perhaps no ribbon. The judges and referee are therefore easily able to indicate a winner by signaling the appropriate color of the winner by use of a flag *(see Appendix, Contest Rules of the Kodokan Judo).*

Judo contests divide into two major categories, individual and team competitions. Depending upon the purpose, we are able to choose a method of competition. The responsibility of pairing should fall to qualified Judo exponents who are familiar with the caliber of the Judo being contested. The type of contest, the time available, contestant capabilities and limitations, purpose of the contest, and other similar modifying factors determine official procedures. Regular problems of seeding, byes, etc., should follow normal patterns. Individual competitions may or may not give regard for weight or Judo skill, but when conducting team competition, the teams line up in order of Judo rank, with the senior man as the team captain. Judo team competition begins with the junior ranked man. This has been a time-honored tradition; however, recent experimentation by Judo officials in Japan has indicated support for disregarding the order of rank in team competition. In the 1960 All-Tokyo University Team Championships, for the first time, competitors were lined up in a team or coach chosen order announced only just prior to the match. This brings additional coaching responsibilities in order to "outguess" the opponents. Where before, the order of team members was established by tradition, under this new method it is possible to introduce many variables effecting the final result. This method has been in use in Europe for years and its popularity will undoubtedly increase.

The *Soatari Shiai* (Round-robin Tournament) permits one of the most thoroughly accurate selections of a winner and place winners. It is particularly well-suited to individual competition rather than team events. It pits opponent against opponent so that at the termination of the event, all contestants have faced each other. The Judo exponent with the highest number of points is the winner. In spite of its accuracy, it finds limited use unless the number of entries is small, generally less than 7. It is too time consuming. Six entries require 30 contests to completion. Small Dojo or Clubs will find it ideal for their use, as will tournament managers who with a small entry list, are able to expand the program via this type of tournament. The Soatari Shiai can be used for purposes of championships, eliminations, evaluations, and promotional contests. See Charts 1(a), 1(b), and 2(a), pages 110, 111, 112.

The *Koten Shiai* (Big Point Tournament) is another type of contest method which in its best application should be restricted to individual purposes rather than team evaluations. Here, as in the Soatari Shiai, no sides (teams) are chosen, but rather, the competitors are lined up in a single line, usually in order of their rank. Beginning with the junior ranked Judo exponent, he competes with the man immediately next to him (on his right). He continues to compete until he loses or is drawn out. Generally decisions of superiority are not given in this type of contest, and a point must be scored to win and advance. Upon loss or draw, he retires as would his opponent. The competition then continues with the next two adjacent Judo exponents who are required to compete similarly, and so on until the line is exhausted. By this method, competitors are trained to be aggressive and seek the "big" point. Most points scored determine the winner. Since all contestants are given a chance to compete, it provides a valuable method to evaluate individual skills. The Koten Shiai can be used in eliminations, evaluations, as the basis of promotional authority, and as a method in training Judo exponents for endurance. See Charts 1(a) and 2(a), pages 110, 112.

The *Tentori Shiai* (Single Elimination) is a popular form of man-to-man competition used in individual and team contests. Used as an individual contest method, Judo exponents are paired in single elimination form and are advanced by victory in each round. No draws are permitted, but victory may be the result of a decision by superiority as well as by a scored point. A winner is finally established in this way. With large entries, brackets will be established, and pairings, seeding, and byes may be necessary. Team contests utilizing the Tentori Shiai bring together equally numbered teams. Starting with lowest ranked Judo exponents, competition commences and regardless of victory or loss, both contestants retire at the end of the bout. Each competitor has one bout. The team with the most points total score is declared the winner. Draws may be awarded but receive no numerical value. Decisions by superiority may be given a one-half point value. Though awarded, they may be discarded unless they are necessary to break a tie. This is a quick method to determine winners and is best adapted to evaluate a team's overall power. However, often the defeated finalist is not the second best team or player. Great numbers of entries may be handled with this type of Shiai. The Tentori Shiai can be used for individual eliminations, individual championships, team evaluations, eliminations, and championships. See Charts 1(b), 2(a) and 2(b), pages 111–113.

The *Kachinuki Shiai* (Winner Continue) is one of the most widely used forms of contest method for Judo. Probably because of this constant use, the term Kohaku Shiai has become synonymous with the method of the Kachinuki Shiai. Its method is somewhat similar to the Koten Shiai *(page 101)* but in this case, two definite sides, or teams, are chosen. One is designated "Red Team" and the other, "White Team." Under individual evaluation purposes, such as is the custom in the Dojo Tsukinami Shiai, these sides or teams do not necessarily have any organizational unity representing some Dojo or Club, but are merely chosen on a deliberately mixed basis. They may be balanced so as to provide accurate evaluations of skills, or they may be deliberately unbalanced in skill, favoring one side. This is often employed by instructors to develop the lower skilled side more rapidly by having them compete against skilled opponents. The contest begins by having the junior ranked Judo exponents from each side compete. The winner will continue to engage the next man from the opposite side until he loses or is drawn out. Losing, or being drawn out requires one to retire, and the next two contestants take their place opposite each other for competition. This process continues until one line is exhausted and the other side has team members remaining. Repairings can be made to afford every contestant a chance to compete, or the contest can be halted. The amount of points scored by each individual determines the superior Judo exponent. Wins by decision of superiority merely allow the contestant to remain on the mat for another chance, and do not necessarily give him point credit. In team competition using the Kachinuki Shiai method, the competition is carried out as is the individual competition, with the winning team determined by the team with the largest number of competitors remaining. If the matches continue so that the final pits the team captains against each other, and they too can bring no decisive score for victory, the tie is broken by having a representative from each side come out for an extra or "overtime" bout. This is continued until victory is achieved. Generally, the team captain is expected to take this extra physical responsibility and compete for the team's honor. In the 1959 All-Japan University Team Championships, Meiji and Nihon Universities faced each other in the semifinals and were forced into 6 overtimes before a tired Meiji team emerged victorious. Nevertheless, Meiji had been drawn beyond its normal recuperative powers, and lost in the final to the powerful Tenri University. The Kachinuki Shiai is especially useful to determine individual skills. It has the drawback that all contestants may not compete, with the members of the stronger side left out of the competition. A weak team with one or two exceptionally strong members can win, but not really show the index of team strength. It may be used as a training device to develop endurance in individuals, or as the basis for promotional action. See Charts 1(a), 2(a), 2(b), pages 110, 112, 113.

The *Kaikyu Shiai* (Rank Tournament) has grown in popularity during the past half decade. European, Central and South American Judo championships are generally decided on the basis of this type of competition. It is limited to individual competition. Contestants are paired in Tentori style (Single Elimination) within their own rank level and are advanced by victory in each round. No draws are permitted though the victory may be the result of a decision for superiority as well as by a scored point. A single champion is finally established in each level of Kyu—White and Brown Belt—and in each level of Dan—Shodan, Nidan, Sandan, and Yodan as a terminal rank. Finally, an All-Category event is conducted which disregards levels of rank and allows both Kyu (usually restricted to Brown Belt) and Dan to compete for honors in Tentori style. The Kaikyu Shiai is useful to establish relative standings in each rank level and follows the general useage, advantages and disadvantages of the Tentori Shiai.

Shinkyu Shiai (Kyu Promotional Tournament) events determine the contest fitness of recommended candidates for advancement in rank among Kyu Judo students. Any of the methods discussed earlier which are adaptable to promotional and evaluation objectives may be employed.

The *Tsukinami Shiai* (Monthly Tournament) is usually a closed event within each Dojo. All trainees within the Dojo are encouraged to participate and improve their contest experience. Here too, the method of competition may be chosen from any of the earlier methods discussed depending upon the objectives in mind.

Miscellaneous devices exist to effect contest and tournament bouts. They conform to normal patterns of consolation, double elimination, Bagnall-Wild elimination, Lombard round-robin, combination, and challenge tournament structures. Officials and instructors should make use of various forms to more intensely develop competitive values of Judo.

Normal competition is arranged on the basis of *Ippon Shobu* (One Point Match) in which victory is determined by the competitor who secures one point. All championships favor this type of contest. However, in training, it is often advantageous to train Judo exponents in the method of *Nihon Shobu* (Two Point Match) in which victory is determined by the competitor who secures two points. This is done for reasons already explained *(see page 91)*.

Scoring systems for team events based on the idea of 7-5-3-0 points for Ippon-Waza ari-Yuseigachi-Hikiwake respectively, are currently in vogue in the U.S.A. This method does not receive favor from traditional Judoka who feel that such a system is purely a device for a "game" and removes the seriousness of having to obtain a point to win. Team events scored entirely on this basis develop a liberal contest philosophy which may find it difficult to keep pace with the traditional aspect. Judo organizations should not exclude traditional scoring.

It is well to avoid the many contest "antics" of modern Judo. They are self-explanatory and need no elaboration beyond simple mention. A strict Referee will invoke Article 28 of the Contest Rules of the Kodokan Judo *(see Appendix, pages 295–96)*. Such antics include: improper wearing of the Judogi; running off the mat continually; "pawing" and "grab and regrabbing" of Judogi in an attempt to confuse the opponent; purely defensive Judo strategy; skirting the edges of the contest area.

Administration of Judo Contests and Tournaments: The contest is an important part of Judo leading to the accomplishment of Judo training objectives. Contests may be a potential source of aid in evaluation of training methods and as such should be exemplary of well-organized and efficient operations. On the other hand, contests easily degenerate into controlled "fights" with little regard for overall training objectives. Occasionally, contests and the necessary preparations bring nothing but utter confusion to participant and spectator alike. For Judo groups sponsoring well-conducted events, this section will be "old hat," but it is recommended that the points listed herein be scanned for possible improvement of efficiency.

Ranging from private Dojo Tsukinami Shiai; dual and multi-team open, closed, and invitational shiai; promotional shiai, up to the various levels of championships; all tournaments must be well-organized if they are to be helpful to Judo training objectives. These preparations may be simple and effected at the tournament site or they may be planned far in advance, but they should never be *last minute* thoughts and actions. The authors well recall the efforts of a group of East Coast colleges who had agreed on an invitational meet. All went well until the first contestants were scheduled when it was discovered that no preparation had been made for qualified referees!

The precise amount of pre-contest, contest, and post-contest preparation is entirely dependent upon the type and level of contest-tournament being conducted. An exhaustive study of each type is beyond the intent of this text, but a checklist may be established on a somewhat maximum set of requirements.

Pre-contest Preparations: Good organizational method places the overall supervision and responsibility for the event in the hands of a tournament director or manager. This job should be assigned to a highly experienced Judo exponent who has both technical and administrative abilities. In lesser level events, the tournament director or manager himself performs almost all duties required to bring off a successful meet, but should wisely delegate various tasks to other personnel. The larger the meet, the more complex the tasks and experience, has proven that separate committees should be appointed to achieve specially assigned tasks for the tournament director, who must then coordinate all committee functions. The tournament director should be a *non-competing* Judo exponent inasmuch as the nature of his job precludes concentration on actual competing. He is, in the last analysis, the source of tournament management and is responsible for all the event does or fails to accomplish. The following check list will suggest a handy reference to guide preparations:

Tournament Director (Manager)

Advises and supervises the overall administration of all activities pertaining to scheduled event. Takes active part in at least one specific assignment. Assigns specific committees.

Shiai Committee

1. prepares, distributes, and receives returned entry blanks.
2. obtains AAU sanction and conducts necessary liaison.
3. obtains officials (referees, judges, timers, scorers, recorders) from local, parent Yudanshakai, or other qualified sources.
4. makes pairings.
5. obtains trophies and medals.
6. obtains necessary equipment for officials (stop watches, time clocks, bell-whistle-gong, red & white flags, red & white ribbons, contest forms (see Appendix, pages 307–308), pencils, contest rules).

Facilities Committee

1. obtains and check tournament site facilities (mat, seating for spectators and participants, showers, lockers, lavatories, tables and chairs for officials, PA systems, scales.
2. appoints ticket sellers-takers, ushers, and announcers.
3. makes accommodations for visiting competitors (refreshments, lodging, meals).
4. arranges for physician and/or first aid.
5. handles finance for necessary disbursements.

Publicity Committee

1. prepares and distribute tickets (complimentary too).
2. prepares programs or throwaways.
3. prepares invitations to guests and officials.
4. solicit publicity in form of TV, radio, magazine, newspaper, poster, exhibition-demonstration-lecture, media.
5. prepare intermission and rest period exhibitions.

Experience has proven that if possible, Yudansha should be assigned to the Shiai Committee, while the Publicity and Facilities Committees can be staffed by any rank levels.

The Contest Day Preparations: The day of the contest should find all in readiness except inevitable last minute details which cannot be attended to earlier. Outstanding among these is the physical checking in of all officials and contestants. Officials should congregate at least an hour before contest time in order to familiarize themselves with all details and to provide the necessary technical assistance for the conduct of the matches. As contestants check in, certain vital statistics must be properly recorded (see Appendix, page 307) such as names, club affiliations, ranks, weights, AAU memberships and travel permits. In the event that pre-contest pairing was not utilized, such vital statistics become increasingly important and strict accuracy must be obtained in their recording. Pairings should be made by experienced Yudansha if possible in order to derive maximum benefit from the combinations of contestants. The following check list may be helpful:

Shiai Committee

1. conducts officials meeting.
2. records check of all competitors (name, rank, club, travel permit, amateurism, weight).
3. makes pairings.
4. provides officials (referees, judges, timers, for Osaekomi, timers for bout duration, scorers and recorders of match results).
5. conducts matches.

Facilities Committee

1. sells and takes tickets (petty cash available).
2. provides usher service.
3. meets and aids visiting competitors.
4. provides announcers.
5. assists Publicity Committee in duties.
6. provides cleaning and police of area.
7. provides physician and/or first aid services.

Publicity Committee

1. aids in ticket selling and taking.
2. aids in usher service.
3. assists in announcing.
4. aids in program distribution.
5. meets and aids invited guests and officials. Makes introductions.
6. arranges for coverage of matches by publicity media.
7. performs intermission and rest period exhibitions.

The actual contest time is one of extreme rapidity of events and the officials actually engaged in the conduct of the matches must be isolated as much as possible from miscellaneous details which tend to hinder proper supervision of the bouts. Facilities and Publicity Committee members should make every effort to respect this fact and utilize their initiative in solving problems that arise.

The physical arrangement of the various official tables should be carefully studied. Efficient operations require that the mat area itself be located so as to permit certain perimeter activities without interferring with the action on the mat. These perimeter activities include viewing of the contests by substitute Referees and Judges, Guests of Honor, Tournament Manager or Director, and Medical Doctor as well as the work of Recorder, Scorer, and Timekeepers. The Announcer or Master of Ceremonies should

also be given a place in the perimeter activities. The pictures above show typical tournament arrangement at Kodokan. Two floor plans have proven functional. The first places all perimeter activity along the Kamiza axis as shown in #1, page 108. An alternate plan provides for a separate location of the Recorder, Scorer, Timekeepers, and Announcer along the Joseki or Shimoseki axis. In this floor plan, it should be noted that provision must be made for two announcer positions, one at the head table at the Kamiza axis, and the other at the Recorder table along the Joseki or Shimoseki axis. #2, page 109.

Specific provision made for competitors along the Shimoza or Joseki axis is desirable in order that the competitors may be grouped in orderly fashion and thus cause no delay in the bouts. Unnecessary mixing of competitors with official tournament perimeter activities, or with spectators, produces straggling and greatly hampers efficient tournament operation.

Post-contest Activities: Somewhat anti-climactic, but nevertheless vital to efficient tournament procedure and in order to obtain maximum benefit from the event within Judo training objectives, post-contest activities often are regarded as activities left to junior members to accomplish. It is here that the overall supervision of the tournament director or manager should continue unabated, and committees continued until all assigned work is completed. The following check list may be helpful:

Shiai Committee

1. awards trophies and medals.
2. conducts officials evaluation meetings.
3. records completely all match records for proper distribution to files, AAU, visiting organizations, etc.
4. prepares necessary reports on match results.

Facilities Committee

1. checks ticket take versus cash.
2. finance and disbursements, reports to appropriate addresses.
3. police and return of all property and facilities to proper owners.

Publicity Committee

1. releases appropriate publicity to TV, radio, newspaper, magazines, etc.
2. prepares and distributes letters of thanks, appreciation.

The Judo Tournament in Retrospect: Regardless of its obvious intended purpose, each contest and surrounding events is a source of training. It is an exercise in both technical and administrative aspects of Judo, and can be made to encompass a valuable area. Whether designed as a championship, a promotional, or whatever, contests should bring a wider understanding to each and every participant, both officials and contestants alike.

Coaches and instructors should insist on transcripts of the match records in order that they may study these records with view toward learning the limitations and capabilities of each competitor. Tournament records will indicate the weaknesses and strong points of trainees, and serve as a direct check on training methods. Intelligent and analytical study of these records is indispensable to all good coaching methods.

Diagram 1

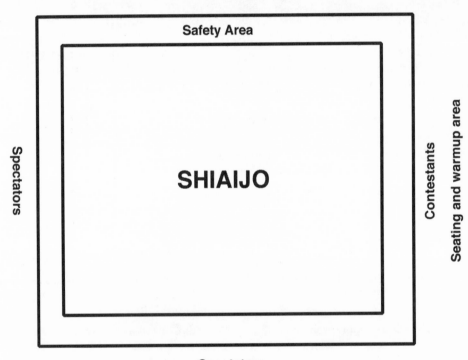

Diagram 2

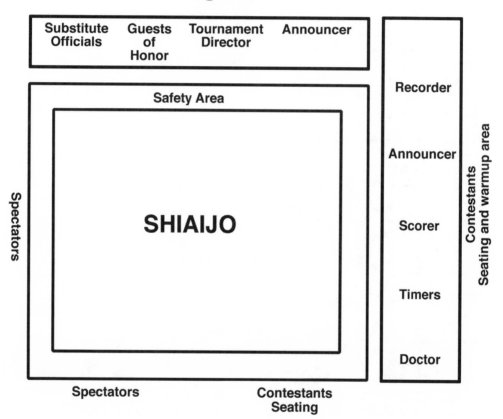

| Substitute Officials | Guests of Honor | Tournament Director | Announcer |

Safety Area

Spectators

SHIAIJO

Spectators

Contestants Seating

Recorder

Announcer

Scorer

Timers

Doctor

Contestants Seating and warmup area

Chart 1a

Scoring of Judo Competitive Types

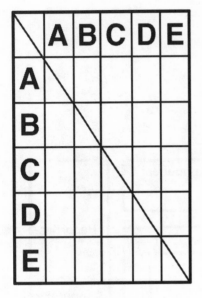

**Soatari Shiai
Record Form**

A B C D E F G H I

**A is winner with 2 points
F is 2nd with 1 point**

**Koten Shiai
Sample Results**

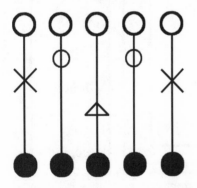

(White side)

(Red side)

**White team is winner
(2 to 1/2)**

**Tentori Shiai
Sample Team Results**

**White team is winner
(3 to 2)
White C is individual
winner**

**Kachinuki Shiai
Sample Team or Individual Results**

CODE

○ Ippon   ✕ Hikewake

△ Waza ari   **E** Team captains or
senior rank

Chart 1b

Scoring of Judo Competitive Types

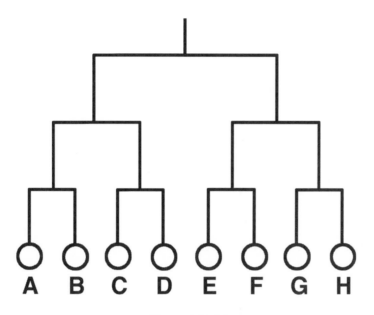

Tentori Shiai
Sample Individual Pairings

Round 1	Round 2	Round 3	Round 4	Round 5
Bye E	Bye D	Bye C	Bye B	Bye A
A vs. D	E vs. C	D vs. B	C vs. A	B vs. E
B vs. C	A vs. B	E vs. A	D vs. E	C vs. D

The Soatari pairings are drawn up by placing as many numbers (letters) as there are competitors in two vertical columns. Arange the numbers (letters) consecutively down the first column and up the second. To obtain pairings for subsequent rounds, rotate the numbers (letters) counterclockwise around one of the numbers (letters) which is kept fixed. Uneven numbers of competitors is balanced by a "bye" which remains fixed as others rotate counterclockwise. *(See soatari record form, chart 1a.)*

Soatori Shiai
Sample pairings for five individual competitors

Chart 2a

Judo Contest Characterisitics (Individual)

PURPOSE	NAME	KIND	REMARKS
Eliminations	Soatari Shiai Koten Shiai Tentori Shiai	Round Robin Big Point Single Elimination	**Kachinuki Shiai:** Shows up individual abilities - point getters. Point scores must be kept except in endurance training. Good for large number of contestants. Not all will necessarily compete. Can provide extreme spectator interest.
Championships	Soatari Shiai Tentori Shiai	Round Robin Single Elimination	**Koten Shiai:** Shows up individual abilities - point getters. Point scores must be kept except in endurance training. Good for large number of contestants. All competitors will take part. Can provide extreme spectator interest.
Evaluations	Soatari Shiai Koten Shiai	Round Robin Big Point	**Soatari Shiai:** Determines true winner and placers. Limited to small entry (under 7). Takes time to run. All competitors will take part.
Promotions	Kachinuki Shiai Soatari Shiai Koten Shiai	Winner Continue Round Robin Big Point	**Tentori Shiai:** Not completely accurate as it does not produce true "best" men or placers. Easy to run; best with large entry.
Endurance Training	Kachinuki Shiai Koten Shiai	Winner Continue Big Point	

Chart 2b

Judo Contest Characterisitics (Team)

PURPOSE	NAME	KIND	REMARKS
Eliminations	Tentori Shiai	Single Elimination	**Kachinuki Shiai:** Not an accurate index of team abilities. Based on individual power. Teams with exceptional individual competitor may utilize best. Good for large number of entries. Not all competitors will necessarily compete. Point score need not be kept. Can provide extreme spectator interest.
Championships	Tentori Shiai Kachinuki Shiai	Single Elimination Winner Continue	
Evaluations	Tentori Shiai	Single Elimination	**Tentori Shiai:** Gives an accurate index of team abilities based on individual member ability. All competitors will take part. Good for large entries, but can be time consuming. Point score must be kept.
Promotions	Tentori Shiai	Single Elimination	

PLATE 6. *Upper:* Ben Campbell, 4 Dan, San Jose State College Judoka and Pacific AAU Judo Champion, an advocate of sensible weight training. *Lower:* James Bregman, 2 Dan, Washington Judo Club Judoka and All-East Coast AAU Judo Champion, currently a Kodokan Kenshusei (special research student), an advocate of sensible weight training.

CHAPTER 5

Judo and Weight Training

Great is the force of custom: Huntsmen will watch all night in snow and endure to be scorched on the hills; fencers bruised with sand-bags or cudgels, do not so much as groan.
Cicero

General: The subjects of weightlifting and weight training have received a considerable amount of bad publicity and subsequent misunderstandings have developed among athletic coaches, trainers, instructors, and athletes themselves. Until a few years ago, most athletes, under fear of removal from the squad, were forbidden to practice weight exercises by firm-minded coaches. Weight movements had little or no place in the training routines of most coaches who argued that continued use of weight exercises would result in "muscle bound," herniated, slow, and possibly "strained heart" athletes.

Today, while this *idée fixe* is rapidly disappearing, many old-school coaches continue to take a strong stand against weight exercises. All of this is due to a lack of understanding of the proper methods of sensible training and the compatibility of these methods in direct application to any sporting form. It is sincerely hoped that this book will aid athletic coaches to further see the applications to which weight exercises can be directed. It is also hoped that by presenting to the Judo world for the first time a systematic method of applying weight training to the normal Judo routines, the already improved performance of Judo exponents undergoing this type of training will bring acceptance from the now indifferent Judo instructors.

Early evidence of the values of weight training were seen in the U.S.A. as far back as 1876 when a weight-trained track and field event man won three national titles. By and large, subsequent athletic achievements of championship status in various sports such as football, baseball, swimming, wrestling, boxing, etc., gained by weight-trained athletes, were entirely due to their own efforts and not to recognized methods of coaching and instruction combining weight training with their individual specialties. In modern times, one of the most truly advanced acceptances of weight training methods applied to sporting competition came in the field of swimming where, almost always, subsidiary exercises had been considered taboo. Until quite recently most coaching methods in swimming forbade the trainee from engaging in any other activities which might tend to "tighten" his muscles. Coach Robert Kiputh of Yale University, developer of numerous National Championship teams and swimmers, as well as Olympic champions, for years coached and conditioned his swimmers by use of "dry land" exercises which included resistance movements. Other swimming coaches have followed suit always with increased success. The co-author, for many years himself a competitive swimmer in the U.S.A., used weight training methods to achieve his moderate success and in later years coached numerous individuals and teams to championship levels utilizing weight-training methods as a complement to the normal training program.

Swimming affords an interesting and related parallel to Judo in that a swimmer must be unusually flexible and develop a supple, strong body, while coupling these qualities into a highly developed technique. The former position of swimming coaches in regard to proper training methods did not include weight training, but rather, specifically condemned it as detrimental to an efficient swimming technique. Judo today, is in the position regarding weight training, that swimming was about 15 years ago. Without further elaboration, let the ever falling swimming records attest to the value of improved training methods which today positively accord weight training a place in the swim training program. There is a parallel "tomorrow" for Judo in weight training methods.

In spite of their attack on resistance exercises, athletic coaches and athletes who have condemned the use of weight training, almost all use some form of resistance exercise. The football coach will require his team members to charge hard and furiously against the "sled;" the baseball and track coach will require "grass drill" which includes duck-walking, jumping squats, push-ups, etc.; while the wrestling coach will make his trainees charge against one another, each one resisting to his utmost. No...these coaches will have none of the resistance exercises!

Athletic coaches in sporting fields other than Judo have developed champions by intelligently applying weight movements as a complement to the normal training routine. Today the list of these pioneers in scientific training is large and steadily growing. To give proper mention to them would be to exceed our purpose, but perhaps the best testimonial and most easily understood results of their foresighted training methods can be summarized by the names of such great champions as: Otis Chandler, Fortune Gordien, Bob Matthias, Don Bragg, Bob Richards, Parry O'Brien, Herb Elliot, John Thomas, Ron Delaney, Mal Whitfield, Bob Backus, Ed Collymore, and Rafer Johnson in track and field world; Allan Ameche, Steve Van Buren, Walter Barnes, Stan Jones, Billy Cannon, and Pete Dawkins in football; Lew Hoad, and Christine Truman in tennis; Ingemar Johansson in boxing; Jackie Jensen, Ralph Kiner, Lee Walls, and Bob Feller in baseball; Bill Simonovich in basketball; Frank Stranahan in golf; Allan Ford, Dick Cleveland, Al Wiggins, and Shelly Mann in swimming; Jack Kelly Jr. in sculling; Henry Wittenberg in wrestling, and scores of other leading names from most every form of endeavor. Now to this list can be added the name of the young man who astonished the Judo world by recently winning the All-Japan Judo title. Isao Inokuma, 21-year old university student from Tokyo and holder of the 4th Grade in Kodokan Judo, bested all challengers to become the youngest champion in the history of Japanese Judo (see Chapter 10, Auxiliary Exercises, page 206).

Major reasons for the current trend toward acceptance of weight training methods applied to all forms of sporting endeavor is largely due to the efforts of Dr. Peter Karpovitch of Springfield College, an eminent physiologist who has removed many of the misconceptions concerning the effects of weight exercises. Sharing the continual efforts for the cause of weight training with Dr. Karpovitch are Dr. Larry Morehouse of Southern California, and the outstanding weight exercise authority and Olympic weightlifting coach, Bob Hoffman of York, Pennsylvania. They are supported actively by a growing list of testimonials from leading physical education specialists, physiologists, and athletic coaches and athletes, who are proving the necessity, both from a physiological and athletic standpoint, for weight training as an adjunct to training for all sports. Outstanding in the development of weight training programs as an official part of the physical education curriculum are the University of Maryland, University of New Mexico, Villanova, Notre Dame, Temple, Stanford, and Michigan State University. There are of course, numerous other schools which have integrated weight training with normal physical education methods and thereby improved varsity sport performances.

That weight training is producing better champions—champions who are bettering records by bettering their strength and physiological functions—cannot be denied. Almost without exception, the greatest athletes and champions in the U.S.A., are *weight trained* athletes. We have established earlier in Chapter 3 the fact that muscular hypertrophy is best stimulated by weight training methods. Further, strength which accompanies this growth is increased and brings the added desirable quality of improved physical fitness. Applied to athletic endeavors, there is not one single event that is adversely affected by an increase in strength. We can think of weight training not just as a form of "pure muscle" building, but the manner in which physical fitness—endurance—can best be promoted.

Weight Lifting and Weight Training: Muscles are designed to operate against resistance. Each time we utilize training methods which use body weight in the form of chining, sit-ups, push-ups, or other pushing and pulling methods, we are using resistance exercises. Whether we use dumbbells, barbells, wall or overhead pulley devices, spring or rubber expanders, we are also using resistance exercises. The principle remains the same ...muscles operating against resistance to perform our exercises. The physiological effects are quite similar, varying only in degree of energy output, muscle contraction and hypertrophic results. When considering these physiological aspects, we have found that the amount of resistance applied will have a great effect on the production of muscle size and its concomitant of strength. It follows then that a system of resistance exercises would be more efficient if it is progressively applied. This implies the gradual increase of resistance within limits, so that the muscles are trained to do more and more work and therefore can exert more efficiently. Such a system of resistance is termed progressive resistance, and exercises patterned after it are termed progressive resistance exercises.

Progressive resistance exercise is best applied through the medium of weight equipments of varying design such as dumbbells, barbells, pulleys, expanders and various other devices. When we apply our muscles to exercise with any of the above equipment, we are in fact "lifting" weight, or operating against resistance. We "lift" weight in a prescribed, organized manner in all methods of weight training. In other words, weight training is a system whereby we make use of weights, lifting them in a particular manner to achieve our training objectives. We also lift weights in the *sport* of weightlifting. Weightlifting is a recognized sport of international proportions which requires participants to lift to their maximum ability in various prescribed manners, the winner to be decided on the basis of his technique, and the total amount lifted in three separate lifts. As such it is a test of strength and athletic ability. Weightlifting makes use of weight training methods to train its advocates. However, weight training is *not* necessarily weightlifting (the sport).

Weight Training Systems: Various systems of resistance exercise, using weights, have been developed based on the fact we have already seen in Chapter 3—muscular hypertrophy is best produced by increasing the blood supply so that the individual cells can assimilate the various nutrients required for their growth. Systems of repetitions and sets, performed in seemingly countless varieties, often bewilder the trainee to the point of frustration. Among such systems, the following are prominent: split, single progressive, double progressive, irregular, limited, compound, "blitz," flushing, super set, super flushing, special, peak contraction, cheating, heavy-light, light-heavy, super speed reps, tri-set, and rest-pause. Much work remains in this area, to determine more specifically just where each of these methods of weight training can best be applied. One thing certain, regardless of terminology, these are different applications of weight movements revolving about the common fact stated earlier in this paragraph. *All these systems work,* individually, or in combination with each other. Let there be no dispute about this, though the relativity of their merit remains largely a matter of personal preference.

The instructor or trainee considering the incorporation of a weight training system into his training routine, must, in the design of a weight training program, give careful thought to many factors which includes the training objectives, facilities available, capabilities and limitations of intended trainees, and quantitative qualities. Regarding the latter, muscle hypertrophy, fatigue, and time, loom as salient considerations.

How much muscle should the trainee attempt to "grow?" His training will usually be conditioned by such remarks as, "Big muscles aren't good for anything except lifting pianos," or, "big muscles can't be used effectively." These statements and the like, are just plain "hog-wash" having no basis in fact. Actually, the opposite has been proven. There is a high degree of correlation between muscular development and athletic ability. The late Dr. C. H. McCloy, Research Professor of Physical Education at Iowa State University, has done considerable work in this area, and all evidence substantiates the fact that bigger muscles can be good for anything they may be assigned to do. Let there be an overall regard for body symmetry in the development of body muscle, however, grow your muscles *as big* as you can.

Programs of exercise, especially those involving weights, must regard the problem of fatigue. Exercise to the point of fatigue is not physiologically sound, yet in systems such as the heavy-light, and others, the muscles are deliberately punished to the extreme. It is so easy to get carried away in a weight training program and wind up with excess exercise and possible disagreeable results. The idea that, "if a little bit is good, more will be better" does not apply necessarily. Sensible application of weight movements must be the guiding feature of your training program. Train...don't strain!

Finally, the authors note that many progressive weight training systems do not regard the physical needs of the exerciser to the extent merited by their devotion to training.

Normal social man cannot, within normal time limits, exercise constantly. A specially dedicated few can realize a full devotion to training, while the majority of the serious athletes must attempt to balance their training with life's routine necessities. Train as you go, progressively, and remember that it takes a lifetime of self-discipline and indefatigable energy to achieve. Let *distributive practice*—that practice which is spread over a period of time under stringent regularity—be the *sine qua non* of success.

Weights and Myths: A word here is deemed necessary concerning the "myths" of exercise associated with weight movements. The first is the term "muscle bound." This term is of generic origin with no definitive meaning, and has been shown by scientific authorities as a misnomer when applied to muscular athletes.[2] If muscles were "bound," implying inability to stretch or contract within normal ranges, it is easy to see that the untrained person would most closely fit the description. He is unable to bend from the waist, without bending his knees, in order to touch the floor with his palms—*or even his finger tips!* (#1). The muscular athlete, properly trained, can readily touch the floor with his palms, and sometimes almost his elbows. (#2). Another example is readily demonstrated by the limited forward bend of the untrained person when seated on the floor with his legs outstretched and knees unbent. (#3). The muscular athlete can bend and place his forehead on the floor between his outstretched legs quite easily. (#4). These examples are only a few that tend to indicate the unqualified pseudo-authoritative support of the muscle-bound theory. Certainly the photographs of the co-author, #5 and #6, display a high state of muscular development, which was gained from the methods described in this book. Yet, speed, flexibility, agility, and coordination have not suffered, nor has he become "muscle-bound" as his feats of flexibility show. The reader is asked to make the tests shown in #1 to #4 before beginning a three month training program of the methods described herein, and to compare the beginning flexibility with that obtained after this exercise period is completed.

A second "myth" is the denouncement that severe exercise, especially weight exercise, will harm the heart. This subject will not be discussed, for it would require intensive scientific background. But it is generally agreed upon by the world's leading heart authorities that "A normal, healthy heart cannot be injured by exercise no matter how strenuous or long continued the effort."[3]

2 Jack R. Leighton, "Are Weight Lifters Muscle-Bound?", *Strength & Health,* March 1956, p. 16.

3 A.M. Gibson, M.D., "Does Exercise Harm the Heart?", *Strength & Health,* March 1959, p. 37.

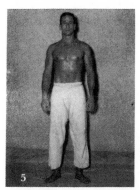

A third "myth" warns against weight exercises which may cause hernia or rupture. Again, an intensive medical background is necessary to adequately discuss this subject, and the interested reader is referred to an excellent article on this subject in the popular magazine, *Strength & Health*.[4] A study made by Dr. Karpovitch showed that only 5 cases of hernias were reported among 31,702 weight trainees, bringing the occurrence of hernia in non-weight trainees to about 20 times that of the weight trainees.

Still another "myth" predicts that weight exercises will result in a "slowing down" of the athlete. Rather than prolong needlessly the discussion for our reader, we merely point to the sensible training methods of the growing list of champions who use weight training methods to establish their record performances. The Judo exponent will not suffer any "slowing" of action or technique. In fact, he will greatly increase his speed under proper training methods. The brilliant work of such men as Chui, Capen, Zorbas, Karpovitch, Wilkins, Masley, and a host of others, definitely disproves this "myth" *(see Bibliography, Selected Readings)*.

Finally, one "myth" refers to weight exercises as "un-natural" exercises, which can find no direct transfer to practical situations in daily life, except possibly ox-like tasks or the like. For this ill-based reason, they are condemned and considered wholly unnecessary. What is apparent here, is lack of understanding of what should be an obvious fact. In performing weight exercises, we sometimes *purposely penalize our muscles* from the standpoint of leverages, fulcrums, and body positions, in order to more fully make them exert. These imposed handicaps, if any, will enhance the full development of the muscles, and make them more effective under normal circumstances. Of course, we must train them to work in Judo unison.

For a fuller discussion of "myths" the interested reader is referred to an excellent article in *Strength & Health*.[5]

Physical Fitness: It would be foolish to contend that physical fitness is not necessary for the Judo exponent. By physical fitness is understood the capacity of an individual to exert hard and relatively long without undue fatigue or undesirable after effects. Surely better physical condition will permit better performance of Judo, as well as other activities, and we must seek training methods to cause our physical condition to develop to a maximum level and be maintained at this point.

The causes of the lack of physical fitness are many, but important among them is the lack of any *positive* plan of training. A properly designed training program will, if persistently followed, add up to a large amount of personal energy on an accumulative basis. Exercise has invaluable ability to build up physical and mental powers and energy reserves, and must be based on a systematic, sensible and progressive conditioning program. Judo exponents are prone to depend entirely upon contact Judo exercise in the form of Randori as a balanced program to achieve both Judo excellence and health. A disregard of subsidiary means of exercising in all but directly related movements of a Judo nature,

4   John C. Grimek, "What to do About Rupture," *Strength & Health,* April 1959, p. 28.

5   A.M. Gibson, M.D., "Is Weight Lifting Dangerous?", *Strength & Health,* October 1959, pp. 24–25 and 46–47.

is prevalent. This is a mistake which must be corrected if increased Judo performance is the goal. Before that correction is to take place, an understanding of the benefits of exercise must be gained.

Benefits of Exercise: In Chapter 3 we determined the physiological basis of improving one's physical condition; that is, muscular exercise and resultant exertion. As a muscle exerts, it grows and becomes stronger. When this strong muscle is "taught" Judo movement by proper training, Judo technique becomes more efficient than before. It is at this point in our discussion that the compatibility of weight training and Judo, and a need for these combined items is further demonstrated.

Physical educators will agree that the most effective and efficient manner in which to increase strength is to exercise in such a way that the muscles will exert against progressively greater resistance. No other form of physical activity provides the means of working every muscle group of the body so completely in the shortest possible time as does weight exercise. Such exercise will move blood, including oxygen, water, and nutrients into the tissues and will flush them with vital supplies. All of the joints will work better, joint membranes will thicken and will be better equipped to withstand shock. Dr. Hardin Jones of the University of California has shown that the better the blood flow, the more young and healthy tissues remain. Scientific evidence demonstrates that physical exercise of the endurance type will manifest in improved muscular endurance, cardiovascular fitness, respiratory efficiency, and good health, *providing the exercise is sufficient and proper.*

Is Weight Exercise Contrary to Kodokan Judo?: Introducing a new form of subsidiary exercise to the established Judo routines of the ages, is from the start resolutely faced with a staunch barrier—the barrier of tradition. Within the Judo world, conservatism abounds, and any encroachment by "foreign" ideas upon its more-or-less sanctified position is apt to be labeled "man-handling" of this lofty art. To the conservative defenders of Judo, with due respect to their puristic attitudes, let it be re-emphasized that true art can withstand an enormous amount of "manhandling" and its survival should never be in doubt. But is the addition of weight exercise to normal Judo training programs in violation of Kodokan principles?

The underlying principle of weight exercises in any form is that of *resistance.* We have already shown that within the underlying principle of Kodokan Judo, there are two facets, one of which is *resistance.* Kodokan Judo further develops the resistance factor by insisting on a careful application of it in accord with *maximum efficiency.* We need only to bring our training methods utilizing weight exercises, into a pattern of maximum efficiency to bring about a complete harmony between Kodokan Judo and weight training. This is feasible and can be accomplished both in the design and application of a weight training program, as well as in correct application of the newly acquired strength when we perform Judo. *There is no disjuncture between weight exercise and Kodokan*

Judo and it can be seen readily that by accepting weight training methods in the normal Judo training routine, we are not going contrary to the teachings of Dr. Kano. Indeed, it is a little known fact that Dr. Kano himself had contact with international weight exercise authorities, and on his return trip from abroad, prior to his death in 1938, had documentation concerning weight exercises. Who can now say just what his intent was? But, by inference, we can allude to his interest in the subject as perhaps a farsighted tentative plan for integration with his beloved Judo.

That old-time Judo exponents regarded resistance exercises as valuable to their daily training can be seen in the current carry-over exercises required of students in most Dojo today. Some of these methods are depicted on the preceding page. While of a resistive nature, these exercises are most inefficient when compared to exercises of a like nature which can be performed using weight apparatus. They do, of course, have the advantage over weight exercises only in that they can be performed without special equipment.

I. Odate, 6 Dan, former Kyoto powerhouse Judoka, recalled for the co-author his early training days when trainees were made to hoist the *Tawara* (rice bales) on a repetition basis, snatching them from the ground to shoulder height or to an overhead position. This type of training was general practice, not an exception, and evidences the support of resistance exercises in early Judo training.

Outlook for Weight Training in Relation to Judo: Weight training is essential to championship level Judo performance in that it will, like no other existing means, improve posture and strengthen postural muscles. Judo is always concerned with a minimum expenditure of energy and the body posture is the basic source of this economy. Good posture by definition in Judo, is the most efficient way to carry the muscles, bones, and organs of the body in order to most effectively apply Judo technique. Weight training movements correctly performed under sensible application will also develop the muscles and bring the body into muscular symmetry. Fatigue is accentuated in underdeveloped muscle areas, and acts as the "weak link" in our Judo performance. An assymmetrical body will result in inefficiency in Judo.

Weight training methods have helped materially to reach Judo training objectives and specifically in terms of improved strength, endurance, and speed, have resulted in increased Judo performances. It is through weight exercises that fatigue has been delayed and circulatory and respiratory systems have been improved, permitting the Judo exponent to exert more and longer. Strength has been increased both in terms of ability to resist force if necessary, and the added capacity for exertion. Speed has been increased by removing obstacles such as fatigue, muscle resistance, and joint resistance. Undesirable fatty weight has been taken off, and underweight conditions replaced by solid useable muscle.

Those Judo exponents who, in the course of weight training programs, gain weight of substantial muscular proportions, often fear a deterioration of Judo skills. It has been the experience of the authors that this fear is ungrounded, though additional body weight brings with it a new "feeling" and any period of clumsiness experienced by trainees is primarily psychological. Jon Bluming, 4 Dan, Amateur Judo Champion of the Netherlands, gained over 40 pounds in one year of weight training and stands as living evidence of improved Judo performance without any loss of original skills.

Weight trained Western Judoka who have been successful in competition include

Europeans J. Bluming and A. Geesink from the Netherlands; M. Gruel from France; G. Kerr from Scotland; Americans J. Bregman, B. Campbell, G. Lebell, R. Nishi, from U.S.A., and D. Rogers, F. Matt from Canada.

Farsighted *Kodansha* (Kodokan High Grade Holders) such as T. Otaki, 8 Dan; T. Daigo, 7 Dan; T. Kawamura, 7 Dan; and Y. Osawa, 7 Dan, advocate the use of sensible weight training as a complement to Judo training. Weights can be found in many Dojo throughout Japan. For many years, Judoka of the Tokyo Metropolitan Police Judo Instructors College were encouraged to weight train by the co-author. One of the strongest police champions of this school who later won the Tokyo Championship was an avid weight training fan. Research by the co-author at Kodokan, using the *Kenshusei* (Special Research Students) Judoka has indicated that additional support for weight exercises by high grade Judo masters is slowly being gained.

As mentioned before, subsidiary exercise is *necessary* for proper Judo performance, and weight training has a very definite place in such subsidiary exercises. Weight training alone will not make a Judo expert, and many hard hours of training on the mat *doing Judo* must be accomplished. But, weight training utilized as a complementary training measure to normal Judo routines, with their more directly purposeful movements of the Preparatory, Supplementary, and Compound Exercises, will bring a new high level of Judo performance. As remarkable as weight exercises are in producing results, they will not perform miracles overnight. Only through intelligent application and sensible training will they demonstrate what has been stated in this book.

PLATE 7. Weight training compliments normal Judo training sessions at Kodokan.

CHAPTER 6

Judo Training
Routines

I have no method and I will have no method.
Leschetizky

General: Much has been said, but much more has remained unsaid about the methods of Judo training. In Japan, this subject is more or less taken for granted, for in the land where Judo developed, there is never a lack of qualified instructors. However, in the Western world it has become increasingly evident that many Judo groups do not understand the proven methods of study.

Judo is a study, and not the mere engagement of physical skills, unscientifically presented with little or no progressive nature. It is to be understood at the outset, that this Chapter offers some tested, systematic, training programs for Judo study. It is not exhaustive nor inflexible. What is advocated here is simply a composite of ideas which have been gleaned from numerous sources in Judo circles all over the world. The collective result produces a unity of methodology which puts stress on competitive excellence, though it will be seen that full regard for the entire scope of Judo is always in sight. The programs to follow are, in their strictest interpretation, intended for serious well-conditioned athletes and application to the average person will require some modification as to the intensity of exercise. They are further intended for the male adult trainees interested in improved Judo performance, though in Japan, male youngsters are subject to these identical methods with superior results.

The old adage, "He who can, does; he who cannot, teaches," may or may not be true. However, it should be added that qualified observation of Judo exponents makes it obvious that Judo skill is not synonymous with a qualified teacher. The mere fact that one is highly skilled in technique, being able to defeat any and all opponents or perform in part or entirety the Judo repertoire, does not guarantee that one is a good teacher. Judo has the unfortunate tendency to rely upon teaching by authority of rank gained as a sole prerequisite. Certainly, rank comes through experience, and experience furnishes the fundamental base from which a qualified teacher must operate, but there are other considerations which go into the makeup of a good teacher (see Chapter 4). All instructors must remember that teaching is a constant revision and expansion of methods based on a training program which is *systematic,* and *progressive.* To build a successful training program, it is necessary to have sound ideas, adequate presentation, and a sensible way of evaluating its success. The program must be a dynamic one, based on trainee needs. motivation, long-ranged planning, and always presented within the scope of Kodokan ideals. Whenever possible, it should be a *written* and *posted* training schedule for the benefit of both instructors and trainees. See page 51 and page 144.

The Judo Training Session: Judo instructors will find that by following the below suggested order for training, each Judo session will present an orderly and efficient class to the student and facilitate the instructor's role. Omissions or additions as required by the situation may find their way into the below order, but basically, what is shown has proven to be adequate for most needs. The length of time of the session will determine what percentage to devote to each subdivision. However, no less than the recommended times should be devoted to the Preparatory Exercises, Ukemi, Supplementary Exercises, and Randori except in unusual cases where time is drastically limited. It is not suggested that the below order must be given at each Judo session; that is, each and every item listed must be practiced. This would necessitate a 3 hour training session which is beyond the needs of most Dojo. If this time is not available, some appropriate abbreviation can be made as shown in other examples to follow:

FULL PROGRAM

1.	Formal opening of class by instructor	⎫
2.	Class announcements by instructors or officials	⎬ .... 5 min.
3.	Preparatory Exercises	........15 min.
4.	Ukemi	........15 min.
5.	Supplementary Exercises	........15 min.
6.	Kata	........30 min.
7.	Randori (emphasis on Nage Waza)	........45 min.
8.	Technical instruction—new techniques—practice	........30 min.
9.	Compound Exercises	.... 5 min.
10.	Katame Waza instruction & practice	........15 min.
11.	Preparatory Exercises to relax (Shumatsu Undo)	⎫
12.	Formal closing of class by instructor	⎬ .... 5 min.

Total time of session: 3 hours

The above routine can most easily be applied to a class of the same level of proficiency. but by splitting the class into different levels, providing mat space is available, this program will meet the needs of mixed-proficiency groups.

MINIMUM PROGRAM

1. Formal opening of class by instructor
2. Preparatory Exercises } . . . . 15 min.
3. Ukemi   . . . . 10 min.
4. Supplementary Exercises   . . . . 10 min.
5. Randori   . . . . 30 min.
6. Preparatory Exercises to relax (Shumatsu Undo) }
7. Formal closing of class by instructor   . . . . 5 min.

Total time of session: 1 hour 10 min.

BASIC BEGINNER PROGRAM

1. Formal opening of class by instructor
2. Lecture on Judo background or history } . . . . 15 min.
3. Preparatory Exercises   . . . . 20 min.
4. Ukemi demonstrations   . . . . 5 min.
5. Practice of ukemi   . . . . 25 min.
6. Lecture-demonstration of Judo fundamentals (shisei, shintai, kumikata, kuzushi, tsukuri, kake, taisabaki) . . . . 10 min.
7. Kuzushi, shisei, shintai, taisabaki, practice   . . . . 15 min.
8. Ukemi practice   . . . . 25 min.
9. Preparatory exercises to relax (Shumatsu Undo) }
10. Formal closing of class by instructor   . . . . 5 min.

Total time of session: 2 hours

NAGE EMPHASIS PROGRAM

1. Formal opening of class by instructor   . . . . 2 min.
2. Preparatory Exercises   . . . . 15 min.
3. Ukemi   . . . . 15 min.
4. Supplementary Exercises   . . . . 15 min.
5. Randori   . . . . 30 min.
6. Technical instruction period for Nage Waza   . . . . 15 min.
7. Randori   . . . . 25 min.
8. Preparatory Exercises to relax (Shumatsu Undo) }
9. Formal closing of class by instructor   . . . . 3 min.

Total time of session: 2 hours

KATAME EMPHASIS PROGRAM

1. Formal opening of class by instructor $\Big\}$ ....20 min.
2. Preparatory Exercises
3. Ukemi ....10 min.
4. Compound Exercises ....10 min.
5. Katame Waza practice ....30 min.
6. Technical instruction period for Katame Waza ....15 min.
7. Katame Waza practice ....15 min.
8. Preparatory Exercises to relax (Shumatsu Undo) $\Big\}$ .... 5 min.
9. Formal closing of class by instructor

Total time of session: 1 hour 45 min.

The use of Ukemi practice as a distinct phase in either the Nage or Katame emphasis programs above may undergo modification at the discretion of the instructor. Since, in Nage, there will be sufficient chance for Ukemi as a result of throwing, it may be minimized if desired, to about a 5 minute period. In Katame emphasis it can be contained within the time devoted to opening the class and Preparatory Exercises. The time thus gained can be added elsewhere in the program at the discretion of the instructor.

KATA EMPHASIS PROGRAM

1. Formal opening of class by instructor $\Big\}$ ....20 min.
2. Preparatory Exercises
3. Ukemi ....15 min.
4. Kata demonstrations ....10 min.
5. Kata practice ....30 min.
6. Technical instruction period for Kata ....15 min.
7. Kata practice $\Big\}$ ....15 min.
8. Formal closing of class by instructor

Total time of session: 1 hour 45 min.

Several points of discussion are appropriate to the Kata emphasis program. Since Kata is prearranged and is easy to modify or control in terms of physical output, some instructors will omit the Preparatory Exercises on the basis that Kata in itself will "warm" the body sufficiently. However, it is preferable to include the Preparatory Exercises as indicated, though the time devoted to them may be somewhat reduced. The Ukemi, as a distinct phase of this program, can also be eliminated or greatly reduced if the Kata performed is one of the following: Nage no Kata; Itsutsu no Kata, Koshiki no Kata, Go no Sen no Kata, or the Goshinjitsu. Kata performed on the basis of *Katachi* (form) only—that is the form of the Kata is executed without making any throwing action or producing a completed action—is a supple practice with little energy output. In this respect it can substitute for the Preparatory Exercises at the opening or closing of the session (Junbi Undo or Shumatsu Undo).

ENDURANCE EMPHASIS PROGRAM

1. Formal opening of class by instructor
2. Preparatory Exercises $\Big\}$ . . . . .30 min.
3. Ukemi . . . . .15 min.
4. Supplementary Exercises . . . . .30 min.
5. Randori . . . . .40 min.
6. Compound Exercises . . . . .20 min.
7. Randori . . . . .40 min.
8. Preparatory Exercises to relax (Shumatsu Undo)
9. Formal closing of class by instructor $\Big\}$ . . . . 5 min.

Total time of session: 3 hours

The alert instructor can with little effort design training programs which promote endurance aspects. All that must be recalled *(page 47)* is that protracted exercise will build endurance. A great variety of ways of exercising suggest themselves immediately, but it should be understood that while disciplined monotonous repetitions provide good training, such training is limited in that it can do no more than give mechanical movement. A balanced training session over a period of time will produce superior Judo exponents. Trainees should not become "robot" Judo exponents, but seek for a higher understanding of Judo technique which is the mark of a true Judoka.

GASSHUKU PROGRAM

7:00 AM	15 minutes Preparatory Exercises as Junbi Undo; 2 mile run outdoors regardless of weather (½ mile jog-½ mile backward 1 mile moderate pace); 5 minutes Preparatory Exercises as Shumatsu Undo.
8:00–10:00	rest—breakfast—rest
10:00–12:00	¼ mile jog around Dojo; 15 minutes Preparatory Exercises as Junbi Undo; 10 minutes Ukemi; Uchikomi (speed repetitions of any Owaza done in sets of 10 repetitions alternating with partner). 10 partners minimum. 3 minutes each partner. Randori (Nage Waza only). 10 partners minimum. 5 minutes each partner. Preparatory Exercises in form of Shumatsu Undo, 5 minutes.
12:00–12:30 PM	rest

12:30–3:00	lunch—rest
3:00–5:00	¼ mile jog around Dojo; Preparatory Exercises in form of Junbi Undo, 15 minutes; Ukemi 10 minutes; Uchikomi (per above); Randori (Katame Waza only). 10 partners minimum. 3 minutes each partner. Kakari geiko. Senior men take on 10 consecutive opponents. 3 minutes time limit; Compound Exercises. 500 yard run around Dojo (50 yards jog-50 yards Duck Jumps-50 yards jog-50 yards Duck Jumps, etc.). Injured knee Judo exponents will jog and do Pushups in lieu of Duck Jumps; Katame Waza Taisabaki 100 yards; Prone Crawling 100 yards; Preparatory Exercises in form of Shumatsu Undo, 5 minutes.
5:00–600	bath—rest
6:00–7:00	supper
7:00–9:00	relax
9:00	lights out

As explained in Chapter 4, the Gasshuku method of training is a severe one, primarily designed to condition the trainee and bring him accelerated learning. The following schedule is one emphasizing "do" Judo, minimizing technical instruction, and is the pattern followed by university Judoka in preparation for serious competition. It should only be undertaken by young athletes who are in sound physical condition. It is a 10 day period of training.

Weight Training Programs: The programs which follow are suggestions for complementary training to normal Judo routines. They have been tested and have proven functional. It would be impossible due to space limitations, to list a great variety of weight programs, but the instructor or trainee may self-design a program after he has a thorough understanding of the scientific principles involved and as discussed elsewhere in this book. An adequate description is perhaps limited by the fact that the variety is great among the different weight exercises, but the user must bear in mind that though certain principles apply (discussed in Chapter 10), *almost any* **weight** *exercise is beneficial if properly performed.*

GENERAL PROGRAMS

Perform the exercises on a 10 repetition—3 set basis.

1. Squat *(page 224)*
2. Calf Raise *(page 228)*
3. Barbell Supine Press (normal grip) *(page 269)*
4. Supine Bent-arm Dumbbell Lateral *(page 232)*
5. Dumbbell Rowing *(page 239)*
6. Supine Straight-arm Dumbbell Pullover *(page 231)*
7. Military Barbell Press *(page 252)*
8. Standing Barbell Triceps Curl *(page 250)*
9. Military Barbell Curl *(page 241)*
10. Situp (any kind) *(page 260)*

1. Jefferson Lift *(page 225)*
2. Supine Straight-arm Dumbbell Pullover *(page 231)*
3. Incline Dumbbell Bent-arm Lateral *(page 229)*
4. Upright Rowing *(page 235)*
5. Seated Barbell Press Behind Neck *(page 235)*
6. Barbell Bent Rowing *(page 268)*
7. Dumbbell Biceps Concentration Curl *(page 241)*
8. Barbell Reverse Curl *(page 250)*
9. French Press *(page 251)*
10. Dumbbell Bend Press *(page 253)*

1. Squat *(page 224)*
2. Supine Straight-arm Barbell Pullover *(page 234)*
3. Hack lift *(page 225)*
4. Barbell Supine Press (narrow grip) *(page 229)*
5. Decline Dumbbell Press *(page 230)*
6. Lat Machine Rowing *(page 240)*
7. Seated Dumbbell Curl and Press *(page 252)*
8. Supine Triceps Barbell Press *(page 245)*
9. Straight-legged Dead Lift *(page 257)*
10. Situp (any kind) *(page 260)*

1. Supine Dumbbell Press *(page 231)*
2. Heavy Dumbbell Clean *(page 266)*
3. Calf Raise *(page 228)*
4. Dumbbell Rowing *(page 239)*
5. Supine Bent-arm Dumbbell Lateral *(page 232)*
6. Decline Dumbbell Press *(page 230)*
7. Standing Barbell Triceps Curl *(page 250)*
8. Standing Alternate Dumbbell Curl *(page 245)*
9. Seated Barbell Press Behind Neck *(page 235)*
10. Seated Dumbbell Lateral Raise *(page 255)*

1. Straight-legged Dead Lift *(page 257)*
2. Upright Rowing *(page 235)*
3. Shrugging *(page 239)*
4. Decline Dipping *(page 233)*
5. Decline Straight-arm Dumbbell Lateral *(page 228)*
6. Barbell Cleaning *(page 270)*
7. Supine Straight-arm Dumbbell Pullover *(page 231)*
8. Lat Machine Pull-down Behind Neck *(page 238)*
9. Incline Dumbbell Biceps Curl *(page 243)*
10. Lat Machine Triceps Press *(page 251)*

1. Squat *(page 224)*
2. Incline Dumbbell Bent-arm Lateral *(page 229)*
3. Barbell Supine Press *(page 269)*
4. Seated Barbell Press Behind Neck *(page 235)*
5. Barbell Bent Rowing *(page 268)*
6. Supine Triceps Barbell Press *(page 245)*
7. Standing Alternate Dumbbell Curl *(page 245)*
8. Swingbar Raise *(page 258)*

1. Barbell Clean and Press *(page 256)*
2. Military Barbell Curl *(page 241)*
3. Squat *(page 224)*
4. Supine Straight-arm Barbell Pullover *(page 234)*
5. Barbell Supine Press *(page 269)*
6. Military Barbell Press *(page 252)*
7. Dumbbell Rowing *(page 239)*
8. Bench Situp and Twist *(page 263)*

1. Barbell Supine Press *(page 269)*
2. Hack Lift *(page 225)*
3. Barbell Bent Rowing *(page 268)*
4. Barbell Clean and Press *(page 256)*
5. Seated Dumbbell Front Raise *(page 254)*
6. Seated Dumbbell Lateral Raise *(page 255)*
7. Bench End Curl *(page 249)*
8. Incline Straight-leg Lift *(page 264)*

1. Barbell Clean and Press *(page 256)*
2. Upright Rowing *(page 235)*
3. Jefferson Lift *(page 225)*
4. Supine Straight-arm Dumbb⁻. Pullover *(page 231)*

5. Decline Dumbbell Press *(page 230)*
6. Military Barbell Curl *(page 241)*
7. Stall Bar Leg Raise *(page 262)*

These general programs may be applied to weight reducing or weight gaining objectives by the proper application of repetitions and sets (described fully in Chapter 10).

Perform the exercises on a 6–8 repetition—3 set basis.

1. Supine Dumbbell Press *(page 231)*
2. Heavy Dumbbell Clean *(page 266)*
3. Supine Bent-arm Dumbbell Pullover
   (page 232)
4. Seated Barbell Press Behind Neck
   (page 235)

1. Barbell Supine Press *(page 269)*
2. Seated Barbell Press Behind Neck
   (page 235)
3. Upright Rowing *(page 235)*
4. Supine Straight-arm Dumbbell Pullover
   (page 231)
5. Dumbbell Triceps Concentration Press
   (page 248)
6. Seated Dumbbell Curl and Press
   (page 252)

1. Incline Dumbbell Bent-arm Lateral
   (page 229)
2. Supine Dumbbell Thrust *(page 233)*
3. Jumping Squat *(page 226)*
4. Supine Bent-arm Dumbbell Pullover
   (page 232)
5. Standing Barbell Triceps Curl
   (page 250)

1. Barbell Supine Press *(page 269)*
2. Incline Dumbbell Bent-arm Lateral
   (page 229)
3. Barbell Cleaning *(page 270)*
4. Barbell Bent Rowing *(page 268)*
5. French Press *(page 251)*
6. Incline Dumbbell Biceps Curl *(page 243)*

1. Barbell Clean and Press *(page 256)*
2. Squat *(page 224)*
3. Barbell Bent Rowing *(page 268)*
4. Incline Dumbbell Biceps Curl
   (page 243)
5. Dumbbell Triceps Concentration Press
   (page 248)

1. Military Barbell Press *(page 252)*
2. Upright Rowing *(page 235)*
3. Supine Dumbbell Press *(page 231)*
4. Standing Alternate Dumbbell Curl
   (page 245)
5. Seated Barbell Press Behind Neck
   (page 235)

1. Barbell Pullover and Press *(page 273)*
2. Squat *(page 224)*
3. Supine Bent-arm Dumbbell Pullover
   (page 232)
4. Military Barbell Press *(page 252)*

1. Barbell Clean and Press *(page 256)*
2. Squat *(page 224)*
3. Supine Straight-arm Dumbbell Pullover
   (page 231)

1. Jumping Squat *(page 226)*
2. Decline Straight-arm Dumbbell Lateral
   (page 228)
3. Barbell Cleaning Curl *(page 273)*

1. Barbell Supine Press *(page 269)*
2. One Hand Dumbbell Swing *(page 269)*
3. Seated Barbell Press Behind Neck
   (page 235)

1. Seated Barbell Press Behind Neck
   (page 235)
2. Upright Rowing *(page 235)*
3. Heavy Dumbbell Clean *(page 266)*
4. Dumbbell Power Pull *(page 267)*

1. Half Squat *(page 265)*
2. Supine Bent-arm Dumbbell Pullover
   (page 232)
3. Heavy Dumbbell Clean *(page 266)*
4. Swingbar Raise *(page 258)*
5. Incline Leg Double *(page 262)*

1. Jumping Squat *(page 226)*
2. Supine Straight-arm Barbell Pullover
   (page 234)

3. Barbell Cleaning *(page 270)*
4. Dumbbell Power Pull *(page 267)*

These abbreviated programs may be applied best to weight gaining objectives by the proper application of repetitions and sets as indicated. They should be utilized primarily by trainees who have undergone about 6 months of general program training and are fully prepared for heavier weight movements. However, in the event that the trainee is limited as to time that can be spent working with weights, these abbreviated programs can be used to some degree of success as a general program. This practice is not to be undertaken by those of unusually frail physique or extreme musculature deficiency.

POWER PROGRAMS

Perform the exercises on a 4 (or less) repetition—4 (or more) sets basis.

1. Heavy Dumbbell Clean *(page 266)*
2. Straight-legged Dead Lift *(page 257)*

1. Straight-legged Dead Lift *(page 257)*
2. Standing Bent-arm Dumbbell Lateral *(page 267)*
3. Shrugging *(page 239)*

1. Barbell End Rowing *(page 268)*
2. Standing Bent-arm Lateral *(page 267)*

1. Half Squat *(page 265)*
2. Supine Bent-arm Dumbbell Pullover *(page 232)*

1. Barbell End Rowing *(page 268)*
2. Half Squat *(page 265)*

1. Barbell Cleaning Curl *(page 273)*
2. Jerk Press *(page 272)*

1. Barbell Clean and Press *(page 256)*
2. Half Squat *(page 265)*

1. Barbell Cleaning *(page 270)*
2. Dumbbell Power Pull *(page 267)*

1. Straight-legged Dead Lift *(page 257)*
2. Dumbbell Power Pull *(page 267)*
3. Jerk Press *(page 272)*

1. One Hand Dumbbell Swing *(page 269)*
2. Half Squat *(page 265)*

1. Jerk Press *(page 272)*
2. Barbell Power Pull *(page 271)*
3. Half Squat *(page 265)*

1. Barbell Clean and Press *(page 256)*
2. Shrugging *(page 239)*

1. Barbell Cleaning *(page 270)*
2. Barbell End Rowing *(page 268)*
3. Standing Bent-arm Dumbbell Lateral *(page 267)*

Power programs are designed for only one thing...to develop superior power in the body. These programs are not to be utilized until the trainee has adequately prepared his body by use of general programs *(see Chapter 10)*.

ARM SPECIALIZATION PROGRAMS

Perform the exercises on a 6–10 repetition—3 (or more) set basis.

1. Military Barbell Curl *(page 241)*
2. Bench End Curl *(page 249)*
3. Barbell Strict Reverse Curl *(page 242)*
4. Dumbbell Triceps Concentration Press *(page 248)*
5. Lat Machine Triceps Press *(page 251)*
6. Dumbbell Triceps Extension *(page 247)*

1. French Press *(page 251)*
2. Supine Triceps Barbell Press *(page 245)*
3. Dumbbell Biceps Concentration Curl *(page 241)*
4. Incline Dumbbell Biceps Curl *(page 243)*
5. Dumbbell Wrist Curling *(page 247)*

1. Barbell Strict Curl *(page 242)*
2. Standing Alternate Dumbbell Curl *(page 245)*

3. Incline Dumbbell Biceps Curl *(page 243)*
4. French Press *(page 251)*

LEG SPECIALIZATION PROGRAMS

Perform the exercises on a 6–10 repetition—3 (or more) set basis.

1. Squat *(page 224)*
2. Hack Lift *(page 225)*
3. Leg Extension Curl *(page 227)*
4. Leg Biceps Curl *(page 227)*

1. Jefferson Lift *(page 225)*
2. Jumping Squat *(page 226)*
3. Calf Raise *(page 228)*
4. Leg Biceps Curl *(page 227)*

1. Squat *(page 224)*
2. Hack Lift *(page 225)*
3. Jefferson Lift *(page 225)*

4. Calf Raise *(page 228)*
5. Leg Extension Curl *(page 227)*
6. Leg Biceps Curl *(page 227)*

CHEST SPECIALIZATION PROGRAMS

Perform the exercises on a 8–10 repetition—3 (or more) set basis.

1. Incline Dumbbell Press *(page 230)*
2. Barbell Supine Press *(page 269)*
3. Incline Dumbbell Bent-arm Lateral *(page 229)*
4. Decline Dipping *(page 233)*

1. Supine Dumbbell Press *(page 231)*
2. Incline Dumbbell Press *(page 230)*
3. Decline Dumbbell Press *(page 230)*
4. Supine Bent-arm Dumbbell Lateral *(page 232)*
5. Decline Straight-arm Dumbbell Lateral *(page 228)*

\# 1. Squat *(page 224)*
* 2. Supine Bent-arm Dumbbell Pullover *(page 232)*

3. Incline Dumbbell Bent-arm Lateral *(page 229)*
4. Supine Straight-arm Dumbbell Pullover *(page 231)*

\# Number 1 can be any exercise which promotes heavy breathing.
* Number 2 to be done immediately after squatting.

SHOULDER SPECIALIZATION PROGRAMS

Perform the exercises on a 8–10 repetition—3 (or more) set basis.

1. Military Barbell Press *(page 252)*
2. Upright Rowing *(page 235)*
3. Seated Barbell Press Behind Neck *(page 235)*

4. Seated Dumbbell Front Raise *(page 254)*
5. Seated Dumbbell Lateral Raise *(page 255)*
6. Incline Dumbbell Side Raise *(page 253)*

1. Seated Barbell Press Behind Neck *(page 235)*
2. Forward Barbell Raise *(page 254)*
3. Incline Dumbbell Side Raise *(page 253)*
4. Standing Bent-arm Dumbbell Lateral *(page 267)*

1. Barbell Supine Press *(page 269)*
2. Incline Dumbbell Press *(page 230)*
3. Vertical Dipping *(page 255)*
4. Incline Dumbbell Side Raise *(page 253)*

WRIST-FOREARM SPECIALIZATION PROGRAMS

Perform the exercises on a 10 repetition—3 (or more) set basis.

1. Barbell Bent Rowing *(page 268)*
2. Barbell Strict Reverse Curl *(page 242)*

3. Dumbbell Wrist Curling *(page 247)*
*4. Barbell Wrist Curling *(page 249)*

* Notice that number 4 is performed somewhat differently than are the other exercises. Follow the repetitions suggested on page 249.

LOWER BACK SPECIALIZATION PROGRAMS

Perform the exercises on a 6–10 repetition—3 (or more) set basis.

1. Forward Straight-legged Bend *(page 257)*
2. Straight-legged Dead Lift *(page 257)*
3. Back Arching *(page 261)*
4. Bench End Straight-leg Lift *(page 264)*

1. Straight-legged Dead Lift *(page 257)*
2. Heavy Dumbbell Clean *(page 266)*
3. One Hand Dumbbell Swing *(page 269)*
*4. Seated Barbell Press Behind Neck *(page 235)*

* This exercise should be performed with both legs lying on the bench.

1. Barbell Clean and Press *(page 256)*
2. Swingbar Raise *(page 258)*

3. Barbell Power Pull *(page 271)*

ABDOMINAL SPECIALIZATION PROGRAMS

Perform the exercises on a 10–15 repetition—3 (or more) set basis.

1. Leg Tuck and Body Lever *(page 263)*
2. Stall Bar Leg Raise *(page 262)*
3. Incline Leg Double *(page 262)*
4. Side Raise *(page 261)*

1. Bench Situp *(page 260)*
2. Barbell Swinging *(page 259)*
3. Dumbbell Side Bend *(page 260)*
4. Incline Straight-leg Lift *(page 264)*

1. Decline Situp *(page 265)*
2. Bench Situp and Twist *(page 263)*

3. Stall Bar Leg Reise *(page 262)*
4. Side Raise *(page 261)*

NECK SPECIALIZATION PROGRAMS

Perform the exercises on a 8–10 repetition—3 (or more) set basis.

*1. Rear Bridging *(page 168)* or Front Bridging *(page 169)*
2. Bridge and Barbell Bent-arm Pullover *(page 237)*
3. Bridge and Barbell Press *(page 236)*
*4. Neck Rotation *(page 167)*

*1. Rear Bridging *(page 168)* or Front Bridging *(page 169)*
*2. Neck Pushing *(page 167)*
3. Shrugging *(page 239)* or Bridge and Barbell Bent-arm Pullover *(page 237)*
*4. Neck Rotation *(page 167)*

*1. Bridge-Turnover and Twist *(page 166)*
*2. Neck Pushing *(page 167)*

3. Bridge and Barbell Press *(page 236)*

* Preparatory Exercises (Chapter 7).

UPPER BACK SPECIALIZATION PROGRAMS

Perform the exercises on a 6–10 repetition—3 (or more) set basis.

1. Lat Machine Pulldown Behind Neck *(page 238)*
2. Barbell Bent Rowing (narrow grip) *(page 236)*
3. Dumbbell Rowing *(page 239)*
4. Seated Barbell Press Behind Neck *(page 235)*

1. Upright Rowing *(page 235)*
2. Dumbbell Bent Lateral *(page 237)*
3. Seated Barbell Press Behind Neck *(page 235)*
4. Barbell Bent Rowing (narrow grip) *(page 236)*

1. Chin Behind Neck *(page 240)*
2. Lat Machine Rowing *(page 240)*

3. Shrugging *(page 239)*
4. Upright Rowing *(page 235)*

CALF SPECIALIZATION PROGRAMS

Perform the exercises on a 20 repetition—3 (**or more**) set basis.

1. Jumping Squat *(page 226)*
2. Calf Raise *(page 228)*

1. Calf Raise *(page 228)*
*2. Rise on Toes *(page 153)*

* Preparatory Exercise (Chapter 7).

The utilization of specialization programs has a limited use in the development of the body. Substituting specialization for general or overall body training is isolated muscle training and will not produce the desired results for Judo exponents *(page 212)*. A harmonious, efficient muscle growth depends upon the use of sensible, progressive training applied to the whole body. Instructors and trainees utilizing specialization methods, must constantly bear in mind the elements discussed in Chapter 10.

Weight Exercises for Specific Judo Waza: Through sensible weight training programs, we are able to improve our body so that it has a greater potential efficiency in the performance of Judo. Each and every exercise we perform properly, will add to this potentiality; however, there are certain specific weight movements which, by experience, have proven directly beneficial to the various waza. Though not intended to be an exhaustive list, the following weight movements will materially improve the Waza indicated.

TACHI WAZA

Te Waza

Ippon Seoinage: Supine Bent-arm Dumbell Pullover; Half Squat; Seated Barbell Press Behind Neck; Straight-legged Dead Lift; Barbell Swinging; Barbell Pullover & Press; Barbell Power Pull; Military Barbell Curl; Lat Machine Triceps Press; Barbell Strict Reverse Curl; Upright Rowing; Barbell Cleaning Curl; Jefferson Lift.

Taiotoshi: Barbell Swinging; Side Raise; Bench Situp & Twist; Squat; Upright Rowing; Seated Barbell Press Behind Neck; Swingbar Raise; Side Raise; Supine Triceps Barbell Press; Barbell Supine Press; Barbell Strict Reverse Curl; Dumbbell Rowing; Dumbbell Bend Press; Dumbbell Triceps Concentration Press.

Koshi Waza

Tsurikomigoshi: Squat; Dumbbell Side Bend; Bench Situp and Twist; Side Raise; Barbell Strict Reverse Curl; Barbell Bent Rowing; Barbell Cleaning; Heavy Dumbbell Clean; Dumbbell Power Pull; Jumping Squat; Military Barbell Press; Standing Bent-arm Dumbbell Lateral; Seated Dumbbell Front Raise; Seated Dumbbell Lateral Raise; Incline Dumbbell Side Raise; Incline Dumbbell Press; Dumbbell Bend Press; Incline Dumbbell Bent-arm Lateral; Upright Rowing; Seated Barbell Press Behind Neck.

*Uchimata: Back Arching; Jumping Squat; Leg Extension Curl; Leg Biceps Curl; Leg Tuck and Body Lever; Bench Situp; Side Raise; Decline Situp; Barbell Bent Rowing; Heavy Dumbbell Clean; Dumbbell Power Pull; Barbell Cleaning; Barbell Strict Reverse Curl; One Hand Dumbbell Swing; Dumbbell Rowing; Upright Rowing; Barbell Clean & Press; Seated Barbell Press Behind Neck.

*See Table B page 181. These weight movements will also be useful in the development of Haraigoshi, Hanegoshi, Sasaetsurikomiashi, Hizaguruma, Haraitsurikomiashi, Tomoenage; Ushirogoshi; Utsurigoshi.

Ashi Waza

Ashiharai: Calf Raise; Leg Tuck & Body Lever; Leg Extension Curl; Swingbar Raise; Barbell Swinging; Bench Situp; Incline Leg Double; Stall Bar Leg Raise; Bench End Straight-leg Lift, Decline Situp; Dumbbell Power Pull; Barbell Cleaning Curl; Heavy Dumbbell Clean; One Hand Dumbbell Swing; Forward Straight-legged Bend.

Osotogari: Leg Extension Curl; Leg Biceps Curl; Barbell Supine Press; Military Barbell Press; Leg Tuck and Body Lever; Bench End Curl; Supine Barbell Triceps Press; Barbell Cleaning; Back Arching; Seated Barbell Press Behind Neck; Incline Dumbbell Press; Decline Dumbbell Press; Supine Dumbbell Press; Barbell Cleaning Curl; Heavy Dumbbell Clean. These weight movements will also be useful in the development of Ouchigari; Kosotogari; Kosotogake; Kouchigari; Taniotoshi.

KATAME WAZA

Osaekomi Waza

Barbell Supine Press; Supine Dumbbell Press; Supine Bent-arm Dumbbell Lateral; Incline Dumbbell Bent-arm Lateral; Incline Dumbbell Press; Supine Bent-arm Dumbbell Pullover; Supine Straight-arm Dumbbell Pullover; Body Lever and Tuck; Vertical Dipping; Decline Dipping; Barbell End Rowing; Barbell Pullover and Press; Leg Extension Curl; Leg Press Machine; Barbell Cleaning Curl; Bridge and Barbell Press.

Shime Waza

Barbell End Rowing; Barbell Strict Reverse Curl; Dumbbell Wrist Curling; Barbell Wrist Curling; Barbell Bent Rowing; Dumbbell Rowing; Barbell Supine Press; Decline Dipping; Vertical Dipping; Leg Press Machine; Leg Extension Curl; Leg Biceps Curl; Seated Dumbbell Curl and Press; Bench Situp; Bench Situp and Twist; Decline Situp; Half Squat.

Kansetsu Waza

Dumbbell Biceps Concentration Curl; Barbell Strict Curl; Incline Dumbbell Biceps Curl; Standing Alternate Dumbbell Curl; Barbell Cleaning Curl; Bench End Curl; Bench Situp; Dumbbell Rowing; Leg Press Machine; Leg Extension Curl; Leg Biceps Curl.

Fusegi and Nogarekata

Bridge and Barbell Press; Bridge and Barbell Bent-arm Pullover; Supine Dumbbell Thrust; Barbell Supine Press (narrow grip); Barbell Supine Press; Stall Bar Leg Raise; Incline Leg Double; Incline Straight-leg Lift; Bench Situp and Twist; Bench Situp; Supine Bent-arm Dumbbell Pullover; Jerk Press; Leg Press Machine; Leg Extension Curl; Leg Biceps Curl.

Japanese Judo Champions Statistics: A recent study of Japanese Judo training programs by the authors brings to light some interesting statistics and data all of which points to the fact that it takes a lifetime of self-discipline and indefatigable energy to attain Judo perfection. The words of that great master of music, Paderewski, ring true here, "Before you are a master, you will be a slave." The process of learning is not a smooth, easy process, but is filled with unspeakable amounts of toil, countless discomforts and self denials, which mold a Judo technique by superior determination to achieve. That the Japanese are devoted to their training can be readily understood by an examination of the following information, all of which is based on the past 14 years.

Judo for the average serious-minded Japanese potential champion, begins almost without exception at an early age, somewhere during his high school days. Of course, for many, this is just a continuation of younger days in grade school where he was introduced to Judo, perhaps as early as the tender age of 5.

By the time he is 15, he has attained the Shodan (1st Grade Black Belt), though this is not always the case. Outstanding Judo exponents are able to attain Sandan (3d Grade Black Belt) or even Yodan (4th Grade Black Belt) at 17 or 18 years of age. After graduation from high school our potential champion enters the university of his choice, or takes a job on the local police force. A limited few are taken on in special research capacities as Kenshusei (Research Student) at Kodokan. It is at this level, the university or the police force, that his Judo potential is fully cultivated. The comrades who chose to or are otherwise forced to enter industry directly after high school, or otherwise take on jobs which require long hours away from Judo training, more or less disappear from the scene in so far as real championship material is concerned. The champions, for the most, always come from the universities and the police forces. This does not limit the possibility that the championship may be attained some years later, after leaving the university and entering industry or while serving on the police force. Refer to the graphs on pages 138, 139.

The intensity of training is another factor which bears directly on championship caliber. It is best understood in a quantitative sense based on the amount of hours spent daily on the Judo mat. This point appears common to all serious Judoka who

Graph 1

Judo source of All-Japan Judo Champions (1948 - 1960)

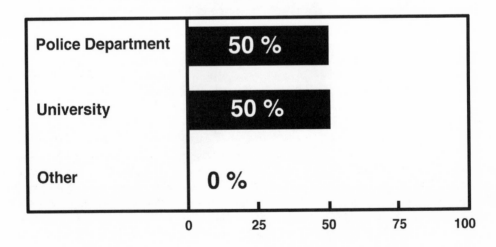

Graph 2

Ages of All-Japan Judo Champions

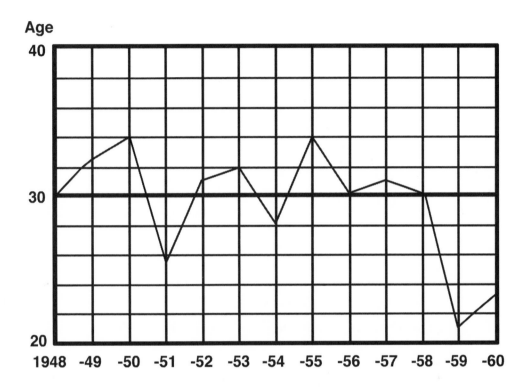

Age

attained the championship...daily training on a 6 day per week basis. This amount of training is strictly adhered to and is reluctantly reduced only in the case of serious injury, school academic or job requirements, religious, political, or domestic affairs which preclude training.

A typical policeman of championship caliber is somewhat older than championship potential from other sources. The average is about 33. He averages daily practice as stated above, which is made up of 1½–2 hours of hard practice and perhaps an additional 2 hour period in which he has teaching responsibilities at some local police Dojo or the metropolitan police training school for Judo instructors. Occasionally, such as during the winter and summer training sessions (Kangeiko and Shochugeiko), he will get additional practice, 1½–2 hours at the Kodokan or some other local central Dojo. On the average, he is on the mat about 3–4 hours daily.

ALL-JAPAN JUDO CHAMPIONS
1948—1961

Year	Champion	Dan	Age	Weight	Height	Source
†1948	Matsumoto	7	30	190 lbs.	6′ 2″	University
†*1949	Ishikawa	7	33	185 lbs.	5′ 8″	Police
†*	Kimura	7	32	185 lbs.	5′ 6″	University
†1950	Ishikawa	7	34	185 lbs.	5′ 8″	Police
†1951	Daigo	6	25	208 lbs.	5′ 10″	University
†1952	Yoshimatsu	6	31	225 lbs.	6′	Police
†1953	Yoshimatsu	7	32	225 lbs.	6′	Police
†1954	Daigo	6	28	215 lbs.	5′ 10″	University
†1955	Yoshimatsu	7	34	242 lbs.	6′	Police
♯⊄1956	Natsui	6	30	216 lbs.	5′ 9″	Police
1957	Natsui	6	31	216 lbs.	5′ 9″	Police
♯†1958	Sone	5	30	190 lbs.	5′ 10½″	University
1959	Inokuma	4	21	179 lbs.	5′ 8″	University
†1960	Kaminaga	5	23	225 lbs.	5′ 9″	University
†1961	Kaminaga	5	24	215 lbs.	5′ 9″	University

* Co-champions
† Graduated from university
⊄ All-Japan not held due 1st World Championships, in which Natsui defeated Yoshimatsu.
♯ also world champion.

The university trained Judoka of championship caliber, somewhat younger, has less responsibilities. His average age is 27 *(see page 139)*. Sometime during the normal school day he will obtain 1½–2 hours of mat time daily, with a special session on Saturdays at the university, Kodokan, or some other central Dojo. Later in the afternoon, on school days, he will perhaps come to Kodokan or some local Dojo where he can practice and put in another 1½–2 hours. Many Judoka will augment this type of daily training with a morning session at the local police Dojo or police Judo instructors college early in the morning for a 1½–2 hour session. On the average, he too is on the mat 3–4 hours daily.

A study of fifty Japanese Universities conducted by the co-author, encompassed some five hundred university Judoka, and reveals some interesting statistics. The university Judoka range in age from 18 to 24 years, while the average age is 20 years. These students range in height from 5′2″ to 6′2″ with the average height being about 5′7″ and weigh between 121 to 242, pounds the average weight being about 170 pounds. Judo ranks range from 1 Dan through 4 Dan with the average rank being about 3 Dan.

Both police and university Judo championship potential are subject to Judo training schedules similar to those shown earlier in this chapter.

Another interesting fact is that the average Dan (Grade) ranking of the Champions is 6 or 7 Dan. This is changing somewhat today, there being a tendency to see lower ranked champions. This is a direct reflection of the fact that champions today are younger. I. Inokuma, 4 Dan, at 21 years of age is the youngest Judo champion in the history of Japan. His training methods are patterned after those described in this chapter. Mr. Inokuma is an avid weight training enthusiast. Actually over 50% of the All-

Graph 3

Judo Dan of All-Japan Judo Champions (1948 - 1960)

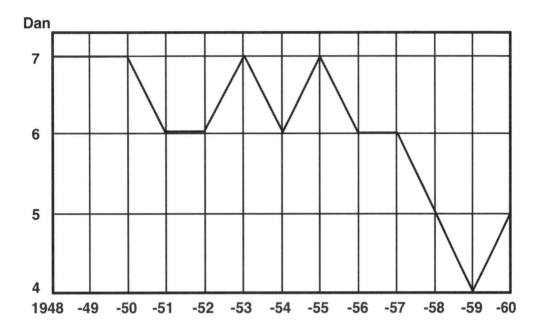

Graph 4

Tokui Waza of All-Japan Judo Champions (1948 - 1960)

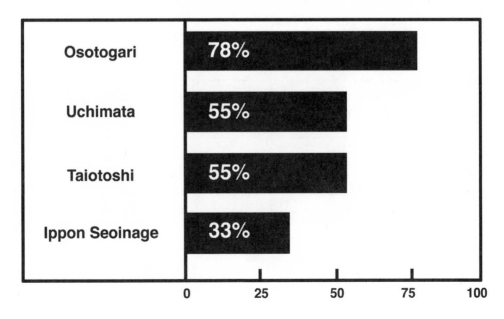

Japan Judo Champions trained with weights in some form or fashion, though in many cases, not under any systematic method.

Essential to a sound understanding of Japanese training methods and the types of men who win the championships is the subject of height and weight. It was earlier stated in Chapter 1 that there never has been a small Japanese Judo Champion. On the average he is 208 lbs. at 5 feet 9 inches *(refer to graphs on pages 142, 143)*. Very obviously there is a relationship between championship ability and size. It is interesting to note that the lightest All-Japan Judo Champion was Isao Inokuma, who weighed 179 pounds at the time he won the championship. The shortest champion was M. Kimura, who stood only 5 feet 6 inches in height.

A final consideration here is the frequency of the Tokui Waza of the All-Japan Judo Champions. Four Waza are predominant: Uchimata, Osotogari, Ippon Seoinage, and Taiotoshi. 55% of the champions had a very powerful and effective Uchimata; 78% an equally powerful and effective Osotogari; while 33% shared the Ippon Seoinage and 55% the Taiotoshi.

Whole broad generalizations are usually dangerous and inconclusive, we are nevertheless, able to draw some important information from the data presented in this discussion. By way of a synthesis, we can see that the following go into the building of a Japanese Judo Champion:

Graph 5

Weight of All-Japan Judo Champions (1948 - 1960)

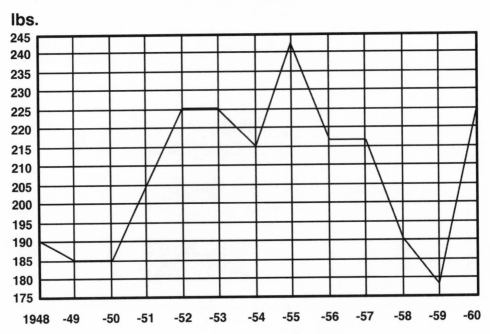

Graph 6

Height of All-Japan Judo Champions (1948 - 1960)

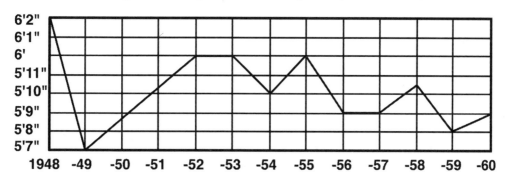

An early age start at Judo, sometime between late grade school and early high school; attainment of 3rd or 4th Dan by the age of 18 years; university or police force Judo training averaging 3–4 hours daily, 6 days per week; 26 to 33 years of age; 6 Dan; over 200 lbs. and about 5 feet 9 inches in height; and the possessor of at least one powerful and effective Waza chosen from Uchimata, Osotogari, Ippon Seoinage, or Tai-otoshi. This is the formidable Judoka of the Orient.

The future success of Western Judo exponents in competition with their Eastern counter-parts depends upon matching, in some fashion, the training and the physical and mental make-ups of these skilled Judoka. This can only be hoped to be approached by intelligent training and devotion to systematic training.

The reader will note that the 1961 All-Japan Judo Championship results are included in List 1, page 140, but are not included in the statistics contained in any of the six graphs of this chapter. The information was received after the graphs had been prepared. Inas-much as Kaminaga retained his title in 1961, the averages borne by the statistics do not change appreciably.

Pre-structured training programs have already been discussed on pages 51 and 126–130. The following sample of such a training program has been successfully used with excellent results and can be used as a guide as to form.

WASHINGTON JUDO CLUB
SHUFU JUDO YUDANSHAKAI

Recognized by
KODOKAN JUDO INSTITUTE, TOKYO, JAPAN
THE JUDO BLACK BELT FEDERATION of the U.S.A.
THE AMATEUR ATHLETIC UNION of the U.S.A.

Office of the   President
726 Upshur St NW DC

TRAINING PROGRAM Pentagon Dojo   1 December–22 December

TRAINING CATEGORY	ITEM	DIVISION
1. Opening Preparatory Exercises	Junbi Undo	A B C D
2. Ukemi	All forms	A B C D
3. Supplementary Exercises	Osotogari 25 repetitions	A B C D
	Seoinage 25 repetitions	B C D
	Tsurikomigoshi 25 repetitions	B C D
	Uchimata 25 repetitions	A B
4. Kata	Ju no Kata	A D
5. Randori	Tachi and Katame Waza	A B C
6. Technical Instruction	Introduction to Ashiguruma	A B
	Study of Taiotoshi	C D
	Renraku Waza—Kouchigari & Ouchigari	A B
7. Kata or Compound Exercises	Prone Crawling	A B C
8. Closing Preparatory Exercises	Shumatsu Undo	A B C D
9. Shiai		
Jr. Tsukinami	8 December 7:30 PM	
Sr. Tsukinami	22 December 7:30 PM	
other	WJC vs U of Md. 17 December 2:00 PM in this Dojo	
10. Special Notices	The Dojo will be closed from 23 December until 3 January 61. Kangeiko begins on 9 January. Best of the Holiday season!	

DIVISIONS   A   Yudansha only
                B   Advanced (Sankyu and higher)
                C   Intermediate (Yonkyu and below)
                D   Women only

JAMES H TAKEMORI

PART II

Practice

*T*HIS PART *of the book deals with the specific exercises beneficial for Judo training. The kinesiological principles established in Part I are herein applied in the various categories of exercises. Historical inertia, which had armored against the energies of progress, has been disturbed by the cutting edge of newly applied knowledge in the form of weight training exercises and applications to Judo training. This is done in the belief that tradition lives by being added to in an orderly, progressive manner. While much of the newly added information is in transition, what is described, is tested and proven training methodology. It is now offered for your comprehension and further elaboration.*

PLATE 8. Isao Inokuma, 5 Dan, demonstrating his favorite Preparatory Exercise—Duck Jumps.

CHAPTER 7

Preparatory Exercises

Just as the twig is bent the tree's inclined.
Pope

General Discussion: The use of this phase of exercise is a prerequisite to all forms of severe exercise. These methods involve the moderate "warm up" exercises of the well-disciplined athlete and team, and are essential to efficient body coordination, minimization of injuries, and top-level competitive performance.

Recently there has been some scientific investigation by physical educators and physiologists attemping to show that "warm-up" exercises are not essentially necessary, and do not result in improved performance of athletes. Such experimentation has had little effect in convincing the majority of athletes and athletic coaches that the "warm-up" should be discontinued, and it can be readily demonstrated that Preparatory Exercises have a vital place in the training programs of all forms of athletic endeavors.

A study of all championship levels of Judo performance shows that without exception, Preparatory Exercises are performed. There are countless such exercises comprised of basic movements and their variations. No attempt has been made to record all of these exercises, but those which are considered by the authors as most beneficial are described in this chapter. To the Judo exponent, these exercises are familiarly known as *Junbi Undo* ("warm-up" exercises) or *Taiso* (calisthenics) used as Junbi Undo.

Equipment: No special equipment is necessary in the performance of the Preparatory Exercises. They may be performed on any clean, level surface, though for some of the exercises, a padded surface or mat is advisable.

Application: Judo instructors conducting a training session should insist on participation of *all students* in the Preparatory Exercises. Individuals practicing as individuals, must take self-initiative and perform these exercises. Preparatory Exercises should be used during a period of from 15 to 30 minutes *before* actual contact Judo exercise is begun. In a well-organized Judo group, class participation in these exercises is always required, and is the first thing on the program after the formal opening of the class by the instructor. Among top level Judo teams in Japan, Preparatory Exercises are performed as a group under the direction of the team captain, for a minimum of 20 minutes before contact work in daily training. Just prior to contest competition, about 15 minutes is devoted to these exercises, which is ample preparation.

A further use of these exercises is found by applying them *after* the normal Judo training program has been completed. Some of the lesser active and exertive movements are used as an aid to relaxation. Such application should be confined to about 1 to 3 minutes of exercise. Preparatory Exercises used in this fashion are termed *Shumatsu Undo* (closing exercises). *(See Table A for recommended exercises p. 149.)*

Each movement should be done thoroughly, without haste, and with a full concentration behind each movement. Speed is not essential at this point; in fact, it is to be avoided. This does not infer that the exercises should be done in a spiritless fashion (just going through the motions), but the body should be exercised until circulation is sufficiently increased and perspiration begins to appear evenly over the body. No attempt should be made to tire or fatigue the body, although each muscle group exercised will experience a period of "healthy fatigue" which will disappear when the repetitions are stopped and the breathing allowed to return to normal. Allow breathing to return to normal between the various exercises.

Selection of Exercises: Utilize at least two exercises from each group shown in Table A, performing enough repetitions to "feel" the exercise. Care must be taken to select wisely within each group. Obviously, the selection of, for instance, the Ankle Walk and the Ankle Flex in the Leg Group, would not bring about adequate stimulation of the major leg muscles. At least one of the exercises selected from each group should involve major muscles and stimulation of those muscles. From time to time, it is well to change exercises to avoid monotony. Do not do the same exercises day-in-day-out, but rather vary them in different combinations. Of course there is a limit to the possible combinations and sooner or later there will be little or no "newness" to the exercises.

Repetitions: Repetitions of each exercise are necessary if the body is to receive adequate stimulation. Just how many repetitions to perform varies greatly with the individual and the conditions under which the training is being performed, as well as the training objectives. Generally, 10–20 repetitions are sufficient to gain benefit from the movements. More repetitions are not recommended unless one or two exercises are being used to establish endurance in a particular muscle group. An example might be for the instructor to require the class to perform two exercises from each group at the normal 10–20 repetitions, adding the performance of 100 squats and 30 pushups. This would be a heavy warm-up, designed to strengthen the leg and chest groups.

After the 10 or 20 repetitions have been performed, it is possible, though not necessary, to repeat the same exercise after a short period of rest before going on to a different exercise. Some instructors will choose this method, performing two or three "sets" of one exercise before going on to another exercise. This is quite a heavy workout and is not generally necessary if the original purpose of the Preparatory Exercises is intended. It is possible to develop endurance by this method however, and with this in mind, this teaching technique becomes a valuable tool.

Order of Exercises: The subject has many solutions, but by experience it has been determined that exercises are best accomplished by working in logical order from a standing position to the lying position and return to the standing position. This allows a great latitude of just what muscle groups to start with and to end with in the "warm-up" routine. In most Japanese Dojo for instance, it is common to begin with neck rotation exercises in the standing position. Then working down the body to the abdominal belt group exercises and the legs before lying down. Each athlete develops his own favorite routine as do many coaches who will direct the "warm-up" of their students. The selection of the order is one of logical progression more than one of physiological necessity and should not cause undue concern to anyone. This order is efficiently arranged to localize "warm-up" and progressively extends to *all* parts of the body in sequence. All major muscle groups and joints should receive adequate exercise during the performance of the Preparatory Exercises as a "warm-up."

Non Judo Exponents: The performance of at least 10 repetitions of a dozen or more of these exercises selected from the different groups, three times per week, will promote noticeable health improvements in less than one month. Flexibility, muscle tone, regulated metabolism, better circulation and general well-being will result. A full program for the average man can be found within this classification of exercises. A period of from 20 to 30 minutes will be sufficient for each workout.

Table A

PREPARATORY EXERCISES

Leg Group *(page 150)*
1. Squats *(page 150)*
2. One-legged squats *(page 150)*
3. Snap ups *(page 151)*
4. Bouncing jumps *(page 151)*
5. Side stretcher *(page 152)*
6. Trunk bobs *(page 152)*
7. Duck walk *(page 153)*
* 8. Rise on toes *(page 153)*
9. Leg stretcher *(page 154)*
10. Reach thrus *(page 154)*
11. Ankle walk *(page 155)*
*12. Knee press *(page 155)*
13. Raised knee bobs *(page 156)*
*14. Thigh stretching *(page 156)*
15. Thigh Spreading *(page 157)*
16. Ankle flex *(page 157)*

Abdominal Belt Group *(page 158)*
1. Taiotoshi exercise *(page 158)*
* 2. Trunk twisting *(page 158)*
3. Trunk circling *(page 159)*
4. Side bends *(page 160)*
* 5. Side reaching *(page 160)*
6. Up and downs *(page 161)*
7. Sit ups *(page 161)*
8. Stiff-legged raises *(page 162)*
9. Rocking situps *(page 162)*
10. Seated trunk twisting *(page 163)*
11. Leg holdouts *(page 163)*
12. Leg doubles *(page 164)*
13. Spread-outs *(page 164)*
14. Pushup leg raises *(page 165)*
*15. Back to back *(page 165)*
16. Arch ups *(page 166)*

Upper Back-Neck Group *(page 166)*
1. Bridge-turnover and twist *(page 166)*
* 2. Neck rotation *(page 167)*
3. Neck pushing *(page 167)*
4. Neck stand *(page 168)*
5. Rear bridging *(page 168)*
6. Spinal doubles *(page 169)*
* 7. Front bridging *(page 169)*

Shoulder-Chest-Arm Group *(page 170)*
1. Catman *(page 170)*
2. Normal pushups *(page 171)*
3. Narrow pushups *(page 171)*
4. Reverse pushups *(page 172)*
5. One hand pushups *(page 172)*
6. Backward running on all-fours *(page 173)*
7. Forward running on all-fours *(page 173)*
* 8. Arm circles *(page 174)*
* 9. Grip and pull *(page 174)*
*10. Wrist rotations *(page 175)*

* Suitable for use after heavy exercise to return the breathing to normal. Considered as "closing exercises" or "cooling-off" exercises (Shumatsu Undo).

LEG GROUP

SQUATS

Purpose: An exercise which is perhaps one of the most important conditioning exercises. Great leg strength, flexibility of knees, ankles, balance, and a general strengthening of the hip and pelvic region is produced by this movement. The entire respiratory system is improved as repetitions are increased, resulting in extraordinary stamina and endurance.

Performance: Stand in the basic natural posture of Judo known as *Shizenhontai*. Relax the body, though keeping it alert. The feet should be placed about the width of the shoulders apart. The body rests squarely over the feet with the weight primarily on the balls of the feet. Fold the arms across the chest. #1.

Lower the body, keeping the back straight so that from shoulder-hip-heel is a straight line. #2.

Sink to the lowest possible position keeping the back as straight as possible. The heels must not leave the ground. Hold the head erect, eyes to the front. Spread the knees as the body is lowered. #3.

Return to the upright starting position, but as you rise, thrust the stomach forward, leaning somewhat backward.

Repeat this movement at least 20 times.

Key Points: The back must never be inclined forward any more than shown in #3. The feet must remain with the full sole in contact with the ground. The toes may be pointing straight ahead or slightly outward for best effect. Repetitions can be beneficially made to 100 or 150 movements without rest.

ONE-LEGGED SQUATS

Purpose: A variation of normal two-legged squatting which is a severe exercise. Used to promote great strength and flexibility in the leg and hip joint muscles.

Performance: Stand on one leg, with the other leg slightly raised to the front. The hand on the side of the leg which is weighted is placed against a wall, a chair, or some other means of support. #1.

Lower the body on the weighted leg, by bending that knee, taking care to raise the extended leg slightly as the body is lowered. #2. Continue the lowering until the lowest possible position is reached as in #3.

Return to the starting position in #1. Repeat this movement at least 10 times.

Key Points: The hand which assists the balance during the performance of this movement should not be used as a power source to control the lowering and raising of the body. The leg which is raised, may be either the farthest away or closest to the means of support. This exercise may be performed without any support. The weighted foot may be flat or raised on the ball of the foot as the body is lowered.

SNAP UPS

Purpose: To promote the development of spring and snap in the legs useful in the completion of various Nage Waza in Judo. Described here only to provide a leg developmental exercise.

Performance: Squat with the feet spaced about the width of the hips. Raise the hands, closed as if gripping of opponent's Judogi. #1.

Snap the legs so as to raise the body, simultaneously swinging the arms together downward sharply toward the knees. #2 and #3.

Return to the starting position in #1 and repeat at least 25 times.

Key Points: The body must be coordinated as a unit in the snapping motion, utilizing a quick motion. As each movement is completed, the feet will slide to the rear, and the body will move backward to a new position. The hands snap downward directly to the area in front of the feet. The final position must be one of balance. Any tendency to finish in the position as shown in #7 is incorrect and is to be avoided. An advanced variation can be made by assuming the throwing position shown in #4 to #6 and performing essentially the same snapping action.

It is well to have the entire class perform this exercise in a "follow-the-leader" line moving backward along the mat.

BOUNCING JUMPS

Purpose: A method of exercising the leg muscles to develop powerful springing action. Also an aid to developing respiratory capacity.

Performance: Stand in the basic natural posture of Judo known as Shizenhontai. Hold the arms along the sides in a relaxed manner. #1.

Jump into the air, about 10 inches, and move the legs into a straddle position with one leg forward and one leg to the rear. #2. As you touch the ground in this straddle position, spring up again immediately into the air and assume a straddle position reversing the position of the legs. Keep the body erect during the entire alternate positions of the legs. #3.

Repeat in alternate order, first one foot forward, then the other, in rhythmic fashion for a least 1 minute. #4 and #5. More advanced trainees may perform this movement for 5–10 minutes without pause.

Key Points: The exercise may be somewhat varied by springing higher into the air and widening or narrowing the straddle, or by straddling sideways. The weight of the body must be maintained on the balls of the feet as contact with the ground is made.

This is a favorite exercise of M. Koga, 5 Dan, former All-Japan University Student Co-Champion who utilized it both as a warm-up for a 3 minute period and as an endurance builder for a 30 minute period.

SIDE STRETCHER

Purpose: An exercise which will produce a severe stretch on the hip muscles, and the muscles along the inside of the legs. Useful in developing ability to spread the legs wide apart without undue strain.

Performance: Stand in the basic natural posture of Judo known as Shizen-hontai. Relax the body though keeping it alert. The feet should be placed about the width of the shoulders apart. The weight of the body now rests primarily on the balls of the feet. Hold the head erect and keep the eyes to the front. Place the hands on the hips. #1.

Simultaneously slide or "walk" both feet outward away from the body, keeping the trunk erect. Continue spreading the feet outward until a wide position is reached that just begins to cause discomfort in the hip joint region. The trunk must be held erect during this movement. #2.

Hold this widespread position for 10 counts and return to the starting position. Repeat this movement at least 3 times, spreading the legs as wide as possible, holding the wide position for 10 counts before returning to the starting position.

Key Points: The trunk must be kept erect; in fact, at the widest spread of the legs, one should attempt to push the stomach forward. It is possible to reach a complete split if extreme flexibility is developed.

TRUNK BOBS

Purpose: An exercise which will promote elasticity in the lower back region and the "ham-string" muscles of the backs of the legs. This exercise aids the all-around development of trunk flexibility.

Performance: Stand in the basic natural posture of Judo known as Shizen-hontai. Relax the body though keeping it alert. The feet should be placed about the width of the shoulders apart. The weight of the body now rests primarily on the balls of the feet. Hold the head erect and keep the eyes to the front. Hold the arms loosely at the sides. #1.

Bend the upper trunk forward at the waist, keeping the legs completely straight, knees locked tightly. #2 *(see Key Points)*.

Continue bending forward with the knees locked. The trainee who is "stiff" should attempt to touch the fingertips or the palms of the hands on the ground, while other trainees who are more flexible should attempt to touch the elbows (from the arms folded position shown in all figures) on the ground. #3.

Return the body to the position shown in #1, using the natural "bob" of the body only after the lowest possible position in #3 is reached. Continue lowering and raising the body in a "bobbing" fashion for at least 35 repetitions.

Key Points: The back must be kept rather "flat" throughout the entire movement, and the knees tightly locked to keep the knees from bending.

DUCK WALK

Purpose: A method for the development of flexible hips, strong leg drive, and improved balance.

Performance: Squat with the haunches close to the heels. Fold the arms across the chest. Hold the back as erect as possible, with a slight lean forward to enhance forward movement. Hold the head erect, with the eyes to the front during the entire movement. #1.

Shift your weight to the right leg, and step forward with the left foot. Keep the upper body as erect as possible. #2.

Continue the stepping, alternately, with each foot, in a duck-like fashion as you move forward. #3.

Repeat the movements described above until you have covered a distance of at least 50 feet. It is sometimes convenient to have the entire group move around the perimeter of the mat area in "follow-the-leader" style.

Key Points: The upper body must not be allowed to incline forward more than shown in the figures. The hands should be kept folded across the chest and not on the floor to maintain balance.

A variation of this exercise is produced by hopping forward with both feet simultaneously from the starting position shown in #1.

This exercise is very severe and should be used only by advanced trainees who are in excellent physical condition. A favorite Preparatory Exercise of All-Japan Judo Champion I. Inokuma, 5 Dan (DUCK JUMPS). See Plate 8.

RISE ON TOES

Purpose: A method designed to stretch, strengthen, and promote flexibility in the muscles of the calf, ankle, arch, and toes. When combined with deep breathing, this exercise is a valuable relaxation exercise and can be used immediately after a severe exercise to bring the respiration back to normal. This exercise also promotes good balance.

Performance: Stand in the basic natural posture of Judo known as Shizenhontai. Relax the body, though keeping it alert. The feet should be placed about the width of the shoulders apart. The weight of the body now rests primarily on the balls of the feet. Hold the arms loosely at the sides. #1.

Keep your weight centered. Raise the heels from the ground by rising on to your toes and fully flexing the ankle. The body weight is now primarily on the balls of the feet as shown in #2.

As you rise on to your toes, raise the arms simultaneously, palms down, forward and upward above shoulder height. As the arms come as high as the shoulders, stretch them to their limit to the sides in a somewhat circular motion, bringing the palms up. Hold the head high, body erect, eyes to the front. #3.

Return to the starting position in #1 by reversing the movement sequence just performed. Repeat this movement at least 20 times.

Key Points: Deep breathing in conjunction with this movement is a valuable supplement, and such breathing should be done by inhaling as the arms are raised, and exhaling as the arms are lowered. The arms must be stretched as widely as possible, and the shoulder blades pushed together by the backward action of the arms in the raised position.

LEG STRETCHER

Purpose: A combination exercise which results in extreme stretching of the "ham-string" leg muscles, ankle, and knee joints. Also promotes balance.

Performance: Stand in a wide-legged straddle stance as shown in #1. Advanced trainees should fold the arms across the chest. Beginning trainees will find it easier to keep the arms free to assist the balance.

Lower the body over the right heel, sinking down until the buttocks almost touch the ground. The right foot is flat in the ground. The left leg is extended, toes upward so that it rests on the ground by heel contact only. The leg is completely extended. #2.

Pushing and driving with the right leg, return to the position in #1.

Lower the body similarly over the left heel, sinking down as before until the buttocks almost touch the ground. The left foot is flat on the ground. The right leg is extended, toes upward so that it rests on the ground with heel contact only. The leg is completely extended. #3.

Pushing and driving with the left leg, return to the position in #1.

Repeat these movements, alternately right and left, until you have done at least 10 movements to each side.

Key Points: This complete movement, from starting position to the right and to the left, should be performed as smoothly as possible, without any delay between the various positions. The weighted foot must be kept flat on the ground. The body should be inclined very slightly to the front to maintain better balance.

REACH THRUS

Purpose: A severe method designed to stretch all major muscle groups of the legs. Extreme hip flexibility and suppleness of the lower back is promoted through constant use of this exercise.

Performance: Stand in a wide-legged straddle stance as shown in #1.

Bend forward from the waist, keeping the legs fully extended, knees locked. Extend the hands so that the arms reach between the widely stretched legs #2.

Continue the forward bend until the lowest possible position, through and behind the outstretched legs is reached. The knees must remain locked in a straightened position. #3.

Return the body to the position shown in #2 by using the natural "bob" of the body only after the lowest possible position shown in #3 is reached. Continue raising lowering the body in a "bobbing" fashion for at least 20 repetitions before stopping.

Key Points: Trainees who find reaching with the hands too easy may add an interesting variation to this exercise by attempting to touch the forehead or chest alternately to each shin bone in a "bobbing" fashion.

154   Judo Training Methods

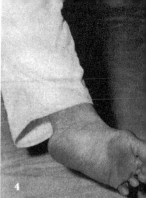

ANKLE WALK

Purpose: One of the best methods of developing complete ankle flexibility for use in the many "hand-like" actions of the feet, and to perfect the *Harai—Gari—Gake* position of the feet, for the various Judo Nage Waza.

Performance: Stand in the basic natural posture of Judo known as Shizenhontai. Relax the body though keeping it alert. The feet should be placed about the width of the shoulders apart. The weight of the body now rests primarily on the balls of the feet. Hold the arms loosely at the sides. #1.

Step forward with the right foot, turning the sole inward (to your left) so that you contact the ground with the outside edge of the right foot. Attempt to place the right ankle bone on the ground. #2.

Bring your full weight over this flexed ankle and step forward with your left foot similarly. #3.

Continue this walking process for at least 50 feet before stopping.

Key Points: The walking and flexing is made easier by crossing each foot over the body center line as you step forward. This facilitates placing the ankle bone on the ground. A fully trained ankle flex is shown in #4.

KNEE PRESS

Purpose: A useful method of exercise which stretches the lower leg muscles, knees, the ankle and all attendant muscles. This exercise is especially useful in developing necessary flexibility of the lower legs for executing the many Judo Nage Waza.

Performance: Stand in the basic natural posture of Judo known as Shizenhontai. Relax the body though keeping it alert. The feet should be placed about the width of the shoulders apart, although in this exercise, the feet are sometimes placed close together *(see Key Points)*. The weight of the body now rests primarily on the balls of the feet. Hold the head erect, eyes to the front. Hold the arms loosely at the sides. #1.

Lower the body slightly by bending the knees. The weight of the body should now be centered approximately over the heels. Do not raise the heels from the ground as the buttocks are lowered. Place the hands on the knees and press the knees down and forward. #2 and #3.

Raise the body slightly by straightening the legs a bit. Return immediately to the lowest position, forcing the knees down and forward without raising the heels. "Bob" the body up and down for at least 10 repetitions, *(see Key Points)*, maintaining the approximate position shown in #2 and #3.

Key Points: The toes must point straight ahead and the heels are never raised during this movement. A variation of this exercise is produced by moving the knees in a rotary motion to the right or left while in the relative position shown in #2 and #3.

RAISED KNEE BOBS

Purpose: A method of promoting flexibility of muscles hard to develop located inside the upper leg and extending into the groin region. Useful development for the execution of Katame Waza.

Performance: Assume a modification of the posture known in Judo as *Kyoshi no Kamae* (kneeling posture). Kneel on your right knee, making sure that the toes of the right foot are in contact with the ground, and the right heel is vertically above them. Your left leg is placed on the ground before you, sole down, knee up with your left arm resting on the upper left thigh. #1.

Bend the upper trunk forward, sliding the left elbow inside the knee of the raised left leg. #2.

Continue the bending forward until you can touch the left elbow to the inside of the left ankle bone. #3.

Return to the position shown in #2 using the natural "bob" of the body only after lowest possible position in #3 is attained. Continue lowering and raising the body in a "bobbing" fashion for at least 20 repetitions before changing into the opposite position to exercise the other leg in a similar fashion.

Key Points: Those trainees who find that touching the elbow is too easy, can make this exercise more severe by touching the forehead to the ankle bone.

THIGH STRETCHING

Purpose: A special exercise performed to assist the stretching of the muscles inside the legs and extending into the groin region. Also promotes hip and knee flexibility necessary in all phases of Judo.

Performance: Seat yourself on the ground with legs bent, feet soles together, knees pointed outward. A partner kneels or stands behind you, close in contact with you, his hands resting on your knees. #1.

Your partner puts pressure downward on your knees in a steady, even manner, leaning forward to bend your body slightly forward. He attempts to touch your knees to the mat. By applying and releasing the pressure alternately, stretching can be achieved.

Repeat at least 20 times.

Key Points: The soles of your feet must be kept together. The pressure must be even and gently applied as this is a severe exercise.

THIGH SPREADING

Purpose: An exercise designed to promote great flexibility in the hip joint regions and the muscles of the inside of the thighs. Also affects the lower back.

Performance: Seat yourself on the ground with both legs outstretched and somewhat widely spread. A partner seats himself facing you and grasps your arms at the wrists, and braces his feet on the inside surfaces of your thighs. He pulls backward with his entire body, thus pulling you forward. #1.

Your partner alternately pulls you forward, while not allowing your legs to close, and lets you rock back to normal sitting position. By bracing his feet, he applies stretching and spreading tension to your legs. He must strive to spread your legs to the utmost.

Repeat at least 20 times.

Key Points: Pressure applied to spread partners legs must be even and gently applied.

ANKLE FLEX

Purpose: A method designed to promote flexibility in the ankle joints, valuable in developing the various "hand-like" actions of the feet in Judo movements of Harai—Gari—Gake.

Performance: Seat yourself on the ground and grip one ankle as shown in #1.

The hand which grips the ankle must firmly support the entire movement, allowing only a minimum of movement. The other hand forces a circular rotation of the ankle joint throughout its normal flex limits. #2. Apply complete circular motion to each ankle joint, varying clockwise and counterclockwise. Make at least 20 repetitions (complete circular motions) with each ankle.

Key Points: Additional flexation may be achieved by forcing the toes up against the leg in the direction of the shin bone. #3. The toes should be limbered too during this exercise.

Preparatory Exercises 157

ABDOMINAL BELT GROUP

TAIOTOSHI EXERCISE

Purpose: A method of developing a coordinated body action, unifying arm, leg, and trunk action similar to the method used in *Taiotoshi* (body drop) technique (*Chapter 8*). Used here only as an abdominal strengthening exercise. Promotes balance and hip flexibility.

Performance: Stand in a wide-legged upright stance, with the weight evenly distributed on both feet. Arms are spread, shoulder high, with the hands lightly clenched as simulating gripping of the opponent's Judogi. #1.

Twist the body to the left, pivoting on the ball of the right foot, and bring the body to face directly over the upraised and bent left knee. The upper trunk must be held upright as shown. Continue to spread the arms, holding them at shoulder height. Lower the body slightly during this movement by bending the extended rearmost leg slightly at the knee. #2.

Reverse the twist by turning fully in a similar fashion to the right until you attain the position shown in #3.

Continue alternately right to left for at least 20 movements (10 on each side).

Key Points: During the performance of this movement, the chest must be held high and actually pushed foward as your body twists to the right and left. The arms and hands assist the twist in a coordinated fashion, "chasing" each other with the left hand "pulling" and the right hand "pushing" an imaginary opponent as the body is twisted to the left (right leg extended rearward), and vice-versa.

TRUNK TWISTING

Purpose: A less severe method than the Taiotoshi exercise (above) designed to strengthen the abdominal muscles and to produce a supple spine.

Performance: Stand in an upright stance, with the weight of the body evenly centered over the feet. The feet are spread as wide as the shoulders. Hold the head erect, with the eyes to the front. Spread the arms to the sides at shoulder height. The fists are clenched lightly. #1.

Twist the body as far as possible to the left, keeping the upper trunk erect, and the knees locked so that the legs are unable to move or bend. The hips are drawn around by the twisting action of the shoulders. #2. Reverse the twist of the body by turning to the right as far as possible in similar fashion. Alternate left to right for at least 20 counts (10 on each side). #3.

Key Points: During the twisting process, the trainee must be sure that the arms do not lead the trunk during the twist, but rather the combined action of the shoulders and abdominal region twisting from solidly fixed legs, bring the arms (held in a fixed position relative to the body) around with the body. The body must remain erect throughout this exercise. The feet must not pivot.

TRUNK CIRCLING

Purpose: The complete exercise for abdominal strengthening and suppleness of the hip and spinal regions. An important exercise to permit adequate abdominal movement for the various *Koshinage* (Waist Techniques) of Judo.

Performance: Stand in the basic natural posture of Judo known as Shizenhontai. Relax the body though keeping it alert. The feet should be placed about the width of the shoulders apart. The weight of the body rests primarily on the balls of the feet. Hold the head erect and keep the eyes to the front. #1.

Bend forward, inclining the upper trunk so that it comes parallel to the ground. The knees are held loosely (not locked). Hold the arms, with a slight bend at the elbows, parallel to the legs in front of you. #2.

Lean your body to the right, raising your head slightly as you shift your weight to the right leg. #3.

Draw your body back in a circular fashion, knees loose and slightly flexed as you describe a big circle with upper body, hands above your head. Make one complete circle with the body as shown in #4 through #9. Repeat this circular movement at least 10 times in this clockwise direction before reversing in the other counter-clockwise direction for the same number of repetitions.

Key Points: This exercised viewed from above would show the head describing a circle around the hips as the center of the circle. It is important to bend the knees slightly, particularly on the rearmost positions in order to allow the body to stretch without losing balance #5 to #7.

SIDE BENDS

Purpose: A method of extreme stretching which fully exercises the abdominal oblique muscles, the major muscle group under the arms, and the abdominals proper.

Performance: Stand in an upright stance, feet as wide as the shoulders apart. The hands are clasped in a crossed-fashion, palm to palm as shown in #1 and #2, and the arms are raised vertically overhead. Press the arms tightly against the sides of the head (ears).

Bend the upper trunk directly to the right side, keeping the arms tightly pressed to the sides of the head. Lower the body as far as possible. #3. Reverse the bend of the upper trunk directly to the left side, in a similar fashion. #4.

Repeat this motion, alternately to the right and left for at least 20 counts (10 on each side).

Key Points: The arms must remain tightly pressed against the sides of the head throughout the exercise, or the stretching effect will be greatly nullified. The bend of the body to the right and left must be directly to the side, or with a slightly backward lean. The body must never be allowed to bend forward.

SIDE REACHING

Purpose: An alternate, less severe method of stretching than Side Bends (above), which fully exercises the abdominal oblique muscles, the major muscle group under the arms, and the abdominals proper.

Performance: Stand in an upright stance, feet as wide as the shoulders apart. Hold the hands above the head as shown in #1.

Bend the trunk directly to the left side, extending the left arm downward along the left leg, and allow the right arm to reach in a curved fashion over the head and as far as it can to your left side. #2.

Return the body to the erect position and repeat this motion on the right side, reversing the above instructions. #3.

Repeat this entire movement for at least 10 repetitions in alternate fashion (10 repetitions on each side).

Key Points: The body must bend directly to the side and not be allowed to twist or lean forward. It is better to permit a slight backward leaning while this motion is performed.

UP AND DOWNS

Purpose: An exercise to stretch and strengthen the abdominal muscles, and those spinal muscles seated in the lower back.

Performance: Bend forward from the stance known in Judo as Shizenhontai, bending the knees slightly as you place both clenched hands on the ground between your legs. #1.

Straighten your body upward, swinging the arms forward as you come to the upright position. #2 .

Continue the motion by arching your body backwards, reaching the arms overhead and behind you as shown in #3.

Return to the position in #1, and repeat this motion for at least 20 counts.

Key Points: The knees remain slightly bent to facilitate the bending and stretching. The head must be thrown back as the body is arched to the rear.

SIT UPS

Purpose: An exercise designed to strengthen the abdominal muscles, and to promote flexibility in the spine and lower back muscles.

Performance: Lie on the ground with the legs spread wide and the arms on the ground overhead, palms up, and behind you. #1.

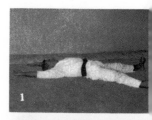

Raise the upper trunk by bending at the waist, swinging the arms forward and upward until they are in front of your face. The legs do not lift from the ground. #2.

Come to a full sitting position with a slight forward lean, head down, arms between the wide-spread legs, fingers touching the toes. #3.

Bend as far forward as possible, attempting to place the forehead on the ground, stretching the arms in front of you between the legs. #4.

Reverse the motion, by lowering the body from the position in #4, until you reach the starting position in #1. This is one repetition.

Repeat this complete movement for at least 10 repetitions.

Key Points: The legs must not be lifted as the body is being raised. Merely sitting up is not enough, and the trainee must make every effort to bend forward and touch his head to the ground. A variation of this exercise can be produced by alternately touching the head to the knees when in the position shown in #4.

Dojo mat space can be greatly economized if this exercise is used on a partner basis, as shown in #5 and #6. Two other trainees can be "hooked" into this combination to save even more mat area, by placing them at right angles to the other trainees (not shown).

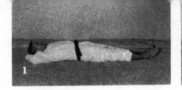

STIFF-LEGGED RAISES

Purpose: An exercise which strengthens the abdominal muscles and exerts a flex on the spine and back muscles lending very extensive suppleness to the spinal region. A necessary exercise in the development of Katame Waza.

Performance: Lie on the ground with your legs extended and joined together. Fold your arms and place the hands behind your head as shown in #1.

Raise the legs, keeping the ankles together, without bending the knees. The buttocks are pressed against the ground and do not lift. #2.

Continue raising the legs without bending the knees, and hold the ankles together. Attempt to keep the lower back in contact with the ground so that the buttocks are not lifted. #3.

Touch the toes behind you and over your head, keeping the legs together. Do not bend the knees. Notice that the back is still very much in contact with the ground, and the body is not just resting on the upper back or shoulder region. #4.

Reverse this raising motion by controlled lowering of the legs, coming to the positions shown in #3 to #1. This is one complete movement.

Repeat this movement at least 10 times.

Key Points: The legs must be kept straight with no bend at the knee, in order to place maximum effect into the abdominal region. The back must be pressed against the ground as the legs pass overhead in order to flex the spine properly.

ROCKING SIT UPS

Purpose: A composite exercise designed to strengthen the abdominal and lower back muscles and promote general flexibility useful in all phases of Judo.

Performance: Sit on the ground with your legs outstretched, ankles together, body bent forward. Reach the arms forward and touch the finger tips to the toes. #1.

Rock backward, raising the legs simultaneously, ankles together, with the arms. #2. Continue rocking backward as shown in #3 and #4, until the final position is reached in #5.

Return to the starting position shown in #1 by rocking forward. Repeat for desired repetitions (minimum of 10).

Key Points: Legs and hands are kept the same distance apart during the performance of the exercise, and the body is actuated as one unit. Do not allow the body to open up, but maintain the jacknife position. A variation may be produced by grasping the ankles and maintaining this grasp during the entire movement.

162   Judo Training Methods

SEATED TRUNK TWISTING

Purpose: A method for stretching the abdominal belt muscles and the inside thigh muscles. Promotes flexibility necessary in all phases of Judo.

Performance: Sit on the ground with the legs widespread, hands resting on your knees as shown in #1.

Bend the body to the side and forward to the right reaching toward the right foot. #2. Continue this forward and sideward bending until you can place your forehead on the ground alongside your right thigh, on the outside. #3.

Return to the starting position shown in #1. Repeat on the left side. Repeat 10 times on each side.

Key Points: The outstretched legs must be kept straightened and locked into position and not allowed to bend or flex as the body is moved from side to side. An aid to this exercise can be had by performing the partner exercise shown in #4. Care must be taken not to over-twist one's partner.

LEG HOLDOUTS

Purpose: A method of strengthening the abdominal muscles, the neck and the back muscles. An exercise necessary in the development of effective Katame Waza.

Performance: Lie on your back with your legs outstretched, ankles together. The head is held off the ground with the chin tucked into the chest. The head remains in this position throughout the whole exercise. #1. Lift the legs about one foot off the ground. The knees are locked so that there is no bend. The eyes watch the belt region. #2.

Hold this position in #2 for one count and lower the legs so that you are again in the starting position shown in #1.

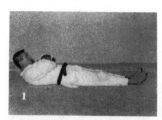

Repeat this movement at least 10 times. *This is not the complete exercise.* Raise the legs again and when in the position shown in #2, hold that position for a count of 20, or until your stomach just becomes tired. Repeat this hold-count procedure at least three times.

Return to 10 more simple leg raises, without any delay between them, to complete the exercise.

Key Points: The head must remain up with the chin tucked into the chest if this exercise is to be fully effective. The upper body can be raised by abdominal power so that the body assumes a sort of U-shaped figure. A variation to this exercise is obtained by twisting the upper body from the hips, alternately raising and dropping each shoulder in a side-to-side fashion, while the position shown in #2 is maintained.

A favorite Preparatory Exercise of T. Ishikawa, 7 Dan, former two-time All-Japan Judo Champion.

LEG DOUBLES

Purpose: An exercise, one of the most valuable to keep the body fit, which strengthens the abdominal muscles and promotes flexibility and suppleness to the spinal regions.

Performance: Lie on the ground with the legs extended and joined together. The arms are folded and are placed under the head. #1.

Bend the knees and draw the heels up close to the buttocks. Note that the feet are only a few inches off the ground. #2. The feet should be drawn up as close to the buttocks as possible before going to the next step. Raise the buttocks from the ground by doubling the knees up toward the chest. The feet remain together, with the heels close to the buttocks. #3.

Continue the doubling action of the knees until the knees touch the chest or the chin (spread the knees to accommodate the chin). The buttocks are now fully off the ground. The weight of the body now rests on the upper-back and shoulder region. #4.

Reverse the doubling action by lowering the buttocks. #5.

Continue lowering the buttocks until they again rest on the ground. The knees are now positioned so as to allow the heels to come close to the buttocks just a few inches off the ground as they did in the earlier stage of the movement. #6.

Return to the starting position, but do not allow the legs to rest on the ground. This is one complete movement.

Repeat this movement at least 10 times.

Key Points: The various positions of the heels and knees in #2 through #6, must be maintained if this exercise is to be fully effective. The entire motion must be done in a smooth, quick fashion for best results. Should the stomach cramp during this exercise, go immediately to Arch Ups (page 166).

SPREAD OUTS

Purpose: A severe exercise for developing unified body tension and strength necessary in Katame Waza. Exercises almost all major muscle groups, but used here as an abdominal belt exercise. Promotes great fixation power.

Performance: Lie face down on the ground with the legs widespread and the arms outstretched to the sides or slightly above shoulder level.

Using the combined power of the body, press the body upward a few inches off the ground, keeping the arms fully extended and locked. Only the toes and palms touch the ground. #1 and #2.

Hold this position for a count of 5 and then return to the ground.

Repeat this movement 10 times.

Key points: The arms must be kept extended and locked. The body must not be allowed to sag in the middle.

A more severe exercise can be obtained by suspending the entire body on the toes and finger tips in similar fashion. Recommended by I. Hatta, 7 Dan.

PUSH UP LEG RAISES

Purpose: A severe exercise which strengthens and makes supple the major muscles of the lower back and hip joints at the same time, affecting the muscles of the arms and chest.

Performance: Take the jackknife pushup position shown in #1. Alternately raise and lower the legs to their highest possible position without much knee bend. #2 and #3.

Repeat at least 10 times with each leg.

Key Points: The body is in a jackknife position, with the arms slightly bent and supporting the body throughout the entire movement. A variation is produced when from the positions of #2 or #3, pushups are performed. This movement as well as the basic exercise requires that the extended leg be kept straight with no bend at the knee.

BACK TO BACK

Purpose: A partner exercise useful in producing spinal flexibility and abdominal stretching. This exercise can be used as a relaxation exercise at the close of a training session.

Performance: Stand back-to-back with a partner, locking arms as shown in #1.

Lower your waist by bending your knees, and begin to lift your partner on to your back. He must not resist, but rather completely relax. #2. Continue to lift him, bending forward and straightening the knees until he is completely suspended on your back. He must relax completely. #3. Return to the starting position.

Repeat this movement at least 10 times before changing and allowing your partner to lift and bend you.

Key Points: When in the position shown in #3, you may add extra stretch and relaxation by bouncing up and down gently.

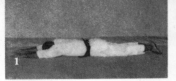

ARCH UPS

Purpose: A complementary exercise for the severe abdominal exercises shown elsewhere in this chapter. Designed to flex the spine and back muscles.

Performance: Lie on the ground, face down with your arms outstretched in front of you. Palms down. Legs should be held together. #1.

Simultaneously lift the legs and arms off the ground, causing an arch in the body. The body now rests on the ground with the weight balanced on the stomach. The knees must not be bent. #2.

Hold this position for one count then lower so that you are again in the position shown in #1.

Repeat this movement at least 10 times. *This is not the complete exercise!* Raise the arms and legs again and when in the position in #2, hold for the count of 20, or until your back becomes tired. Repeat this hold-count procedure at least three times.

Return to 10 more simple archups without any delay between raising and lowering to complete the exercise.

Key Points: The knees must not be bent as such motion will completely nullify the exercise.

UPPER BACK-NECK GROUP

BRIDGE-TURNOVER AND TWIST

Purpose: A method of strengthening the neck and upper back muscles. Also useful in promoting a sense of balance and direction useful in Katame Waza.

Performance: Assume a front bridging position with the legs widespread and the hands placed on the ground as shown in #1.

Using driving power from the legs, turn the body over forward in somersault fashion, but keep the body in a layout position as shown in #2. Continue the forward fall, and arch the body so as to come down on the soles of the feet. The body is now balanced on the head and the feet with the hands held as shown in #3. Immediately upon landing, twist the body by spinning on the head (as in #4), and come into the front bridging position as shown in the starting position and in #5.

Repeat 10 times.

Key Points: A more advanced variation may be performed by clasping the hands in front of the body throughout the entire exercise. In this variation, the hands do not assist the motions. #6.

NECK ROTATION

Purpose: A gentle exercise to loosen and warmup the neck muscles for more severe exercise to come. Useful in promoting flexibility in the neck region. Can be utilized at the end of a training session to relax the body.

Performance: Stand erect in the basic natural posture of Judo known as Shizenhontai. Relax the body though keeping it alert. The feet should be placed about the width of the shoulders apart. The body rests squarely over the feet with the weight primarily on the balls of the feet. The head is erect and the eyes are to the front. #1.

Lower the head so that the chin touches the chest as shown in #2. Rotate the head clockwise progressively as shown in #3 to #6, finally returning to the starting position shown in #2. Repeat with a counterclockwise rotation.

Repeat at least 5 times in each direction.

Key Points: Every effort should be made to stretch the neck muscles and no speed in rotation is necessary. The head should describe a big circle in its rotational movement.

NECK PUSHING

Purpose: A severe method of developing the neck muscles to resist force useful in Katame Waza.

Performance: Take a position on all-fours. Your partner stands (or kneels) somewhat to your side, placing the palms of his hands against one side of your head. #1.

Move your body sideways against your partners hands, fixing the muscles in your neck so you are able to apply strong resistance to his efforts to keep you in place. Use your whole body in an unified effort to move your partner. Your partner resists sufficiently with his whole body, allowing you just enough movement so that you are able to move circularly. Make one complete circle against your partner's resistance. Repeat this movement, resisting with the other side of your head in similar fashion. After you have completed this movement on both sides, your partner places his hands on the back of your head, and provides resistance directly downward against the back of your head. Attempt to raise and lower the head in a "nodding" fashion. Your partner should allow you to move your head very slowly against resistance. Repeat this movement at least 10 times. #2.

Key Points: Care must be taken by the partner providing the resistance, to give a steady pressure to the partner on all-fours. Also, care must be taken so as not to injure the ear or face in any way.

NECK STAND

Purpose: A partner exercise which will develop strong neck muscles useful in all phases of Judo.

Performance: Take the position shown in #1.

The inverted partner must make an attempt to rotate his head, from side to side, front to back, causing the neck muscles to undergo a severe stretching action.

Repeat this movement, the erect partner taking care to maintain his inverted partner's balance for about 30 seconds. Change positions.

Key Points: This exercise is severe and caution must be used in performing it.

REAR BRIDGING

Purpose: A method of strengthening the neck and upper back region. Also affects the abdominal muscles. Especially useful in the performance of the various *Nogarekata* (escape forms) of Katame Waza.

Performance: Lie on your back on the ground, with your feet well under your buttocks. The toes point outward, the weight of the body rests on the upper back and the balls of the feet. The buttocks are free of the ground. #1.

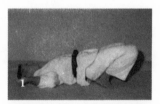

Lift your buttocks higher by pushing the feet against the ground, folding your arms across your chest. Your body is rocked backward, pivoting on the back of your head, by a pushing action of the feet. Lift the abdominal region. #2.

Continue lifting the buttocks, raising the stomach high, and rocking backward onto the top of your head. Attempt to touch your nose to the ground behind you. The arms are reached overhead, stretching them as far as possible away from the body. The weight is now balanced on the top of the head and the balls of the feet. #3.

Reverse this action by controlled lowering until the position shown in #1 is reached. Do not allow the body to rest on the ground.

Repeat this movement (bridge up and lower) at least 20 times.

Key Points: This type of bridging is directly to the rear. It is possible to vary the movement by bridging to the right and left sides, coming up onto the sides of the head. In all bridging, the starting position is very important. A firm base is provided for strong bridging only if the feet are placed well under the buttocks before beginning. The weight must never rest on the heels. The stomach must be raised as high as possible at the height of the bridging action.

SPINAL DOUBLES

Purpose: A severe exercise for increasing the flexibility of the upper back, spinal, and neck regions. Useful in avoiding Katame Waza attacks of the opponent.

Performance: Lie on the ground on your back. Place the feet, soles down on the ground, knees raised in the air. The arms are on the ground behind you. #1.

Raise your buttocks off the ground by doubling the knees up toward the chest until the kneecaps touch the mat behind your shoulders. Spread the knees to facilitate touching the ground with your knees. The head must be placed between the knees (kneecaps resting on the ground). #2.

A variation of this movement is provided by keeping the knees together as they double, and placing them both on one side (either side) of the head, alternately shifting them from one side to the other. #3. and #4. The basic movement or the variation should be continued for at least 1 minute with the body in this doubled position for that period of time.

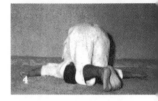

Key Points: The head can be turned so that one ear is placed on the ground (the side on which the leg or legs will be placed). This greatly facilitates the movement. Advanced trainees may find that inverting the body in this position and allowing it to remain there for as much as 3–4 minutes, provides a strong flexing of the spinal regions. This position is an excellent one in which to practice the abdominal breathing known as Kiai (see page 41).

FRONT BRIDGING

Purpose: A complimentary exercise of the bridging variety which strengthens the neck and upper back muscles.

Performance: Lie on the ground, face down. Spread your feet so that only the toes are in contact with the ground. Place your hands palms down on the mat, directly under your shoulders. Your arms should be bent. #1.

Jackknife the body backward by pushing hard against the ground with your hands. The body is pushed backward until your heels touch the ground. Your legs are slightly flexed at the knees. Your head rests lightly on the ground on its forehead. #2.

Adjust the balance of the body so that the weight is supported solidly on the forehead and the balls of the feet. Remove the hands as a means of support. Rock the body forward until the chin touches the chest. #3. Rock back and forth with the body, touching the nose to the ground at one end of the motion (#4), and the chin to the chest at the other (#3). Continue this rocking motion for at least 20 repetitions (back and forth).

Key Points: The knees may be slightly bent to facilitate balance and rocking action. The beginning trainee should allow the hands to be close to the ground to aid in supporting the body until the balance is perfected in this position.

Preparatory Exercises 169

SHOULDER—CHEST—ARM GROUP

CATMAN

Purpose: One of the most effective and useful of all Judo exercises. Designed to strengthen the shoulders, arms, upper back, and the chest. Promotes fixation power of the body useful in all phases of Judo.

Performance: Lie on the ground, face down. Spread your legs so that only the toes are in contact with the ground. Place the palms of the hands on the ground directly under your shoulders. #1.

Jackknife the body backward by pushing hard against the ground with your hands. The body is pushed backward until your heels touch the ground. Your knees are locked. The body now rests on the hands and the soles of your feet. Hold the head face down between the arms. #2. This is the starting position.

Lower the body forward, just brushing the ground with your face as you come forward. The arms bend enough to lower the body. The head, face down, is lifted slightly. The weight of the body rests on the hands and the balls of the feet. #3.

Straighten the arms, arching the back, carrying the head high so that the mid-section of the body is allowed to sag. The upper thighs just brush the ground. The full weight of the body rests on the hands and the balls of the feet. #4.

The motion is continued from this position (#4) by jackknifing the body backward, pushing hard against the ground with your hands. The body is pushed backward until your heels touch the ground. Your knees are locked. Your body rests on the hands and the soles of your feet. The head is folded down between your arms. #5.

Continue the jackknifing action until you reach a position similar to the one shown in #2. This completes one movement.

Repeat this movement at least 10 times.

Key Points: The body must be carried fully on the hands and balls of the feet at all times throughout this exercise. The body must be alternately jackknifed and sagged, stretching to the fullest.

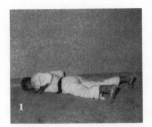

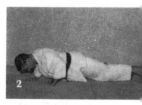

NORMAL PUSH UPS

Purpose: An exercise which develops the arms, shoulders and chest. Promotes power in pushing which is useful in Nogarekata methods of Katame Waza.

Performance: Lie on the ground, face down. Spread your legs so that the feet touch the ground with the balls of the feet firmly on the ground. Bend the arms and place the hands, palms down, directly under the shoulders. The face touches the ground. #1.

Lock the body at the hips and knees. The body must be stiff as a board from head to toe. Push hard with the hands against the ground, lifting the body from the ground. #2.

Extend the arms to their fullest range, locking the elbows. This action will raise the body fully off the ground, with the weight resting on the hands and the balls of the feet. The head faces the ground. #3.

Reverse this action with controlled lowering until you reach the position shown in #2. Do not allow the body to rest on the ground. This is a complete movement.

Repeat this movement at least 15 times.

Key Points: The body must not be allowed to sag in the middle, or jackknife during any phase of this exercise. A straight line should be maintained from head-hip-foot.

NARROW PUSH UPS

Purpose: Primarily designed to strengthen the pushing action of the arms and chest. Concentrates on development of the arms, though promoting fixation power of the body.

Performance: Lie on the ground, face down. Spread your legs so that the feet touch the ground with the balls of the feet firmly on the ground. Hold the body somewhat lifted, head held back, from the waist. The arms are folded. Place the palms downward on the ground in front of the body. #1. The hands overlap one another or form the diamond shaped position shown in #2 and #3.

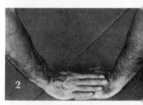

Lock the body at the hips and knees. The body must be stiff as a board from head to toe. Push hard against the ground with the hands, causing the body to rise from the ground. #4.

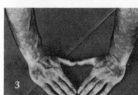

Extend the arms to their fullest range, locking the elbows. This action will raise the body fully off the ground, with the weight resting on the hands and the balls of the feet. The head faces the ground. #5.

Reverse this action with controlled lowering until you reach the position in #4. Do not allow the body to rest on the ground at any time during this exercise.

Repeat this movement at least 10 times.

Key Points: The body must not be allowed to sag in the middle, or jack-knife during any phase of this exercise. A straight line should be maintained from head-hip-foot.

REVERSE PUSH UPS

Purpose: A severe method used to strengthen the shoulders and arms.
Performance: Sit on the ground with the legs outstretched and spread. Incline the body slightly backward. Balance is maintained by placing the hands, palms down, on the ground, fingers away from the body #1.

Lift the buttocks from the ground, arching the body and lifting the stomach high. The weight of the body is on the heels and the hands. The shoulders should be centered directly above the hands to facilitate balance. The head is thrown back. #2.

Return to the position in #1.

Raise the body as described above for at least 10 repetitions.

Key Points: The stomach must be raised high. The legs must be spread wide. The body must not be allowed to rest during the performance of this exercise.

ONE HAND PUSH UPS

Purpose: A severe method of developing arm and shoulder strength and body fixation muscles useful in Katame Waza.
Performance: Take the position shown in #1. The legs are spread to afford greater stability. Begin to lower the body, keeping the body fixed as shown in #2. Continue the lowering supporting the entire body on the toes and the one hand until the low position in #3 is reached. Return to the starting position shown in #1.

Repeat 10 times. Reverse arms and repeat 10 times.

Key Points: The body must not be allowed to sag or rest on the ground during the performance of this exercise. Recommended by K. Takata, 6 Dan.

BACKWARD RUNNING ON ALL-FOURS

Purpose: A severe exercise used to develop the body generally, but with emphasis on the arms and shoulders. Develops endurance.

Performance: Take the position as shown in #1. The body is held from sagging and the weight is thrown over the hands. Begin moving backwards in any fashion. #2 and #3. Arms and legs alternate or move in unison. Continue this movement for a distance of at least 50 feet. Since this exercise requires linear displacement, it is well to form columns and do a "follow-the-leader" method of movement across the mats in any good-sized class, or the trainees may "follow-the-leader" in a circular fashion around the perimeter of the mat.

Key Points: The body must not be allowed to sag. The stomach should be kept high as the movement progresses. This can be made into a partner exercise by having a partner grasp and lift the ankles of the performer, walking in "wheelbarrow" fashion (not shown).

FORWARD RUNNING ON ALL-FOURS

Purpose: A severe exercise used to develop the body generally, but with emphasis on the arm and shoulders. Develops endurance.

Performance: Take the position as shown in #1. The body is held in a slight jackknife position and kept from sagging. The weight of the body is thrown over the hands. Begin moving forwards in any fashion as shown in #2 and #3. Arms and legs alternate or move in unison. Continue this movement for a distance of at least 50 feet. Since this exercise requires linear displacement, it is well to form columns and do a "follow-the-leader" method of movement, or trainees may move in a circle about the training area.

Key Points: The body must not be allowed to sag. The buttocks should be kept high as the movement progresses. This can be made into a partner exercise by having a partner grasp and lift the ankles of the performer, walking in "wheelbarrow" fashion (not shown).

ARM CIRCLES

Purpose: To provide adequate stimulation to the shoulders in the promotion of flexibility. This exercise can also be used at the end of a training session to relax the body.

Performance: Stand upright with the arms outstretched to the side, palms up, at shoulder height. The feet are spread as wide as the shoulders. Hold the head erect, eyes to the front. #1.

Keep the arms straight and begin to describe small circles with the fingers, swinging the whole arm in a straight, outstretched manner. The circular motion is made slowly in a clockwise direction, pulling the outstretched arms backward as far as possible. #2. Continue this motion for at least 20 complete circles.

Turn the palms down and continue the circling in a reverse direction (counter-clockwise) for at least 20 complete circles. Reverse once again, and complete 20 more circular motions in a clockwise direction.

Key Points: The arms and the circles must not be allowed to drop below shoulder level. Pulling the arms back during the circular motion increases the benefit of the exercise.

GRIP AND PULL

Purpose: A method of developing gripping ability and speed in pulling. Especially good for the wrists and forearms.

Performance: Stand in the basic Natural Posture of Judo (Shizenhontai) or with the legs slightly wider. The body rests squarely over the feet with the weight primarily on the balls of the feet. The head is erect, eyes to the front. Hold the arms straight to the front, without stiffness, but fully extended, palms down, fingers extended. #1.

Keeping your body in place, begin to draw your hands to the rear, bending your elbows and turning your hands so that the palms face inwards. #2. Continue pulling with your arms until your hands are near your chest, palms upward. Clench the fingers together making a fist. #3.

Thrust both arms forward, rotating the hands so that the palms again face downward, fingers open, as in the original starting position in #1. Repeat this complete movement at least 20 times.

Key Points: As the arms are pulled back, the arms rotate, dropping the elbows and bringing the palms upward. The fingers are forcibly clenched into a fist. This rear motion must be done quickly and with a snap. The forward thrusting motion need not be speedy.

WRIST ROTATIONS

Purpose: A gentle exercise to loosen and make flexible the wrist joints and associated muscles.

Performance: A great variety of these exercises exist and the above pictures will suggest some of the most used. #1–6.

Key Points: It is absolutely essential to obtain a full rotation, flex, or movement of the wrist joint. In all exercises, this emphasis must be borne in mind. This exercise is useful at the close of heavy exercise, to relax the forearms and is used as Shumatsu Undo.

PLATE 9. Isao Inokuma, 5 Dan, demonstrating his favorite Supplementary Exercise—Uchikomi for Ippon Seoinage.

CHAPTER 8

Supplementary Exercises

A man who goes over what he has already learned and gains some new understanding from it, is worthy to be a teacher.
Confucius

General Discussion: Exercises in this classification are primarily for the Judo exponent's use, since the movements are purposeful and are adapted toward developing a pattern and technique. Each movement must be performed on the basis of understanding the technique implied.

The study of Judo techniques which require the operator to stand on his two feet, such as the various Nage Waza, should be given at least 90% consideration during the first six months of a beginners study of Judo, the remainder of time or 10% being applied to a study of Katame Waza. In the latter study, the Osaekomi Waza are emphasized. The second six months of study should be devoted to a 75–80% study of Nage Waza. Judo students with more than one year of experience should devote about 75% of their time to the study of methods of throwing. Advanced Judo trainees should strive for a 70–30% study of throwing and grappling respectively.

It is generally conceded that the perfection of throwing techniques requires constant application of Judo fundamentals, and is more difficult to master than the grappling techniques. The truth of this declaration is open to discussion, but is of little consequence here. More important to the instructor and the trainee is the fact that the throwing techniques do not allow the use of great strength as do the grappling techniques. While true technique in either category, throwing or grappling, uses strength wisely in accordance with Judo principles, beginners are more apt to apply *excess strength* in grappling, where it is easier to obtain effect by the use of physical force. For this reason, most instructors discourage Katame study, insisting that beginning trainees perform the characteristic light, fast, movements of Judo most easily made in throwing. All beginning emphasis should center around the techniques of throwing.

All levels of true Judo performance make use, without exception, of Supplementary Exercises. There can be little or no real progress without constant practice of this type of exercise. Japanese champions, both individual and team, make daily use of these movements to achieve the perfection they possess. The exercises that follow in this chapter are not exhaustive, but represent the basic and common movements considered adequate for training under all but highly specialized conditions. These exercises are indispensible in developing a proper use of the body in the execution of throwing techniques. To the Judo exponent, these exercises are practiced by the method known as *Uchikomi* (fitting action), or *Butsukari*.

Equipment: Very little equipment is necessary to perform the Supplementary Exercises. Actually, an adequate training program can be built upon those movements requiring no equipment. However, if elastic materials, bicycle inner tubes, etc., *(see below)* are used, safety must be a keynote of observance. The use of worn or badly weakened elastic is to be discouraged, and instructors should frequently check all equipment used and insist on keeping all in good repair. A proper mat surface should be provided, though the exercises which follow can be performed on unpadded surfaces.

Application: In the performance of these exercises, like the Preparatory Exercises, instructors should insist upon *class participation* of all trainees in the Supplementary Exercises. Individuals practicing as individuals, must take self-initiative and perform these exercises. Supplementary Exercises should be used during a period of from 15 to 40 minutes directly following the Preparatory Exercises and the practice of Ukemi. Among champions, these exercises are never excluded from the daily training routine, and immediately after a suitable warm-up and the practice of falling techniques, these movements are practiced either in *Tandoku Renshu* (solo practice) or *Sotai Renshu* (partner practice) style. Just prior to contest, about 5 minutes are devoted to Supplementary Exercises, usually in Sotai Renshu style, using the method of Uchikomi (fully described in this chapter).

Each selected movement must be done with precision and quickness. Lightness of motion is to be sought in order to develop the grace and harmony of all body parts working as a unit. The student should begin a movement somewhat slowly and "pick up" speed as he carries out the repetitions. Attention must be paid to the fundamental qualities of the technique implied, the Kuzushi, Tsukuri, and though not actually carried out, the transference of your body power to the Kake phase of the technique. The emphasis is always placed on proper from—then speed. Performance of Supplementary Exercises as Tandoku Renshu may utilize any of the throwing techniques of Judo or the characteristic movements of Judo for body management and postural control such as Taisabaki (body turning), Tsugi Ashi (follow-foot), Ayumi Ashi (normal Judo walking), and Sukashi (evasive action). In this book we will treat only a fundamental Taisabaki exercise and representative throwing techniques. Also see pages 82–83.

Solo performance of the various throwing movements by beginners can be regulated by the count control of the instructor. At the count of "one," the trainees should apply Kuzushi, at the count of "two," the trainees should apply Tsukuri, and on the count of "three," the trainees complete the movement, imitating a completion of Kake. The use of such a controlled study should be discontinued just as soon as the basic mechanics of the movements are understood and the training should be carried out with

each trainee moving at his own rate of speed without a count as a guide. This is necessary because true efficient technique in Judo is not just a mechanical "one-two-three" process, and must be thought of and developed as one continuous and harmonious body action. The beginning student who is left to perform the Supplementary Exercises without supervision will not usually derive benefit from his performance due to a lack of enthusiasm and "loose" or "unspirited" movement. Then too, improper form cannot always be detected by the performer who may develop bad habits from such improper performance. More advanced trainees can of course, do these exercises without supervision. The solo exercises can be made with or without equipment. (See exercises, pages 182–189.)

Performance of the Supplementary Exercises as Sotai Renshu may also utilize any of the throwing techniques of Judo or the characteristic movements of Judo for body management and postural control, except that certain movements do not easily lend themselves to such partner study. The instructor will by experience determine those techniques which are most easily performed as a partner movement. The throwing techniques can be performed in the method of Uchikomi or Butsukari, which is without rival in the development of correct Judo performance and is the basis of all championship levels of excellence. Uchikomi is a light, fast, coordinated movement in the style of a Judo throwing technique, repeated over and over against an opponent without actually throwing that opponent. The partners are termed *Tori* (active partner who executes the throwing motion) and *Uke* (passive partner who receives the throwing motion). Tori executes a throwing technique movement against Uke, using a light, fast motion, and concentrating on good form. Tori actually should apply Kuzushi and Tsukuri and then return to his starting position without throwing Uke. This process is quickly repeated over and over again for the desired amount of repetitions. The partners then reverse roles. Generally, Uke should allow Tori to secure his technique without resistance. In this case, Uke may actually be lifted off his feet or otherwise severely unbalanced. Uke should not in his desire to cooperate with Tori, anticipate Tori's movement and turn his body or in any way become too easy a target for Tori. While allowing Tori to enter and obtain his technique, Uke should nevertheless attempt to maintain proper Judo posture without extreme stiffness of body or arms. Under special training conditions, Tori may greatly exaggerate his form, or Uke may stiffen trying to block Tori's attempt at a technique, or may offer evasive action in the form of Taisabaki or Sukashi movements. Such Uchikomi becomes a powerful and "slambang" affair, and can only be used by advanced Judo exponents if benefit is to be derived. Occasionally Uchikomi will be performed against two opponents who are fitted closely together. This method is utilized in only the Owaza (major techniques) such as the *Tsurikomigoshi*, the *Hanegoshi*, the *Uchimata*, the *Seoinage*, etc. Heavy resistance is offered in this manner, and Tori must be well versed in applying correct Kuzushi and Tsukuri if he is to succeed, for if two big opponents are utilized, no amount of strength humanly possible will avail on a strength alone basis. This method should only be used by expert Judo exponents. A more suitable method providing ample resistance to Tori's efforts can be had if another partner will hold Uke's obi from the rear as Tori applies his technique. In the practice of Uchikomi, the Japanese Judo champions utilize a refinement which has proven to be one of the most progressive and practical methods of developing proper and powerful throwing technique. Uchikomi is practiced as normal, but on periodically spaced movements, usually the 5th or 10th, Uke is thrown to the mat. If for example, Tori performs Uchikomi for 25 consecutive repetitions of a movement, he will "throw away" his Uke every 5th movement. This process provides a strong workout and allows Tori to "feel" his technique and determine his progress. See #1 to #8, p. 181, and #1 to #12 page 189 and also refer to page 82 for additional information about Uchikomi.

Selection of Exercises: The choice of which exercises to perform depends largely on the experience of the Judo exponent. Beginners should perform at least 3 different throwing movements, selecting one from each classificatior. of hand, waist, and leg categories (page 181). These may be made Tandoku Renshu, with or without equipment, or Sotai Renshu in Uchikomi style. More advanced exponents may follow the same general pattern or may specialize on one or two movements. Those movements listed in Table B are considered adequate for general training, though many other good movements can be selected. Beginners should spend more time on the Taisabaki than advanced students, but should not neglect the throwing techniques. It should be noted that the *Ashiharai* movement is best suited for Tandoku Renshu and is often included in the Preparatory Exercises, but is categorically included in this chapter as a throwing technique.

Repetitions: The conditions under which training takes place—age, sex, physical condition, and the seriousness of purpose are all factors which affect the number of repetitions of the Supplementary Exercises. The instructor must be intelligently guided by these factors and should require repetitions in proportion to the circumstances. Serious Judo exponents and Judo champions will daily specialize in one of the basic throwing techniques, usually their "pet" throw, and perform it at least 400 times during the course of a day's training. The authors can recall their own training methods, in which, daily, 1000 repetitions would be performed in a 2–3 hour period before commencing actual Randori. Indeed, the authors have, for short periods of time, specialized on the Ashiharai movement and have performed as many as 10,000 repetitions in one day! These are "limit" performances and should not be considered as generally advisable, nor should they be imitated by those persons whose physical condition is not at the peak of excellence. Aside from harm to the body which might occur, it is physiologically established that extreme muscle fatigue does not allow for proper muscular contraction and while the student may have good intentions by his intense study and practice, his bodily fatigue will actually prohibit him from making proper responses and movements. Basic needs are met by performing 50 to 100 repetitions of a movement in good form, daily, or at each training session. Exception to this is the Ashiharai which must be performed at least 200 times alternately with each foot, for a total of 400 repetitions, if the proper pattern is to develop. (1000 repetitions—500 each side—takes 25–30 minutes.) In any case, *form* of the movement should be the key stress.

Order of Exercises: Instructors should feel free to take unlimited latitude in choosing the order of exercises. The actual movements will be determined by the level of experience of the class or individuals, or their needs at the time. Since the body has already been adequately "warmed-up" by the use of the Preparatory Exercises and Ukemi, there is no danger of injuring the muscles by performing a more severe movement. Should specialization in one movement be desired to emphasize the fundamentals of that movement, select one movement and perform it for the desired repetitions. Take a short rest and re-perform it. After another short rest, perform it once again, using this "set" method to achieve your purpose. The workout, in this manner, can be regulated from a very light one to an extremely heavy one as more and more "sets" are performed.

Non Judo Exponents: These movements may be lacking in purpose for other than Judoka, but if these movements are utilized to obtain body coordination, and stretching of muscles, they will constitute an interesting diversion from the usual exercises. The use of the solo performance is recommended, using the movements of Taisabaki, Ashiharai, and Uchimata as selections.

Table B
SUPPLEMENTARY EXERCISES (page 182)

Body Turning (Taisabaki) (page 182)
1. Composite Exercise (page 182)

Waist Techniques (Koshi Waza) (page 185)
1. Tsurikomigoshi (Lift-pull Loins) (page 185)
*2. Uchimata (Inner Thigh) (page 186)

Leg Techniques (Ashi Waza) (page 183)
1. Ashiharai (Foot Sweep) (page 183)
2. Osotogari (Major Outer Reaping) (page 184)

Hand Techniques (Te Waza) (page 187)
1. Ippon Seoinage (Shoulder Throw) (page 187)
2. Taiotoshi (Body Drop) (page 188)

* The Uchimata is correctly classified by Kodokan as a Leg Technique (Ashi Waza) in its pure form, but execution can be performed whereby the loins are deeply inserted with close contact against the opponents abdominal region. Such is the understanding the student should have when executing the Uchimata under the conditions of these exercises.

COMPOSITE EXERCISE

Purpose: A method of developing facility for management of the body primarily concerned with the turning action of the body, useful in attack or defense methods of Judo.

Performance: Stand in the basic Natural Posture of Judo known as Shizenhontai. The body is relaxed, though alert, with the feet about the width of the shoulders apart, toes pointed slightly outward. Rest the body squarely over the feet, with the weight falling primarily on the balls of the feet. Hold the head erect with the eyes to the front. The arms hang loosely at the sides. #1.

Step circularly to your left front, the toes of your left foot pointed slightly inward. #2.

Shift your weight from your right foot to your left foot, drawing your right foot toward your now firmly weighted left foot. #3.

Continue drawing your right foot until it comes to rest under your body in the position of the basic Natural Posture. #4. You now face 90° to the right and a pace forward from your beginning position in #1.

Return to the starting position in #1 by reversing the movements shown, finally arriving at the desired position. Move similarly to the right as described by #5 to #7, returning to the original starting position, #1, to complete the movement.

This movement, from starting position to the left and return, and to the right and return, is *one complete movement*. Repeat this movement at least 25 times.

Key Points: The turning must be circular, actually gaining a pace forward from the starting position. The body must turn as if it were a hinged door. The head must be held erect, with the eyes to the front. The weight of the body is centered over the feet, but should feel as though a sheet of paper could be slid under the heels at all times. The entire movement, must be made with a rhythm so as to "flow" smoothly and evenly. Avoid jerky movement.

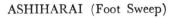

ASHIHARAI (Foot Sweep)

Purpose: A method of developing an effective sweeping action useful in various throwing and countering techniques of Judo. Promotes flexibility and coordination of the entire body power applied via the abdominal region through the leg.

Performance: Stand in the basic Natural Posture of Judo known as Shizen-hontai (fully described on page 182). #1.

Step wide, slightly to your oblique left front with your left foot, bending the knee slightly forward, with the toes pointing outward. #2.

Sweep the right foot circularly to your left, by shifting your body weight to the left foot. Your right foot is curved so that the edge of the little toe brushes lightly over the mat surface. The sole of the foot is directed vertically along the mat. #3.

Continue the sweeping action of your right foot to a point beyond your left foot, bending the weighted left leg slightly to allow you to dip your body to the right. The body is straight from head to the toes of the right foot. The edge of the little toe of the right foot contacts the mat throughout the entire arc of the sweep. #4.

Return the body to an erect position by withdrawing the extended right foot, and as the body rights, #1, step the right foot widely to your right oblique front, with your toes pointing outward. Your right knee is slightly bent. #5.

Sweep the left foot circularly to the right, by shifting your body weight to the right foot. Your left foot is curved so that the edge of the little toe brushes lightly over the mat surface. The sole of the foot is directed vertically along the mat. #6.

Continue the sweeping action of your left foot to a point beyond your right foot, bending the weighted right leg slightly to allow you to dip your body to the left. The body is straight from head to the toes of the left foot. The edge of the little toes of the left foot contacts the mat throughout the entire arc of the sweep. #7.

Reverse the performance, sweeping again to the left, then right, etc. Repeat this movement at least 200 times to each side.

Key Points: It is essential that the sweeping be done with the power of the *entire body*. The leg held straight, only transmits the power of the body. To ensure this, the body must be made to move, abdominal region forward, in the direction of the sweep. A *wide* step will accomplish this. The foot must be curved as shown. #8. Power is concentrated in the little toe of the sweeping foot. The sweeping foot should not leave the mat. Hands may be moved in coordination with the legs (not shown), simulating hand action the opponent's Judogi.

OSOTOGARI (Major Outer Reaping)

Purpose: A method of developing a coordinated body and leg action useful in attacking the opponent with Osotogari. Promotes body coordination and strength in back, legs, and abdominal region. Promotes good balance.

Performance: Stand in the Right Natural Posture of Judo known as Migi Shizentai. The body is relaxed, though alert, with the feet about the width of the shoulders apart toes pointing slightly outward. The right foot is advanced about twelve inches. The body rests squarely over the feet. Hold head erect and the eyes to the front. Outstretch the right arm as if grasping the opponent's left lapel at the level of the collarbone. Hold the left arm lower and closer to your body as if grasping the opponent's sleeve, just below his elbow. #1.

Step forward with the left foot, knee bent, the weight of the body over the left foot. The chest is held high, head erect. Bend the right arm so as to bring the right hand alongside your right shoulder, permitting your body to contact the opponent's right side with your right side. Hold the left hand low alongside your left hip. Visualize pulling the opponent slightly upward and to your right chest with your right hand, while twisting his body to your left by pulling backward and down with your left hand (pull toward your belt). #2.

Swing the right leg forward and behind the right thigh of the imaginary opponent. Center your hip over your left foot. Your hip should be visualized touching and slightly passing behind the opponent's right hip. The toes of your attacking foot are pointed downward. The entire weight of your body must be centered over your left foot, knee slightly bent. Press your right chest hard against your opponent. #3.

Reap the right leg backward, toes pointed downward, leg held straight, as you lower your upper body forward and downward. Your body now describes a letter T, balancing over the left foot. The right arm pushes the opponent backward, quickly downward and to the opponent's right rear corner, with the edge of the arm from elbow to the wrist, while the left hand pulls the opponent in to your belt region. #4. Return to the starting position in #1, and repeat the movement at least 50 times.

Key Points: The performer must visualize his body action as one which will place his opponent in a broken-balance position to the opponent's right back corner. The upper body and leg motion must be executed as one motion. The left leg must be placed on a line with the opponent's two feet. The foot of the weighted leg must be turned slightly inward. This movement can be executed on the left side by reversing the instructions. (Recall points pages 82–83.)

TSURIKOMIGOSHI (Lift-pull Loins)

Purpose: A method of developing a coordinated body and leg action useful in attacking the opponent with Tsurikomigoshi. Promotes body coordina tion and strength in back, legs, and abdominal region.

Performance: Stand in either the basic Natural Posture or Right Natural Posture of Judo known as Shizenhontai and Migi Shizentai respectively (fully described on pages 182 and 184). Outstretch the right arm as if grasping the opponent's left lapel at a point just at the collarbone. Hold the left arm lower and closer to your body as if grasping the opponent's sleeve, just below his elbow. #1.

Step forward with the right foot, placing the foot in front of the imaginary opponent's right foot. Twist the body slightly to the left. The toes of your right foot are slightly turned to your left. Your weight rests on the toes of your right foot, and the ball of the left foot. With your right hand, draw the opponent onto the toes of his right foot, as you pull the opponent forward with your left hand. #2.

Turn your body to your left by circularly sliding the left foot behind your right foot, sinking down by lowering the knees as you place your feet inside and parallel to the opponent's feet. Your right elbow is thrust under the opponent's left armpit, while your left hand pulls the opponent's body across your chest. Your back is kept straight in a deep crouch designed to bring the back of your hips in contact with the thighs of the opponent. #3. Shown from opposite side (left).

Straighten the legs, pushing your hips backward as you pull your right hand into your ear and your left hand and arm around your chest just under your chin. Lean your head to the left and turn to the left as your left hand pulls across your chest. As your body twists, the right hand drives upward and forward. #4.

Return to the starting position in #1 and repeat the movement at least 50 times.

Key Points: The performer must visualize his body action as one which will place his opponent in a broken-balance position to the opponent's right-front corner. The initial step forward with your right foot must not be too close to the opponent, but should rather be 6–10 inches in front of his advanced right foot. The right side of your body must be kept in close contact with the opponent's chest at all times. Get down low and pull hard. This movement can be executed on the left side by reversing the instruction (recall points, pages 82–83).

UCHIMATA (Inner Thigh)

Purpose: A method of developing a coordinated body and leg action useful in attacking the opponent with Uchimata. Promotes balance, coordination, and strength in the back, legs, and abdominal region.

Performance: Stand in the basic Natural Posture or Right Natural Posture of Judo known as Shizenhontai and Migi Shizentai respectively (fully described on pages 182 and 184). Your right hand rests against a wall at shoulder height, while your left hand simulates gripping the opponent's Judogi at a point just below the elbow. #1.

Draw your left foot circularly behind your right heel, so that the left foot makes an approximate right angle with the right foot. Twist your body to the left as you do this, shifting the weight of your body to the left foot. Your right hand acts as a stabilizer in this movement, but should be visualized as pulling the opponent upward onto his toes. Your left hand pulls across your waist. #2.

Place the full weight of your body on your left and reap your right leg backward and up between the thighs of the imaginary opponent. Lower the head and upper part of the body as though trying to place your forehead on the mat. With your right hand, push outward and upward as your left hand pulls hard across your waist. Twist your body to the left. Your head should now be lower than your right foot, and your body assumes the position of a slanted T. #3.

Return to the starting position in #1, and repeat the movement at least 50 times.

Key Points: The performer must visualize his body action as one which will place his opponent in a broken-balance position to the opponent's right-front corner. Initially, as your weight is shifted onto your left leg, the left leg must be slightly bent. Your hip must be deeply inserted in this action so as to simulate touching the opponent's lower abdominal region. The toes of the weighted left leg must be pointed in the direction of the intended throw. The upward reap of the leg must be coordinated with the downward lowering of the upper body and head. Concentrate on a strong hip movement and a powerful lifting action of the rear thigh of the outstretched leg which must not be bent at the knee. Point the toes. This movement can be executed on the left side by reversing the instructions.

IPPON SEOINAGE (Shoulder Throw)

Purpose: A method of developing a coordinated body, arm, and leg action useful in attacking the opponent with Seoinage. Promotes general body development with emphasis on the legs, back, and arms.

Performance: Stand in the basic Natural Posture or the Right Natural Posture of Judo known as Shizenhontai and Migi Shizentai respectively (fully described on pages 182 and 184). Outstretch the right arm as if grasping the opponent's left lapel at a point just below the collarbone. Hold the left arm lower and close to your body as if grasping the opponent's sleeve, just below his elbow. #1.

Step forward with the right foot, placing the foot in front of the imaginary opponent's right foot. Twist the body slightly to the left. Turn the toes of your right foot slightly to your left. Your weight now rests on the toe of your right foot and the ball of the left foot. Using your right hand, draw the opponent onto the toes of his right foot, as your left hand pulls the opponent forward. #2.

Turn your body to the left by circularly sliding the left foot behind your right foot, sinking down by bending the knees as you place your feet inside and parallel to the opponent's feet. Simultaneously, as you turn your body to the left, release your grip of the opponent's left lapel with your right hand, and insert your right arm under your opponent's right armpit, thrusting your arm so that you are able to put your right shoulder into his right armpit. Bend your inserted right arm and turn the hand so that the palm faces you. With your right hand grasp his right upper-sleeve or right shoulder. Keep your back straight in order to bring the opponent's chest firmly against your back. #3.

Continue turning your body to the left, as you straighten your legs, pushing your hips slightly backward. Pull the opponent with both hands so that he comes up and over your right hip and shoulder region. The feet pivot slightly to the left on the balls of the feet as you straighten the legs. Lean your head to the left and twist to look behind you. #4. Return to the starting position in #1, and repeat the movement at least 50 times.

Key Points: The performer must visualize his body action as one which will place his opponent in a broken-balance position to the opponent's right-front corner. Initially, as your weight is shifted onto your right leg, the right leg must be slightly bent. As your body twists around to your left and during the course of the actual throwing movement, your right shoulder must be held in the opponent's right arm pit by a strong pulling action of the left hand which pulls the opponent's right arm around your chest just under your chin. Any gap between your back and your opponent' chest will lessen the effectiveness of the throw. Try to draw your left shoulder around far enough so that your left side of your back touches the opponent's left chest. This will automatically ensure back-chest contact. The straightening of the legs and the pulling of the arms must be a well-coordinated action. This movement can be executed on the left side by reversing the instructions (recall points, pages 82–83).

TAIOTOSHI (Body Drop)

Purpose: A method of developing a coordinated body, arm, and leg action useful in attacking the opponent with Taiotoshi. Promotes general body development, coordination, balance, and strength in the arms, legs, and abdominal region.

Performance: Stand in the basic Natural Posture or the Right Natural Posture of Judo known as Shizenhontai and Migi Shizentai respectively (fully described on pages 182 and 184). Outstretch the right arm as if grasping the opponent's left lapel at the collarbone. Hold the left arm lower and closer to your body as if grasping the opponent's sleeve, just below his elbow. #1.

Step forward with the right foot, placing the foot in front of the imaginary opponent's right foot. Twist the body slightly to the left. Turn the toes of your right foot slightly to your left. Your weight now rests on the toe of your right foot and the ball of the left foot. Using your right hand, draw the opponent onto the toes of his right foot, as your left hand pulls the opponent forward. #2.

Turn your body to the left by circularly sliding the left foot behind you so that the left foot comes to rest slightly in front of and a bit wider than the opponent's left foot. Your body is presented with its back to the opponent's front. Simultaneously, your right hand pulls and lifts the imaginary opponent upward to his right-front corner while your left hand pulls the opponent forward. #3.

Lower your body quickly by bending your left knee. Twist your body to the left and stab your right leg in front of and close to the right leg of the imaginary opponent at a point just above his ankle, but below his knee. Simultaneously, your right hand pushes the left chest of the opponent with the edge of the right arm from elbow to the wrist, while the left hand pulls the opponent forward and slightly downward #4 and #5. Return to the starting position in #1, and repeat the movement at least 50 times.

Key Points: The performer must visualize his body action as one which will place his opponent in a broken-balance position to the opponent's right-front corner. Initially, as your weight is shifted onto your right leg, the right leg must be slightly bent. As your body twists around to your left and during the course of the actual throwing movement, your left leg is bent considerably so that your body may be placed across the front of your opponent at a low position. The right knee is placed across the right leg of the opponent with the knee slightly bent *(see #5)*, and rests on the toes or the ball of the foot with the heel raised. The placing (stabbing action) of the right leg and the twisting of the body to the with the action of the hands. The point at which the right hand changes with the action of the hand. The point at which the right hand changes from an upward pull to a push (edge of the right arm from elbow to wrist) *outward* and forward, is critical in effective timing of this throw. Notice that the left hand continues pulling during the entire course of the movement. Care must be taken not to pull downward too much as this will nullify the throwing efforts. Study #5 carefully to determine the correct direction of pull with the left hand. In this position, #5, the body describes a straight line from head to the extended right foot. Any marked forward bend or sway from the hips will result in failure of the throw. The performers hip or buttocks do not touch the opponent at any point. This movement can be executed on the left side by reversing the instructions.

Sotai Uchikomi—Ippon Seoinage

Sotai Uchikomi—Taiotoshi

Sotai Uchikomi—Tsurikomigoshi

PLATE 10. Isao Inokuma, 5 Dan, demonstrating his favorite Compound Exercise—Bridge and Spin.

CHAPTER 9

Compound Exercises

A good system is twice blessed—it blesses him that trains and him that's trained.

Spenser

General Discussion: Designed as severe conditioning exercises which develop endurance and afford precision movements for special situations in Judo, these exercises will give the student increased facility in Katame Waza.

General study of Katame Waza should consume only about 10% of training time during the first six months of the students Judo study, the remainder of the time being devoted to the Nage Waza. During this first period study of grappling, the Osaekomi Waza (holding techniques) should be emphasized as this is the basic category of grappling study and success with Shime and Kansetsu Waza (choking and joint locking techniques) depends almost entirely upon facility with Osaekomi Waza. The second six months of the student's learning should mark the increase in study of Katame Waza to about 20–25% of the training time. Students with over one year of Judo experience should give at least 25% of their study to this category of Judo technique. The tendency to ignore Katame Waza is disastrous to finished Judo technique, and is often the result of the instructor being led to believe that true Judo technique is only found in the throwing category. This is completely erroneous and the Judo exponent who is lacking proficiency in grappling is on insecure footing. Then too, some instructors believe that grappling is uninteresting to the student who is usually more intrigued by the visually spectacular throwing techniques. Finally, the teaching of grappling requires much exertion and energy expenditure on the part of the instructor when compared to the teaching of throwing, and many instructors are prone to refrain from such heavy contact work.

Judo performance can be likened to a two-wheeled coach. One wheel—Nage Waza, the other, Katame Waza. The absence or malformation of either wheel produces an inferior and usually highly unsatisfactory journey no matter how smooth the path—the instructor

—provided. Judo students must develop their grappling abilities, and will come to realize the beauty and sense of accomplishment in this sometimes neglected category. There can be no mastery of Judo without proficiency in this department. A study of all top level competitive Judo revealed that the strongest champions were masters at both throwing and grappling. These exercises are indispensable to the study of the Katame Waza.

Equipment: No special equipment is necessary for the study of the Compound Exercises; however, the mat surface should meet the normal requirements of size, cleanliness, and serviceability.

Application: Instructors should insist on *class participation* of all students in the performance of the Compound Exercises. Individuals practicing as individuals must take self-initiative and perform these exercises. Compound Exercises can be used in a variety of ways in the normal training routine or when grappling is not in a particular study period. These exercises can be left out entirely, though this is not particularly advisable as a general practice. Some instructors see fit to use the Compound Exercises as part of the normal "warm-up" early in the training period. While this is permissible, it is assumed that the normal Preparatory Exercises provide all the stimulation to the muscles that is necessary for a "warm-up," and the Compound Exercises can better be utilized within their intended purpose of developing special abilities for special situations in Judo. On this basis, the Compound Exercises should be performed somewhere "inside" the training program, just prior to grappling study or free exercise in grappling. A period of from 10–15 minutes is usually sufficient in all but specialized training emphasizing grappling.

Since these exercises are usually performed as an endurance exercise type, they should be avoided until conditioning is receptive to strenuous exertion. Each movement must be done with precision and rhythm characteristic to applications on the ground. Special effort must be made to orient oneself continually even though in an inverted or twisted position. Balance similar to standing must be developed. Breathing must be coordinated with movement for efficient coupling of upper and lower major body muscles. It is well if the performer understands just what the motion being applied is related to and of what situation it is indicative. To merely exercise mechanically is of little value.

The exercises are usually performed in one spot on the mat, but certain movements require actual linear movement. Instructors will have to organize the class according to the needs of the exercises selected.

Selection of Exercises: Here to, as in the Supplementary Exercises, order of the exercises is dependent upon the level of experience of the performers and their current needs. Generally, at least two of the exercises shownin Table C (page 193) should be selected and performed just prior to contact grappling practice. Special training involving extensive grappling study should utilize four of five of these exercises in one Judo training period. The movements listed in Table C are not exhaustive, but are considered adequate for most training needs.

Repetitions: The mixed nature of these exercises makes a generalization about performance of repetitions impossible. Since these movements are in part an endurance developer, high repetitions should be utilized. In the case of the stationary exercises, requiring no linear displacement, 25–100 repetitions are adequate, while the exercises requiring movement should be performed for a distance of from 20 to 50 feet. Some instructors ignore repetition count and require the performance of all movements for a period of time—one, two, or three minutes without rest. This is quite severe and will provide a heavy workout.

Order of Exercises: Instructors should feel free to take unlimited latitude in choosing the order of the exercises.

Non-Judo Exponents: These exercises can be used as a method of developing increased stamina and a sense of balance while very actively stimulating the internal organs. It is not recommended that these exercises be performed until a relatively good physical condition is achieved.

Table C
COMPOUND EXERCISES (page 193)

PRONE CRAWLING

Purpose: A method of developing great strength in the arms, shoulders, and upper back. The abdominal muscles are taught to coordinate with the entire body. This exercise will develop tremendous holding power for the Osaekomi Waza of Judo.

Performance: Lie face down on a smooth surface, extending the arms forward, making a fist of each hand and placing the little finger side of each fist on the ground. Hold the head erect. Spread the legs wide, with the toes pointed outward. Arch the back slightly. #1 and #2.

Using only the pulling power of the arms, drag the body forward until the fists come under the shoulders. Keep the feet and lower body in contact with the ground at all times. The body must remain in an arched position as the arms pull. #3 and #4.

Again extend the arms forward and resume the position shown in #1 and #2.

Repeat the pulling with the arms as described above, dragging the body forward. Crawl at least 20 feet by this method before finishing this movement.

Key Points: This method can be made less severe by keeping the legs together, and slightly bending the knees so that the arches of the feet are off the ground (only the kneecaps touch) as you drag the body forward.

PRONE CRAWLING (alternate)

Purpose: A method of developing strength in the arms, shoulders, and upper back. The abdominal muscles are taught to coordinate with the entire body. This exercise is an alternate method of prone crawling, less severe, and is useful as an exercise for young children or those trainees who lack sufficient strength in the arms to perform the regular method. Develops holding power for Katame Waza.

Performance: Lie face down on a smooth surface, extending the arms forward, making a fist of each hand and placing the little finger side of each fist on the ground. Hold the head erect. Spread the legs wide, with the toes pointed outward. Arch the back slightly. #1.

Reach forward with one arm, making contact with the elbow of that arm. Using the power of the arm, pull the body forward until the elbow comes under the body. Then, reach forward with the other arm, making contact with the elbow of that arm. Using the power of that arm, pull the body forward as before, until the elbow comes under the body once again. #2 and #3.

Alternately reach forward, using the elbow as a point of contact to pull the body, and crawl at least 20 feet by this method before finishing the movement.

Key Points: This method can be made still less severe by keeping the legs together, and slightly bending the knees so that the arches of the feet are off the ground, (only the kneecaps touch) as you drag the body forward. The body must remain in an arched position, head erect. In this alternate method, the body will wiggle as you move forward. Recommended by S. Sato, 6 Dan.

BODY TURNING (Taisabaki)

Purpose: A method of developing coordinated twisting of the body, affording python-like ability to escape an opponent (Nogarekata) who is attempting to control your body on the ground. The entire body is strengthened by this exercise.

Performance: Lie on your back on a smooth surface with your knees bent and feet flat on the ground. Hold your head off the ground, chin into the chest. Rest your hands vertically above the elbows, which rest on the ground. #1.

Turn onto your right shoulder by pressing the left foot against the ground and draw your right knee toward your chest. Thrust your arms downward toward your right knee. Jackknife your buttocks backward. #2.

Raise your buttocks into the air by pressing hard with both feet against the ground. Swing your body slightly to the right, bringing the feet close together as you rock up onto the right shoulder and neck region. Turn your head, right ear down to the ground. Your hands support you as in #3. Continue to swing your body around to the right, bringing the weight of your body onto the back of your right shoulder. #4.

Allow your body to roll to the left, and come into position as shown in #5.

Continue rolling to the left and repeat the movements shown in #2, #3 and #4, reversing the directions so that your body is in the positions shown in #6 and #7.

Come back to the position shown in #1 and without hesitation, repeat the entire sequence, from right to left, until you have actually moved your body for at least 20 feet by this method.

Key Points: This motion must be rhythmic and continuous without any jerky movements. Only practice will establish this pattern of exercise.

Recommended by Chugo Sato, 7 Dan.

SIT THRUS

Purpose: A method of developing coordinated shifting of weight useful in changing techniques of holding (Osaekomi Waza). The arms, shoulders, and abdominal regions are strengthened by this exercise.

Performance: Lie face down on a smooth surface with your hands flat on the ground, fingers pointed forward, hands a little wider than, but directly under, your shoulders. Spread your legs wider than your hips. Push up to arms length. #1.

Thread your left leg under your body, twisting slightly to the right. Maintain pressure with the hands as a point of support. #2.

Sit down on your left flank, with your left leg outstretched. #3.

Push hard with both hands, lifting your body slightly upward so that you are able to twist your hips to the left, and return your left leg to its starting position as shown in #1.

Repeat this movement to the left, sitting on your right flank. #4 and #5.

Return to the starting position shown in #1. Repeat this movement (to the left and to the right) at least 15 times.

Key Points: This motion should be rhythmic and continuous without any jerky movements. The buttocks should be kept as close to the ground as possible, so that a quick transfer of hips can be made.

LEG THRUST

Purpose: A method of developing a controlled directional pushing action of the legs, useful in evading and controlling an opponent who is making an attempt to enter (Hairikata) into Katame Waza with you. Strengthens the legs and abdominal muscle groups.

Performance: Lie on your back, head up, chin in, on a smooth surface with your legs slightly raised, knees bent. Rest your hands on your abdominal region. Flex your feet, toes up. #1.

Begin by drawing your right leg and knee to your chest, while simultaneously lowering the left leg and thrusting it forward. Maintain the flexed position of the feet. #2.

Continue drawing your right leg and knee up to a maximum position near the chest, and simultaneously extend your left leg to its fullest position, making sure that it is a few inches off the ground. #3.

Raise the extended left leg slightly, and bend the knee as you bring your left knee to your chest, simultaneously lowering your right leg and thrusting it forward. #4.

Final position shown in #5. Repeat this movement (right and left side alternately) at least 20 times.

Key Points: Your head must be kept off the ground throughout the exercise. The feet must be kept flexed, toes up. The legs describe a reverse rotary "bicycle" action, and thrust with a snapping action at the final extension of each leg. The thrust is made with the sole of each foot.

BRIDGE AND LIFT

Purpose: A method of developing a coordinated pushing, twisting, and pressing action of the body, useful in escaping the grappling attempts of an opponent. Promotes a supple and strong back. Also strengthens the legs and abdominal region.

Performance: Lie on your back on a smooth surface with your feet resting close to your buttocks, soles flat on the ground. Your head is on the ground, while your arms rest on the elbows alongside your body. #1. Lift your buttocks off the ground by pressing hard with both feet. Twist slightly to your right as you turn your head to the right. #2.

Continue lifting your buttocks, causing your stomach to rise high as you increase the body twist to your right. Your head now rests on the ground, right ear down. Push with your hands in a coordinated effort toward your right shoulder using an upward and backward direction. Support your weight in this new position by pressing with your feet. In this completed position, your weight rests on your feet, your right shoulder, and the right side of your head. #3.

Control your lowering to the original starting position. #1.

Repeat this movement to the left side. Return to the starting position and repeat (right and left) at least 15 times.

Key Points: This action must be done with exaggeration and with the feeling that a heavy weight were on your chest. Stretch fully as you bridge and lift, pushing with your arms. Your feet must be kept close under you at all times, with the weight on the toes.

BRIDGE AND SPIN

Purpose: A method of developing a coordinated lifting and turning action of the body, useful in escaping the grappling attempts of an opponent. Produces a strong neck and supple back and abdominal region.

Performance: Assume a low bridging position with your body weight resting on the top of your head and the balls of your feet. Your feet must be brought deeply under your body. Rest your arms on your body. #1.

Raise your stomach high, by pressing the ground with your feet, coming up onto the toes. Swing your arms up and over your body. #2.

Draw your right shoulder under your body as you twist quickly to your right. Swing your left leg over your right knee and place it in a new position on the ground. Your right arm and shoulder aid your body. #3.

Turn over so that you now face the mat, your body weight resting on the balls of your feet and your forehead. Your hands do not aid this support. Feet are widely spread for balance. #4.

Repeat by twisting back from whence you came, and then twist back again, only this time to the left. Repeat at least 6 times (to each side).

Key Points: Beginners can use their hands and arms to aid the support and balance as the twist is made, but the most benefit is derived if the hands are not used. This twist-over must be done quickly and without delay in order to keep the body from falling over. A favorite Compound Exercise of I. Inokuma, 5 Dan, 1959 Judo Champion of Japan.

HIP SHIFTING

Purpose: A method of developing the correct and powerful pressure of the body useful in holding an opponent to the ground. Promotes flexibility in the hip joints and strengthens the abdominal region.

Performance: Lie face down on a smooth surface with the legs widely spread, toes pointed outward. Raise your upper body (chest) by arching your back. Your abdominal region touches the ground. Hold your head erect and support your weight on the elbows and forearms. #1.

Shift your weight onto your left hip as you slightly raise your right buttock. Slide your right leg toward your head, stiff-legged, sole of the foot pressing the ground. The knee is off the ground, thus preserving the rigidity of the leg. Cast your entire weight onto your left side by pressing hard with your right leg and forcing your breathing into your lower abdominal region. Push your stomach into the mat as you arch. #2.

Return to the starting position. #1.

Repeat this performance on the left side (shifting your weight to your right side, extending the left leg, etc.). #3.

Repeat this movement at least 10 times to each side.

Key Points: This transfer of weight from hip to hip and side to side must be done quickly, and smoothly. The legs must never buckle, but must be held rigid.

LEG CIRCLING

Purpose: A method of developing the correct and powerful use of the legs to evade, control, and unbalance the opponent in Katame Waza. Promotes suppleness of the knees.

Performance: Lie with your back on the mat, knees bent, and feet raised as shown in #1. Fold your hands on the chest. Raise your head off the mat.

Spread your legs slightly, #2, and keep your chin tucked tightly into your chest.

Begin describing large circles, each foot independently of the other. Circle the left foot clock-wise and the right foot counter-clockwise. Then, reverse the action. #3–4.

Repeat these movements at least 25 times, starting slowly and gaining speed as you progress (25 times clockwise, etc.).

Key Points: The knees must be kept supple and not relatively fixed in one place. The body must be slightly arched by keeping the head up off the mat, and chin tucked into the chest.

LEG SWINGING

Purpose: A method of strengthening the abdominal region and to develop a coordinated body action useful in Nogarekata in Katame Waza.

Performance: Lie on your back on the mat. Raise your feet slightly from the mat. Keep your legs together, knees flexible, but legs straight. Hold your head off the mat, chin tucked into your chest. Raise your arms over your head, but keep them slightly bent and flexible. #1.

Roll on to your right side slightly, swinging your legs together to the right. Swing your hands downward together as if to meet your feet. #2. Continue swinging your legs and arms, keeping them together, until your body reaches a jackknife position as shown in #3. Reverse the movement and return to the starting position shown in #1.

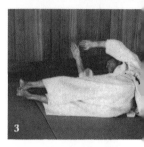

Immediately repeat this movement on the left side by reversing the instructions.

Repeat this movement (to the right and the left sides) at least 10 times.

Key Points: This movement must be a coordinated one in which the entire body is utilized. If done at a rather fast pace, the body will actually move around on the mat, and much mat space will be needed to perform this movement. The chin must remain tucked in to the chest, and the upper back region must be kept free of the mat surface to reduce friction. Recommended by S. Takagaki, 9 Dan.

POLE HANGING

Purpose: A severe method designed to strengthen the muscles necessary to effect powerful holding in Osaekomi Waza.

Performance: Hang from a bar of suitable material (bamboo, metal, etc.) which will support your weight. Either of the two basic positions shown in #1 or #2 will provide a good workout. The legs may be held in either the tuck or right-angled position as shown in #3.

Hang in this position until you become quite tired. The exact amount of time will vary with the individual. Do not stop the hanging at the first sign of fatigue, but rather seek to extend the period as long as you possibly can.

Key Points: The muscles of the arms, back, and abdominal areas must contract and hold this contraction forcibly for the entire time of hanging. Professor Ushijima, 7 Dan, teacher of M. Kimura, 7 Dan, former All-Japan Judo Champion, used this method to train his famous students to develop powerful Osaekomi.

LEG FOLDING (Ashi Sankaku)

Purpose: A method of developing leg action useful in controlling the opponent's actions to prohibit his freedom and thereby reduce his Katame attacking power. Also used to restrict an opponent's action while attacking in Katame Waza.

Performance: Lie on your back on a smooth surface, knees bent and feet raised with the legs slightly apart. Hold your head off the ground, keeping your chin tucked into your chest. Hold your hands on your abdominal region. #1.

Raise one leg (right shown) and fold the other (left shown) so that the instep of that foot is brought in contact with the back of the knee of the raised leg. Your toes of this foot (left) must extend and hook onto the outside surface of your other leg (right). #2 and #3.

Lower the raised leg (right shown), clamping down forcibly on the foot (left shown) which is hooked behind your knee. #4. Unfold your legs and return to the starting position shown in #1. Reverse the instructions and repeat on the other side.

Repeat these movements at least 25 times on each side, starting slowly and gaining speed as you progress.

Key Points: The knees must be kept supple and relatively fixed in one place. Keep the body slightly arched with the head off the ground. The toes of the hooking foot must hook onto the outside of the leg being hooked as shown in #3. Speed in performance of this movement is essential as is strong fixation power once the hold is taken.

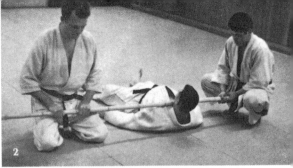

NECK PRESSING

Purpose: A severe method designed to strengthen the muscles of the neck useful in resisting the effects of Shime Waza.

Performance: Lie on your back on a smooth surface. A bamboo pole is placed across your throat and held at each end by a partner. #1.

Both partners apply resistance by pressing down on the ends of the pole causing pressure on your neck. Attempt to sit up, forcing your neck against the pole. The partners should apply enough resistance to just keep you from rising. #2.

Repeat this sit-up attempt at least 5 times.

Key Points: The abdominal region must be tensed in order to bring a strong sit-up action against the pole. A variety of different pressures may be brought against the neck by placing the pole along the sides of the neck, or from a face-down position, on the back of the neck. The force of the pressure can be regulated by the length of the pole used. The longer the pole, the more flex will be present, and the less resistance can be applied. (#1 and #2). Bamboo is recommended as a safe material to use. Regardless, care must be taken not to injure the throat or neck of the trainee. Recommended by K. Shibayama, 6 Dan. If a bamboo pole is unavailable, Neck Pushing (see Preparatory Exercises, page 167) or a variation of that exercise can be satisfactorily used here. #3 to #5 clearly show the necessary details. It is important here to apply steady pressure to the training partner's head so that he is unable to move his head and must resist with all his neck power. A small face towel can be used to keep from slipping off the partner's head.

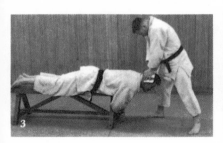

PLATE 11. Isao Inokuma, 5 Dan, demonstrating his favorite Auxiliary Exercise—Barbell Supine Press.

CHAPTER 10

Auxiliary Exercises

I have seen the future, and it works.
Steffens

General **Discussion:** Considered the "aid to strength" exercises, these movements should be performed as augmentation to a normal Judo training program. As such, they are a training complement acting in direct support of the non-special equipment exercises of the normal Judo training program. These exercises are indispensable in building those parts of the body which are lacking in strength or suffer some developmental weakness, but must not be confined only to this application. Utilization as a method to condition the *whole* body should be the primary consideration in mind. A fuller discussion is found in Chapter 5.

All of these movements are of a resistive nature, utilizing weight or other special apparatus and should be though of as methods of increasing body strength—promotion of joint and tendon resistance to injury by developing the ligament cartilages, tendons, and even adding size and thickness to the bones; building vital forces—by strengthening the internal organs and improving their functions of digestion, assimilation, elimination, circulation, and efficiency. They are further, exercises to increase speed, prevent possible slowness of movement and stiffness which sometimes is the result of an improper training program, aids to adequate muscle tonus and tone which keeps the body more supple, flexible, and allows it to develop efficient timing or coordination. No attempt is made in the suggested programs listed separately in Chapter 6 or in the following discussion within this chapter, to offer these exercises as "physique" or "body-building" methods that strive for the immense and proportionate perfection of the human torso, although these exercises will have great developmental effects along those lines. Though not precisely so, Auxiliary Exercises can be termed "weight exercises." All Auxiliary Exercises operate on the principle of resistance exercise, which makes use of the physiological fact that short bursts of activity followed by frequent rest produces muscular hypertrophy.

The use of progressive weight training as a complementary means of improving Judo performance is completely new. While individual Judo exponents have in the past used weight equipment to improve their Judo movements, these individuals have been in the vast minority and their methods have been generally unprincipled and unsystematic. To-day, with the successes of a variety of competitive forms of atheletic endeavor being vast-ly improved by means of weight training, there is a growing awareness of the need for weight training methods applied to Judo to increase contest efficiency. The exercises which follow in this chapter are those exercises which have been investigated by the authors and which have been established as compatible with the needs of Judo. They are not exhaustive, but are considered as adequate for training under most all circum-stances.

Kinesiological studies made on the comparison of the Oriental and Western bodies reveal that almost without exception, the Oriental is stronger in the legs, hips, and ab-dominal region, while the Westerner will sometimes demonstrate superior strength in the arm, shoulder and chest regions. This is partially explained by the fact that in the Orient, particularly Japan and Korea, daily life requires a squatting position for long periods of time such as eating, reading, studying, etc. This action, carried out from infancy, pro-duces in the mature adult an extreme condition of flexibility in the arches, ankles, knees, and hips, combined with extremely powerful fixation muscles in the legs, hips, and ab-dominal belt region. Western Judoka are often amazed at the nonchalant attitude of the Japanese Judo exponent when assuming the traditional sitting posture required in formal Judo discipline. While the Westerner squirms in discomfort and even pain, or is unable to hold this position for more than a few minutes, his Eastern counterpart will rest comfort-ably. The Westerner can never hope to change the unequal ability to utilize the lower trunk muscles with the Western habits of soft chairs and beds. Nor is this necessarily de-sirable except in the case of the athlete, particularly the Judo exponent. If Western Judo exponents will broaden their squatting power, with sensible weight training methods, the now obvious gap will be appreciably closed and with it, the excellence of Western Judo materially increased.

Equipment: Weight training requires special equipment, and most any commercial product can be considered as functional. The variety of barbells, dumbbells, pulley ma-chines, special benches, and other pieces of equipment is great, and offers no problem. However, where unavailability or economic reasons preclude the ownership or use of the necessary equipment, certain homemade equipment will suffice. Improvised apparatus is certainly functional, but the emphasis must be placed on *safety*. The use of weak benches, teetering seats or boxes, and ill-designed bars or bells is to be discouraged. Take time out to construct or supervise the construction of proper equipment and your efforts will be rewarded. Select enough poundages to enable you to move along to the various exercises without long rests in between the movements or sets caused by changing or breaking down and setting up new poundages on the bars and bells. The ambitious trainee will seek the benefits of all types of bars, bells, pulleys, expanders, and pieces of accessory equipment. Variety and interest can be increased with the use of special equipment demonstrated in this book.

The use of a training suit or a sweat suit has been mentioned in Chapter 4. It is equally important as an aid to weight training methods. *Always train warm.* The use of a sweat suit while performing weight training routines is highly recommended. Of course, the Judogi can be used as a substitute, but it is not as satisfactory for this type of exercise as the sweat suit.

Application—General: The nature of the exercises within this category, and the need for specialized equipment makes it nearly imperative that trainees perform these exercises individually, or in groups. Only in institutions which are lavishly equipped can trainees perform in large groups. Instructors should encourage their students to follow weight training whether or not the individual concerned is physically weak or physically exceptional. As far as the authors have been able to determine, beginning or advanced Judo students may enter into progressive weight training exercises without detriment to their Judo study. It is assumed that *sensible* weight training methods are employed, and that a sensibly planned and systematically followed training program be established. Auxiliary Exercises should not form a part of the normal Judo practice. The body will experience fatigue after a use of a balanced program of progressive weight training and it would not be advisable to enter directly into Judo exercise. However, when anything less than a full balanced weight training program is utilized, this may be somewhat modified.

Individuals respond unequally to progressive weight training exercises. What is often good for one, is ill-suited for another. However, we have been able to draw some general guide-signs which can easily be observed. Only experimentation by the individual performing these Auxiliary Exercises can establish what is best for that individual. The trainee is urged to carefully perform and observe his progress over a period of time, and to determine his own optimum routines. This implies that he should never permit himself to be force-driven beyond his natural capabilities. If he does, he will be sapping his vital nerve force which strains and drains the system so that instead of improving, he is actually worsening his physical condition. There is such a thing as "overdoing." The old adage, "...if a little bit is good, more is better," doesn't apply, except within very well-established limits.

There is considerable cleavage between East and West in many respects, Judo notwithstanding. The serious Japanese Judo exponent would no more think of missing his daily Judo session than the Westerner would his "3 squares." For this reason, the authors have conducted considerable experimentation on the subject of how often Auxiliary Exercises of a resistive nature should be performed; when, or what time they should be performed; and how long such a training program should be. Since Eastern World Judo is a daily affair and quite severe, and Western World Judo is more often than not an occasional affair, we have taken special note of this, emphasizing that there is a different approach required to progressive weight training applied to these two dissimilar philosophies.

Application—Daily Judo Training: For the serious minded Judo exponent who makes daily hard Judo training a "must," best results will be had by using progressive weight training on a two to three time per week basis. These workout periods should not be scheduled on consecutive days. Increasing the workouts to four or more per week has in all cases proven impractical and detrimental to the best interests of the Judo exponent. This reference implies that the progressive weight training programs used are full, balanced programs and not merely modified, abbreviated, or specialized programs of short duration. If an abbreviated program is followed, then it is permissible to train more than the two or three periods recommended, although three weight training workouts per week is probably the most satisfactory. Remember that weight training is a *complement* to your Judo training and must not replace it. The former All-Japan Judo Champion, Mr. I. Inokuma conducts three weight workouts per week on alternate days as a complement to his daily Judo workout, which consists of two heavy practice mat sessions totaling 3–4 hours of Judo.

Judo practice on a daily basis demands careful selection as to when the weight training will be performed. A variety of possibilities suggest themselves, but after considerable investigation, the authors believe that either of two methods which have proven workable, produce optimum results. A weight workout performed at least two or three hours before the normal Judo training period will not interfere with Judo training, providing that the trainee is in good physical condition. Another satisfactory method, and the one preferred by Mr. Inokuma, All-Japan Judo Champion, is taking a weight workout after the normal Judo training routine. In both cases, it is understood that the workout is a full, balanced program. Any reduction or modification in the weight program where considerably less than a full balanced program is utilized, lessens the seriousness of choosing the time to perform the weight exercises. In this case, if the weight exercises are performed prior to Judo training, allow a 30 minute minimum rest period before going on to the Judo workout.

The length of the weight training period when complementing a daily Judo session has proven adequate and functional when limited to less than one and one-half hours. A full and balanced program can be accomplished when working individually or in small groups, in from one to one hour and one-half. Of course under modifications of a lesser program, the length of time will decrease proportionately and offers no great problem. Mr. Inokuma averages a one hour workout each time he weight trains.

Application—Occasional Judo Training: When Judo workouts are limited to less than daily, say two or three per week, the advice for daily Judo training can be followed, but it has proven more functional to schedule the Auxiliary Exercises on days when no Judo is anticipated or on days of very light practice. Combining two or three Judo days with two or three weight days, scheduled on different days, will satisfy the average Judo exponent and should provide the necessary progress and all-around betterment for increased Judo performance and health. This applies to a full, balanced weight training program, as before. Weight training, here too, should not be scheduled on consecutive days.

A full and balanced program of weight training may be had in less than one and one-half hours as was stated earlier, though the ambitious trainee performing Judo on an occasional basis may wish to extend the weight session another 30 minutes or so. It is probably better to limit to less than two hours and test cases conducted by the authors showed no material benefits gained beyond a two hour weight training period.

Application—Exercise Principles: Weight exercises should be considered as muscle-building tools and in this role it is physiologically possible to use the same exercise to perform different jobs such as losing weight and gaining muscle definition, adding bulk, gaining weight, and gaining power, provided that the principles by which the exercises are applied are altered. This interchangeable application allows the user to perform weight exercises for a wide latitude of objectives and is equally important in the design of a weight training program as is the consideration of whether or not the trainee will perform Judo daily. The design of various programs is discussed elsewhere in this chapter.

In Chapter 3 various kinesiological facts about muscle were established. In the application of the Auxiliary Exercises, trainees should perform all exercises on the basis of *concentric* contraction. That is, the muscle is allowed to contract and return to normal through a *full range* of motion *without* any controlled lowering or raising. This is the most applicable type of contraction to Judo in all but special cases which will be separately pointed out. Don't hurry the motion, but seek to make a complete motion and concentrate on form. The muscles must work through their entire range of intended motion. The heaving or "cheating" variety of movement has undergone considerable debate among weight authorities. Its use should be restricted to power programs, but programs which are designed solely on this type of movement are not recommended. Muscles must work through their entire range for proper development. Heaving causes muscles, the weaker ones, not to enter the entire movement. As a result, they can never fully develop under programs confined to heaving or cheating movements. Yet, these cheating movements find application in teaching muscles to work together to achieve a teamwork necessary to apply extreme power, forcing various other muscles to "take over" for the weaker ones unable to make a full contraction. In this light, the additional burden placed on muscles doing more than their share of the work, is valuable. The use of heaving or cheating movements requires a very thorough knowledge of kinesiology if they are to be effective and bring predictable results. Generally, as stated for the exception in power routines, movements should be conducted through a full range of motion. *Reduce the weight* when form conditions are not being met. Do not place undue emphasis on "how much" weight you use. It is not directly important in that you are not trying to prove how heavy a weight you can lift.

Application—Safety in Lifting: Most persons know the basic steps in lifting a weight, but it is amazing just how many will ignore them only to suffer injury or inability to perform the desired movements. Since some exercises require special body positions, it is difficult to cover all of them with simple, general, safety rules. Yet, certain basic things must be observed. As discussed under *Equipment* in this chapter, ensure that the equipment you use and any accessories are in good repair. Do not perform your exercises with faulty equipment. Ensure that all collars and clamps holding the various weights in place are properly placed and secured. Make it a rule never to lift a bar or bell without securing the collars or clamps. When lifting, feet should be placed on a line about 12 to 18 inches apart, feet pointed slightly outward. The bar should rest quite near the shins. The back should be straight, and the hands spaced normally to allow a balanced lift. Most lifting of heavy weights should be done by the legs initially, not the back. When in inverted positions or supine positions, take care that you are able to support the chosen weight. In all limit lifting, it is well to have one or two persons standing by to act as "spotters" in case you should require assistance. Another consideration under this subject is the necessity of warming up prior to heavy weight exercise. Any suitable exercise which will adequately stimulate all major muscles of the body is recommended. Trainees can draw from the many exercises listed in Chapter 7, or can perform such Auxiliary Exercises as the squat, press, and clean for a warmup. Of course, when using weight warmups, the weight used should be extremely light and less than 50% of one's maximum lift. Many muscle injuries can be eliminated by proper warmup.

Application—Repetitions and Sets: Throughout the use of Auxiliary (and other for that matter) Exercises, reference is made to repetitions and sets. A *repetition* is the performing of a selected movement or motion. Successive repetitions of that movement for the desired number of times forming a series of repetitions is termed a *set*. The purpose of our weight training program will determine the number of repetitions and sets performed. As discussed in *Exercise Principles* in this chapter, weight training can be performed with various objectives in mind. Generally, if we wish to lose weight and gain definition, we must perform high repetitions and high sets; if we wish to add bulk and gain weight, we must perform low repetitions and low sets; and if we wish to gain tremendous power, we must perform extremely low repetitions and high sets. These objectives will be discussed each in turn.

All exercises described in this chapter are on the basis of sets and repetitions desireable for *general* training. Purposes other than general training, such as weight gaining, weight reducing, power gaining, etc., should make use of the same exercises utilizing the principles of design discussed elsewhere in this chapter. Perform all exercises on the basis of good form. When this is impossible, reduce the weight, not the sets or repetitions. An exception to this is seen in power routines, where poundages and sets are high, repetitions low, and form somewhat less strict.

A raw beginner in Judo and weight training should complement his Judo training with Auxiliary Exercises utilizing ten repetitions for one set for at least the first month to five weeks. The second month he should increase the sets to two, keeping the repetitions at 10. The third month period should bring a full 3 sets to each workout, using 10 repetitions as before. This three month period is considered a slow, but sensible start. It is especially recommended for beginners in weight training methods, or those who are in a weakened physical condition, who should not attempt more than the recommended amount of repetitions and sets. *Train—not strain,* would be a good motto to follow. After a three month introductory period, the trainee should be able to enter more advanced training without undue depletion of the body reserves. In extreme cases, it would be well to repeat another three month period utilizing 3 sets and 10 repetitions after which advanced training is in order. In all cases, except under special instruction applicable to the individual case, the raw beginner should undertake only a *general program.* Advanced trainees in excellent physical conditions may enter directly into the program of their choice; generally the abbreviated program.

Applicable at this point is an understanding of just how much rest should be taken between sets and change of exercises. Considerations important in this determination are the physical condition of the trainee, and the training objective. Weight authorities vary their advice from a minimum of 1 minute to a maximum of 5 minutes between sets and change of exercises. Trainees who are under par physically will require more recuperation time than highly trained athletes. Also, perhaps one of the purposes of the training objective is to achieve increased endurance and therefore, the period of waiting between sets and change of exercises will border the minimum of 1 minute. Trainees under a power program will require more rest time in order to achieve limit lifts and may thus approach the 5 minute limit. Regardless, for general purposes, the authors have found that by waiting for breathing to return to normal between sets and changes of exercises is adequate time. This usually is in the vicinity of 2–3 minutes.

Application—Selection of Exercises: A sound beginning routine complementing the normal Judo training sometimes poses a problem for the instructor or trainee. A balanced weight training program should consist of between 8 to 15 exercises, covering the entire body. They should be arranged in such a manner so as to stimulate all major muscle groups in a logical and efficient order. It is well to fully exercise each muscle group before going on to another muscle group. That is, one to three exercises are done which primarily affect one major muscle group before going on to another series of exercises affecting a different muscle group. The actual order of the exercises in so far as what major muscle groups to begin with, is also important, however not critical. There are several approaches to this problem, but one which has proven quite efficient in general programs is a progression from legs-chest-back-arm/shoulders-abdominals. Select one to three exercises from each of these major muscle groups and perform one-two-three sets of each, depending upon your level of advancement. The number of repetitions will depend on the purpose of your training. Remember... *almost any exercise* can be used, but the way of applying the exercise principles (repetitions, sets, contraction) is important. The anatomical categories are for convenience.

More advanced weight trainees may follow the same order of progression or may enter into specialization work which confines the workout to a major muscle group or two. Those who utilize the specialization programs must thoroughly understand the capabilities and limitations of such a routine. Those who train to lose or gain weight, should follow the same progression, but always within the framework of the particular pattern of the training objective. Those trainees desiring power must confine their workouts to only one or two major muscle groups and utilize only one or two exercises for each such selected group. This book describes sufficient exercises to prevent boredom and gives a wide latitude for design of all the programs. *(Refer to Table D, page 222.)*

Application—General Program: This might be called "balanced" weight training since the object of the program under this design is to provide suitable stimulation to all major muscle groups, and to generally improve the body equally and proportionately. This type of training is always a one, two, or three set method, with repetitions more or less fixed at 10. The instructor should assign such a program to those individuals who are beginning Judo, and who have no weight training experience. Those advanced students of Judo who are in a relatively weak body condition, should also be assigned to this kind of program. Under no circumstances should other types of programs be used until at least 3 months of training under a general program has been completed. Additional principles which apply to this type of weight training are:

Use a variety of different exercises. One or two exercises for each muscle group will be adequate. As many as 8 to 15 different exercises should be performed for the entire body, ensuring that each major muscle group is worked from different angles.

Train no more than 2 or 3 periods per week, allowing a day of rest between each weight training day.

Continue normal good eating habits.

Enjoy a minimum of 8 hours sleep.

Use poundages which are 60–75% of your total ability in each lift. (See pages 213–215.)

Application—Weight Losing Program: More correctly, this process should be understood as a process of burning off fatty tissue via weight exercise and to increase muscle definition. It will be necessary to severely exercise the body so that more tissue is used up than is stored. The principles which apply to this type of weight training are:

Use a high variety of different exercises. One or two exercises for any general muscle group will not produce the desired result. As many as 15 to 20 different exercises should be performed for the entire body, ensuring that each major muscle group is worked from different angles.

Perform high repetitions of each exercise. At least 15 to 20 repetitions each exercise, 3 or 4 sets, will break down the fatty tissue rapidly and result in greater muscularity. This high repetition routine will tend to tire the body greatly, but this is to be considered natural. Fatty tissue must be broken down in large quantities so that it cannot replace itself during your rest periods.

Train more than 3 periods per week, which will limit rest periods and the rebuilding of fatty tissues.

A low calorie diet should be followed, limited to 3000 calories daily. Stay away from starchy and fatty foods by substituting lean meats, vegetables, fruits, etc.

Enjoy a minimum of 8 hours sleep. At other times, you should be active and avoid periods of inactivity.

Use poundages which are 50–60% of your total ability in each lift. (See pages 213–215.)

Application—Weight Gaining Program: By weight, we understand the addition of useful muscle to the body and the gaining of muscular definition. Here it is necessary to conserve as much of the body energy as possible. The principles which apply to this type of weight training are:

Exercise periods are of moderate duration. One or two exercises for each muscle group will suffice. From 6–10 different exercises should be performed for the entire body, ensuring that each major muscle group is exercised.

Avoid high repetitions. From 6–10 repetitions, 3 sets each exercise, are best. The energy of the body is conserved in this manner, and muscle tissue stimulated to grow.

Never train more than 3 times per week.

A substantial diet is important, and calorie intake in the neighborhood of 4000–6000 calories. Ample quantities of fresh fruits and vegetables, plenty of lean meat, and the usual healthful foods are necessary to make the body grow. Protein is most essential and foods which are high in this content are absolutely necessary.

Enjoy a minimum of 8 hours restful sleep, although 9–10 hours will greatly improve chances of gaining weight. Aside from actual training periods, one should try to rest as much as possible and avoid undue strain and depletion of energies.

Use poundages which are 70–85% of your total ability in each lift. (See pages 213–215.)

Application—Abbreviated Program: These programs are modifications of a balanced, full routine usually patterned under a general program. While of a general nature, they nevertheless are not as all-encompassing, and as such, are primarily intended for advanced trainees who wish to gain weight and improve their physical condition, and who have had a minimum of 3 months of weight training, or by whose Judo experience, posssess physical condition above average. These programs are especially valuable for those Judo exponents who train daily and whose time is considerably limited. The principles which apply to abbreviated training are:

Exercise periods are of short duration. Exercises are selected from those which emphasize use of the major groups (legs, back, chest). From 3–6 different exercises should be performed.

Utilize moderate repetitions. From 6–8 repetitions, 3 sets each exercise are adequate. The energy of the body is conserved in this manner, and muscle tissue stimulated to grow.

Never train more than 3 times per week.

A substantial diet is important, and calorie intake in the neighborhood of 4000–6000 calories.

Ample quantities of fresh fruits and vegetables, plenty of lean meat, and the usual healthful foods which are high in protein content, are absolutely necessary.

Enjoy a minimum of 8 hours of restful sleep.

Use poundages which are 70–80% of your total ability in each lift. (See pages 213–215.)

Application—Power Program: This type of program affords the method by which we are able to obtain maximum strength. While all weight training programs will develop strength to some degree, it is within the power program that our capacities can be realized. It is a program for advanced trainees only. Trainees will find for their convenience that exercises suitable for power routine treatment have been taken out of the usual anatomical categories and listed separately. The exercises within this group are described in terms of power training principles (repetitions, sets, poundages), but, although somewhat difficult, may be classified under appropriate anatomical categories. They may be also converted to other training aims such as general training, specialization, etc., by the proper application of exercise principles (repetitions, sets, poundages). Other exercises from within the anatomical categories may be similarly adapted to power training if so desired. In power training we seek to develop all-around body strength. The principles which apply to power training are:

Perform only 2 or 3 different exercises during the entire workout. Train with the same exercises until you reach peak performance beyond which you can make no advance. (this is sometimes in excess of 3 months).

Avoid high repetitions. Use 2–4 repetitions, unlimited (minimum of 4) sets, until the weight being used allows you only one repetition.

Do not set a definite schedule to train, but utilize days of high energy to exceed past workout poundages. Never exceed 3 workouts per week. It is common to train every third day and thus only twice per week.

Here too, a substantial diet is necessary such as noted in the weight gaining program *(see page 210)*.

Enjoy a minimum of 8 hours sleep.

Use near maximum or maximum poundages. Start with poundages which allow you to perform only 4 repetitions. Rest briefly (2 to 5 minutes), then, add weight which will bring you down to two or three repetitions.

Rest briefly again (another 2 to 5 minutes), and add more weight which will bring you down to one repetition. Rest once again (2 to 5 minutes), add weight, and try to exceed your previous performance.

Use poundages which are 85–100% plus of your total ability in each lift. (See pages 213–215.)

Application—Specialization: A common physiological phenomenon in weight training is the "training plateau" or "sticking point." This is the period in our training that we seem to make no progress. The muscles refuse to respond to ordinary methods and they require a more advanced application of weight training methods to stimulate them. If this is the case, we are justified in applying specialization.

Specialization is a system whereby we place intense and concentrated physical emphasis on the muscles selected with the purpose of making them respond. It is obvious that specialization is not a sensible program for beginners, except as noted in the following.

Sometimes, parts of our muscular development are not up to par. We cannot function effectively with this "weak link" in our muscular chain. To effect growth in these below par areas, we apply specialization. It is through this process we acquire muscle response and stimulate the body to gain its proportionality. Specialization, in this case, should be used only to develop the sub-par portion, and once this area responds, a general routine or one of the other formerly described programs should be used. Specialization in this vein of bringing some areas of the body up to par can be used by beginners if properly applied. However, experience has shown that such practice often runs astray. The beginner, whose body may be all or nearly all sub-par, will with good intentions, apply a series of specialization routines to each major muscle group in turn. He will, for example, begin training with arm specialization, concentrating on bicepses and tricepses development for a period of one-two, or three months before moving on to the chest muscle group. And so on until all major areas have been covered. His routine will always contain only exercises concerned with the part of his anatomy he is specializing in, and thus his training method can never bring his body to the desired effective unity necessary in Judo. And this is not the only danger, as such a specialization application often leads to overwork and no muscular development. Applying 8 to 10 different exercises for the muscle group receiving specialization, he is likely to overwork the muscle with negative results. Even though the muscles respond, and some growth is established, a series of programs of specialization used in this manner are leading to disastrous results and can be labeled *non-sensible training*.

Training which is *all* specialization is *isolated muscle training*, and will not result in a harmonious body to be used effectively in Judo. The muscles thus produced are developed in isolation from each other, and never receive the experience of working in cooperation in major muscular effort under conditions of weight training. As such, muscles so developed can never match the effectiveness produced by proper application of specialization and other program objectives.

Specialization for beginners should always be based on the need to bring some exceedingly sub-par muscle group to the necessary standard. "Training plateaus" or "sticking points" can occur in the beginning trainee's program, but they almost always can be traced to improper application of exercise principles relative to the trainee. The solution of this "plateau" lies within a restudy of a *general program* and should not be focused on specialization unless absolutely necessary.

Applying specialization routines to sub-par muscle areas is best handled by designing, for the beginner, a specialized program to be performed *after or as a part of* a general routine. This will necessitate extending the training period somewhat. Care must be taken not to exceed the physical limts of the trainee with this additional work, and each case must be individually studied and applied. It has been found exceedingly helpful to introduce specialization only after 2 months of general training has been accomplished, and the trainee's body is more receptive to increased energy output.

Advanced weight trainees or those Judo exponents who are well above average in physical condition may enter specialization programs with the purpose of improving sub-par muscle areas, or getting over the "training plateau." While many weight training enthusiasts of advanced experience utilize with varying degrees of effectiveness programs which are all specialization, this practice cannot be recommended for Judo exponents. Experience has shown that the best results for the Judo exponent who enters specialization for either of the two purposes already stated, comes from specialization which is included as *a part* of an established training objective such as a general program, weight gaining or weight losing program, power program, or abbreviated program. Performed at the *end* of such programs, the specialization further adds to the stimulation of the muscle group which may already have been stimulated earlier by the basic program. Such specialization may be directed at the same area for as long as the basic program is continued, or may be directed to new areas each time the basic program is undertaken.

Some readers will notice that even within a basic program such as one designed for weight gaining, each muscle group is exercised in a "specialized" way before passing on to the next group. In this sense, all programs are "specialized," but it must be noted that basic programs *connect* muscle actions and do not produce isolated muscle training. This is particularly evident when composite exercises such as the clean and press or repetition cleaning are used within the basic program.

The principles which apply to specialization are:

Perform at least 3 different exercises which will strongly stimulate the muscle or muscles considered in need of the extra work.

Use from 6–10 repetitions, at least 3 sets of each exercise. An exception to this is specialization for the calves of the legs, an exceedingly difficult muscle to stimulate by ordinary means. 20–30 repetitions are necessary when exercising this muscle area. The abdominal muscles, likewise an exception, require 10–15 repetitions.

Specialization should be confined to one major muscle, or a major group, depending upon the goal in mind. Care must be taken to choose exercises which will work the muscles from all angles.

Use specialization as a *part* of the basic training program. Placed at the end of your basic program, specialization will take better effect.

Follow the general rules of your basic training objective (program).

Use poundages which are 70–80% of your total ability on each lift. (See below.)

Application—Selection of Poundages: After you have selected the exercises to be utilized within your training objective in a particular fashion (repetitions and sets), next important is the amount of weight you should use. This subject has many controversial aspects among physiologists, coaches, physical educators, and trainees themselves, and is still open to debate. However, we can draw some very secure guidance by recalling our principles of exercise. In general, high repetitions using good exercise form and moderate weight will trim excess poundages and bring muscular definition; lower repetitions, heavier weights and less strict exercise form produces weight gains; while concentrating entirely on one or two exercises, using maximum poundages, and unlimited sets of exceptionally low repetitions, results in the development of maximum power.

We have then, set a guide for ourselves depending upon our weight training objectives. We must fully understand our objective and then use poundages accordingly. Once we have decided this, we still must insist on an honest evaluation of our physical abilities. If the weights we choose are too light, the muscles will not work enough and the resultant lack of stimulation will be of little benefit. If the weights are too heavy, we will not be able to perform the exercises properly and can overload the muscles, causing injury.

The proper poundage, within our training objective, is the one with which we can correctly perform the desired number of repetitions. The first few repetitions often seem very easy, but as we approach our final repetitions, we must put forth considerable effort. Generally, except when we are training on an exclusive power routine, it is not good to have to strain with an "all out" effort in order to make our desired repetitions. We should have some ability left to make one or two more repetitions if necessary. By the same token however, our desired repetitions should not be effortless.

Correct usable poundages must be determined by a workout or two as a test case, and is best done by starting light and adding a bit of weight until you find the weight which just reaches the exercise performance desired. Be honest with yourself...use weights which allow you to perform the desired repetitions. Trying to keep up with a more powerful training partner can bring injury or other undesirable results. The weight you choose for each movement should be recorded or otherwise remembered to facilitate subsequent sessions. Remember that you have very definite physical limitations. Work within them, and gradually, under a progressive weight training system, you will find these limitations broadened. Recommended weights listed in the exercises are guides for adult trainees.

In Chapter 3 we learned that a muscle can perform contraction with maximum efficiency only at about 50% of its maximum contraction force. To develop strength rapidly, we must exert with a weight which is at least 60% of our maximum contraction ability in any one exercise. This means that if we are able to squat with 100 lbs. ten times and really feel the exercise, we should drop the weight to a minimum of 60 pounds when we do our repetitions. What has been stated is a *minimum* and individual differences will often make the use of heavier weights necessary for rapid muscular hypertrophy. At any rate, it is advisable to perform with weights which lie within the 60–85% range of our total abilities. An exception to this is of course seen in the power routines which are performed within the 85–100% or more range of total abilities. Working muscles continually at 100% of their contraction ability will result in unsatisfactory muscle conditions, yet it is at this point in weight training that most mistakes are made.

As a muscle grows in strength, its ability to use more weight will increase and we must apply a progressive system of training, one which permits us to periodically increase the weight we are using for each movement if we are to fully exploit our physical potential. These additions of weight should fall within the 60–85% range as stated earlier, or, as within power routines, the 85–100% or more range.

The exact method of adding weight to the barbell or dumbbell in a progressive system of weight training need not concern the trainee unduly. The process should not be time consuming nor should it require the precise calculations that enter into an engineering problem. Too often, the trainee will become involved in complicated methods of adding weight at the expense of his actual training. However, it is important that there be some provision made for recording or otherwise remembering just what weight has been used so that some progression may be obvious in subsequent workouts. For all-around convenience, the following method has proven adequate. Take a poundage with which you can just perform the desired repetitions required by your training objective—use this poundage for all sets and do as many repetitions (within the recommended limit) as you can. Usually, as your muscles become increasingly tired with more sets, you will fall short of the repetitions performed in the first set. With training, as the second and third sets become easy and the repetitions become the same in number as the first set, add weight, usually 5–10 pounds for most muscle groups. The legs require 10–20 pounds more due to the greater strength of those muscles. The second and third sets will now become difficult again in so far as repetitions are concerned. In this way, you will realize a direct progression in strength gains. This method of adding weight is useful when applied to programs of a general, weight gaining or losing, abbreviated, or specialization nature. Power routines should utilize a different approach.

Power programs are conveniently and effectively performed on the basis of what is sometimes known as the single progressive system. It is performed as follows. Use a poundage with which you can just perform the desired repetitions required by the power routine training objective—usually 2-4 repetitions. For subsequent sets (minimum of 4 sets), add weight, 5-10 pounds each set. As a result, in short order, the number of repetitions you are able to perform will be reduced. The variation in repetitions should be controlled so as to produce one less repetition each time a set is performed. However, several sets may be performed with a like number of repetitions before it is impossible to match the preceeding one. In this way, sets may be carried on to 10 or even 12 before obtaining just one repetition with a poundage which is in excess of 100% of the maximum total ability. With continued training, your strength will increase and your training objective of increased power will be realized.

The authors are aware of the many methods of weight training which make use of various lines of progression concerning poundages used. Whether they are single, double, or whenever they follow increase or decrease progressions, it is noted that the common ground of each is based on *progression*. What is more, all the systems work! Effective results have been registered by advocates of all these and other systems. Gradual progression from lighter poundages to heavier ones remains as the basis of systems of weight training designed to develop strength and better physical condition.

Application—Breathing: Oxidation is, for the physiologist, the sole source of animal energy. Without breathing air, we cease to transform energy and we die. Oxygen exchange, which replenishes consumed nutritives in the blood, is a vital process which stimulates muscle growth. Cardio-vascular and respiratory systems are mechanisms of our internal transport system necessary to life. Aside from complicated physiological reasons, simpler anatomical considerations make breathing an important part of the weight training program.

Trainees will find that many exercises cause no great concern for just what rhythm to apply to breathing. Breathing as exertion demands will fit many of the situations. However in various exercises such as contained in the leg, chest, and the power groups particularly, the use of rhythmic breathing is essential to the performance. Trainees should follow the breathing instructions for each movement described. In some cases as described *(page 40, Kiai)*, breathing will make a unified body effort an efficient one. This is especially important to trainees performing exercises within movements requiring maximum body power. Additionally, rhythmic breathing will expand the lungs and stretch the rib-box, contributing to the complete development of the chest.

Application—Change of Exercises and Program: Aside from an adjustment within a program for reasons of practicability, injury, etc., a change of exercise should mean a change of weight training program. It has proven more efficient if each weight training program embarked upon is continued for a minimum of 3 weeks and more preferably 5 weeks, after which time, a change of program can be instituted. This change of program will bring a fresh group of exercises and reduce the chance of boredom or possible nonprogress. Physiologically, a change of exercise will permit the muscles to be worked from other angles and thus provide more adequate stimulation.

It should be pointed out that a change of exercise, and thus program, may or may not mean a change of training objective. It is perfectly possible and functional to set up an objective of training for bulk or gaining weight and after 5 weeks of performing those selected exercises, to change the exercises and the program, *continuing* the training objective of gaining weight. Under no circumstances would it be possible to fully realize the original training objective in such a short time as 3 to 5 weeks, and if we are to completely reach our training objective, it would be well to figure on one or two more 5 week periods of weight gaining routines. Switching from one training objective to another too frequently will not bring the best progress. It has been found that a minimum of three months confined to one training objective is generally suitable and brings superior results.

Application—Expander Exercises: Exercises described under this category of Auxiliary Exercises have been grouped together purposely for convenience and have not been placed in the various muscle group divisions.

Expanders, sometimes referred to as "cables," can be used advantageously only for the upper body, and it is with this in mind that the exercises are presented. Neck and leg movements can be made, to be sure, but they are for the most, sub-standard movements which can better be performed with other pieces of equipment or even without any special apparatus (see Leg and Upper Back-Neck Groups of Preparatory and Auxiliary Exercises). Athletes have long realized the value of expander type of exercise in the development of the arms, chest, shoulders, upper back, and abdominals. Expanders are convenient to handle, highly portable, and provide a moderate to heavy workout if the appropriate tension and exercises are chosen. Judo exponents the world over have used this style of exercise for many years with success and most all Dojo today contain some form of expander equipment.

The authors have experimented with various expander or cable types and personally prefer the flat rubber band type with clamp handles *(see below)*. These expanders are durable, easily adjustable, do not pinch, will not rust or tear, and should provide many years of useful service. The authors have personally carried this kind of expander for a score of years throughout their travels in various climates, and are to this day, using the original expanders.

Expander exercises, like all other exercises, should be performed sensibly and with regard to safety. The flat type of expander will provide perfectly safe movements if used properly. The use by Judo exponents of bicycle inner tubes as expanders is all right from the safety standpoint, but inasmuch as these tubes do not allow for a variety of tension adjustments, they are less efficient.

Expander exercises can be used on the basis of various exercise principles discussed earlier in this chapter. This will permit the exercises to be used for training objectives of gaining weight, losing weight, specialization, general routines, and abbreviated routines. While they do develop strength, they are not ideally suited to power routine training objectives. The trainee will find them valuable in various warmup, specialization, and weight losing applications. They are additionally valuable in abbreviated training, on the days when access to weight equipment is impossible. Trainees recovering from injuries may well use expanders to increase blood flow to the injured area and thus promote healing. The expander exercises should follow the same general principles of exercises as stated before, but training programs restricted to expander exercises will never fully develop the potential of the trainee.

Application—Obi Exercises: The standard Judo obi can be utilized to provide a useful form of moderate exercise of a stretching nature and is ideally suited for warmup routines. Any material of lightweight construction may be used, such as towels, cloth, trouser belt, sticks, or wands. The trainee or instructor is left to utilize his imagination in the design of exercises not shown in this chapter.

Application—**Pulley Exercises:** Special apparatus of the wall pulley type can offer a valuable augmentation to Auxiliary Exercise programs. For many years pulley exercises have played an important part in the training of athletes from almost all fields of endeavor. Pulleys are almost always standard equipment for any training site, and are often found in Judo Dojo.

The use of pulleys can best be adapted to resistance movements of a moderate degree which are applied to the upper body. A few ideas of exercises are shown in the following pages and exercises of the pulley type have been grouped together for convenience, rather than placed in anatomical categories. An exception to this is the use of the Lat Machine, a pulley device, which has been retained within the anatomical groupings.

Pulley exercises may be used on the basis of various exercise principles discussed earlier in this chapter. In this manner, the exercises can be applied to training objective of gaining weight, losing weight, specialization, general routines, and abbreviated routines. These exercises will develop strength to some degree, but are not suited to power routines. Better application is made as warmup and specialization exercises. Trainees recovering from injuries may also use pulleys. Pulley exercises should follow the same general principles of exercise as stated before, but training restricted to pulley exercises will never fully develop the potential of the trainee. The authors are of the opinion that Judo movements of a Supplementary Exercise nature, while they can be performed using pulleys, can more efficiently be performed by the partner or elastic band methods.

The Post-Workout Shower or Bath: The use of hot water for a prolonged period of time in the form of either a shower or a bath in which the trainee can soak, can and does affect the results of a weight workout. The body, after a stimulating workout, will experience increased blood flow to the muscle groups exercised. This is often referred to as a "pumped up" condition. This flooded tissue gives the feeling of "tightness" in the muscle area which will persist until the tissues so inundated become more nearly "normal." It is a temporary condition. This is a normal result of adequate stimulation, though the "tightness" it produces within the muscle group will vary in intensity.

Hot water has a relaxing effect on the flooded muscle tissue and will rapidly dissipate the hard-worked for effects and all but nullify the workout. Trainees should most certainly take a shower or bath after finishing a workout, but by avoiding *prolonged* immersion in hot water, and finishing with a cold shower, long-lasting benefits from the workout will accrue. An occasional prolonged immersion in a hot shower or bath is both welcome and necessary for trainees, but it should not become the rule after each weight training session.

Muscular Soreness: This topic is discussed only in the light of muscular exertion, though there are various other sources of this sometimes painful condition. Any adequate simulation of a muscle by means of resistance exercise to promote its growth, will bring about the condition of muscular soreness. It is the varying degrees of this condition that sometimes makes it important.

Muscular soreness is sometimes painful and always annoying. It can result in reduced efficiency in Judo, and, therefore must be minimized. The use of Preparatory Exercises to warmup and cool down the body will reduce muscular soreness resulting from severe exertion. Additional massage and the use of alcohol and liniment rubs after severe exertion also aid in eliminating extreme muscular soreness. Hot baths or showers, turkish baths, and steam treatments can also greatly relieve the suffering caused by muscle soreness. The use of vitamin C to reduce post-exercise soreness has not been fully investigated.

Particularly when utilizing weight training movements, the trainee can expect muscular soreness to develop some 20–30 hours after training has been completed. This is particularly evident if the training program is the first one for the trainee, or if an advanced weight trainee, a new program. The change of programs, involving either new muscle groups or the same ones exercised from new angles, will always result in some degree of muscle soreness. It is natural and to be expected. However in the training of Judo exponents, consideration must be given to any possible potential muscle soreness when considering the approaching Judo contest. It is obvious that changing programs near contest time is a risky thing and to be avoided. Since muscle soreness of an extreme nature can endure for a period of up to 4–5 days, it is well to greatly limit any heavy weight training about 5 days prior to the contest. Mr. Inokuma, All-Japan Judo Champion uses this rule-of-thumb and has never suffered adversely from it.

Muscle Growth and Progress: Individual differences, types, and intensity of weight training are key factors in muscular hypertrophy. More directly and simply, muscular growth seems to lie in increased blood circulation from energetic activity, most rapidly from methods of weight training. We can do little about our physiological differences and so by varying our exercise principles (see page 208) we can to some degree, control and adjust our muscular growth.

Trainees can expect to experience muscle growth at the rate of 1–2 pounds per week. A somewhat lesser gain, such as 2–5 pounds per month can also be considered as a substantial gain and should be no cause for discarding the program producing such a result. Weight gains of 10 pounds or more per month are probably maximum beneficial gains, but it is to be noted that after the second month, these gains will be reduced by one half, or 5 pounds per month, and after the fourth month, weight gains of less than 5 pounds per month are average. Obviously there is a limit to the amount of steady increase in weight that can be produced, and trainees are advised to keep this factor in mind so as not to cause frustration or discontent.

The entire subject of weight gaining is impossible to express in terms of an exact formula. The average gains mentioned above have seen many exceptions, but in general, may be used as a basis for training evaluation. As such they are predicated on the assumption that the trainee concerned has balanced body chemistry, and is meeting the adequate amounts of nutrition, exercise, and sleep, the vital triad of training.

Questions are often directed toward the differences in muscular growth and subsequent weight gaining of adolescents as compared to adults. Let it be understood that weight gains of adolescents produced by weight training methods must be planned by systematic progressive training methods and are not considered as "forced" growth, but rather "stimulated" growth. While the adolescent can sometimes make steadier and more rapid growth in muscle, the adult is by no means unable to duplicate or even excel that growth. It is possible under ideal conditions of body chemistry and training methods for adults in their forties to evidence like gains, and almost always, substantial gains.

A final consideration under this heading is the topic of losing weight. We have briefly discussed cutting weight in Chapter 4. This discussion applied to the well-conditioned Judo exponent who for purposes of competition under weight category systems imposed by the AAU in the U.S.A., had to lose weight. Such case begins from an already fit and well-muscled body, with little surplus fatty tissue. However, in the discussion which follows, our starting point is the body with large quantities of fatty tissue.

Normal Judo training complemented by Auxiliary Exercises of the weight training variety will quickly reduce overweight persons. All this reduction process must be carefully supervised if the trainee concerned is to remain in a healthy condition. Too rapid a loss will result in drastic changes which may cause difficult adjustment problems. Experience has shown that gradual losing of surplus weight is best. 2–4 pounds per week seem to be ideal. This can be carried on until the desired amount of weight has been removed from the body. A 4–6 month period of weight reduction programs usually is adequate to bring the overweight trainee down to more normal body weight without adverse effects. The trainee must of course adhere to proper amounts of nutrition, exercise, and sleep and have a balanced body chemistry.

Exercise Terminology: The exercises listed in Table D, page 222, are those generally known to all familiar with weight exercises. For the most, they follow basic patterns of exercise form, but in certain cases, they will appear to be slightly at variance with known forms of performance. This is an intended variance, and is not to be interpreted otherwise. For this reason, *read the exercises carefully, noting all the details of performance, even though the pictures suggest an exercise "well-known" to you.* Slight variations are important. Do not omit them. Terminology, or exercise names, likewise follow commonly accepted names of exercises, but are not intended to adhere strictly to the common names found in most any weight gym. The names are merely a convenience with which to catalog the exercises.

Exercise Potpourri: In the design of exercise programs various factors which affect the intended results are important, though they will appear to be more or less insignificant. The trainee and instructor must have full cognizance over such factors if proper training programs are to be constructed.

The effect of the incline bench versus the decline bench is quite relevant to our program design. Generally, it should be understood that exercises performed on the incline bench affect the upper portion of the pectoral muscles and the anterior deltoid muscles, while exercises performed on the decline bench to affect the lower portion of the pectoral muscles. A balanced effect is generally attained by exercising from a flat or normal bench. In the design of weight training programs, make use of all benches. The angle of incline or decline will vary with the exercise, but usually falls within the 5°–60° range.

The manner of holding dumbbells prior to pressing action, and the very position of the dumbbells during the pressing action also is worthy of consideration and affects the design of our exercise programs. Holding dumbbells wide with the bar axis pointed to the sides at the shoulders, #1, will affect the deltoids more during pressing action, while dumbbells held with the axis of the bar pointing from front to rear will affect the triceps more during similar pressing action. #2.

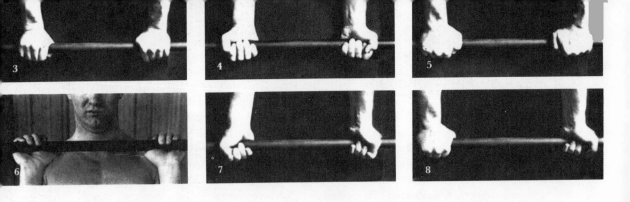

The manner in which the bar of a barbell is gripped can also be relevant to our design of a training program. Normal pulling, cleaning, and pressing actions can be made with a normal grip. #3–4. A variation pressing grip termed the "thumbless" grip is sometimes useful in maximum pressing attempts. #5–6. Cleaning or pulling maximum weights will be facilitated by using the "hook" grip in which the thumb is placed next to the bar and encircled by the forefinger and second finger while the remainder of the fingers grip normally. #7. Normal curling can be achieved with the grip shown in #4, although the "hook" grip can be used with maximum poundages. Lifting heavy weights from the floor for only a short distance upward can be accomplished by the grip shown in #8. This grip is good for use with the Jefferson Lift (see page 225).

Hand spacing also bring various effects dependent upon the exercise used. Throughout this chapter, the terms wide, normal, and narrow are used to designate grip spacing. Wide spacing refers to a grasp taken wider than the shoulders out to a maximum position of next to the plates of the barbell. Normal spacing refers to a grip taken shoulder or hip width apart. Narrow spacing refers to a grip taken with the hands 10 inches or less apart. Wide gripping (spacing) used in supine pressing will affect the outer pectoral muscles and deltoids; normal gripping (spacing) gives a balanced effect to the chest muscles; and narrow gripping (spacing) tends to work the inner portion of the pectorals and triceps. A wide grip in supine pressing, as is its opposite extreme, the narrow grip, is not efficient in handling maximum poundages. For maximum lifts, the normal grip must be used. A wide grip must be used to pull down behind the neck. The wider the hands are spaced in pulling actions, the shorter the distance the weight has to move, but the arm and shoulder muscles will not be able to assist efficiently in the lift. For full cooperation of the arm and shoulder muscles, the grip must be normal or narrow. Pressing is easier with a normal grip, at least during the initial stage of the motion, but as the weight rises a wide grip affords more efficiency. Curling action is affected by gripping also. Wide grips will tend to emphasize action on the inner side of the arm muscles while narrow grips will throw the emphasis on the outside portions of the arm muscles. Trainees and instructors must use all varieties of gripping (spacing) in their programs over a period of time.

Various exercises are described in straight-arm manner while others are described in terms of bent-arm action. Generally, it must be understood that lighter weights are best used in straight-arm action and that any exercise designed to use a heavy weight involving the arms, must be designed on the basis of bent-arm action. This will prevent overloading the elbow joint, a potential source of injury.

Foot spacing directly affects our efficiency in leg exercises as well as emphasis on the

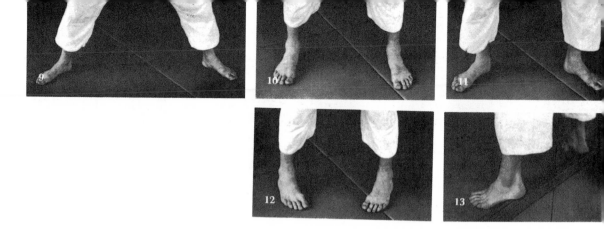

various muscles of our legs (#9–12.) Wide stances will give severe stretching action to the muscles on the inner portion of the thigh as well as the upper thigh and hip muscles. Stability is increased by a wide stance, and we are able to best exercise fixation muscles of the body in this position. Generally, we should attempt to perform the exercises from the Judo stance of Shizenhontai or its right and left derivatives, except as noted in the exercise descriptions. Pointing the toes slightly outward will be a normal method in our stance. However, pointing the toes directly forward or slightly inward throws emphasis on different areas not normally reached by the normal stance. This is particularly true in calf exercises. Trainees should take advantage of variation in pointing the toes to achieve full development of the legs. Raising the heels on a block of 1, 2, or 3 inches will increase balance and throw emphasis on the calf muscles which is not received when the feet are flat on the floor. Squat action from a raised block #13 is beneficial.

Carrying heavy poundages across the back of the neck and shoulders is sometimes disagreeable, especially when maximum weights are being used. The wearing of sweat shirts is not sufficient to protect the skin and cervical bone structures from the pressure of the bar and trainees often find that padding provided by sponge rubber, toweling or the like, is necessary.

Emphasis on correct breathing in various exercises cannot be overemphasized. The beneficial effects of breathing have already been discussed, but one effect sometimes neglected, will often cause the trainee considerable concern. Rapid breathing can lead to dizziness. This "over breathing" is termed hyperventilation and has a logical physiological explanation which will not be discussed here. It is sufficient to know that the condition is a normal result of rapid and prolonged heavy breathing, and that it can cause discomfort and injury if the trainee actually passes out. Any signs of discomfort and dizziness from hyperventilation should promptly be checked by terminating the exercise, putting the weight down and lowering the head between the legs until the head becomes clear once again.

A full understanding of anatomical considerations is necessary for a successful continuation of program design. Trainees and instructors who will be responsible for training programs of Judo exponents should have formally studied elementary physiology, anatomy and kinesiology in preparation for this responsibility. Being fully acquainted with the human body musculature will make for intelligent planning not otherwise possible except by a stroke of luck. By way of example, the commonly known muscles of the body such as the tricepses and deltoid muscles are vital to Judo training methods. They must be fully developed if full efficiency is to be realized. Yet, it is not commonly known that those muscles are tri-part muscles and require exercise for all three parts if full development is to take place. Singling out the deltoid muscle as a concrete example, proper training will, over a period of time, utilize exercises such as the Incline Dumbbell Press which works the anterior portion of the deltoid; the Incline Dumbbell Side Raise which works the lateral portion of the deltoid; and the Dumbbell Bent Lateral which works the posterior portion of the deltoid. Thus exercise is provided for the three parts of the deltoid and full development can be realized. There are of course other exercises which can be used to accomplish this, but without this special knowledge of the anatomical construction of the deltoid and the kinesiological understanding of exercise methods to stimulate the tri-part muscle, it is evident that full development would probably not be achieved. Instructors and trainees must understand that sensible training is no "hit or miss" process, but is based on sound facts and principles.

Non-Judo Exponents: The regular use of these exercises will bring amazingly fast developmental response. Excess weight may be trimmed off, underweight frames packed with solid muscle, and general body conditition and subsequent improved health can be had within a relatively short time. The program of exercise for a beginner should be sought from within the exercise principles for a *general program*, devoting as much as 3 periods per week, one hour each period, to these movements. A program of exercise may be self-designed, but until the beginner has a thorough understanding of the kinesiological principles involved, it is well that the suggested programs in Chapter 6 be followed.

Advanced trainees and well-conditioned athletes may enter programs of their choice, although it is advisable to practice a general program for at least one month. These exercises have been successfully used in the sporting fields of track, football, basketball, swimming, wrestling, boxing, fencing, and other well-known endeavors.

Table D

AUXILIARY EXERCISES *(page 224)*

LEG GROUP *(page 224)*

1. Squat *(page 224)*
2. Hack Lift *(page 225)*
3. Jefferson Lift *(page 225)*
4. Jumping Squat *(page 226)*

5. Leg Press Machine *(page 226)*
6. Leg Extension Curl *(page 227)*
7. Leg Biceps Curl *(page 227)*
8. Calf Raise *(page 228)*

CHEST GROUP *(page 228)*

1. Decline Straight-arm Dumbbell Lateral *(page 228)*
2. Barbell Supine Press (narrow grip) *(page 229)*
3. Incline Dumbbell Bent-arm Lateral *(page 229)*
4. Incline Dumbbell Press *(page 230)*
5. Decline Dumbbell Press *(page 230)*
6. Supine Dumbbell Press *(page 231)*
7. Supine Straight-arm Dumbbell Pullover *(page 231)*

8. Supine Bent-arm Dumbbell Lateral *(page 232)*
9. Supine Bent-arm Dumbbell Pullover *(page 232)*
10. Supine Dumbbell Thrust *(page 233)*
11. Decline Dipping *(page 233)*
12. Supine Straight-arm Barbell Pullover *(page 234)*
13. Incline Dumbbell Cris-cross *(page 234)*

Auxiliary Exercises   223

LEG GROUP

SQUAT

Purpose: The "king" of exercises basic to general body improvement and powerful legs. Affects the respiratory capacity and is an aid to developing endurance and chest size. Performed in many variations, but described here as a breathing squat.

Performance: Stand erect, feet shoulder width apart and flat on the floor, toes pointed slightly outward. Hold a barbell across the back of the neck and shoulders. Hold the head erect with your eyes to the front #1.

Lower the body by bending the knees. Part the knees. Maintain an erect upper body and continue to keep the head erect. #2. Continue the lowering until a deep position is reached. #3.

Rise from this deep position to the starting position in #1. This is one repetition. Pause and repeat for the desired number of times.

Breathing: Inhale at the starting position. Hold your breath as you lower your body to the deep position. Exhale as you approach the return to the starting position.

Recommended Weight: 80–100 lbs. 10 repetitions.

Key Points: The body should be kept as erect as possible in order to make this movement effective. The use of too much weight will cause the body to lean forward, and thus become a back exercise reducing the effect intended. Varying the width of the feet and the positional direction of the toes in combination, affords variety and beneficial effects. Placing the heels on a raised block (2 or 3 inches high) will also give additional variety and benefit. #4. The barbell may be held in front of the chest. #5. As the weight increases, it is sometimes necessary to utilize a partner or squat racks (#6) to bring the bar into the starting position.

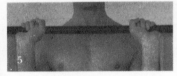

224

HACK LIFT

Purpose: A severe exercise to strengthen the leg muscles near the knees and inside the thighs. Necessary in all phases of Judo.

Performance: Stand erect, heels about 10–20 inches apart on a 2 inch raised block, toes pointed slightly outward. Hold a barbell behind the back, against the buttocks with the hands comfortably spaced, palms to the rear. #1.

Lower the body as in performing Squats, parting the knees. Maintain an erect upper body by keeping the head erect. Keep the barbell close against the buttocks at all times. #2. Continue lowering the body until a deep position is reached. The head may be tilted slightly forward. #3.

Rise from this deep position to the starting position #1. When the starting position is reached, lock the knees fully and tense the thigh muscles for the count of two. Relax the muscles. This is one repetition. Pause and repeat for the desired number of times.

Breathing: Inhale at the starting position. Hold your breath as you lower your body to the deep position. Exhale as you approach the return to the starting position.

Recommended Weight: 40–60 lbs. 10 repetitions.

Key Points: Do not emphasize the forward lean, but try to keep the body upright. The barbell must be kept tightly against the buttocks.

JEFFERSON LIFT

Purpose: An unusual leg exercise designed to promote leg power and flexibility. It also develops lower back strength. Necessary in all phases of Judo.

Performance: Stand erect, astride a barbell, feet comfortably apart (about the width of the shoulders). The left foot is advanced about 10–12 inches. Hold the barbell with both hands, the left hand in front of the body, palm inward; the right hand behind the body, palm also inward. With the arms at full length, the bar rests just under the crotch. The head may be tilted slightly forward. #1.

Lower the body by bending the knees, keeping the body as erect as possible. The arms retain their relative positions. #2. Continue lowering the body until the deep position shown in #3 is reached. The plates of the barbell just touch the floor, but the barbell is not rested at this point. Immediately, return to the starting position in #1. This is one repetition. Pause and repeat for the desired number of times.

Breathing: Inhale at the starting position. Hold your breath as you lower your body to the deep position. Exhale as you approach the return to the starting position.

Recommended Weight: 60–80 lbs. 10 repetitions.

Key Points: An erect posture must be maintained for best results. Attempt the deepest possible squat position before returning to the upright stance. Do not rest the barbell on the floor at any time. Exceptionally flexible trainees will have to pull the barbell up with the arms into the crotch in order to obtain their deepest position in #3. The stance and the grips may be reversed to perform this exercise on the "other" side.

JUMPING SQUAT

Purpose: An exercise which will develop endurance and powerful springing ability in the legs. Necessary in all phases of Judo.

Performance: Start in a deep squat position with a barbell across the back of your neck and shoulders. Feet spread about shoulder width apart, toes slightly pointed outward. #1.

Using a strong drive from your legs, jump as high as you can into the air from the position shown in #2. Point the toes toward the floor as you leap into the air, taking full advantage of the assistance of the calf muscles. Be sure to maintain a tight grip on the barbell. #3.

When the feet touch the ground again, give way with the downward momentum created and drop into the deep squat position (#1) again. This is one repetition. Spring up immediately and repeat for the desired number of times.

Breathing: Breathe as exertion demands.

Recommended Weight: 30–50 lbs. 10 repetitions.

Key Points: This movement may be done with a "side straddle-hop" or forward and backward "split" position by varying the width and position of the feet.

LEG PRESS MACHINE

Purpose: A developmental exercise which primarily affects the legs, but also the abdominal belt region. Necessary in all phases of Judo.

Performance: Lie on your back under a leg press machine. Raise your buttocks slightly by lying on an incline board. Place your feet flat on the push board. Grip the safety bars with your hands. Spread your knees. #1. Begin pushing the push board with your feet, raising the weights as in #2. Continue this pushing action until the legs are fully outstretched. #3. Lower the weights until you reach the starting position shown in #1. This is one repetition. Pause and repeat for the desired number of times.

Breathing: Breathe as exertion demands.

Recommended Weight: 150–250 lbs. 10 repetitions.

Key Points: When in the positions shown, that is, under the weights, the safety bars should be utilized. These bars keep the weights from complete descent and are safety devices.

From the position shown in #3, it is possible to obtain good calf stimulation by fixing the legs and flexing the ankles—pointing the toes repeatedly. Judo exponents will note the similarity of the position in #1 to that commonly attained in Katame Waza. Develop push power from this position.

LEG EXTENSION CURL

Purpose: An exercise designed to further develop the muscles of the thigh. Useful in post-injury exercise for weak knees. Also affects the fixation power of the abdominal belt region.

Performance: Sit with your feet placed as shown on a Leg Curl Machine. Lean your body slightly backward. Fold your arms across your chest. #1. Extend your legs so that the feet are raised. Maintain your body position of the upper body by fixing the abdominal muscles. Continue the extension until your legs are straight in front of you in a fully extended and locked position. #2. Return your legs to the starting position shown in #1. This is one repetition. Pause and repeat for the desired number of times.

Breathing: Breathe as exertion demands.

Recommended Weight: 50–100 lbs. 10 repetitions.

Key Points: The backward lean of the body is important in this exercise. The body should not "bounce" to aid the legs. The arches of the feet may be protected by padding as shown in the illustrations. Iron boots can be used in lieu of the Leg Curl Machine.

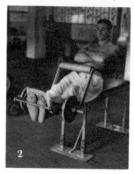

LEG BICEPS CURL

Purpose: To develop the bicepses muscles of the legs necessary in all "pulling" actions of Katame Waza (Sankaku, etc.).

Performance: Lie prone with your feet placed as shown on a Leg Curl Machine, legs fully extended. Hook your heels on the cross bar. Hold the bench or the grip bar with your hands. The head is held slightly off the bench. #1.

Begin to curl the legs toward your buttocks, keeping the toes pointed. #2. Continue this curling action until your legs reach the maximum position of contraction as shown in #3. Return your legs to the starting position shown in #1. This is one repetition. Pause and repeat for the desired number of times.

Breathing: Breathe as exertion demands.

Recommended Weight: 50–100 lbs. 10 repetitions.

Key Points: The buttocks must not be allowed to rise during the curling action. Keeping the head raised and the back slightly arched will help eliminate this undesirable action. The toes may be cocked upward toward the shin to provide a variation exercise. Iron boots can be used in lieu of the Leg Curl Machine.

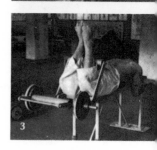

CALF RAISE

Purpose: An aid to the development of the usually stubborn leg muscles (calf). Also promotes ankle flexibility. Necessary in all phases of Judo.

Performance: Stand on one leg on a two or three inch wood block or a similar height of weight plates. Center the weight of the body over the part of the foot where the toes join the sole, and primarily on the ball of the foot. Hang the heel over the block or other means of support. Fold the other leg and rest it on the rear portion of the weighted leg. The body is held erect and aided in its balance by a wall, post, or some other support. #1.

Rise up on the toes to the fullest possible contraction of the calf muscle. #2. Immediately lower your body, without bending your knee, so that the heel touches the floor behind the block. #3. This is one repetition. Pause and repeat for the desired number of times. Change legs and repeat similarly.

Breathing: Breathe as exertion demands.

Recommended Weight: Body weight. 20–30 repetitions each leg.

Key Points: Varying the height of the block, positioning the toes inward, straight ahead, extremely outward, and reversing this motion by placing the heel on the block and the toes off, all provide possible variations of this exercise. A dumbbell may be held in the free hand in order to increase resistance, but this is not absolutely necessary. This exercise which exercises the calves singularly is considered by the authors as superior to those exercises which exercise both calves at once.

CHEST GROUP

DECLINE STRAIGHT-ARM DUMBBELL LATERAL

Purpose: Promotes chest development necessary in the execution of powerful Osaekomi Waza.

Performance: Lie on your back on a bench which is on a slight decline (10°–15°). Hold a dumbbell in each hand, straight-armed, and slightly above your abdominal region. The dumbbells or the arms must not rest on the body. #1.

Move the dumbbells backwards, with straight arms, away from the body, but on the same plane as the body. #2. Continue lowering the dumbbells until they are even with the shoulders. #3.

Return the dumbbells to the starting position in #1, keeping the arms straight. This is one repetition. Pause and repeat for the desired number of times.

Breathing: Inhale as you move the dumbbells backward from the starting position. Exhale as you return the dumbbells to the starting position.

Recommended Weight: 10–20 lbs. (each dumbbell). 10 repetitions.

Key Points: The arms must be kept straight during the entire movement. The dumbbells never rest on the body. Notice that the dumbbell ends touch in the starting position.

228

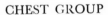

BARBELL SUPINE PRESS (narrow grip)

Purpose: A developmental exercise designed to effect the muscles of the chest necessary in pushing actions useful in defensive movements of Tachi Waza and Katame Waza. Also affects the muscles of the arms.

Performance: Arrange a sturdy bench either on the level ground, or on a slight incline as shown. Take a supine position, holding a barbell at arms length with a narrow grip, palms facing forward. Place your feet on the floor for stability. #1.

Lower the barbell to the chest, spreading the elbows as shown in #2 and #3. Return to the starting position shown in #1. This is one repetition. Pause and repeat for the desired number of times.

Breathing: Inhale as the barbell is lowered and exhale as it is pushed upward.

Recommended Weight: 50–100 lbs. 10 repetitions.

Key Points: This exercise can be performed on either the level, incline, or decline. Spacing the hands as widely as possible or at a normal spaced grip (shoulder width) provides variety to this exercise and should be utilized. *(See page 269.)*

INCLINE DUMBBELL BENT-ARM LATERAL

Purpose: To develop the muscles of the upper chest and shoulders which strengthen holding actions necessary in Osaekomi Waza.

Performance: Lie on an incline bench (about 45°), holding dumbbells overhead with the arms slightly bowed. Place the feet flat on the floor. The dumbbells are held parallel. #1. Begin lowering the dumbbells with the arms bent at the elbows. #2. Continue lowering the dumbbells, keeping the elbows bent in approximately the same relative position. Pull the elbows back as the weights reach the lowest position shown in #3. Return the dumbbells to the starting position #1, being careful to use the chest muscles to effect this return motion. The arms remain bent at the elbows during the entire motion. This is one repetition. Pause and repeat for the desired number of times.

Breathing: Inhale as the dumbbells are lowered, exhale as the dumbbells are brought back to the starting position.

Recommended Weight: 15–30 lbs. (each dumbbell). 10 repetitions.

Key Points: This lateral action is not a pressing action and the chest muscles should effect the movement. Care must be taken to maintain the relative angle of bend in the arms during the entire movement, or the value of the exercise will be lost.

INCLINE DUMBBELL PRESS

Purpose: A developmental exercise designed to increase power and flexibility in the chest and shoulders. Necessary in all phases of Judo.

Performance: Lie on an incline bench (about 45°), holding dumbbells overhead with the arms straight. Place your feet flat on the floor. The dumbbells are held end-to-end. #1.

Begin lowering the dumbbells with the weights directly over the shoulders, elbows pointing downward. #2. Continue lowering the dumbbells until the weights just touch the shoulders. The elbows are now pointing downward. #3. Press the dumbbells upward and return to the starting position shown in #1. This is one repetition. Pause and repeat for the desired number of times.

Breathing: Inhale as the dumbbells are lowered; exhale as the dumbbells are brought back to the starting position.

Recommended Weight: 35–50 lbs. (each dumbbell). 10 repetitions.

Key Points: The dumbbells may be started in a parallel position instead of end-to-end as described. The pressing should be made in the direction of the vertical line directly above the shoulders.

The extreme stretching of the chest can only be achieved by bringing the elbows into the low position shown in #3.

DECLINE DUMBBELL PRESS

Purpose: A stimulating exercise which flushes the muscle areas of the lower chest and shoulders, aiding the promotion of muscle growth and strength necessary in all phases of Judo.

Performance: Lie on a decline bench (5°–10°) holding a pair of light dumbbells overhead end-to-end as shown in #1.

Lower the dumbbells to the lowest position so that the weights just touch the shoulders. Point the elbows downward. #2. Press the dumbbells to the starting position shown in #1. This is one repetition. Pause and repeat for the desired number of times.

Breathing: Breathe as exertion demands.

Recommended Weight: 15–25 lbs. (each dumbbell). 10 repetitions.

Key Points: The weights in this exercise should be pressed and returned rather rapidly to cause a quick flushing action in the muscles. The pressing action should be in the vertical direction directly above the shoulders.

SUPINE DUMBBELL PRESS

Purpose: Designed to increase the chest size and flexibility. Promotes tremendous pushing power necessary in various phases of Tachi Waza and Katame Waza.

Performance: Lie on your back on a bench holding a dumbbell in each hand. Position the dumbbells so that the inside plates are end-to-end. Hold your arms at full length, with the dumbbells vertically above your shoulders. Place your feet flat on the floor for stability. #1.

Lower the dumbbells, keeping them a little wider than shoulder width apart. Point the elbows downward. Keep the dumbbells vertically above your elbows. #2. Continue lowering the dumbbells until the low position which allows the inside plates to touch the shoulders is reached. Elbows must continue to point downward. #3. Return the dumbbells to the starting position shown in #1. This is one repetition. Pause and repeat for the desired number of times.

Breathing: Inhale as the dumbbells are lowered; exhale as the dumbbells are brought back to the starting position.

Recommended Weight: 30–60 lbs. (each dumbbell). 10 repetitions.

Key Points: The pressing action must be in a vertical direction directly above the shoulders. At the starting position, after each return from the low position, the dumbbells must be brought together.

SUPINE STRAIGHT-ARM DUMBBELL PULLOVER

Purpose: A breathing rhythm exercise designed to stretch the rib-box and chest muscles. Develops flexibility in the back and shoulder muscles. Particularly useful in Katame Waza.

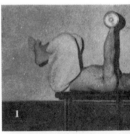

Performance: Lie on your back on a bench holding a dumbbell in each hand so that the palms are pointing toward your feet. Fold the legs to keep the back straight and in contact with the bench. #1.

Lower the dumbbells simultaneously with the palms upward, keeping the dumbbells relatively close together (end plates a few inches apart). #2. Continue lowering until the lowest possible position is reached by straight-arm lowering. #3. Return to the starting position in #1. This is one repetition. Pause and repeat for the desired number of times.

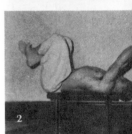

Breathing: Inhale slowly as you lower the dumbbells to the lowest position. You should have taken only *half* a breath when you arrive at the position shown in #3. *Continue inhalation* as you return the dumbbells so when you reach the starting position (#1), you reach capacity inhalation. Expel air forcefully at this time.

Recommended Weight: 10–20 lbs. (each dumbbell). 10 repetitions.

Key Points: The arms must be kept straight and the legs doubled to retain the intended purpose of this exercise.

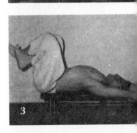

SUPINE BENT-ARM DUMBBELL LATERAL

Purpose: To develop the muscles of the chest which strengthen holding actions necessary in Osaekomi Waza.

Performance: Lie on your back on a bench holding a dumbbell in each hand. The arms are not straight, but slightly bowed as though you were reaching around a large barrel. The inside plates of the dumbbells touch. Hang the head slightly over the end of the bench. Place the feet flat on the floor. #1. Lower the dumbbells simultaneously keeping the elbows fixed so that the approximate angle of the upper arm and lower arm is always the same. #2. Continue lowering the dumbbells until the lowest position possible is reached. The angle of the arms is as it was in the starting position. #3. Return the dumbbells to the starting position (#1) by action of the chest muscles (not pure arm power). This is one repetition. Pause and repeat for the desired number of times.

Breathing: Inhale as you lower the dumbbells from the starting position; exhale as you return the dumbbells to the starting position.

Recommended Weight: 20–45 lbs. (each dumbbell). 10 repetitions.

Key Points: See Incline Dumbbell Bent-arm Lateral *(page 229)*. The back must not be allowed to arch from the bench. To avoid this, fold the legs as per Supine Straight-arm Dumbbell Pullover *(page 231)*.

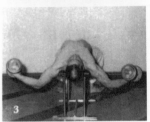

SUPINE BENT-ARM DUMBBELL PULLOVER

Purpose: To develop greater flexibility in the chest and shoulders as an aid in Nogarekata for Katame Waza.

Performance: Lie across a bench with the upper part of your back and neck touching the bench. Hold a dumbbell cupped in both hands, plams away from the body. Keep the buttocks low, and arch the back. #1. Lower the dumbbell to a position behind the head by bending the arms. The dumbbell just grazes the head and face as it passes. #2. Continue lowering the dumbbell until the lowest possible position is reached. #3. Pull the dumbbell to the starting position. This is one repetition. Pause and repeat for the desired number of times.

Breathing: Inhale as you lower the dumbbell from the starting position; exhale as you return the dumbbell to the starting position.

Recommended Weight: 35–60 lbs. 10 repetitions.

Key Points: The breathing should be forceful, and the body should be forced down to the floor at the buttocks as much as possible. Do not let the abdominal region rise. The feet may be straightened out for more severe stretching.

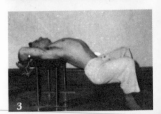

SUPINE DUMBBELL THRUST

Purpose: A method of developing strength in pushing and thrusting necessary in Tachi Waza and Katame Waza.

Performance: Lie on your back on the ground, holding a dumbbell in each hand. The dumbbells must not be allowed to rest on the body and are held end-to-end at arms length just above the upper thigh region. Lift your head off the floor, chin tucked in to the chest. Raise your feet off the floor, legs straight, feet together. #1.

Bring the dumbbells up to the chest, bending the arms and keeping the elbows off the ground. Maintain the body position originally assumed. #2. Continue bringing the dumbbells up to the chest until the position shown in #3 is reached. Return to the starting position with a forceful thrusting action. This is one repetition. Pause and repeat for the desired number of times.

Breathing: Breathe as exertion demands.

Recommended Weight: 10–20 lbs. (each dumbbell). 10 repetitions.

Key Points: The body must be kept in the starting position during the whole exercise as the arms execute the thrust. The thrust is a "scooping" or slightly circular (concave) action. To increase the severity of this exercise, lift the shoulders from the floor and hold them up throughout the entire movement.

DECLINE DIPPING

Purpose: Designed to promote great flexibility in the chest, upper back, and shoulder muscles, and an aid to arm power. Necessary in developing tremendous pushing power for Nage Waza and Katame Waza.

Performance: Position your body between two benches, and place your hands flat on the benches. Place your feet on another bench or support *higher* than your hands. This is similar to a "push-up" position. Maintain your body in one plane. Extend your arms fully. #1.

Lower your body, taking care to maintain a rigid, straight-line position, as shown in #2. Continue lowering the body until you reach the lowest possible position. Your body will now be in a rigid straight-line position, but your head will be lower than your feet. #3. Return the body to the starting position by straightening the arms fully. This is one repetition. Repeat for the desired number of times.

Breathing: Breathe as exertion demands.

Recommended Weight: Body weight. 10 repetitions.

Key Points: The body must not be allowed to sag or arch. Holding the position shown in #2 for 10 counts on the last return repetition develops tremendous fixation power in the body. Advanced trainees may have a partner place additional weight (plates) on their back before commencing this exercise.

Auxiliary Exercises 233

SUPINE STRAIGHT-ARM BARBELL PULLOVER

Purpose: To develop extreme flexibility of the chest, back, and shoulder muscles necessary in Nage Waza and Katame Waza.

Performance: Lie on your back on a bench, holding a barbell with an extra wide grip (out to the plates) above the body, palms facing forward. Place your feet on the floor. #1.

Lower the barbell with straight arms to a position behind your head. #2. Continue lowering the barbell to the lowest possible position. #3. Return the barbell to the starting position, keeping the arms straight throughout the movement. This is one repetition. Pause and repeat for the desired number of times.

Breathing: Inhale as you lower the barbell; exhale as you return the barbell.

Recommended Weight: 15–30 lbs. 10 repetitions.

Key Points: As the barbell is lowered, stretch the arms fully. The back must not be allowed to arch or the abdominal region to lift. To eliminate this, the legs may be folded as per Supine Straight-arm Dumbbell Pullover (*page 231*). Do not hurry the cadence of this exercise. Concentrate on breathing.

INCLINE DUMBBELL CRIS-CROSS

Purpose: A stimulating exercise which flushes the muscle areas of the upper chest and shoulders, aiding the promotion of muscle growth and strength necessary in all phases of Judo.

Performance: Lie on an incline (5°–10°) bench holding a pair of light dumbbells crossed arm over arm (either arm uppermost). Place your feet flat on the floor. #1.

Simultaneously raise the dumbbells by lifting your arms and begin to uncross them. #2. Continue this action and as the dumbbells come into the approximate position shown in #3, pull the elbows backward. Continue the motion until the low position shown in #4 is reached. Return to the starting position shown in #1. This is one repetition. Pause and repeat for the desired number of times.

Breathing: Breathe as exertion demands.

Recommended Weight: 8–15 lbs. (each dumbbell). 10 repetitions.

Key Points: The arms may be alternated as to position (uppermost-lowermost) in the performance of the repetitions. The dumbbells should be moved rather rapidly to effect a flushing action in the muscle areas.

UPPER BACK-NECK GROUP

SEATED BARBELL PRESS BEHIND NECK

Purpose: To develop pushing power in the upper body and great shoulder flexibility. Also develops fixation power in the abdominal belt region. Necessary in all phases of Judo.

Performance: Sit on a bench and place your feet flat on the floor, somewhat widespread. Hold a barbell overhead, spacing your hands wide (out to the plates), palms facing forward. #1.

Lower the barbell so that the bar reaches the lowest possible position on the upper back. Pull the shoulders back to accomplish this. #2. Press the barbell up overhead until the starting position is reached. #1. This is one repetition. Pause and repeat for the desired number of times.

Breathing: Breathe as exertion demands.

Recommended Weight: 40–80 lbs. 10 repetitions.

Key Points: The grip must be very wide. The upper body must be kept erect. This exercise may be increased in severity by bringing the feet up so that they are outstretched on top of the bench. *(See Plate 4, page 30.)* The exercise may also be performed from a standing position, but in this way, some of the fixation value for the abdominal belt is lost.

UPRIGHT ROWING

Purpose: Designed to develop the muscles of the upper back, shoulders, and neck for increased efficiency in pulling and lifting motions of Nage Waza.

Performance: Stand erect with the feet slightly apart, feet flat on the floor, toes pointed outward. Hold a barbell with a narrow grip, palms facing the body as shown in #1.

Raise the barbell to the height of the chin by arms and shoulder power. Force the elbows to a high position. #2. Lower the weight to the starting position shown in #1. This is one repetition. Pause and repeat for the desired number of times.

Breathing: Inhale as you raise the barbell; exhale as you lower the barbell.

Recommended Weight: 35–50 lbs. 10 repetitions.

Key Points: The body must be maintained in an erect position and not allowed to sway or in any way assist the pulling motion. Concentrate on strict form. The elbows must be spread and pulled high at the high point of the movement. Some variety can be introduced by pulling the bar high enough to allow the hands to come to the height of the forehead. This exercise may be done with dumbbells.

Auxiliary Exercises   235

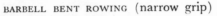

BARBELL BENT ROWING (narrow grip)

Purpose: A developmental movement which severely affects all major muscles of the upper body, with emphasis on upper back and arms. Necessary in all phases of Judo, but particularly good in promoting pulling power useful in Osaekomi Waza and Shime Waza.

Performance: Stand bent over from the waist. Hold a barbell, bar resting next to your shins, with a narrow grip, palms inward. Lock the legs. Spread the feet slightly wider than your shoulders and point the toes outward. #1. Using arm power, bring the barbell off the ground and begin pulling it to the belt. #2. Continue the pulling until the bar reaches the belt region of the body. #3. At this position, the body is still in the same relative position as the starting position—knees locked, back straight—as shown in #4. Return the weight to the lowest position, but reach *outward* and forward with it, maintaining the body in relatively the same position. #5. This is one repetition. Pause and repeat for the desired number of times.

Breathing: Breathe as exertion demands.

Recommended Weight: 50–75 lbs. 10 repetitions.

Key Points: Do not allow the body to sway up and down to assist the movement. Keep the knees locked and back relatively straight. *(See page 268.)*

BRIDGE AND BARBELL PRESS

Purpose: To strengthen the neck muscles and to coordinate body power especially useful in Katame Waza.

Performance: Assume a bridge position, holding a barbell over your body with arms fully stretched. The weight of your body rests on the top of your head and feet which are flat on the floor, and well under your body. Spread the feet slightly wider than the shoulders. #1.

Lower the barbell to the chest while maintaining the bridge position. Point the elbows downward. #2. Return the barbell to the starting position in #1. This is one repetition. Pause and repeat for the desired number of times.

Breathing: Breathe as exertion demands.

Recommended Weight: 35–75 lbs. 10 repetitions.

Key Points: In the starting position, hold the barbell in a position over the body which brings the bar slightly forward of the vertical line. The body must not aid the pressing action. Fix the body as shown in the illustrations. Note that this bridge is somewhat lower than that assumed for the Bridge and Barbell Bent-arm Pullover, page 237. The hands may be spaced wide, normal, or narrow for variety. This exercise may be performed with dumbbells.

BRIDGE AND BARBELL BENT-ARM PULLOVER

Purpose: A severe exercise designed to strengthen the neck muscles and to coordinate body power especially useful in Katame Waza.

Performance: Assume a bridge position, holding a barbell over your body with arms fully stretched. The weight of your body rests on the top of your head, but more toward your forehead (a somewhat higher bridge than executed in the Bridge and Barbell Press, page 236), and your feet which are flat on the floor, well under your body. Spread the feet slightly wider than the shoulders. #1.

Lower the barbell to a position in front of your face by bending your arms and reaching backward (away from your face), maintaining the bridge position. Do not fully extend your arms, but keep flex in them. #2. Continue lowering the barbell with bent arms until the barbell plates just touch the ground. #3. Return to the starting position shown in #1. This is one repetition. Pause and repeat for the desired number of times.

Breathing: Breathe as exertion demands.

Recommended Weight: 25–60 lbs. 10 repetitions.

Key Points: In the starting position, hold the barbell in a position over the body which brings the bar vertically over the throat. The body must not aid the pullover action. The barbell can be gripped with the palms up or down. Space the hands a little less than shoulder width apart.

DUMBBELL BENT LATERAL

Purpose: A severe exercise designed to promote the growth of muscles in the upper back and shoulders, developing great power necessary in all phases of Judo.

Performance: Stand bent over, upper body parallel to the floor. Hold a pair of dumbbells together (parallel) in front of you so that your arms are vertical to the floor. Bow the arms slightly as shown in #1.

Raise the dumbbells laterally, maintaining the bend in the body. Keep the arms bowed in relatively the same position as when you started. #2. Continue to raise the dumbbells laterally, pulling the elbows upward high above the shoulders. Both the bend in the body and the bowed position of the arms is maintained. #3. Return the dumbbells to the starting position. This is one repetition. Pause and repeat for the desired number of times.

Breathing: Breathe as exertion demands.

Recommended Weight: 10–20 lbs. (each dumbbell). 10 repetitions

Key Points: The arms must be kept in the bowed position throughout the movement. The body must not sway to assist the lifting of the dumbbells. To ensure this, keep the knees slightly flexed, but fixed. In extreme cases, the head may be placed on a high bench or against the wall. The elbows must be pulled high.

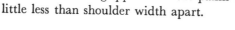

PRONE INCLINE DUMBBELL STRAIGHT-ARM RAISE

Purpose: Designed to fully flush the muscles of the upper back and shoulders promoting growth and strength necessary in all phases of Judo.
Performance: Lie prone on an incline bench (about 45°) holding a pair of light dumbbells with arms hanging vertically downward. Brace your body with your feet flat on the floor and rest your forehead on the upper part of the bench. #1.
Raise the dumbbells laterally with straight arms. This lateral raise is slightly forward of the shoulders. #2. Continue the raising of the dumbbells until they reach the highest point possible with straight arms. This point is lateral, but slightly above shoulder height. #3. Lower the dumbbells to the starting position shown in #1. This is one repetition. Pause and repeat for the desired number of times.
Breathing: Breathe as exertion demands.
Recommended Weight: 8–12 pounds (each dumbbell). 10 repetitions.
Key Points: The dumbbells must not be raised backward and laterally. As the repetitions increase and fatigue sets in, a strong effort must be made to bring the dumbbells above the shoulder height at the highest position.

LAT MACHINE PULL-DOWN BEHIND NECK

Purpose: A severe exercise designed to promote great strength in the upper back, arms, and shoulders, necessary in all phases of Judo.
Performance: Seat yourself under a lat machine, and extend your legs forward. Grasp the bar with a wide grip as shown in #1.
Pull the bar down behind the neck, keeping the elbows well back and pointed outward. #2. Continue pulling the bar until the bar comes to rest on the upper-back-neck region. #3. Return the machine weights to the starting position by allowing the bar to rise until you reach the position shown in #1. This is one repetition. Pause and repeat for the desired number of times.
Breathing: Inhale before pulling the bar down; exhale as the bar rises.
Recommended Weight: 50–80 lbs. 10 repetitions.
Key Points: Various postures may be assumed under most lat machines, but sitting will emphasize the functioning of the upper back-shoulder-arm regions. If the weight used becomes so heavy as to lift you from the floor, a partner may sit across your legs to hold you in place. An extremely wide grip will allow the bar to be pulled down to a position similar to that in Seated Barbell Press Behind Neck *(page 235)*. #2.

DUMBBELL ROWING

Purpose: To strengthen the pulling muscles of the upper back, shoulders, and arms for improvement in pulling power necessary in Nage Waza and Katame Waza.

Performance: Bend the body from the waist so that one hand rests on a bench or other low support. The upper body is parallel to the floor. Spread the feet about shoulder width apart, feet flat on the floor, toes pointed outward. Grasp a dumbbell with the other hand, so that the arm hangs vertically. #1.

Pull the dumbbell up, bending the arm so that the elbow is pointed upward and outward. Continue pulling the dumbbell until a high point is reached which brings the elbow higher than the body, still pointing upward but slightly behind the body (see Key Points). #2. Lower the dumbbell to the hand position, but in front of the foot on the *opposite side* (left foot in #1). This is one repetition. Pause and repeat for the desired number of times. Repeat using the other arm.

Breathing: Breathe as exertion demands.

Recommended Weight: 25–50 lbs. 10 repetitions (each arm).

Key Points: The supporting arm should be kept straight, not allowing the body to assist in lifting the dumbbell. The path of the dumbbell is diagonal and circular. Beginning from a point next to or in front of the opposite side foot, to a point high under the armpit.

SHRUGGING

Purpose: To flush the muscles of the upper back-neck and shoulder groups promoting growth and flexibility for greater suppleness necessary in all phases of Judo.

Performance: Stand erect, holding a dumbbell in each hand. Spread the feet slightly apart, feet flat on the floor, toes pointed outward. #1.

Simultaneously, lift your shoulders, shrugging them so that you describe a circular motion from front to rear in a counter-clockwise motion. Take care to draw the shoulders high to the ears before lowering them. #2. Continue lowering the dumbbells and throw your head backwards slightly as you do until you come to the starting position as shown in #3. This is one repetition. Pause and repeat for the desired number of times.

Breathing: Inhale as you shrug the shoulders upward; exhale as you lower them.

Recommended Weight: 50–90 lbs. (each dumbbell). 10 repetitions.

Key Points: The arms must not offer assistance in lifting the dumbbells. This exercise may be performed using a barbell.

LAT MACHINE ROWING

Purpose: To develop pulling power using the upper back muscles and arms. Also affects the fixation ability of the abdominal belt region. Necessary in all phases of Judo.

Performance: Sit on the floor in front of a lat machine, feet spread and straight in front of you. Grasp the bar of the lat machine with a narrow grip. Arms must be fully stretched upward and slightly in front of your body. #1.

Pull the bar in to your waist, using the muscles of the arms and back to accomplish this. The elbows will point downward, but must be spread to accommodate the body trunk. #2. Continue the pulling until the bar touches your belt region or the thighs. #3. Allow the machine weights to raise the bar to the starting position shown in #1. This is one repetition. Pause and repeat for the desired number of times.

Breathing: Breathe as exertion demands.

Recommended Weight: 40–75 lbs. 10 repetitions.

Key Points: Various positions of your body which change the angle of pull have beneficial effects. The trainee is invited to experiment. Sit far enough in front of the lat machine to allow a full stretch of the arms without allowing the weight to touch the floor. If the weight used is too heavy, a partner may sit across your legs to keep you in place.

CHIN BEHIND NECK

Purpose: A developer of the upper back, shoulder, and arm muscles necessary in all phases of Judo.

Performance: Hang from a chinning bar, using a very wide grip. #1.
Pull the body with arm and shoulder power. #2. Continue pulling upward until the bar touches the body *behind* the neck. Keep the feet together and the body vertical. #3. Lower the body to the starting position as shown in #1. This is one repetition. Pause and repeat for the desired number of times.

Breathing: Breathe as exertion demands.

Recommended Weight: Body weight. 10 repetitions.

Key Points: The width of the grip can be varied to produce different beneficial effects. The body must remain vertical and should not be allowed to swing. Should more resistance be desired, a dumbbell may be held with the feet.

A severe variation of this exercise which strongly affects the abdominal belt region can be performed by keeping the legs in an outstretched position at a right angle to the upper body and parallel to the floor.

ARM-SHOULDER GROUP

MILITARY BARBELL CURL

Purpose: To develop powerful forearms, wrists, and arms (bicepses) necessary in all phases of Judo.

Performance: Stand erect with a barbell held in the hands, palms upward with the backs of the hands resting on the thighs or just slightly wider than the thighs. Spread the feet about shoulder width apart, feet flat on the floor, toes pointed outward. #1.

Raise the barbell in an arc upward toward the chest using only arm power. Keep the body erect. #2. Continue this curling action until the barbell touches the chest at the sternun or comes just across the neck (in this case, the elbows will come forward and upward slightly). #3. Lower the barbell to the starting position as shown in #1. This is one repetition. Pause and repeat for the desired number of times.

Breathing: Inhale at the starting position. Hold your breath as you curl the barbell. Exhale only as you lower the barbell to the starting position.

Recommended Weight: 40–75 lbs. 10 repetitions.

Key Points: The body must not sway to assist the curling action. Different spacing of the hands—wide-normal-narrow—will produce a variety of effects.

DUMBBELL BICEPS CONCENTRATION CURL

Purpose: An extreme developmental exercise for the arm biceps promoting strength necessary in all pulling actions of Judo.

Performance: Sit on a bench, holding a dumbbell in one hand. Fix the elbow of that arm with the other arm as shown in #1.

Begin curling the dumbbell, taking care not to let the elbow move. The arm providing the fixation to the curling arm, must be held rigid. #2. Continue curling the dumbbell until the hand just reaches the chin. #3. Return the dumbbell to the starting position in #1. This is one repetition. Pause and repeat 8 times before changing to the other arm. Execute 8 repetitions with this arm also. Return the dumbbell to the other hand and execute 7 repetitions. Continue this curling motion with each arm, each time, decreasing by one repetition until the last movement is made for one repetition.

Breathing: Breathe as exertion demands.

Recommended Weight: 15–30 lbs. Repetitions as described.

Key Points: The palm of the curling arm must continue to be turned upward throughout all the motions. Maintain the arc of curl as shown. The fixing arm must be rigid enough to keep the curling arm elbow from moving.

BARBELL STRICT CURL

Purpose: A severe exercise designed to isolate the (bicepses) muscle action (useful in specialization), promoting growth and strength necessary in all phases of Judo.

Performance: Lean upright against a wall or some solid support. Place your feet away from the wall and spread them slightly wider than the shoulders apart, toes pointed outward. The knees are slightly bent, but fixed. Hold a barbell with a normal grip, palms up, the elbows against the wall. #1 and #2.

Curl the barbell to the chest, but keep the elbows tight against the wall. #3. Continue the curling until the bar reaches the chest. #4. Return the barbell to the starting position in #1. This is one repetition. Pause and repeat for the desired number of times.

Breathing: Breathe as exertion demands.

Recommended Weight: 35–60 lbs. 10 repetitions.

Key Points: Keep the back pressed against the wall by bracing with the feet. The elbows must not be allowed to move away from the wall. Variations may be produced by varying the spacing of the hands (wide-normal-narrow).

BARBELL STRICT REVERSE CURL

Purpose: A severe exercise designed to isolate forearm muscle action (useful in specialization), promoting growth and strength necessary in all phases of Judo.

Performance: Lean upright against a wall or some solid support. Place your feet away from the wall and spread them slightly wider than the shoulders apart, toes pointed outward. The knees are slightly bent, but fixed. Hold a barbell with a normal grip, palms down, the elbows against the wall. #1 and #2.

Reverse curl the barbell to the chest, but keep the elbows tight against the wall. #3. Continue the curling until the bar reaches the neck. #4. Return the barbell to the starting position in #1. This is one repetition. Pause and repeat for the desired number of times.

Breathing: Breathe as exertion demands.

Recommended Weight: 25–40 lbs. 10 repetitions.

Key Points: Keep the back pressed against the wall by bracing with the feet. The elbows must not be allowed to move away from the wall. Variations may be produced by varying the spacing of the hands (wide-normal-narrow).

INCLINE DUMBBELL BICEPS CURL

Purpose: A severe development exercise for the arm (bicepses) muscles, promoting growth and strength necessary in all phases of Judo.

Performance: Lie on an incline bench (about 45°), holding a dumbbell in each hand, arms hanging vertically downward, palms up. Brace the feet on the floor in front of you. #1.

Begin curling the dumbbells simultaneously, taking care to keep the elbows well back. #2. Continue curling until the dumbbells come up to shoulder level, and as they do, allow the elbows to rise. They now point to the front. The dumbbells are just above the shoulders. #3. Return the dumbbells to the starting position shown in #1. This is one repetition. Pause and repeat for the desired number of times.

Breathing: Breathe as exertion demands.

Recommended Weight: 15–25 lbs. (each dumbbell). 10 repetitions.

Key Points: The elbows must be kept back during the curling action. They are permitted to rise only when the curl reaches maximum position, after which they are again lowered to the position well-back. This must be done prior to returning the dumbbells to the starting position.

DUMBBELL FIXED ELBOW CURL

Purpose: A severe exercise which isolates the arm biceps muscle action (useful in specialization), promoting growth and strength necessary in all phases of Judo.

Performance: Sit behind an incline bench holding a dumbbell in one hand. Outstretch this arm on a decline (about 45°), palm up. #1.

Curl the dumbbell, palm up, elbow fixed on the incline board. #2. Continue curling the dumbbell until it just touches your chin as shown in #3. Lower the dumbbell to the starting position in #1. This is one repetition. Pause and repeat for the desired number of times. Repeat this movement using the other arm.

Breathing: Breathe as exertion demands.

Recommended Weight: 15–25 lbs. 10 repetitions (each arm).

Key Points: The elbow should be protected by some padding. This exercise may be performed on the basis of *eccentric* contraction if so desired (see page 34).

If the decline is more than 45°, this exercise becomes more like the Bench End Curl on page 249.

BAR TRICEPS EXTENSION

Purpose: A severe contraction and extension exercise affecting the tricepses muscles of the arms and the muscles of the shoulder and chest region, promoting flexibility necessary in all phases of Judo.

Performance: Stand bent front the waist so that the upper body is parallel to the floor. Hold a barbell behind the legs as shown in #1. Spread the feet about shoulder width apart, toes outward.

Begin raising the bar upward and pushing away from the body so that the arms are straightened. #2. Continue raising the bar until it is brought above the body as shown in #3. Return the bar to the starting position in #1. This is one repetition. Pause and repeat for the desired number of times.

Breathing: Breathe as exertion demands.

Recommended Weight: Weight of bar (15–45 lbs.). 10 repetitions.

Key Points: The arms must be kept straight during the entire movement. This exercise can be performed on the basis of *eccentric* contraction if so desired *(see page 34).*

SUPINE TRICEPS BARBELL EXTENSION

Purpose: Designed to develop the tricepses muscles of the arms, promoting growth and strength necessary in all phases of Judo.

Performance: Lie on a bench holding a barbell with a grip spaced about as wide as your shoulders. Hold the barbell overhead, palms up, so that the bar touches the top of your head. Place your feet flat on the floor. #1 and #2.

Push the barbell backward on the same plane as the body. #3. Continue pushing the barbell backward, keeping it on the same plane as the body, until the arms are completely extended. #4. Return the barbell to the starting position shown in #1 and #2. This is one repetition. Pause and repeat for the desired number of times.

Breathing: Breathe as exertion demands.

Recommended Weight: 20–50 lbs. 10 repetitions.

Key Points: The barbell must remain on the same plane as the body throughout the entire exercise. This exercise may be performed on the basis of *eccentric contraction* if so desired *(see page 34).*

SUPINE TRICEPS BARBELL PRESS

Purpose: Designed to develop the tricepses muscles of the arms, promoting growth and strength necessary in all phases of Judo.

Performance: Lie on a bench holding a barbell with a grip spaced about as wide as your shoulders. Hold the barbell overhead, palms up, so that the bar touches the top of your head. Place your feet flat on the floor. Point your elbows upward. #1 and #2.

Begin pressing the barbell upward, taking care to keep the elbows fixed. #3. Continue pressing the barbell upward until it reaches the approximate position shown in #4. Notice that the elbows have not moved. Return the barbell to the starting position shown in #1. This is one repetition. Pause and repeat for the desired number of times.

Breathing: Breathe as exertion demands.

Recommended Weight: 25–50 lbs. 10 repetitions.

Key Points: Study the position of the elbows very carefully. This relative position must be maintained during the pressing action. Note also the final position of the bar at the height of the movement at which the arms are fully stretched and locked.

STANDING ALTERNATE DUMBBELL CURL

Purpose: To promote a flushing action for the arm (bicepses) muscles necessary to growth and the development of strength necessary in all phases of Judo.

Performance: Stand erect holding a dumbbell in each hand. Place the feet together. #1.

Curl one dumbbell, palm upward, keeping the other arm along your side. #2. Continue curling this dumbbell until the dumbbell is brought up to the ear. Raise the elbow high. #3. Return the dumbbell to the starting position in #1. Begin curling the other dumbbell only after the original dumbbell comes to complete rest, as shown in #4. Continue curling this dumbbell until it is brought up to the ear. Raise the elbow high. #5. Return the dumbbell to the starting position in #1. This is one repetition. Pause and repeat for the desired number of times.

Breathing: Breathe as exertion demands.

Recommended Weight: 25–40 lbs. (each dumbbell). 10 repetitions.

Key Points: The common fault of exercise in this particular movement is the use of the body to assist the curling action. The body must not be allowed to sway in any fashion. The dumbbell which is lowered, must be fully lowered to its starting position and must come to *complete* rest before the other dumbbell is curled. Any premature curling action by one arm as the other is being lowered, will destroy the intended effect. Be careful not to control the lowering. Maintain *concentric* contraction *(see page 33).*

DUMBBELL CIRCULAR SWING CURL

Purpose: A composite exercise designed to promote flushing action to the arms and shoulders, promoting growth and strength in these regions. Necessary in all phases of Judo.

Performance: Stand erect holding a pair of dumbbells so that the arms hang along your sides, palms inward. Spread your feet about shoulder width apart, toes outward. #1.

Raise the right arm and hold the arm vertically with the dumbbell alongside your head, palm inward. The left arm is raised so that the dumbbell is vertical and close to the abdomen, palm inward. #2. Extend the right arm, turning the palm outward as the arm assumes a right-angled position. Reverse curl the dumbbell in the left hand, palm inward, to a point near the upper chest. #3. Continue extending the right arm, palm down, so that the dumbbell is thrust outward and high above shoulder level. The left arm continues to reverse curl the other dumbbell, palm inward #4.

Lower the right arm fully extended, palm down, as the left arm begins to extend with the palm turned outward. #5. Continue to extend the left arm, palm down, thrusting the dumbbell outward and high above shoulder level. The right arm now brings the dumbbell in circularly to a position in front of the abdomen, palm inward. #6. Continue extending the left arm palm down as the right arm reverse curls the dumbbell, palm inward, to a point just at the upper chest. #7. Lower the left arm fully extended, palm down, as the right arm comes into a vertical position with the dumbbell alongside your head, palm inward. #8. Bring the dumbbell in the left hand into your abdomen, using a circular motion, palm inward, as your right arm takes a vertical position alongside your head, palm inward (this is like original position in #2). #9.

This is one repetition. Pause and repeat for the desired number of times.

Breathing: Breathe as exertion demands.

Recommended Weight: 15–30 lbs. (each dumbbell). 10 repetitions.

Key Points: This motion must be circular and rhythmic. Only practice can bring this action. (A variation of the old Zotman exercise). The arm that is thrust and thus fully extended, must be thrust *above* shoulder height. Turn the head to follow the dumbbell in its extension and circular path.

DUMBBELL WRIST CURLING

Purpose: A developmental exercise for the muscles of the wrist and fore-arm, producing strength necessary in all phases of Judo.

Performance: Stand erect holding a dumbbell in each hand, palms inward. Spread your feet about shoulder width apart, toes pointed outward. #1. Begin reverse curling the dumbbell in one hand, keeping the palm down and the elbow close to your side. Allow your wrist to "gooseneck" and flex to its fullest. The other arm remains at your side. #2. Continue the reverse curling action, palm down, until the dumbbell is brought to a position near the shoulder. Keep the "gooseneck" flex in the wrist. #3 and #4. Lower the dumbbell to the starting position shown in #1. Perform this movement on the other side. This is one repetition. Pause and repeat for the desired number of times.

Breathing: Breathe as exertion demands.

Recommended Weight: 15–25 lbs. (each dumbbell). 10 repetitions.

Key Points: When the dumbbell is brought to the high position shown in #3, the wrist may be straightened and flexed to the other extreme and then returned to the "gooseneck" position before the dumbbell is lowered.

DUMBBELL TRICEPS EXTENSION

Purpose: A flushing exercise designed to promote growth and strength in the arm triceps muscle, necessary in all phases of Judo.

Performance: Stand with the body bent from the waist. The upper body is parallel to the floor. Hold a dumbbell in one hand, palm inward, so that the elbow is in a fixed position at your side and the arm is fully flexed (the arm makes an angle of just less than 90°). Support your body with the other hand resting on a wall or some other solid support. #1.

Keep your elbow fixed and close to your body as you extend your arm backward, palm inward. The dumbbell moves backward. #2. Continue the extension until the dumbbell reaches the position shown in #3. Return the dumbbell to the starting position shown in #1. This is one repetition. Pause and repeat for the desired number of times. Change arms.

Breathing: Breathe as exertion demands.

Recommended Weight: 10–20 lbs. 10 repetitions.

Key Points: The elbow must remain fixed as the extension is made. Ensure that the arm is fully extended.

Auxiliary Exercises 247

DUMBBELL TRICEPS CONCENTRATION PRESS

Purpose: A composite exercise which is designed to strengthen the arm triceps, necessary in all phases of Judo.

Performance: Take a position on the floor, legs spread similar to the manner for Kesagatame (Scarf Hold). Rest the far side arm, elbow to fist, on the floor for support. Hold a dumbbell in the other hand so that it is directly above your head, palm forward. Keep the biceps tight against your head. The arm is fully stretched. #1.

Lower the dumbbell keeping the palm forward so that the dumbbell ends point downward. Keep the biceps tight against your head. #2. Continue lowering the dumbbell until a low position somewhat behind your shoulder is reached. The biceps remain tight against your head, and the palm is forward. #3. Return to the starting position shown in #1. Repeat 20 times. Change arms and perform the same motion for an equal number of repetitions.

Immediately take a lighter dumbbell and perform the same general motion, but at the position shown in #3, pause for a full count of 3 before returning to the starting position shown in #1. Repeat 15 times. Change arms and perform the same motion for an equal number of repetitions.

Immediately take a still lighter dumbbell and begin with the position shown in #4. (Same as starting position in #1). Lower the dumbbell to a half-way position shown in #5. Return the dumbbell to the starting position in #4. Repeat 10 times. Change arms and perform the same motions for an equal number of repetitions.

Breathing: Breathe as exertion demands.

Recommended Weight: Select three dumbbells and have them near you to avoid delay in changing. Combinations of: 20–15–10 lbs. or 15–12–10 lbs. are adequate. Repetitions as described.

Key Points: The elbow must remain flexed with the arm biceps tight against the side of the head throughout the entire exercise. The dumbbell is turned and held with one end upward and is raised and lowered in a plane along its long axis.

BARBELL WRIST CURLING

Purpose: A composite exercise for the fingers, wrists, and forearms, promoting powerful lower arms necessary in all phases of Judo.

Performance: Squat down, flat-footed with the feet about hip width apart, toes pointed outward. Hold a barbell in your hands so that you are able to rest your forearms on your thighs. Your hands, palms upward, project beyond your knees. #1.

Lower the barbell downward using only wrist power, the arms remaining in full length (elbow to wrist) contact with your thighs. Allow the fingers to extend to their limit so that they "hook" the bar at the lowest possible position. #2. Curl the fingers back to a normal clenched grip and then curl the barbell upward using only wrist power (arms again remain in contact—elbow to wrist—with thighs) until the highest position is reached. #3. Hold this position for 3 counts. This is one repetition. Repeat for the desired number of repetitions.

This is not the complete exercise.

Reverse the grip taken in the above movement, so that the palms face downward in the starting position shown in #1. Perform the same movements as made with the first grip, except that the palms are now reversed. Repeat for the desired number of times.

Breathing: Breathe as exertion demands.

Recommended Weight: 20–50 lbs. 20 repetitions for each style of curling (total of 40 repetitions).

Key Points: The starting position may be taken alongside a bench or low flat surface, with the performer kneeling on both knees. In this case, padding under the arms is advisable. The extension of the fingers in the low position in #2 is important to the exercise.

BENCH END CURL

Purpose: A severe exercise designed to promote extra power in the arms (bicepses). Necessary in Nage Waza.

Performance: Lie prone on a *high* bench with your feet on top of the bench. Center your weight so that you have some stability. Position yourself at one end of the bench so that your arms are free to hang vertically at that end and hold a barbell with a narrow grip, palms upward. Fix your elbows so that they cannot move. #1.

Curl the barbell to the high position which brings the bar (and your hands) to your chin. #2-#3. The elbows remain fixed, pressed against a solid support. Lower the barbell to the starting position in #1, taking care to fully extend the arms *(see Key Points)*. This is one repetition. Pause and repeat for the desired number of times.

Breathing: Breathe as exertion demands.

Recommended Weight: 35–65 lbs. 10 repetitions.

Key Points: The width of the grip may be varied to give different beneficial effects. The bench must be high enough to allow the arms to fully lower the barbell. #4 shows an improper lowering action in that it does not allow the bicepses to work through their full limit of extension.

BARBELL REVERSE CURL

Purpose: Designed to develop gripping and forearm strength necessary in all phases of Judo.

Performance: Stand erect, feet slightly apart, flat on the floor, toes pointed outward. Hold a barbell in your hands, palms downward, across your thighs with the grip spaced about hip width as shown in #1.

Raise the barbell toward the chest with a reverse curling action, fixing the elbows against the sides. #2. Continue reverse curling the barbell until the bar comes just under the chin and the palms point forward. #3. Lower the barbell to the starting position in #1. This is one repetition. Pause and repeat for the desired number of times.

Breathing: Breathe as exertion demands.

Recommended Weight: 30–50 lbs. 10 repetitions.

Key Points: The body must remain erect and not sway to assist the reverse curling action. The elbows, though they remain fixed against your sides, will move slightly as the highest position is reached. The wrists must remain fixed (do not allow the wrists to "gooseneck").

STANDING BARBELL TRICEPS CURL

Purpose: A developmental exercise designed to promote growth and strength in the arm (tricepses) muscles. Necessary in all phases of Judo.

Performance: Stand erect, feet slightly apart, flat on the floor, toes pointed slightly outward. Hold a barbell overhead, arms fully outstretched, palms forward, hands holding with a close grip. #1.

Lower the barbell behind the head by bending the arms. Fix the elbows so that only the portion of the arm above the elbow is moved. The elbows will have a tendency to move outward slightly. #2. Continue lowering the barbell until the lowest possible position is reached. The elbows remain fixed as before. #3. Return the barbell to the starting position shown in #1. This is one repetition. Pause and repeat for the desired number of times.

Breathing: Breathe as exertion demands.

Recommended Weight: 40–60 lbs. 10 repetitions.

Key Points: The body must not sway to aid the curling action. Fix the elbows and maintain that rigidity throughout the exercise.

FRENCH PRESS

Purpose: A developmental exercise for the tricepses muscles of the arms which increases pushing power necessary in many phases of Judo.

Performance: Sit on a bench, upper body erect, feet on the floor. Hold a dumbbell cupped in your hands, palms upward directly overhead. The arms must be fully outstretched. #1.

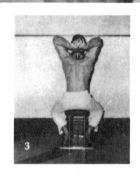

Lower the dumbbell behind the head, keeping the elbows relatively fixed. The back must be kept erect during this movement. #2. Continue lowering the dumbbell until the lowest possible position is reached. #3. Return the dumbbell to the starting position as shown in #1. This is one repetition. Pause and repeat for the desired number of times.

Breathing: Breathe as exertion demands.

Recommended Weight: 30–50 lbs. 10 repetitions.

Key Points: Keep the body erect as the movement is performed. The arms must be fully outstretched when in the position shown in #1.

LAT MACHINE TRICEPS PRESS

Purpose: A severe developmental exercise to promote pushing and pressing power ability in the tricepses muscles of the arms. Necessary in all phases of Judo.

Performance: Stand in front of a lat machine, body slightly inclined forward, feet slightly spread, flat on the floor, toes pointed slightly outward. Grasp the bar with a narrow grip, palms downward. Bend the arms so that the bar (and the backs of your hands) is just in front of your chin. #1. Press the bar down to the thighs, fixing the elbows against the sides of the body so that only the portion of the arm below the elbow moves. The body, inclined forward, exerts a fixation by tensing the abdominal muscles. #2. Continue pressing downward until the bar touches the thighs. The arms are relatively straight. #3. Return the bar to the starting position, by allowing the lat machine weights to be lowered, as shown in #1. This is one repetition. Pause and repeat for the desired number of times.

Breathing: Breathe as exertion demands.

Recommended Weight: 25–40 lbs. 10 repetitions.

Key Points: The body must remain fixed and not sway to assist the pressing action.

Auxiliary Exercises   251

MILITARY BARBELL PRESS

Purpose: A basic upper body developer with emphasis on arm and shoulder areas, developing pushing power necessary in all phases of Judo.

Performance: Stand erect, feet shoulder width apart, flat on the floor, toes pointed slightly outward. Hold a barbell across the upper chest, palms upward cradling the bar. The elbows are slightly forward, but close to the sides. Hold the head erect, eyes to the front. #1.

Press the barbell upward so that the bar passes very close to the face. The head may be tilted very slightly backward to allow this passage. However, keep the eyes to the front (do not follow the bar as it is being raised). #2. Continue the pressing until the bar is overhead at the full extension of the arms. The head is moved slightly forward. #3. Return the barbell to the starting position shown in #1. This is one repetition. Pause and repeat for the desired number of times.

Breathing: Inhale at the starting point. Exhale as the position in #3 is reached.

Recommended Weight: 55–100 lbs. 10 repetitions.

Key Points: As the pressing action is started, the body is locked at the mid-section and knees. The back must not be allowed to bend backward to assist this pressing action. The knees also remain locked and do not assist the pressing action. *(See page 220 for gripping.)*

SEATED DUMBBELL CURL AND PRESS

Purpose: A composite exercise designed to promote pulling and pushing power in the upper body. Necessary in all phases of Judo.

Performance: Sit on a bench holding a dumbbell in each hand, palms forward. Place your feet flat on the floor, close together. Keep your back erect. #1.

Curl the dumbbells simultaneously to the shoulders, palms upward. The body remains fixed and erect. #2. Continuously press the dumbbells above the head so that the palms face each other or face slightly to the front. The arms are fully outstretched. #3. Return the dumbbells to the starting position shown in #1, by reversing the motions. This is one repetition. Pause and repeat for the desired number of times.

Breathing: Breathe as exertion demands.

Recommended Weight: 20–40 lbs. (each dumbbell). 10 repetitions.

Key Points: The body must not be allowed to sway to aid the curling and pressing actions. During the curling and lowering actions, the palms must be faced upward.

252 Judo Training Methods

DUMBBELL BEND PRESS

Purpose: A severe exercise designed to promote shoulder and arm pressing power and flexibility as well as fixation power in the trunk and legs. Necessary in various Nage Waza.

Performance: Stand erect with the feet shoulder width apart, flat on the floor, toes pointed outward. Hold a dumbbell in one hand at shoulder height, palm forward. Turn your head to watch the dumbbell. Your body leans very slightly away from the dumbbell. #1.

Bend your body to side away from the dumbbell, simultaneously pressing the dumbbell vertically upward. The other arm may rest on your leg *(see Key Points)*. #2. Continue bending the body and pressing the dumbbell until the arm is fully outstretched, vertically overhead. Your body is in a low position, knees bent. You continue to watch the dumbbell. #3. Raise the body slowly to the starting position simultaneously lowering the dumbbell to the shoulder as the body becomes erect. This is one repetition. Pause and repeat for the desired number of times. Repeat similarly on the other side.

Breathing: Inhale at the starting position. Hold your breath as you bend your body and press. Exhale only after the dumbbell reaches its highest position.

Recommended Weight: 25–45 lbs. 10 repetitions (each side).

Key Points: Watch the weight, fixing your eyes on the dumbbell to give you greater balance. More advanced trainees may assume the exact position for Tsurikomigoshi (see page 185).

A variation of this exercise is performed as follows. When in the position of #3, continuously lower and press the dumbbell 10 repetitions before bringing your body to the starting position. This is repeated on the other side.

INCLINE DUMBBELL SIDE RAISE

Purpose: A severe developmental exercise designed to promote growth and strength in the shoulder muscles. Necessary in all phases of Judo.

Performance: Lie sideways on an incline (about 50°) holding a dumbbell in one hand, arm along your free side. Brace your body with your feet. #1. Begin raising the dumbbell laterally with a straight arm, keeping the wrist straight, palm downward. #2. Continue raising the dumbbell until it reaches the height of the shoulder. The arm continues to be straight. #3. Return the dumbbell to the starting position shown in #1. This is one repetition. Pause and repeat for the desired number of times. Change arms and perform the exercise on the other side.

Breathing: Breathe as exertion demands.

Recommended Weight: 12–20 lbs. 10 repetitions.

Key Points: The arm must be fully outstretched during the entire exercise. Do not raise the dumbbell above shoulder height. This exercise may be done on the basis of *eccentric* contraction if so desired *(see page 34)*.

FORWARD BARBELL RAISE

Purpose: Designed for the partial development of the shoulder muscles promoting strength and fixation power necessary in many phases of Judo.

Performance: Stand erect holding a barbell across your thighs, hands spaced about shoulder width apart, palms down. Spread your feet a little wider than shoulder width, toes pointed slightly outward. #1.

Raise the barbell with straight arms, keeping the wrists fixed. The body must be locked in the knees and abdominal region. #2. Continue raising the barbell until the position of the bar is just above shoulder height. #3. Return the barbell to the starting position shown in #1. This is one repetition. Pause and repeat for the desired number of times.

Breathing: Breathe as exertion demands.

Recommended Weight: 20–45 lbs. 10 repetitions.

Key Points: The body must not be allowed to sway and assist the arms. The arms must continue to remain in an outstretched position during the entire exercise, and the wrists not allowed to "gooseneck." This exercise may be performed on the basis of *eccentric* contraction if so desired (*see page 34*).

SEATED DUMBBELL FRONT RAISE

Purpose: Designed to promote shoulder strength and flexibility necessary in all phases of Judo.

Performance: Sit on a bench, holding a dumbbell in each hand, palms to the rear. Keep the body erect, feet flat on the floor, with toes pointing slightly outward. Your arms hang along your sides. #1.

Raise the dumbbells simultaneously to the front, palms downward, with straight arms until the dumbbells come to a position just above shoulder height. Pause at this point for the count of one. #2. Continue raising the dumbbells simultaneously until they reach a position overhead with the palms facing to the front. #3. Lower the dumbbells to the starting position as shown in #1. This is one repetition. Pause and repeat for the desired number of times.

Breathing: Inhale while raising the dumbbells overhead. Exhale while lowering the dumbbells.

Recommended Weight: 5–15 lbs. (each dumbbell). 10 repetitions.

Key Points: The body must not sway to assist the raising of the dumbbells. Keep the arms straight during the entire exercise.

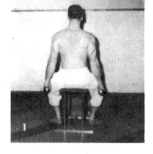

SEATED DUMBBELL LATERAL RAISE

Purpose: Designed to promote shoulder strength and flexibility necessary in all phases of Judo.

Performance: Sit on a bench, holding a dumbbell in each hand, palms to the rear. Keep the body erect, feet flat on the floor, slightly spread and with the toes pointing slightly outward. Arms hang along your sides. #1. Simultaneously raise the dumbbells laterally, palms downward, straight-armed, to a position where the dumbbells are just above shoulder height. The wrists are fixed (do not allow them to "gooseneck"). Pause at this point for the count of one. #2. Continue raising the dumbbells simultaneously until they reach a position overhead with the palms facing outward. #3. Lower the dumbbells to the starting position as shown in #1. This is one repetition. Pause and repeat for the desired number of times.

Breathing: Inhale while raising the dumbbells overhead. Exhale while lowering the dumbbells.

Recommended Weight: 5–15 lbs. (each dumbbell). 10 repetitions.

Key Points: The body must not sway to assist the raising of the dumbbells. Keep the arms straight during the entire exercise. The dumbbells must be tipped slightly downward to the front as they are raised.

VERTICAL DIPPING

Purpose: Designed to develop great flexibility, growth, and strength in the muscles of the shoulders, arms, and upper back. Necessary in all phases of Judo.

Performance: Position your body between two dipping or parallel bars. Your body hangs somewhat vertically, with arms fully extended and locked. Keep your legs together. #1.

Lower the body vertically by bending the arms. Your body will hang in a somewhat slanted position. #2. Continue lowering your body by bending your arms until you come to the lowest possible position. #3. Return the body to the starting position by pushing with and fully extending the arms. #1. This is one repetition. Pause and repeat for the desired number of times.

Breathing: Breathe as exertion demands.

Recommended Weight: Body weight. 10 repetitions.

Key Points: The arms must be fully extended in the highest position shown in #1. Take care to reach the lowest possible position after lowering. The body may be "bounced" up and down while in this low position in order to obtain more stretch. Do not allow the body to swing. Bend the legs at the knees if necessary to avoid touching the floor.

Purpose: A composite exercise designed to develop arm and shoulder muscles in pulling and pushing, promoting growth and strength necessary in all phases of Judo. Also stimulates the muscles of the legs and back.

Performance: Stand close to a barbell which rests on the floor. Your feet are spread about shoulder width apart, toes pointing slightly outward. Lower your hips by bending your knees so that you are able to grasp the bar, palms toward your body, with your hands spaced about shoulder width apart. Keep your back straight, head up, eyes to the front, arms fully extended. #1.

Pull the barbell off the floor by using an initial drive of the legs, which begin to straighten. Keep the back flat, hips low, and your head up. Your arms remain straight and do not pull. #2. Continue the drive of the legs. As the back straightens up and the bar passes the knees, pull very hard with your arms, keeping your body forward in the hips and close to the bar. Continue pulling the bar upward, taking care not to move your feet and as the bar comes high up on the chest (elbows high, palms in toward the body), your hands snap the bar up to the chest in a reverse curling (but faster) action. This whipping action of the hands brings the bar over and the elbows are thrust forward to stabilize the weight at shoulder level. #3.

Set your weight evenly and lock your hips and knees. Press the barbell overhead, thrusting the hips forward slightly. As the bar passes in front of the face, the head may be tilted slightly backward, but the eyes do not follow the bar. Continue pressing the barbell upward vertically to a high position overhead in which your arms are fully extended. #4. Lower the barbell to the position shown in #1, to a hang position just below your knees (plates just touching the floor) by bending the kness, keeping the back straight, head up, as your arms extend palms downward. This is one repetition. Immediately repeat for the desired number of times.

Breathing: Inhale before beginning the cleaning action (#1). Exhale when you reach the position shown in #3. Inhale once again at this position and hold your breath until #4. Exhale as you lower the barbell to the hang position.

Recommended Weight: 75–125 lbs. 10 repetitions.

Key Points: At the starting position in #1, the feet should be *under* the barbell. The legs straighten slowly, and the arms must not pull until the bar just *passes* the knees. A slight dip of the knees coordinated with the whipping action of the arms and snap of the wrists will attain the position in #3. Do not hold the bar at the chest (#3) for more than a few seconds. Press the barbell vertically and not away from the body.

256 **Judo Training Methods**

ABDOMINAL BELT GROUP

STRAIGHT-LEGGED DEAD LIFT

Purpose: Designed to develop lower back power and flexibility contributing to all-around torso strength necessary in all phases of Judo.

Performance: Stand erect with your feet about shoulder width apart, flat on the floor, toes pointed slightly outward. Your feet rest under the bar of a barbell. Bend forward from your waist, knees locked (no bend in your knees), and grasp the bar with both hands, palms toward you. #1. Raise the barbell from the floor by lower body power alone (the arms do not assist by pulling). Keep the back straight. #2. Continue raising the barbell by bringing the body to the erect position and the barbell across the thighs. Bend backward, allowing the knees to flex slightly in order to maintain balance. The arms do not lift the barbell, but merely fix the barbell at thigh level. #3. Lower the barbell by bending the body forward from the waist, without bending the knees. Lower to the position as shown in #2. Do not allow the barbell to rest on the floor. This is a hang position. This is one repetition. Repeat for the desired number of times.

Breathing: Inhale as you raise the body; exhale as you lower the body.

Recommended Weight: 75–125 lbs. 10 repetitions.

Key Points: The back must be kept flat. Keep the knees locked except as noted in the above instructions.

FORWARD STRAIGHT-LEGGED BEND

Purpose: Designed for the strengthening of the lower back and abdominal regions, but also affecting the legs, promoting flexibility necessary in all phases of Judo.

Performance: Stand erect, feet shoulder width apart, flat on the floor, toes pointed slightly outward. Rest a barbell across the back of your shoulders and neck. Hold the barbell with your hands spaced wide (out to the plates), palms forward. #1.

Bend the upper body forward from the waist. Keep the knees straight and locked. The back must be kept flat. #2. Continue bending forward to the lowest possible position without bending the knees. #3. Return to the starting position shown in #1. This is one repetition. Pause and repeat for the desired number of times.

Breathing: Inhale at the starting position; exhale as you begin to raise your body.

Recommended Weight: 25–50 lbs. 10 repetitions.

Key Points: The back must be kept as flat as possible during the bending forward and the knees locked in a straightened position. The body may be "bounced" when in the deep position to enhance flexibility.

Auxiliary Exercises 257

SWINGBAR RAISE

Purpose: To develop upper body power and flexibility and a coordinated action of the abdominal muscles with general body motion necessary in various phases of Nage Waza.

Performance: Stand erect, feet shoulder width apart, flat on the floor, toes pointed slightly outward. Hold a swingbar in both hands, palms toward your body as shown in #1.

Raise the swingbar to one side (right shown) with a straight-arm action, twisting the body slightly and pivoting on the toes of the rearmost foot. #2. Continue this twisting action until you face directly to the side(right shown). #3. Raise the swingbar, with straight arms, until it comes to a position about shoulder height, #4, and continue the straight-arm raising action until the swingbar is overhead. At this highest position, the body is arched, chest high, and the swingbar is somwhat behind the body. #5. Return to the starting position shown in #1, by reversing the movements that brought the bar overhead. As you reach the starting position (#1), take advantage of the momentum to swing the swingbar up to a high position on the other side in similar fashion. Similarly, return the swingbar to the starting position shown in #1. This is one repetition. Without pause, repeat for the desired number of times.

Breathing: Inhale as the swingbar is raised; exhale as you lower it.

Recommended Weight: 15–30 lbs. 10 repetitions (on each side).

Key Points: Maximum benefit can be had from this movement if the body acts with a swinging rhythm, pendulum-like swingbar action, and if, at the highest position, the body is allowed to arch as much as possible. The abdominal region must be thrust forward during the raising of the swingbar.

BARBELL SWINGING

Purpose: Designed to develop abdominal strength, flexibility, and a coordinated action necessary in various phases of Nage Waza.

Performance: Stand erect, feet shoulder width apart, flat on the floor, toes pointed slightly outward. Hold a barbell across your thighs, hands spaced widely (out to the plates), palms toward your body. #1.

Twist the body to one side (left shown), pivoting on the toes of the rearmost foot. As you face to the side, move the barbell into a somewhat vertical position by pulling the barbell upward with the hand on the side to which you are turning (left hand shown). Lift that elbow high. The other hand (right hand shown) pushes the barbell to a position in front of your abdomen, close to your body. #2. Continue twisting your body (left direction shown) and pull the barbell closer to the body and around the body (left hand shown pulling) as your other hand keeps the barbell somewhat fixed (right hand shown). #3. Return to the starting position shown in #1 by reversing the movements that brought the barbell to its high position. As you reach the starting position (#1), take advantage of the momentum to pull the barbell up to a high position on the other side in similar fashion. Similarly, return the barbell to the starting position. This is one repetition. Without pause, repeat for the desired number of times.

Breathing: Breathe as exertion demands.

Recommended Weight: 25–45 lbs. 10 repetitions (on each side).

Key Points: Maximum benefit can be had from this movement if the body acts with a swinging rhythm. The abdominal region must be thrust forward during the pulling of the barbell. The head is turned to follow the barbell. A severe variation may be performed when at the final position shown in #3, the barbell is moved to the position shown in #4. This exercise is a favorite of T. Daigo, 7 Dan, All-Japan Judo Champion in 1951 and 1954.

DUMBBELL SIDE BEND

Purpose: Designed to promote strength and flexibility in the oblique muscles of the abdominal region. Necessary in all phases of Judo.

Performance: Stand erect, feet shoulder width apart, flat on the floor, toes pointed slightly outward. Hold a dumbbell in one hand (right shown), along your side, palm inward. Your other hand (left shown) is placed behind your head, bending the arm, and pointing the elbow outward. #1. Bend your body *directly* sideward and downward on the side which holds the dumbbell (right side shown). Allow the dumbbell to effectively pull the trunk to its lowest possible position. Keep the legs straight and knees locked. #2. Return the body to the starting position shown in #1, but continue bending the body to the opposite side as shown in #3 (left side shown). Return to the starting position shown in #1. This is one repetition. Pause and repeat for the desired number of times. Perform this movement on the other side similarly.

Breathing: Breathe as exertion demands.

Recommended Weight: 25–50 lbs. 10 repetitions (each side).

Key Points: During the bending of the body to the side, care must be taken not to bend forward. The body may be "bounced" up and down when in the position shown in #3. The raised elbow must be pointed outward and drawn backward as the bending takes place. Pulling the dumbbell upward with the arm is undesirable and will reduce the effect of this movement.

BENCH SITUP

Purpose: A general exercise designed to develop the muscles of the mid-section, promoting trunk flexibility and body power necessary in all phases of Judo.

Performance: Sit on a bench with your feet hooked under a bar or strap. Keep your body erect, and fold your arms across your chest. #1.

Lower your body backward, keeping the feet immobilized under the bar or strap. The arms remain folded across the chest. #2. Continue lowering your body backwards until the lowest position (head may touch the ground) is obtained. #3. Return to the starting position shown in #1. This is one repetition. Pause and repeat for the desired number of times.

Breathing: Breathe as exertion demands.

Recommended Weight: Body weight. 15 repetitions.

Key Points: The body must be kept straight when in the process of lowering and raising (do not hump or bend the spine). If a high bench is used, more backward bend can be made possible. If such is the case, the position of the feet will affect the severity of the exercise. The lower they are placed, the more flex will be imparted to the spine. The bench can be moved closer to the feet so that the buttocks hang over the edge. This too will increase the severity. Holding the arms higher has an additional effect on the severity also. Pad the arches for protection.

SIDE RAISE

Purpose: A severe exercise designed to develop powerful oblique muscles in the mid-section and trunk flexibility necessary in all phases of Judo.

Performance: Take a position, lying on your side with your legs securely anchored on a bench by your partner. Place your hands behind your neck and allow your body to hang directly to the side in the lowest possible position. #1.

Begin to raise your body upwards (directly to your side) as your partner keeps your legs securely anchored and your body positioned on its side. #2. Continue the raising action until you reach a maximum height. #3. Return to the starting position as shown in #1. This is one repetition. Pause and repeat for the desired number of times. Change sides and repeat similarly.

Breathing: Breathe as exertion demands.

Recommended Weight: Body weight. 10 repetitions (each side).

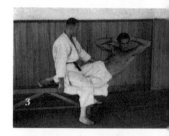

Key Points: Your partner must securely anchor your legs and keep your body from twisting. Perform your action directly sideways and do not allow your body to twist. Keep your elbows well up and slightly backwards, drawing the shoulders back. The body may be "bounced" when in the position shown in #3. The bench must be adequately padded.

BACK ARCHING

Purpose: A severe hyperextension exercise designed to promote strength and flexibility in the lower back and mid-section. Necessary in all phases of Judo.

Performance: Lie prone over a bench with your arms clasped behind your neck. Your belt line just reaches the leading edge of the bench. A partner anchors your legs, which are held together securely on the floor. Your forehead rests lightly on the floor. #1.

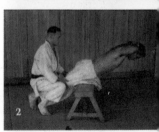

Begin raising the body upward as your partner keeps your lower body securely anchored. #2. Continue raising your body until you reach a maximum arched position as shown in #3. Return your body to the starting position as shown in #1. This is one repetition. Pause and repeat for the desired number of times.

Breathing: Breathe as exertion demands.

Recommended Weight: Body weight. 10 repetitions.

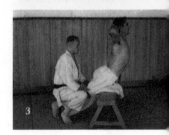

Key Points: The bench must be padded adequately under your body. Your partner must not allow your legs to lift or your body to twist. At the high point in your body arch, #3, pull the elbows back.

INCLINE LEG DOUBLE

Purpose: A severe exercise designed to develop strength and flexibility in the mid-section and lower back necessary in various phases of Katame Waza.

Performance: Lie on an incline board with your legs together and holding yourself on the board with your hands overhead. #1.

Begin doubling your legs, keeping the feet together. The knees may be allowed to spread slightly. Bring your heels up close to your buttocks. #2. Continue from this doubled position by tucking the body and raising the buttocks from the incline board by drawing the knees toward the chest. #3. Continue this tucking action and draw the knees up to the ears as in #4. Reverse the action, keeping the feet together and bringing the heels once more close to the buttocks before extending the legs to the starting position (#1). This is one repetition. Pause and repeat for the desired number of times.

Breathing: Breathe as exertion demands.

Recommended Weight: Body weight. 10 repetitions.

Key Points: The position shown in #2 must be attained both as a step in the upward doubling action and in the downward return to the starting position. The heels must be brought *close* to the buttocks in both cases. See Leg Doubles, Preparatory Exercises, page 164.

STALL BAR LEG RAISE

Purpose: A severe exercise designed to further promote the mid-section flexibility and strength necessary in all phases of Judo.

Performance: Hang from a stall bar either at full length or as shown in #1. Raise the legs, keeping the legs together, pointing the toes forward. Do not bend the knees. The back is kept against the bars. #2. Continue raising the legs, keeping the knees locked, until the feet touch the bar you are holding. #3. Return to the starting position shown in #1, without bending the knees. This is one repetition. Pause and repeat for the desired number of times.

Breathing: Breathe as exertion demands.

Recommended Weight: Body weight. 10 repetitions.

Key Points: The knees must be locked and the legs held straight during the entire exercise. As the legs are lifted to the position in #3, the back will move away from the bars. A variation of this exercise may be performed when, in the position shown in #2, the legs are opened and closed several times.

LEG TUCK AND BODY LEVER

Purpose: A severe exercise designed to strengthen the abdominal belt region. Promotes fixation power of the body necessary in all phases of Judo.

Performance: Lie on a bench in a tuck position, holding the bench overhead as shown in #1.

Stretch the legs vertically above the body, keeping them together. Balance on the upper back-neck region. Continue holding firmly with the hands to maintain balance. #2. Keep the body rigid and lower the body toward the bench in layout fashion. #3. Continue lowering your body until the position shown in #4 is reached (or lower). Hold this position for 5 counts. Allow your body to settle slowly to the bench (layout) and assume the starting tuck position shown in #1. This is one repetition. Pause and repeat for the desired number of times.

Breathing: Breathe as exertion demands.

Recommended Weight: Body weight. 10 repetitions.

Key Points: In the actual lowering (#2 to #4), the legs must remain together and straight, knees locked.

BENCH SITUP AND TWIST

Purpose: A severe exercise designed to develop the abdominal region with emphasis on the oblique muscles, promoting strength and flexibility necessary in all phases of Judo.

Performance: Sit on a bench with your feet hooked under a bar or strap. Keep your body erect, and fold your arms across your chest. #1.

Begin twisting your body sideways and lean back, coming up on to your hip slightly. #2. Continue twisting and lowering your body until the lowest position is reached. #3. Return to the starting position shown in #1. Perform this movement similarly on the other side and return to the starting position, #1. This is one repetition. Pause and repeat for the desired number of times.

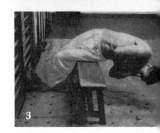

Breathing: Breathe as exertion demands.

Recommended Weight: Body weight. 10 repetitions (each side).

Key Points: The position of the feet will affect the severity of the exercise. The lower they are placed, the more flex will be imparted to the spine. The bench can be moved closer to the feet so that the buttocks hang over the edge. This too will increase the severity. Holding the arms higher has an additional effect on the severity also. Pad the arches for protection.

INCLINE STRAIGHT LEG LIFT

Purpose: Designed to develop flexibility in the lower back and abdominal strength necessary in all phases of Judo.

Performance: Lie on an incline board with the legs together and straight. Hold yourself on the board with your hands overhead. #1.

Begin to raise your legs, keeping the knees locked and the legs straight. #2. Continue raising your legs until the position shown in #3 is reached. Return to the starting position shown in #1, keeping the legs straight and knees locked. This is one repetition. Pause and repeat for the desired number of times.

Breathing: Breathe as exertion demands.

Recommended Weight: Body weight. 10 repetitions.

Key Points: The legs must be kept straight and knees locked during the entire exercise. A variation may be performed when in the position shown in #2 by spreading and closing the legs for several repetitions.

BENCH END STRAIGHT LEG LIFT

Purpose: Designed to develop flexibility in the lower back and lower abdominal strength necessary in all phases of Judo.

Performance: Lie supine on a high bench with the buttocks completely off the bench. The edge of the bench should be placed above the belt level, in the small of the back. Extend your legs, keeping them together, so that they hang downward, but remain suspended off the floor. Grasp the bench with your hands overhead. #1.

Begin raising your legs, keeping the knees locked, legs straight, and the toes pointed outward. #2 and #3. Continue raising your legs until the position shown in #4 is reached. Return the legs, straight with knees locked, to the starting position shown in #1. This is one repetition. Pause and repeat for the desired number of times.

Breathing: Breathe as exertion demands.

Recommended Weight: Body weight. 10 repetitions.

Key Points: The legs must be kept straight, knees locked, during the entire exercise. Pad the bench end to avoid discomfort. The buttocks must hang over the edge of the bench.

DECLINE SITUP

Purpose: Designed to develop abdominal strength necessary in all phases of Judo.

Performance: Sit on the low end of a decline board so that your feet are at the highest end and are secured by a strap, partner, or some appropriate device. Fold your hands behind your head, elbows forward. Lean forward so that your elbows touch your knees. The body is bowed slightly, and the legs are *not* fully extended. #1.

Lower the body backward, keeping the knees slightly flexed, but locked. Keep the elbows pointed forward. #2. Continue lowering your body until the approximate position shown in #3 is reached. Return to the starting position by raising the body. This is one repetition. Pause and repeat for the desired number of times.

Breathing: Breathe as exertion demands.

Recommended Weight: Body weight. 10 repetitions.

Key Points: The legs must not be completely straight, but the knees may be locked. The body remains somewhat bowed (forward) throughout this movement.

POWER GROUP

HALF SQUAT

Purpose: A severe exercise designed to quickly promote tremendous leg strength and body fixation power. Necessary in all phases of Judo.

Performance: Stand erect, feet spread as wide as the shoulders apart, flat on the floor, toes pointed slightly outward. Rest a barbell across the back of the neck and shoulders. Space your hands comfortably apart to steady the barbell. #1.

Lower the body by bending the knees. Maintain your upper body in an erect posture, head up. Lower your body only to a half squat (or less) position. Hold this position for at least one count. #2. Return the body to the starting position shown in #1 by a powerful drive from both legs. Fully extend the legs and lock the knees, tensing the leg muscles. Relax the leg muscles. This is one repetition. Pause and repeat for the desired number of times.

Breathing: Breathe as exertion demands.

Recommended Weight: 200–300 lbs. 4 repetitions.

Key Points: Very heavy weight can be handled in this exercise and it may be necessary to take the weight from squat or some device of support in order to assume the starting position. Additional safety is afforded by placing a bench between your legs so that you can sit down should it become necessary. Observe all safety precautions. It is advisable to have a training partner or two stand by to assist you.

HEAVY DUMBBELL CLEAN

Purpose: Considered by the authors as the best all around power development exercise for Judo. Designed to promote all-around body power, especially terrific pulling power necessary in Nage Waza.

Performance: Assume a deep squatting position between two heavy dumbbells placed on the floor. Spread the feet about shoulder width apart, flat on the floor, toes pointed slightly outward. Keep your buttocks low, back straight but inclined forward. The dumbbells lay outside, but slightly in front of your feet. Grasp the dumbbells firmly, palms inward. #1.

Straighten the body upward, by driving hard with the legs, pulling each dumbbell (cleaning action) quickly to the chest without moving the feet. Your body must rise on its toes and your mid-section is snapped forward to assist the lifting action. #2. Continue driving hard with the legs, straightening the legs fully, coming up on the toes as the dumbbells come up to shoulder height. Push your mid-section forward and hold your head erect, chin into the chest. The dumbbells now rest over the shoulders with the elbows high and pointed forward. #3. Settle down to a flat-footed position. Return the dumbbells to the starting position shown in #1, by reversing the action. *However,* do not let the dumbbells rest on the floor, but merely touch. This is one repetition. Immediately repeat for the desired number of times.

Breathing: Breathe as exertion demands.

Recommended Weight: 50–100 lbs. (each dumbbell). 4 repetitions.

Key Points: A definite rhythm must be established to this cleaning action so that the entire exercise is performed without any delay in between the various stages shown in the pictures. The dumbbells must be literally "torn" off the floor to a height of the head as though you wished to throw the dumbbells over your shoulders. The whole body must cooperate in this exercise if the intended benefit is to be attained. The use of *heavy* weights which preclude the mere slow-motion lifting action of the arms is essential to the success of this exercise.

The body must attempt to rise on to the toes at the height of the cleaning action. Bringing the mid-section forward will assist this motion. The feet must not move.

It is beneficial to perform this exercise with a starting position of either Migi Shizentai or Hidari Shizentai by placing the lead leg between the dumbbells.

STANDING BENT-ARM DUMBBELL LATERAL

Purpose: Designed to develop a powerful upper body, with emphasis on shoulders and upper back. Necessary in all phases of Judo.

Performance: Stand erect, feet shoulder width apart, flat on the floor, toes pointing slightly outward. Hold a dumbbell in each hand, palms inward. Rest the dumbbells on the front of your thighs. #1.

Swing the dumbbells laterally and upward, keeping the elbows slightly bent. Turn the palms up as the dumbbells rise and come to shoulder level. #2. Continue the action until the dumbbells reach a position overhead, the arms remaining slightly bowed. #3. Lower the dumbbells by reversing the actions performed and return to the starting position shown in #1. This is one repetition. Immediately repeat for the desired number of times.

Breathing: Inhale as you swing the dumbbells laterally and upward; exhale as you return the dumbbells to the starting position.

Recommended Weight: 30–50 lbs. (each dumbbell). 4 repetitions.

Key Points: The arms must be bent during the performance of this entire exercise. The body should assist the raising of the dumbbells by using abdominal and lower back power to accomplish this. The body may sway, but the feet must be kept in place.

DUMBBELL POWER PULL

Purpose: Designed to develop maximum pulling power of the arms, necessary in Nage Waza.

Performance: Stand erect with the feet spread as wide as the shoulders apart, flat on the floor, toes pointed slightly outward. Hold a dumbbell in each hand, arms along your sides, palms inward. #1.

Pull the dumbbell in one hand (left shown) to shoulder height with a powerful and quick motion so that the end plates of the dumbbell are held in position by your hands which grip with palms facing inward during the entire movement. #2. Immediately, lower this dumbbell (left side shown) and simultaneously begin pulling the dumbbell in the other hand (right shown) to the shoulder in a similar manner. #3 and #4. Continue this pulling and lowering action until the position shown in #5 is reached. This is one repetition. Immediately repeat for the desired number of times.

Breathing: Breathe as exertion demands.

Recommended Weight: 40–60 lbs. (each dumbbell). 4 repetitions.

Key Points: This motion must be done with rhythm, power, and speed. Do not attempt slow motion action. Pull powerfully and as quickly as you can. The body may sway to assist this action, but the feet must not move.

It is beneficial to perform this exercise with a starting position of either Migi Shizentai or Hidari Shizentai. Care must be taken not to strike the face with the dumbbells.

BARBELL BENT ROWING (*normal grip*)

Purpose: A basic exercise which affects many major muscle groups including the arms, the upper and lower back, and the legs, developing strength necessary in all phases of Judo.

Performance: Stand bent over from the waist. Spread your legs about shoulder width apart. Hold the back flat, locking the legs in a straight position. Grasp the barbell with a grip slightly wider than shoulder width, palms toward the body. The arms are held straight. #1.

Pull the barbell off the ground using arm power only. The body does not move to assist and the legs remain straight and locked, the back flat. #2 and #3. Continue pulling the barbell upward until the bar just touches your chest. #4. Return the barbell to the starting position by extending the arms fully, maintaining a fixed body position (legs straight and locked, back flat), #1, but do not allow the barbell to rest on the ground. This is one repetition. Pause and repeat for the desired number of times.

Breathing: Breathe as exertion demands.

Recommended Weight: 125–200 lbs. 4 repetitions.

Key Points: The straight-legged position must be maintained together with a flat back during the entire exercise. Be careful not to pull the bar too hard so that it slams into the chest and causes injury. *(See page 236.)*

BARBELL END ROWING

Purpose: Designed to affect the major muscles of the legs, lower and upper back, abdominal region, as well as the arms, wrists, and fingers, promoting strength in these parts. Develops powerful pulling and holding power necessary in the various Osaekomi Waza and Shime Waza.

Performance: Arrange a barbell with all the weights placed on one end. Rest the opposite end against some solid support to block its movement. Stand straddling the loaded end so that your position is just behind the last plate of the barbell. Spread your feet wider than shoulder width apart, flat on the floor, toes pointed slightly outward. Lower your body by bending the knees so that you are able to grasp the bar with both hands (baseball bat fashion, either hand on top), the arms remaining slightly bent. #1. (With heavy weights, stand ahead of the plates.)

Using power from the legs and back, lift the loaded end of the barbell from the ground. The arms do not pull. #2. Continue lifting the barbell, combining leg and back power, until the body is somewhat straightened and the bar comes up into the crotch region. Lean slightly backward. #3. Lower the weight to the starting position shown in #1, but do not allow the weight to rest on the ground. This is one repetition. Immediately repeat for the desired number of times.

Breathing: Breathe as exertion demands.

Recommended Weight: 200–300 lbs. 4 repetitions.

Key Points: The arms do not pull the weight, but merely serve to connect the power of the body with the barbell. Keep the arms slightly bowed. Change the top hand frequently when you perform sets.

BARBELL SUPINE PRESS *(normal grip)*

Purpose: A basic exercise designed to develop upper body power necessary in all phases of Judo.

Performance: Lie supine on a bench with your legs spread, feet flat on the floor. Hold a barbell straight above your upper chest, at arms length. Grip the bar with a spacing which is slightly wider than your shoulders. #1.

Begin to lower the barbell to your upper chest, elbows pointing downward. #2. Continue lowering the weight until the bar just touches the chest. #3. Using the power of the arms and the chest, press the barbell upward and return it to the starting position shown in #1. This is one repetition. Pause and repeat for the desired number of times.

Breathing: Inhale as the barbell is lowered; exhale as you press the barbell upward.

Recommended Weight: 100–200 lbs. 4 repetitions.

Key Points: The body must not arch to assist the arm and chest muscles in pressing the weight. Variations in grip spacing (wide-normal) are beneficial, but generally the normal or the slightly wider than shoulder grip should be used. This exercise is a favorite of I. Inokuma, 5 Dan, All-Japan Judo Champion. *(See page 229.)*

ONE HAND DUMBBELL SWING

Purpose: Designed to severely affect the major muscles of the legs upper and lower back, abdominal region, and shoulders, developing all-around body power necessary in all phases of Judo.

Performance: Straddle a heavy dumbbell which is resting on the floor. Spread your feet slightly wider than shoulder width apart, flat on the floor, toes pointed slightly outward. Lower your buttocks by bending your knees so that you are able to grasp the dumbbell in one hand (right shown), palm inward. Your free hand (left shown) rests on your knee. #1. Swing the dumbbell upward with a straight arm, using the combined power of the legs and upper body. Your mid-section snaps forward. #2. Continue the upward swinging action until the dumbbell comes to a point directly overhead. #3. Return the dumbbell to the starting position shown in #1, but do not allow the dumbbell to rest on the ground. This is one repetition. Taking advantage of the momentum, immediately swing the dumbbell upward and repeat for the desired number of times. Change hands and repeat similarly on the other side.

Breathing: Breathe as exertion demands.

Recommended Weight: 50–100 lbs. 4 repetitions each side.

Key Points: The snapping action of the mid-section must be properly timed to assist this movement. The arm must maintain a straight position during the entire exercise.

BARBELL CLEANING

Purpose: Designed to develop arm-shoulder muscles in pulling, and the all-around power of the legs and upper body in coordinated movement necessary in all phases of Judo.

Performance: Stand close to a barbell which rests on the floor. Your feet are spread about shoulder width apart, toes pointing slightly outward. Lower your hips by bending your knees so that you are able to grasp the bar, palms toward your body, with your hands spaced about shoulder width apart. Keep your back straight, head up, eyes to the front, arms fully extended. #1–2.

Pull the barbell off the floor by using an initial drive of the legs, which begin to straighten. Keep your back flat, hips low, and your head up. Your arms remain straight and do not pull. #3. Continue the drive of the legs. As the back straightens up and the bar passes the knees, pull very hard with your arms, keeping your body forward in the hips and close to the bar. Continue pulling the bar upward, taking care not to move your feet. As the bar comes high up on the chest, (elbows high, palms in toward the body), your hands snap the bar up and to the chest in a reverse curling (but faster) action. #4. This whipping action of the hands brings the bar over and the elbows are thrust forward to stabilize the weight at shoulder level.

Lower the barbell to a hang position just below your knees (plates just touching the floor) by bending the knees. Keep the back straight and head up as your arms extend, palms downward, similar to the position shown in #1–2. The barbell should not rest on the floor. This is one repetition. Immediately repeat for the desired number of times.

Breathing: Inhale before beginning the cleaning action (#1–2). Exhale when you reach the position shown in #4.

Recommended Weight: 125–200 lbs. 4 repetitions.

Key Points: At the starting position in #1–2, the feet should be *under* the barbell. The legs straighten slowly, and the arms must not pull until the bar just *passes* the knees. A slight dip of the knees coordinated with the whipping action of the arms and snap of the wrists will attain the position in #4. Additional benefit, by way of variation, may be had by controlling the lowering of the barbell (reverse curl action on the basis of *eccentric* contraction (see page 34).

BARBELL POWER PULL

Purpose: Designed to develop pulling power and gripping strength necessary in all phase of Judo.

Performance: Stand close to a barbell which rests on the floor. Spread your feet about shoulder width apart, toes pointed slightly outward. Lower your hips by bending your knees so that you are able to grasp the bar, palms toward your body, with your hands spaced about 6–10 inches apart. Keep your back straight, head up, eyes to the front, arms fully extended. #1.

Pull the barbell off the floor by using an initial drive of the legs, which begin to straighten. Keep your back flat, hips low, head up. Your arms remain straight and do not pull. #2. Continue the drive of the legs. As the back straightens and the bar passes the knees, pull very hard with your arms, keeping your body forward in the hips and close to the bar. Continue pulling hard, and snap the mid-section forward as you attempt to pull the bar up (without cleaning) as high as you can. The elbows are pointed outward. #3. Lower the weight to a hang position just below your knees (plates just touching the floor) by bending the knees, keeping the back straight, head up, as your arms extend palms downward, similar to the position shown in #1. The barbell should not rest on the floor. This is one repetition. Immediately repeat for the desired number of times.

Breathing: Inhale before beginning the pulling action, #1 and exhale when you reach the position shown in #3.

Recommended Weight: 150–300 lbs. 4 repetitions.

Key Points: At the starting position in #1, the feet should be *under* the barbell. The legs straighten slowly, and the arms must not pull until the bar just *passes* the knees. A snapping action of the mid-section, forward, close to the bar, will assist the pull attempt. The head must be erect, chin in, at the height of the pull. The pull should attempt to bring the barbell as high as possible, and with limit poundages, any pull which is limited to below the belt is not within the intended purpose of this exercise. This is a pure "pull" exercise. Do nothing but pull! This is a favorite exercise of Jon Bluming, 4 Dan, amateur Judo champion of the Netherlands.

JERK PRESS

Purpose: Designed to develop maximum pushing power ability and fixation power of the body. Especially useful in Katame Waza.

Performance: Stand erect, feet spread about shoulder width apart, flat on the floor, toes pointed slightly outward. Hold a heavy barbell across the front of your body (upper chest) with a grip spaced just slightly wider than your shoulders, palms facing forward and upward away from the body. Thrust the elbows forward to stabilize the weight. Thrust the mid-section slightly forward and hold the head somewhat back. #1.

Bend the knees slightly, lowering the body a few inches, but maintaining the forward position of the mid-section. Simultaneously, lower the barbell to a position at the sternum. #2. Stop this "dipping" action suddenly, and snap the legs back to the straightened position as you drive the barbell upward taking advantage of this momentum. Press-out the barbell overhead as your legs come to a locked and straight position. #3–4. Lower the barbell to the position shown in #1. This is one repetition. Immediately repeat for the desired number of times.

Breathing: Inhale before you begin the dipping action. Exhale as you lock the barbell overhead.

Recommended Weight: 100–200 lbs. 4 repetitions.

Key Points: The weight may be cleaned to the starting position or taken from squat racks. At any rate, do not hold the barbell in the starting position for more than one or two seconds as it will result in an ineffective lift when maximum poundages are used. The press must start from a low position near the sternum. The dip of the legs must be a fast action with a sudden stop and rapid recovery to the straight leg position. The simultaneous pressing action must be well-timed to take advantage of this momentum. The barbell must be *pressed* vertically. The position of your mid-section thrust forward and head held somewhat back, will allow this. If the barbell gets away from a vertical pressing direction, you will fail. A strong drive, utilizing the full momentum of the dipping action of the body must be used to achieve the overhead position. *Do not* follow the bar with your eyes as it passes in front of your face. Look forward only. Hold your elbows in as the press takes shape. Once your legs have recovered from the dipping action and are locked straight, your hips must also be fixed to afford a stable base for the pressing action.

BARBELL PULLOVER AND PRESS

Purpose: A composite exercise designed to assist in the development of maximum upper body power necessary in various phases of Nage Waza and Katame Waza.

Performance: Lie supine on a decline bench (5°–10°), spreading your feet and placing them comfortably on the floor. Reach overhead and grip a barbell, which rests on the floor, with your hands spaced slightly less than shoulder width apart, palms upward. Your arms are bent. #1. Begin pulling the barbell off the ground, with bent arms, so that the bar just passes over your face. #2. Continue pulling until the bar comes to a position across the upper chest. #3. Press the barbell upward to a position directly above your upper chest.

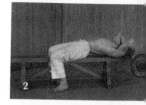

Extend the arms fully. #4. Lower the barbell to the position shown in #3. Return the barbell to the starting position on the floor shown in #1. This is one repetition. Pause and repeat for the desired number of times.

Breathing: Inhale before beginning to pull the bar to the chest; exhale as the bar reaches its maximum high position over the chest.

Recommended Weight: 100–200 lbs. 4 repetitions.

Key Points: Gripping the bar with too wide a grasp will cause discomfort and possible injury to the shoulders. However, the grip must be sufficiently wide to allow a strong pressing action. This exercise may be performed on incline and level benches. The barbell may be rested on the floor between repetitions.

BARBELL CLEANING CURL

Purpose: Designed to develop maximum pulling strength in the arms in cooperation with all-around body power especially useful in Katame Waza.

Performance: Stand close to a barbell which rest on the floor. Your feet are spread about shoulder width apart, toes pointed slightly outward. Lower your hips by bending your knees so that you are able to grasp the bar, palms upward, with your hands spaced about shoulder width apart. Keep your back straight, head up, eyes to the front, arms somewhat bent. #1.

Pull the barbell off the floor by using a combined action of leg drive, back power, and arm curling action. Keep the bar close to the body and thrust the mid-section forward as the barbell is brought above the knees. #2. Continue this curling action until the bar rests across the chest. #3. Return the bar to the starting position #1. This is one repetition. Pause and repeat for the desired number of times.

Breathing: Inhale prior to beginning the curling action #1; exhale after the weight is brought into the position shown in #3.

Recommended Weight: 100–200 lbs. 4 repetitions.

Key Points: The arms are bent at the starting position. This is a "cheating" action in which the arms are assisted by the body. As such, it is a coordinated movement and correct timing is essential. Curl the barbell *close* to the body, and ensure that the mid-section is snapped forward. The elbows may be lifted after the curl is completed in order to stabilize the weight. The may be rested briefly on the floor between repetitions. This "rest" should not exceed more than one count.

EXPANDER EXERCISES

NORMAL PULL DOWN

Purpose: Designed to promote flexibility and strength in the arm-shoulder, chest, and upper back-neck groups. Necessary in all phases of Judo.

Performance: Stand erect, feet spread as wide as the shoulders apart, flat on the floor, toes pointed slightly outward. Hold an expander at arms length overhead, grasping with the palms facing inward. #1 and #2. Start the pull down, using straight arms, stretching the expander so that it comes down in front of the body. #3. Continue the stretching until the position in #4 is reached. Return to the starting position in #1. Immediately pull the expander down in similar fashion *behind* the body as shown in #5 and #6. Return to the starting position shown in #1. This is one repetition. Repeat in alternate fashion for the desired number of times.

Breathing: Breathe as exertion demands.

Recommended Weight: Number 1 strand. 5 repetitions (5 front–5 back).

Key Points: Keep a steady pulling and returning action. Do not allow the expander to jerk the arms back to the starting position. A variation exercise may be performed, termed Reverse Pull Down, by taking the grasp shown in #7, and performing the exercise above.

FORWARD STRAIGHT-ARM SPREAD

Purpose: Designed to promote strength and flexibility in the arm and chest groups, necessary in all phases of Judo.

Performance: Stand erect, feet spread as wide as the shoulders apart, flat on the floor, toes pointed slightly outward. Hold an expander at arms length in front of your body, parallel to the floor, grasping with the palms facing inward. #1.

Pull the expander, using straight arms, stretching the expander so that it comes across the chest. #2. Return the expander to the starting position shown in #1. This is one repetition. Pause and repeat for the desired number of times.

Breathing: Breathe as exertion demands.

Recommended weight: Number 1 strand. 10 repetitions.

Key Points: Keep a steady pulling and returning action. Do not allow the expander to jerk the arms back to the starting position. A variation exercise may be performed by taking the grasp as shown in #7 above. This exercise, if performed slowly, is valuable as a breathing exercise. Inhale as you spread the expander and exhale as you return it to the starting position.

ONE ARM DIAGONAL PRESS

Purpose: Designed to develop strength and flexibility of the arm-shoulder group, necessary in various phases of Nage Waza.

Performance: Stand erect, feet spread as wide as the shoulders apart, flat on the floor, toes pointed slightly outward. Hold an expander diagonally across your back. One hand, the arm extended alongside the body (right shown), grasps the expander, palm inward, so that the expander band passes over the wrist. Lock this arm. The other arm is bent, elbow down, with the back of the hand next to the shoulder (left shown), palm forward. #1.

Start pressing the upper hand upward (left shown). The other arm (right shown) remains extended alongside the body and locked. #2. Continue pressing upward until the highest position of the arm is reached. #3. Return to the starting position shown in #1. This is one repetition. Pause and repeat for the desired number of times. Perform this movement similarly on the other side.

Breathing: Breathe as exertion demands.

Recommended Weight: Number 1 strand. 10 repetitions (each side).

Key Points: Keep a steady pulling and returning action. Do not allow the expander to jerk the arms back to the starting position.

HORIZONTAL PRESSING

Purpose: Designed to develop strength and flexibility in the arm-shoulder, upper back, and chest groups, necessary in all phases of Judo.

Performance: Stand erect, feet spread as wide as the shoulders apart, flat on the floor, toes pointed slightly outward. Hold an expander horizontally across your back. Grasp the expander, palms forward. Draw the shoulders together and pull the elbows together behind your back. #1. Press the arms directly sideward, to the maximum extent of the arms, stretching the expander as shown in #2. Return to the starting position shown in #1. This is one repetition. Pause and repeat for the desired number of times.

Breathing: Breathe as exertion demands.

Recommended Weight: Number 1 strand. 10 repetitions.

Key Points: Keep a steady pulling and returning action. Do not allow the expander to jerk the arms back to the starting position. The shoulders should be pulled together before pressing.

Auxiliary Exercises **275**

UPRIGHT ROWING

Purpose: Designed to develop the arm-shoulder and upper back-neck group, necessary in all phases of Judo.

Performance: Stand erect, feet spread as wide as the shoulders apart, flat on the floor, toes pointed slightly outward. Hold an expander under one foot (right shown), and grasp the other end with the arm (same side) extended downward in front of the body, palm toward the body. #1.

Pull the expander vertically upward, raising the elbow high, until the hand is under the chin. #2. Return the expander to the starting position shown in #1. This is one repetition. Pause and repeat for the desired number of times. Change sides and perform the exercise similarly on the other side.

Breathing: Breathe as exertion demands.

Recommended Weight: Number 1 strand. 10 repetitions (each side).

Key Points: Keep a steady pulling and returning action. Do not allow the expander to jerk the arm back to the starting position. The elbow must be pulled high. The body should not sway to assist the arm in pulling. Be sure that you hold the one end of the expander securely under your foot.

DIAGONAL ROWING

Purpose: Designed to develop strength and flexibility in the arm-shoulder, upper back-neck, and abdominal belt groups, necessary in all phases of Judo.

Performance: Stand erect, feet spread as wide as the shoulders apart, flat on the floor, toes pointed slightly outward. Hold an expander under one foot (right shown), and grasp the other end, palm toward the body, with the opposite side hand (left shown) so that the expander is diagonally across the lower body. #1.

Pull the expander diagonally upward across the body, raising the elbow high. #2. Continue pulling diagonally until your hand comes near the chin. Keep the elbow pointed upward. #3. Return the expander to the starting position shown in #1. This is one repetition. Pause and repeat for the desired number of times. Change sides and perform the exercise similarly on the other side.

Breathing: Breathe as exertion demands.

Recommended Weight: Number 1 strand. 10 repetitions (each side).

Key Points: Keep a steady pulling and returning action. Do not allow the expander to jerk the arm back to the starting position. The elbow must be pulled high. Be sure that you hold the one end of the expander securely under your foot. The head may be turned to follow the pulling hand.

ONE ARM CURLING

Purpose: Designed to strengthen the biceps, forearm muscles, and wrist, necessary in all pulling action of Judo.

Performance: Stand erect, feet spread as wide as the shoulders apart, flat on the floor, toes pointed slightly outward. Hold an expander under one foot (right shown), and grasp the other end, palm facing forward, with the arm extended downward (same side) alongside the body. #1. Fix the elbow and curl the arm upward, palm up, until the fist touches the chest as shown in #2. Return the expander to the starting position shown in #1. This is one repetition. Pause and repeat for the desired number of times. Change sides and perform similarly on the other side.

Breathing: Breathe as exertion demands.

Recommended Weight: Number 1 strand. 10 repetitions.

Key Points: Keep a steady pulling and returning action. Do not allow the expander to jerk the arm back to the starting position. The elbow must be fixed. Be sure that you hold the expander securely under your foot.

VERTICAL TRICEPS PRESS

Purpose: Designed to develop strength in the tricepses muscles of the arms, necessary in all pushing actions of Judo.

Performance: Stand erect, feet spread as wide as your shoulders apart, flat on the floor, toes pointed slightly outward. Hold an expander vertically along one side. One hand, the arm extended alongside the body (left shown), grasps the expander, palm inward, so that the expander band passes over the wrist. Lock this arm. The other arm is bent, the biceps along the side of your head (right shown) and the forearm over the top of your head grasping the expander with the palm upward. #1.

Press the expander upward, palm up and outward, keeping that pressing arm biceps tight alongside the head. The arm must not move away from the head. The other arm, extended down alongside the body must be kept locked. Continue pressing upward until the position in #2 is reached and the arm is at its maximum extension. Return the expander to the starting position shown in #1. This is one repetition. Pause and repeat for the desired number of times. Perform this exercise similarly on the other side.

Breathing: Breathe as exertion demands.

Recommended Weight: Number 1 strand. 10 repetitions (each side).

Key Points: Keep a steady pulling and returning action. Do not allow the expander to jerk the arms back to the starting position. The raised arm must be kept tight alongside the head and not allowed to move away.

HORIZONTAL TRICEPS PRESS

Purpose: Designed to develop strength in the tricepses muscles of the arms, necessary in all pushing and pulling motions of Nage Waza.

Performance: Stand erect, feet spread as wide as your shoulders apart, flat on the floor, toes pointed slightly outward. Hold an expander horizontally across the upper body, close to the body. One arm (left shown) is extended directly to your side, parallel to the floor and grasps the expander with a palm forward grip. The other arm is bent, elbow pointing outward, hand in front of your face, palm toward the body. Your arm is parallel to the floor. #1.

Begin pulling the expander with the bent arm (right shown), keeping the elbow high, arm parallel to the floor, palm facing toward the extended arm (left). #2. Continue pulling until the arm reaches its maximum extended position and is symmetrically extended as is its mate. The palm now faces forward. #3. Return the expander to the starting position shown in #1. This is one repetition. Pause and repeat for the desired number of times. Change sides and perform this exercise similarly on the other side.

Breathing: Breathe as exertion demands.

Recommended Weight: Number 1 strand. 10 repetitions.

Key Points: Keep a steady pulling and returning action. Do not allow the expander to jerk the arms back to the starting position. The arms must be kept parallel to the floor during the entire exercise. The head may be turned to follow the pressing action.

STRAIGHT-ARM RAISE

Purpose: Designed to develop strength in the shoulder and arm muscles, necessary in all phases of Judo.

Performance: Stand erect, feet spread as wide as your shoulders apart, flat on the floor, toes pointed slightly outward. Hold an expander in front of your upper thighs, arms extended fully downward, palms inward. #1. Pull the expander with straight arms, directly to your sides and upward. #2. Continue pulling the expander by raising your straight arms upward directly to the sides, palms down and slightly forward. #3. Return the expander to the starting position shown in #1. This is one repetition. Pause and repeat for the desired number of times.

Breathing: Breathe as exertion demands.

Recommended Weight: Number 1 strand. 10 repetitions.

Key Points: Keep a steady pulling and returning action. Do not allow the expander to jerk the arms back to the starting position. The arms must be kept straight and locked during the entire exercise.

DIAGONAL TRICEPS PRESS

Purpose: Designed to develop strong pulling power necessary in various phases of Nage Waza.

Performance: Stand erect, feet spread as wide as the shoulders apart, flat on the floor, toes pointed slightly outward. Hold an expander diagonally across and close to your body. One arm extends alongside your body (left shown), is locked at full length, and grasps the expander with the palm facing to the rear. The other arm is bent (right shown), raised high and pointing outward, while the hand grasps the expander with the palm facing forward. #1.

Pull the expander diagonally upward and outward as your other arm (left shown) remains fixed alongside your body. #2. Continue pulling the expander upward and outward until the arm reaches the fully extended position, palm outward, as shown in #3. Return the expander to the starting position shown in #1. This is one repetition. Pause and repeat for the desired number of times. Change hands and perform the exercise similarly on the other side.

Breathing: Breathe as exertion demands.

Recommended Weight: Number 1 strand. 10 repetitions (each side).

Key Points: Keep a steady pulling and returning action. Do not allow the expander to jerk the arm back to the starting position. The wrist must be kept fixed and straight.

TRUNK EXERCISE

Purpose: Designed to aid the development of the abdominal belt group muscles necessary in all phases of Judo.

Performance: Stand erect, feet spread slightly wider than the shoulders, flat on the floor, toes pointed slightly outward. Hold an expander under one foot (right shown). Grasp the expander with your hand on the same side as the foot which is anchoring the expander. Bend that arm, keeping the elbow down and close to your body while your hand is held at shoulder level, palm facing to the opposite side. Your free hand hangs alongside your body. #1.

Bend your body toward the free side and slightly forward (left side shown). Keep your elbow close to your side. Bend as far as the expander will permit you. #2. Return to the starting position shown in #1. This is one repetition. Pause and repeat for the desired number of times. Change sides and perform the exercise similarly on the other side.

Breathing: Breathe as exertion demands.

Recommended Weight: Number 1 strand. 10 repetitions (each side).

Key Points: Keep a steady pulling and returning action. Do not allow the expander to jerk your body back to the starting position. A variation exercise may be performed when in the position shown in #2, by pressing the bent arm upward in the direction of your bending. The foot must hold the expander securely.

DIAGONAL STRAIGHT-ARM PULL UP

Purpose: Designed to promote strength and pulling power in the arms and shoulders, necessary in various phases of Nage Waza.

Performance: Stand erect, feet spread as wide as the shoulders apart, flat on the floor, toes pointed slightly outward. Hold an expander diagonally across your body with one arm (left shown) extended downward, straight and locked, grasping the expander with a palm down grip. Hold that hand against your upper thigh. The other hand (right shown) is extended directly in front of you, parallel to the floor, palm down. #1. Pull the expander upward with the upper arm (right shown). Maintain both arms in a straight and locked position. #2. Continue pulling upward and diagonally outward until the position with arm fully extended is reached as shown in #3. Return the expander to the starting position as shown in #1. This is one repetition. Pause and repeat for the desired number of times. Change sides and perform this exercise similarly on the other side.

Breathing: Breathe as exertion demands.

Recommended Weight: Number 1 strand. 10 repetitions (each side).

Key Points: Keep a steady pulling and returning action. Do not allow the expander to jerk your arm back to the starting position. Both arms must be kept straight and locked. Keep the wrists fixed and straight.

OBI EXERCISES

SHOULDER STRETCHING

Purpose: Designed to promote extreme flexibility in the shoulders and upper back-neck muscles, necessary in all phases of Judo.

Performance: Stand erect, feet spread as wide as your shoulders apart, flat on the floor, toes pointed slightly outward. Hold an obi, which has been doubled, at arms length in front of the body, grasping the ends with your palms facing your body. Your arms should be straight and pointing toward the floor, making about a 45° angle with the sagittal plane of the body (plane which divides the body vertically into two symmetrical halves, left and right). #1.

Raise your arms forward and upward, keeping your arms straight and locked, as shown in #2. Continue this motion, carrying the arms overhead and behind the body, keeping them straight and locked. #3. Carry this motion further until the final position shown in #4 is reached. Return your arms to the starting position shown in #1. This is one repetition. Pause and repeat for the desired number of times.

Breathing: Inhale as your arms are raised and until you reach the position in #4. Exhale as you return your arms to the starting position.

Recommended Weight: None. 10 repetitions.

Key Points: The arms must not be allowed to flex or bend throughout the entire exercise. The arms must draw *outward* as if to pull the obi apart during the entire movement. Varying hand spacing will increase or decrease severity of this exercise. Any length of material that is light-weight can be used, such as: towel, belt, stick, etc.

TRUNK STRETCHING

Purpose: A severe method of stretching the upper body designed to promote flexibility necessary in all phases of Judo.

Performance: Stand erect, feet spread as wide as your shoulders apart, flat on the floor, toes pointed slightly outward. Hold an obi, which has been doubled, at arms length in front of the body, grasping the ends with your palms facing your body. Your arms should be straight and pointing toward the floor, making about a 45° angle with the sagittal plane of the body. #1. (See shoulder stretching, page 280.)

Twist your body to one side (right shown), keeping your feet in place. Raise the trailing arm (left shown) to your front as your leading arm (right shown) pulls the obi down, back, and around your body. #2. Raise the trailing arm (left shown) to a position directly overhead as the lead arm (right shown) elevates a little. #3. Twist your body to the left and simultaneously swing the now lead arm (left shown) downward and behind your body as the now trailing arm (right shown) begins to lift. #4. Continue this action until your trailing arm (right shown) is raised directly overhead and your lead arm (left shown) elevates a little. #5. Bring the trailing arm (right shown) over to your front lead arm (left shown) which comes forward. #6. Twist your body to the right assume the starting position as shown in #1. This is one repetition. Immediately repeat for the desired number of repetitions. Perform both clockwise and counterclockwise.

Breathing: Breathe as exertion demands.

Recommended Weight: None. 10 repetitions (each, clockwise and counter-clockwise).

Key Points: The arms must not be allowed to flex or bend throughout the entire exercise. The arms must draw *outward* on the obi, as if to pull the obi apart, during the entire movement. Varying hand spacing will increase or decrease severity of this exercise. Any length of material that is lightweight can be used, such as: towel, belt, stick, etc. This exercise should be performed in a rhythmic fashion with no delay between the various stages.

BALANCE EXERCISE

Purpose: To provide an interesting form of exercise designed to teach the principles of Judo based on body coordination, resistance, and non-resistance.

Performance: Two opponents stand erect, feet completely together, facing each other. They hold a Judo obi, which is wrapped once around their hands, to their chests so that there is just a slight amount of slack. #1. By combined action of arms and body, they attempt to unbalance the opponent and make him take a step or lose his balance. The one losing his balance or the one who takes a step or in any way moves his feet, or touches the ground with any part of his body but his feet, is declared the loser.

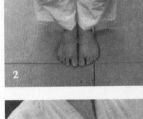

Breathing: Breathe as exertion demands.

Recommended Weight: Body weight. Two out of three points.

Key Points: Correct application of resistance and non-resistance is essential to achieve victory. The feet must be kept together as in #2. The grasp is illustrated by #3.

NECK CARRY

Purpose: A method of developing the muscles of the neck necessary in resisting the pressures of Shime Waza.

Performance: Stand back to back with a training partner, looping a Judo obi around his neck so that the obi crosses behind his neck and can be held by you as shown in #1–2. Lower your body slightly as shown in #2, and bend forward carrying your partner up onto your back. Keep your arms pulling hard on each end of the obi. #3. Walk forward, keeping the position shown in #3, until you have covered at least fifty feet or until your training partner gives the signal of defeat (see page 94).

Breathing: Breathe as exertion demands.

Recommended Weight: Body weight.

Key Points: Before picking up your training partner, be sure to lower your body so that your obi is lower than his. This will make the carrying much easier. Do not bend forward more than shown in #3 or it will nullify the exercise.

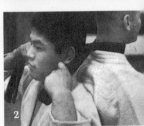

PULLEY EXERCISES

PULLEY WARMUP

Purpose: A moderate exercise ideally used to warm up the upper body, promoting flexibility particularly in the chest and shoulder muscles.

Performance: Stand erect, facing away from the wall pulleys, with your feet spread slightly wider than your shoulders. Hold the pulley handles in your hands with your palms facing forward. Your arms are straight and extended along your sides. #1.

Keeping your arms straight, begin to activate the pulleys forward and backward in a smooth continuous movement, #2 and #3. As you continue this action, gradually, laterally raise the position of the arms so that you travel from the starting position shown in #1, through positions shown in #2 and #3, finally arriving (after about 25 repetitions) at the maximum position shown in #4 and #5. Immediately reverse the motion by lowering the arms downward laterally while activating the pulleys forward and backward (another 25 repetitions) until you return to the starting position, #1.

Breathing: Breathe as exertion demands.

Key Points: The arms must be kept straight during the entire exercise, and the lateral raising must be gradual and performed with a continuous and smooth forward and backward activation of the pulleys.

PULLEY SPREAD

Purpose: A moderate exercise designed to warmup the upper body, promoting flexbility in the chest muscles.

Performance: Stand erect, facing the wall pulleys, with your feet spread slightly wider than your shoulders. Hold the pulley handles in your hands with your palms facing to the rear. Your arms are straight and extended diagonally to your front. #1.

Keeping your arms straight, begin to activate the pulleys forward and backward in a smooth continuous movement, ensuring that your palms continue to face to the rear. The arms should be laterally raised slightly during this activation (not to exceed 45°). #2 and #3. Continue this movement at least 25 times.

Breathing: Breathe as exertion demands.

Key Points: The arms must be kept straight during the entire exercise, and the movement a smooth and continuous one. If the arms are laterally raised beyond about a 45° angle, the palms can be rotated to face forward.

PULLEY HIGH PULL

Purpose: A moderate exercise designed to warmup the upper body with promotion of shoulder flexibility and abdominal strength.

Performance: Stand erect, facing the wall pulleys, with your feet spread slightly wider than your shoulders. Hold the pulley handles in your hands with your palms facing to the rear. Your arms are straight and extended diagonally to your front. #1.

Raise your arms simultaneously forward and upward, #2, until you come to the maximum position shown in #3. Immediately, return the arms to the starting position shown in #1. This is one repetition. Pause and repeat at least 25 times.

Breathing: Breathe as exertion demands.

Key Points: The arms must be kept straight during the entire movement, and the raising and lowering of the arms must be a continuous and smooth movement. As an alternate method, the arms may be raised and lowered alternately.

ONE-HAND PULL

Purpose: Designed to aid the development of pulling power necessary in many Nage Waza of Judo.

Performance: Stand erect at right angles to the wall pulleys. Hold both pulley handles in one hand (left shown), palm facing your chest, your forearm approximately parallel to the ground. #1.

Begin pulling, keeping your elbow high, so that your hand describes an arc around your upper chest. Rotate your body slightly to aid this pulling action. #2. Continue pulling and rotating your body until the position shown in #3 is reached. Return hand to the starting position shown in #1. This is one repetition. Repeat at least 25 times. Perform this exercise on both sides.

Breathing: Breathe as exertion demands.

Key Points: Your legs must remain in place, body rotation coming primarily from above. Your hand may be rotated during the pulling action to allow the palm to face outward.

Appendix

#1

World Judo Organization
Note: as of August 1961

```
                    ┌─────────────────┐
                    │  International  │
                    │      Judo       │
                    │   Federation    │
                    └─────────────────┘
```

Asian Judo Federation	European Judo Union	Pan-American Judo Confederation	Oceanian Judo Union
Cambodia	Austria	Argentina	Australia
Ceylon	Belgium	Bermuda	New Zealand
China (Taiwan)	Czechoslovakia	Brazil	
Indonesia	Denmark	Canada	
Japan	France	Chile	
Korea (South)	Great Britain	Costa Rica	
Phillipines	Italy	Cuba	
Thailand	East Germany	El Salvador	
Singapore	West Germany	Mexico	
	Luxembourg	Panama	
	Netherlands	Uruguay	
	Spain	U.S.A.	
	Switzerland	Guatemala	
	Jugoslavia	Nicaragua	
	Poland	Venezuela	
	Hungary		
	Portugal		

Appendix

#2

U.S.A Judo Organization

To:
International Judo Federation
Pan American Judo Confederation

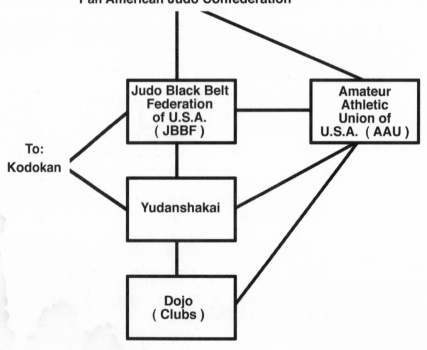

To:
Kodokan

Judo Black Belt Federation of U.S.A. (JBBF)

Amateur Athletic Union of U.S.A. (AAU)

Yudanshakai

Dojo (Clubs)

Appendix
#3
JBBF Organizational Diagram

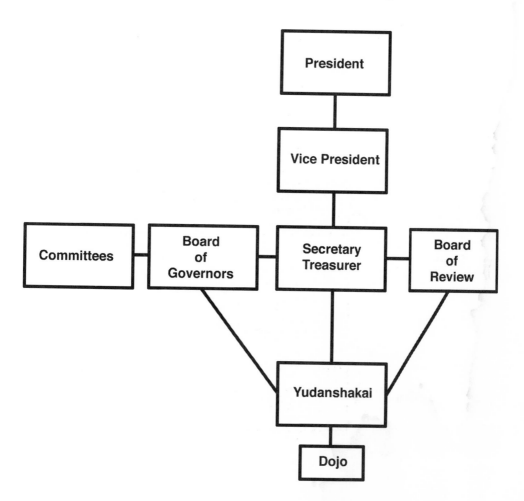

List of Kodokan Judo Yudanshakai in USA
and their jurisdictions.

THE FOLLOWING Judo Yudanshakai are officially Kodokan chartered and carry national recognition from the only official national Judo body in the USA, the Judo Black Belt Federation of the USA (JBBF). The administrative jurisdiction of each Yudanshakai is also shown. Persons residing within these respective areas will be able to obtain answers to their Judo questions by contacting the local Yudanshakai.

SHUFU JUDO YUDANSHAKAI

306 Lamond Pl.
Orchard Valley
Alexandria, Virginia

Administers: Maine, New Hampshire, Vermont, Connecticut, Massachusetts, Rhode Island, New York, New Jersey, Pennsylvania, Delaware, Maryland, Washington, D.C., West Virginia, Virginia, North Carolina, South Carolina, Georgia, Alabama, Mississippi, Louisiana, Puerto Rico.

KONAN JUDO YUDANSHAKAI

4444 Joy Road
Detroit 4, Michigan

Administers: Michigan, Ohio, Kentucky, Tennessee.

CHICAGO JUDO YUDANSHAKAI

334 South Wabash Ave.
Chicago, Illinois

Administers: Minnesota, Wisconsin, Illinois, Indiana, Iowa, Missouri, Arkansas.

ROCKY MOUNTAIN JUDO YUDANSHAKAI

3444 Alcott
Denver, Colorado

Administers: North Dakota, South Dakota, Nebraska, Kansas, Colorado, Utah, New Mexico, Wyoming, Oklahoma, Texas.

NORTHWESTERN JUDO YUDANSHAKAI

14211 S.E. 272d St.
Kent, Washington.

Administers: Alaska, Washington, Oregon, Montana, Idaho.

HOKKA JUDO YUDANSHAKAI

24 Rosewood
San Francisco. California

Administers: Northern California, Nevada.

CHUKA JUDO YUDANSHAKAI

P.O. Box 145
Del Rey, California.

Administers: Central California, Fresno area.

NANKA JUDO YUDANSHAKAI

3201 W. 27th St.
Los Angeles, California.

Administers: Southern California, Arizona.

HAWAII JUDO YUDANSHAKAI

2138 Kapiolani Blvd.
Honolulu, Hawaii.

Administers: Hawaiian Island group.

SAC-ARDC JUDO YUDANSHAKAI

HQ, SAC, Offutt, AFB,
Omaha, Nebraska.

Administers: All Air Force Judo activities regardless of geographical location.

FLORIDA JUDO YUDANSHAKAI

248 First Ave., North,
St. Petersburg, Florida.

Administers: Florida.

#5   Judo Black Belt Federation—Promotional Policy

THE FOLLOWING is an excerpt from the Constitutions & By-Laws of The Judo Black Belt Federation of the United States of America (Beikoku Judo Yudansha-kai Renmei):

CHAPTER VII

Section I   *Promotions*

Promotions or recommendations for change in Judo rank shall be made only by authorized member Yudanshakai who are recognized by the Kodokan Judo Institute and this Federation.

Section II

(a) Recommendations for change in Judo rank and promotions shall be subject to the following provisions:

1. Promotions below the rank of Nikyu shall be effected by individual instructors (Yudansha) who are recognized by member Yudanshakai, and submitted to the member Yudanshakai for administrative record.

2. Promotions to the rank of Nikyu and above shall be effected only by member Yudan-shakai (Boards of Promotion).

Section III

(a) Member Yudanshakai unable to promote certain grades of Yudansha shall forward their recommendations to the Chairman of the Board of Review for action.

(b) All promotions to Shodan or higher will be properly recorded by the originating Yudanshakai, who shall immediately notify the Secretary-Treasurer of the Federation.

6   JBBF Rank and Belt Colors

THE FOLLOWING Judo ranks and belt colors are those of the Kodokan and are enforced within the U.S.A. by the Judo Black Belt Federation of the U.S.A. (JBBF).

SEINEN MEN (17 years and over)

Rank	Belt Color	Grade
Rokkyu	White	6 Kyu
Gokyu	White	5 Kyu
Yonkyu	White	4 Kyu
Sankyu	Brown	3 Kyu
Nikyu	Brown	2 Kyu
Ikkyu	Brown	1 Kyu
Shodan	Black	1 Dan
Nidan	Black	2 Dan
Sandan	Black	3 Dan
Yodan	Black	4 Dan
Godan	Black	5 Dan
Rokudan	Red & White Sections	6 Dan
Shichidan	Red & White Sections	7 Dan
Hachidan	Red & White Sections	8 Dan
Kudan	Red	9 Dan
Judan	Red	10 Dan

YONEN BOYS (Age 12 years and under)

Yonen Rank	Belt Color	Shonen Rank	Belt Color
		Conversion to Shonen Rank Upon Reaching 13 Years of Age	
Rokkyu	White	———	———
Gokyu	White		
Yonkyu	White	———	———
Sankyu	Green	Rokkyu	White
Nikyu	Green	Gokyu	White
Ikkyu	Green	Yonkyu	White
		Sankyu	Purple

SHONEN BOYS (Age 16 years and under)

Conversion to Seinen Rank
Upon Reaching 17 Years of Age

Shonen Rank	Belt Color	Seinen Rank	Belt Color
Rokkyu	White	———	———
Gokyu	White	———	———
Yonkyu	White	Rokkyu	White
Sankyu	Purple	Gokyu	White
Nikyu	Purple	Yonkyu	White
Ikkyu	Purple	Sankyu	Brown

Female ranks are the same as for male, except that the colored belts will be those with a thin white stripe along the length of the belt midway between the width edges.

The above does not preclude in exceptional circumstances, the awarding of junior ranks of a higher age group to a boy or girl although he has not yet attained the chronological age of that rank group.

#7   Contest Rules of The Kodokan Judo

(Recognized Officially by the All-Japan Judo Federation)
Revised March 26, 1951
Revised May 6, 1955
Revised February 25, 1961

CONTEST AREA

Article 1. The Contest Area shall, as a rule, be a square platform, 30 feet (Approximately 9.09 meters) in length and width, raised to such a height as conditions (note) require, and covered with 50 pieces of "Tatami." (See Appendix A for "Tatami"). To prevent injuries and other dangers, the area around the perimeter of the Contest Area, shall further be bordered by either "Tatami" or mats for a width of 6 feet (approximately 1.82 meters) and lowered by 6 inches from the said platform.

If and when, for lack of space or other circumstances, sufficient area cannot be provided, the conditions prescribed in the preceding paragraph may not necessarily be followed strictly. However, the demarcation line between the Contest Area and the area around the perimeter must be marked distinctly. It is permissible to substitute canvas or vinyl matting or the like for "Tatami-omote" or rush matting.

Note: Governing conditions will depend upon size and scope of the contests, number of spectators, arrangement of seating, etc.

COSTUME

Article 2. The contestant shall wear "Judo-gi" or Judo Costume. (See Appendix B for "Judo-gi"). Both contestants shall, as a rule, wear a red or white cord or strap respectively, as their own signs, tied over around their regulation belts. The Judo-gi to be worn by the contestant shall comply with the following conditions;

(a) The jacket shall be long enough to cover the hips, when tied at the waist by a belt or sash;

(b) The sleeves shall be loose, (there must be an opening or play of at least more than one and a quarter inches (approximately 3 centimeters) between the cuff and forearm) and shall extend more than half way down the forearms;

(c) The trousers shall be loose, (there must be an opening or play of at least more than one and a quarter inches (approximately 3 centimeters) between the bottom of the trousers and the leg) and shall reach more than halfway down the legs;

(d) The belt or sash must be tied properly with a square knot, tight enough to prevent the jacket from coming loose, and must be long enough to go twice around the body with its two ends left free at least 6 inches (approximately 15 centimeters) from the knot when tied.

Article 3. The contestants must keep their finger and toe nails cut short; and must not wear any articles, such as rings, ornaments, etc., liable to cause injury to the opponent.

CONTEST

Article 4. The contestants shall stand approximately twelve feet (approximately 3.64 meters) apart, at the center of the Contest Area, facing each other, and exchange a salute by bowing to each other simultaneously. After finishing the salutation, the contest shall be started immediately upon the announcement of "Hajime" ("Start" or "Go") by the Referee.

As a rule, the salutation for the contest shall be made in standing posture; however, the salutation in formal Japanese kneeling posture may be used instead. In the latter case, the contestants shall finish the salutation, stand up facing each other, and then the contest shall be started immediately at the announcement of "Hajime" by the Referee.

Article 5. When a contest comes to an end, the contestants shall return to the position originally taken at the start of the contest, facing each other and, following the indication or declaration by the Referee, the contestants shall make the standing or kneeling salutation simultaneously.

Article 6. The result of a contest shall be judged on the basis of "Nage-waza" (Art of Throwing or Throwing Techniques) and "Katame-waza" (Art of Grappling or Grappling Techniques).

Article 7. The result of a contest shall be decided on the basis of not more than "Ippon" (one point).

Article 8. The contest shall be started with both contestants in standing posture.

Article 9. In the following cases, a contestant may shift into techniques in a lying position. However, if any technique applied is not continued properly, the Referee may, at his discretion, make the contestants stand up.

(a) When a contestant, after obtaining some result by his throwing techniques, shifts without interruption into techniques in a lying position and takes the offensive;

(b) When a contestant falls while applying a throwing technique against his opponent; or when a contestant takes the offensive when his opponent falls down;

(c) When a contestant, after obtaining, in a standing position, some result by "Shime-waza" (strangling technique) or "Kansetsu-waza" (bonelocks), shifts without interruption into techniques in a lying position and takes the offensive.

Article 10. The time limit for a contest shall be from 3 to 20 minutes and such limit shall be fixed beforehand. However, the above limit may be extended, in certain special cases.

Article 11. When the time allotted for the contest is expired, the Referee shall be notified by the ringing of a bell or some other means.

Article 12. Any technique applied simultaneously with the signal notifying expiration of the time limit shall be judged as valid. In the case of an "Osaekomi" (holding) officially announced, the time limit shall be extended until the "Osaekomi" is completed or broken.

Article 13. Any technique applied when one or both of the contestants are outside of the Contest Area, shall be judged as null and void.

Article 14. When a throwing technique is successful, and, at the moment, the contestant applying the technique stays within the Contest Area, and more than half of the body of his opponent remains within the Contest Area, the technique shall be judged as valid.

Article 15. If an "Osaekomi" (holding) is officially announced and the contestants are judged as getting outside of the Contest Area, the Referee shall announce "Sono-mama" ("Do not move," or "No movement") to the contestants, order them to remain motionless, pull them well within the perimeter of the Contest Area with their relative positions unaltered, and make them continue the contest by announcing "Yoshi" ("Go" or "All right").

In this case the time between the announcements of "Sono-mama" and "Yoshi" shall be taken out from the time required for completing the "Osaekomi" (holding).

JUDGMENT OF CONTEST

Article 16. The Referee shall have the sole responsibility for the conduct of the bout. His decisions shall be final and without appeal.

Article 17. As a rule, there shall be one Referee and two Judges. However, depending upon the scope and nature of the contest, there may be only one Referee. Also the employment of one Referee and one Judge is permissible.

Article 18. The Referee shall stay inside of the Contest Area, and administer the progress and the judgment of the contest.

Article 19. The Judges shall assist the Referee. The two Judges shall take positions at opposite corners and outside of the Contest Area and shall not encroach upon the Contest Area.

Article 20. The Referee shall start the contest by announcing "Hajime" ("Start" or "Go"), after the contestants have finished their salutation.

Article 21. If a contestant wins a contest by a throwing or grappling technique, the Referee shall announce "Ippon" or "One Point," stop the contest, make both contestants return to the position originally taken at the start of the contest, and indicate the winner by raising his hand towards him.

Article 22. If a contestant scores a "Waza-ari" or "Half Point," the Referee shall announce "Waza-ari." Should the same contestant gain a second "Waza-ari," the Referee shall announce "Waza-ari, Awasete Ippon" or "One Point by Two Techniques," stop the contest, make both contestants return to the positions originally taken by them at the start of the contest, and indicate the winner by raising his hand toward him.

Article 23. When the Referee judges that a contestant secures a complete hold by "Osaekomi-waza" (holding technique), he shall announce "Osaekomi" (holding). When the hold is broken after it was announced as "Osaekomi," the Referee shall announce "Osaekomi Toketa" or "Hold Broken."

Article 24. If a Judge takes an exception to the announcement of the Referee, the Judge shall submit his opinion to the Referee. In this case, the Referee may rescind the announcement made by himself, and adopt the opinion of the Judge. However, this last decision of the Referee, as indicated to or declared on the contestant, shall be final.

Article 25. When the time limit expires without the contest having been decided with "Ippon" (one point), the Referee shall announce "Sore-made" or "That is all," stop the contest, and make both contestants return to the position originally taken at the start of the contest. Then the Referee shall take the position which he had originally taken at the start of the contest and raise his hand high, calling "Hantei" or "Judgment" towards the two Judges. At this signal the two Judges shall manifest their judgment by hoisting the red or white signs simultaneously. In the case of "Hikiwake" or "Draw," both the red and white signs shall be hoisted at the same time.

Article 26. The Referee shall add his own opinion to those of the two Judges, regarding the superiority or inferiority or draw, make a decision upon it by the majority opinions of the three officials, and indicate or declare the "Yusei-gachi" or "Win by Superiority," or "Draw." In case the opinions of the three officials differ, the judgment of the Referee shall prevail.

When a Referee and one Judge are used, the Referee shall take the opinion of the Judge into consideration and indicate or declare the decision of "Yusei-gachi" (win by superiority) or "Hikiwake" (draw).

Article 27. In the following cases, the Referee shall announce "Mate" or "Wait," and halt the contest temporarily. To resume the contest, he shall announce "Hajime" (start or go). In this case, if it is specifically announced as "Jikan" or "Time," the time passed shall be taken out from the time limit of the contest.
(a) When a contestant goes out of the Contest Area, or is about to go outside of it;
(b) When a contestant commits any prohibited acts;
(c) When a contestant is injured, or some accident or difficulty takes place;
(d) When a contestant is required to adjust his costume;
(e) When in lying position the contest comes to a standstill, with the contestants clinging together in "Ashi-garami" (a leg of a contestant coiled against a leg of the opponent) or in other such positions;
(f) In cases other than those mentioned above, when deemed necessary by the Referee.

Article 27-2. The Referee shall, when he has decided the result of the contest by "Hansoku" or "Violation of Rules," "Fusen" or "Default of the Opponent," injury or other reasons, indicate the winner. In the case of "Hikiwake" (draw), he shall declare to the same effect to the contestants.

PROHIBITED ACTS

Article 28. Concerning the contestant's techniques and actions, the following things shall be prohibited:

(a) When a contestant is attacked by his opponent with "Harai-goshi" (Sweeping Hip or Loin) or the like, to sweep from inside, the leg with which his opponent is supporting his weight;

(b) To apply "Kawazu-gake" to the opponent;

(c) "Do-jime" (Squeezing Abdomen), or squeezing the head or neck directly with the legs (Scissors);

(d) Applying "Kansetsu-waza" (Bonelocks) on joints other than the elbow;

(e) To apply any hold or lock which is liable to injure the vertebrae of the opponent;

(f) When a contestant lifts his opponent who is lying with his back on the mat, to drop him onto the mat;

(g) When the opponent clings fast to a contestant from behind, for the contestant thus caught to hold his opponent to him and to purposely throw himself backwards;

(h) To release the opponent's hand or hands grasping a contestant's costume by "kicking" or "wrenching" with the knee or foot or any other part of the leg;

(i) Deliberately avoiding contact or holds with the opponent in order to prevent action in the contest;

(j) To deliberately go outside of the Contest Area or to push the opponent outside of it meaninglessly;

(k) To adopt a purely defensive posture in order to avoid defeat, (crouching, retreating, etc.);

(l) To continually adopt a stance holding the lapel and sleeve on the same side of the opponent's jacket, or a stance holding the belt of the opponent with a rigid stretched arm;

(m) To grip the opponent's end of the sleeves or bottom of the trousers by inserting finger or fingers in them;

(n) For both contestants to continue in standing position with their fingers of both hands interlocked;

(o) To untie and tie again the belt arbitrarily, without the Referee's permission;

(p) Dragging an opponent into techniques in a lying position without attempting a definite technique from the standing position;

(q) To grab the opponent's leg from a standing position in order to shift into technique in a lying position;

(r) To apply techniques by binding any part of the opponent's body with the end of the belt or the bottom of the jacket;

(s) To hold the opponent's costume in the mouth or to put one's foot or hand directly on the face of the opponent;

(t) In "Katame-waza" (grappling techniques), to put a foot or both feet on the belt or the flap or lapel of the jacket of the opponent, or to take the hand grip of the opponent off bending his fingers in the wrong way;

(u) When a contestant is lying with his back on the floor, and his opponent is standing on his feet or kneeling on his knee or knees, in a position able to lift the lying contestant, for the lying contestant to strangle the neck of the standing contestant or to apply "Kansetsu-waza" (bonelocks) against him by scissoring aslant both the neck and armpit with his legs;

(v) To make meaningless cries, remarks or gestures derogatory to the opponent;

(w) Any act which is liable to cause danger to the person of the opponent, other than specified above, and all other acts which might be prejudicial to the spirit of Judo.

Any contestant shall constitute a "Violation of Rules," if and when he violates any one of the items (a)—(w) of the preceding paragraph of this Article.

Article 28-2. The Referee shall notice the contestant if and when he violates any one of the prohibited acts provided in the preceding Article. The Referee shall, in case where he deems that if and when the said contestant violates again, it would subject him to a "Loss by Violation of Rules," warn him to the same effect.

JUDGMENT OF THE MATCH

Article 29. Judgment of "Ippon" (one point) shall be made on the basis of the following conditions:

A. Nage-Waza (throwing technique):

(1) When a contestant applying a technique, or countering his opponent's attacking technique, throws down his opponent on to his back with sufficient force;

(2) When a contestant skillfully lifts his opponent, who is lying with his back on the floor, up to about the height of his own shoulders.

B. Katame-waza (grappling technique):

(1) When the opponent of a contestant says "Maitta" ("I give up" or "I give in"), or taps his or his opponent's body or the mat, with his hand or foot twice or more;

(2) In the case of "Osaekomi" (holding), when the opponent cannot break the hold within 30 seconds after the announcement of "Osaekomi;" provided, however, that as long as the contestant holds his opponent under his control, the "Osaekomi" shall be regarded as continuous even though the technique of holding is changed;

(3) In the case of "Shime-waza" (strangling techniques) and "Kansetsu-waza" (bonelocks), when the effect of the technique is sufficiently apparent.

Article 30. Judgment of "Waza-ari" (half-point) shall be made on the basis of the following conditions:

A. In the case of "Nage-waza" (throwing technique), when a contestant throws his opponent in good form which merits closely "Ippon" (one point) but not to the extent of scoring a complete "Ippon";

B. In the case of "Osaekomi-waza" (holding technique), when a contestant holds his opponent successfully for more than 25 seconds; however, should the contestant who has already scored "Waza-ari" secure "Osaekomi" in the same contest, it shall only be necessary for him to hold for 25 seconds to obtain a full point or "Ippon."

Article 31. Judgment of "Yusei-gachi" (win by superiority) shall be made on the basis of the following conditions:

A. When a contestant was awarded a "Waza-ari" or displayed a technique close to a "Waza-ari;" provided, however, even if he had scored a "Waza-ari," the contestant shall not necessarily be awarded "Yu-sei-gachi," if he stalled throughout the match;

B. The two contestants' attitude in the contest, their skill in techniques, the existence of violation of rules in their acts and other conditions shall be compared, in the case of lack of decisive counts for the Judgment on the basis of the results of techniques in accordance with the preceding paragraph A.

Article 32. Judgment of "Hikiwake" (draw) shall be made on the basis of the following conditions:

A. When no result is reached in a contest within the regulation limit of time;

B. When the superiority or inferiority of the two contestants can not be judged.

Article 33. Judgment of "Hansoku-make" (loss by violation of rules) shall be made on the basis of the following conditions:

A. When a contestant violates any one of the major items of the prohibited acts such as techniques or actions which are dangerous to the person of the opponent or, remarks or gestures which might be prejudicial to the spirit of Judo;

B. When a contestant violates any item of the prohibited acts repeatedly in disregard of the warnings given by the Referee.

Article 34. When a contestant waives a contest, the opponent shall be judged as "Fusen-gachi" or "Fusen-sho" (win by default).

Article 35. In the event that a contestant cannot continue the contest because of injury, accident or attack of illness, the Referee shall, after consultation with the Judges, judge the result of the contest on the basis of the following conditions:

A. In the cases of injury:

(1) When the cause of a contestant's injury is his own carelessness, the injured shall be the loser;

(2) When the cause of contestant's injury is his opponent's carelessness, the opponent shall be the loser;

(3) When the cause of contestant's injury is judged that neither one of the contestants can be held responsible, the result of the contest shall be judged as "Hikiwake" (draw);

B. When the contestants cannot continue a contest because of an accident, the result of the contest shall, as a rule, be judged as "Hikiwake" (draw);

C. When a contestant cannot continue a contest because of an attack of illness, the attacked shall, as a rule, be the loser.

Article 36. Any situations not covered by these rules shall be decided in consultation by all Referees and Judges concerned.

Note:—In the event of a disagreement between the original Japanese text of these rules and any translation thereof, regardless of the languages used, or any ambiguity in any such translation, the Japanese text shall prevail.

APPENDICES

A. "Tatami." The accepted "Tatami" or Judo-mat shall answer to the following description:—

Size: 3'×6'×2½" that is, about 2½ inches thick and nearly 3 feet wide by 6 feet long. Manufacture (Method of): In order to provide additional strength to the "Tatami" or Judo-mat which is made of "I-omote" (grass matting or rush matting) and "Toko" (rice-straw padding), single stitches of hemp or linen string shall be woven through the material of the mat, 14 lines lengthwise and 33-35 stitches in a line.

Padding: To make a piece of padding, about 50-55 pounds of rice straw shall be pressed to a thickness of about 2½ inches and single stitches of hemp or linen string shall be woven through the material of the padding, so that the stitches shall be 28 lines lengthwise on the back and 56 lines sidewise on the top.

B. "Judo-gi." The accepted "Judo-gi" or Judo costume which comprises a jacket or coat, trousers, and belt or sash shall follow this description:—

Jacket: The entire jacket shall be of two layers of cotton material. In order to provide additional strength to the jacket, double stitches of cotton string shall be woven through the material of the jacket, covering the entire upper half of the garment, both front and back, from the neck to the waist. The sleeves of the jacket shall also be woven in this manner.

From the waistline to the bottom of the jacket, both front and back, shall be woven in a small, diamond-shaped design. The size of each diamond shall be approximately two inches by three inches. This design shall be woven with the same cotton string in double, in order to provide further stability to the jacket.

From the bottom of the right side of the jacket, up the right side, around the back of the neck and down the left side of the jacket to the bottom of the left side, shall run a continuous lapel which shall be made of cotton canvas and shall be stitched to the body of the jacket with five lines of stitching by machine. The lapel shall be approximately two inches wide, the outside 3/4" to be filled with cotton canvas padding in order to provide strength for the lapel.

A rectangle of extra heavy stitching which shall be approximately two inches by five inches shall be woven into each armpit of the jacket in order to prevent opening of seams and deterioration by perspiration.

There shall be a slit of approximately seven inches up each side of the jacket, in order to prevent the jacket binding the hips when the contestant is moving.

Trousers: The trousers with binding straps shall be made of single cotton fabric, either woven through the material with cotton string in a small, diamond-shaped design or unwoven,

Belt: The belt shall be made of cotton fabric and cotton canvas padding, about 1½ inches wide and 8 or 9 feet long to enable it to be wound twice around the contestant's waist and tied in a double knot in front, and shall be woven through the material with 8-10 lines of stitching by machine.

Remarks:—In case such "Tatami" and/or "Judo-gi" as mentioned above are not readily available, it is permissible to makeshift with any mat and/or costume which may be available, if suitable for Judo contest; provided, however, that as to the costume, it shall conform to the provisions (items a, b, c & d) of Article 2 of these Contest Rules of the Kodokan Judo.

#8   Go Kyo no Waza

JIGORO KANO established the Go Kyo no Waza in 1896, utilizing the technical skills of the following high Dan Judoka: Yokoyama, Yamashita, Nagaoka, and Iizuka. In 1920, the Go Kyo was revised and stands to this date as a well-founded, but little understood by Westerners, *guide* to the teaching of Judo. The Go Kyo no Waza is based on complex theory of the dynamics of Judo and involves patterns of Taisabaki, Ukemi, Kuzushi, and lends a systematic approach to the teaching of Kodokan Judo. Used as a guide, the trainee will be ensured a progressive method of the study of Nage Waza, from the simpler movements (1st Kyo) to the more complex (5th Kyo).

Dai Ik-Kyo (1st)	Dai Ni-Kyo (2nd)
Deashiharai	Kosotogari
Hizaguruma	Kouchigari
Sasaetsurikomiashi	Koshiguruma
Ukigoshi	Tsurikomigoshi
Osotogari	Okuriashiharai
Ogoshi	Taiotoshi
Ouchigari	Haraigoshi
Seoinage	Uchimata

Dai San-Kyo (3rd)	Dai Yon-Kyo (4th)
Kosotogake	Sumigaeshi
Tsurigoshi	Taniotoshi
Yokootoshi	Hanemakikomi
Ashiguruma	Sukuinage
Hanegoshi	Utsurigoshi
Haraitsurikomiashi	Oguruma
Tomoenage	Sotomakikomi
Kataguruma	Ukiotoshi

Dai Go-Kyo (5th)

Osotoguruma	Ushirogoshi
Ukiwaza	Uranage
Yokowakare	Sumiotoshi
Yokoguruma	Yokogake

ARTICLE I

NAME

This organization shall be known as the_____.

PLACE

The headquarters of this organization shall be located in_____.

PURPOSES AND OBJECTIVES

(a) To encourage the art and science of Kodokan Judo in_____.

(b) To provide guidance and leadership in Kodokan Judo for advocates residing in

_____.

(c) To provide means for better relationship between Judoka and to in general unify local Judo activity.

(d) To foster and to maintain competition among its members on a high plane of sportsmanship and friendly endeavor.

(e) To establish and maintain relations with Judo activities in the national organization.

GOVERNMENT

This organization shall be an independent organization, officially recognized by the Kodokan via the national Judo body and——Judo Yudanshakai, but governed by its own Constitution and By-Laws. It shall cooperate fully with the national Judo body with official recognition by the Amateur Athletic Union of the USA. It shall be administratively responsible to_____Judo Yudanshakai as required by the national Judo body.

MEMBERSHIP

The members of this organization shall be persons advocating Kodokan Judo and now residing in_____and other such persons who shall be recognized by this organization in accordance with the national Judo organization.

OFFICERS

The officers of this organization shall consist of the following:

President, Vice-President, Secretary, Treasurer.

Additional officers may be elected but must be chosen from member Yudansha only:

Examiner, Technical Advisor

CHAPTER IV   *Duties of the Officers*

(a) The President shall direct the activities of this organization and shall preside at all meetings.

(b) The Vice-President shall assist the President in the direction of this organization and shall perform all the duties of the President in case of absence or inability to preside.

(c) The Secretary shall keep the minutes of all meetings of this organization and shall perform all duties required of him by this organization.

(d) The Treasurer shall keep full and accurate accounts of the receipts disbursements of funds of this organization.

CHAPTER V   *General Policies*

This organization shall at all times in matters of rules of competition, ranks and promotions, standards of practice and administrative matters, conduct its functions in Kodokan ideal as required by the national Judo organization and supervised by_____ Judo Yudanshakai.

CHAPTER VI   *Order of Business*

The order of business of the meetings of this organization shall be as follows:
1. Roll call and accrediting of new members.
2. Reading, correction and adoption of minutes.
3. Reports of officers and committees.
4. Unfinished business.
5. New Business.
6. Amendments to Constitution and By-Laws.
7. Election of Officers.

CHAPTER VII   *Dissolution*

Only by a majority vote of two-thirds or more of the total membership may this organization be dissolved. In case of such dissolution, the members will decide the future of the organizational funds.

♯ 10   Requirements for Kodokan Male Dan Ranks

THE REQUIREMENTS set forth herein are those of Rule No. 16 of the Kodokan Ranking Committee and are the basis of all ranking policies of the Judo Black Belt Federation of the U.S.A. and its member Yudanshakai.

PART I: *Shodan through Rokudan*
The following aspects are to be considered and requirements contained therein before a candidate may be promoted:
1. Character.
    (a) A candidate must have a good moral character.
2. Proficiency in Judo.
    (a) posture, sportsmanship, randori, overall impression.
    (b) technique and kata (consult chart I).
    (c) tournament record and time (chart II).

3. Principles of Judo.
   (a) sound understanding of the principles of Judo as explained in the book "Illustrated Kodokan Judo."
4. Age: minimum age limit. (chart III).

PART II: *Shichidan and Hachidan*
  1. Character: living in accordance with the principles of Judo.
  2. Proficiency in Judo.
     (a) tournament record. (chart IV).
     (b) present day randori. (chart V).
     (c) kata. (chart VI).
  3. Contributions.
     (a) instructional record, spread and promotion of Judo.
     (b) research towards the advancement of Judo.
  4. Time and Age.
     (a) time requirement. (chart VII).
     (b) minimum age requirement. (chart III).

PART III: *Honorary Dan*
Honorary Dan may be presented as recognition of meritorious effort for the cause of Judo. (chart VIII).

CHART I: *Various kata required for each Dan*
Shodan ....Nage no Kata
Nidan ....as above
Sandan ....Nage no Kata and Katame no Kata
Yodan ....as above
Godan ....as above
Rokudan ....Kime no Kata or Goshinjitsu
Shichidan ....Itsutsu no Kata or Ju no Kata
Hachidan ....Koshiki no Kata

CHART II: *Tournament record and time requirements*
Shodan
a. batsugun by defeating 6 Ikkyu consecutively in kohaku contest. No time requirement.
b. 10 points accumulated from contests; no time requirement.
c. 6 points accumulated from contests; 1 year as active ikkyu.
d. 3 points accumulated from contests; 2 years as active ikkyu.
Nidan
a. batsugun by defeating 6 Shodan consecutively in kohaku contest; 6 months required as active Shodan.
b. 10 points accumulated from contests; 1 year as active Shodan.
c. 6 points accumulated from contests; 2 years as active Shodan.
d. 3 points accumulated from contests; 3 years as active Shodan.

Sandan

a. batsugun by defeating 6 Nidan consecutively in kohaku contest; 1 year as active Nidan.
b. 10 points accumulated from contests; 1½ years as active Nidan.
c. 6 points accumulated from contests; 2 years as active Nidan.
d. 3 points accumulated from contests; 3 years as active Nidan.

Yodan

a. batsugun by defeating 6 Sandan consecutively in kohaku contest; 1 year as active Sandan.
b. 10 points accumulated from contests; 2 years as active Sandan.
c. 6 points accumulated from contests; 3 years as active Sandan.
d. 3 points accumulated from contests; 5 years as active Sandan.

Godan

a. batsugun by defeating 6 Yodan consecutively in kohaku contest; 2 years as active Yodan.
b. 10 points accumulated from contests; 3 years as active Yodan.
c. 6 points accumulated from contests; 5 years as active Yodan.
d. 3 points accumulated from contests; 7 years as active Yodan.

Rokudan

a. batsugun by defeating 6 Godan consecutively in kohaku contest; or if exceptional ability shown; 5 years as active Godan.
b. 10 points accumulated from contests; 7 years as active Godan.
c. 6 points accumulated from contests; 9 years as active Godan.
d. 3 points accumulated from contests; 12 years as active Godan.

Supplemental Data

Batsugun (instant promotion) conditions:

a. 5 of the 6 wins must be attained by Ippon and not by Yuseigachi or addition of Waza-ari.
b. defeating 4 opponents a Dan higher merits batsugun.
c. defeating 3 opponents two Dan higher merits batsugun.
d. defeating 10 opponents a Dan lower merits batsugun.
e. defeating 17 opponents two Dan lower merits batsugun.
f. to qualify a batsugun, the kohaku tournament must be a major city, sectional, regional or national tournament recognized by the JBBF or its member Yudanshakai.

Definition of a point:

a. defeating an opponent of the same Dan credits 1 point.
b. defeating an opponent of a Dan higher credits 1.5 points.
c. defeating an opponent of two Dan higher credits 2 points.
d. defeating an opponent a Dan lower credits 0.5 points.
e. defeating an opponent two Dan lower credits 0.3 points.
f. Yuseigachi is to be recognized as a win.
g. a point must be won in a contest officially recognized by the JBBF or its member Yudanshakai.

CHART III: *Minimum Age Limit*

Dan Grade	1	2	3	4	5	6	7	8
Age	15	#	#	20	22	27	33	42

\# in accordance with ability.

CHART IV: *Tournament Record*

"A" rating ....outstanding record as contestant in International or National tournament.

"B" rating ....good record in the above tournaments.

"C" rating ....fair record in the above tournaments and a very good record in minor tournaments.

"D" rating ....participant in above tournaments as well as good record in minor tournaments.

CHART V: *Present Day Randori*

"A" rating ....active randori 6 days a week.

"B" rating ....randori 6 days a week.

"C" rating ....randori at least 20 days a month.

"D" rating ....randori at least 15 days a month.

CHART VI: *Kata*

"A" rating ....performed in International or National tournament and possesses exceptional ability.

"B" rating ....performed in National tournament and possessing good skill.

"C" rating ....performed in National and in minor events.

"D" rating ....performed in minor events.

CHART VII: *Time Requirements for Shichidan.*

"A" rating ....6 years or more.

"B" rating ....9 years or more.

"C" rating ....12 years or more.

"D" rating ....15 years or more.

Time Requirements for Hachidan.

"A" rating ....9 years or more.

"B" rating ....12 years or more.

"C" rating ....15 years or more.

"D" rating ....18 years or more.

Supplemental Data for procedures for Shichidan and Hachidan Promotions.

Class "A" ....candidate must have an "A" rating in three of the requirements including 2 (a) along with "B" ratings in two other requirements.

Class "B" ....candidate must have a "B" rating in 3 other requirements including 2 (a) along with "B" rating in two other requirements.

Class "C" ....candidate must have three "B" ratings and two "C" ratings.
Class "D" ....candidate must have six "C" ratings.
note: uncharted requirements are to be rated carefully by Board of Examiners.

CHART VIII: *Time Chart for Honorary Dan.*
Shodan to Nidan .... 7 years of service.
Nidan to Sandan .... 8 years of service.
Sandan to Yodan .... 9 years of service.
Yodan to Godan ....10 years of service.
Godan to Rokudan ....15 years of service.
Rokudan to Shichidan ....18 years of service.
Shichidan to Hachidan ....21 years of service.
Although a candidate has no tournament record but has been practicing diligently, a year may be deducted from the above chart. Recommendation for promotion may be for one Dan at a time but if there be any special reason, a Dan may be skipped.

#11   Requirements for Kodokan Male Kyu Ranks

THE PRECISE requirements for each Judo rank effective within the U.S.A. are based on Kodokan requirements. These have been strictly enforced by the official national Judo body, the JBBF, via each Kodokan Yudanshakai, and all candidates for ranks are expected to meet these requirements. It is impossible to list each and every specific detail which goes into the determination of each rank level, however, the following data is among the complete information possessed by qualified examiners and should be used as a guide in preparing candidates for examinations.

Rokkyu (6 Kyu): Any person of unquestionable moral character, regardless of age, accepted by a nationally affiliated Judo activity as a student. Must declare intentions to study diligently and should possess motivation for study of Judo.

Gokyu (5 Kyu): Sufficient study of the *Ik-Kyo* (1st Principle of *Go Kyo no Waza*) with the ability to demonstrate these forms to a reasonable degree of skill. Basic *Katame Waza* knowledge of *Osaekomi* and *Shime Waza*. Background and history of development of Kodokan Judo knowledge with the awakening of the Judo spirit. Contest experience on a limited basis. Some knowledge of Judo terminology.

Yonkyu (4 Kyu): Continuation of junior rank qualities with additional knowledge of Judo rationale. A reasonable degree of proficiency with the *Ni-Kyo* (2nd Principle of *Go Kyo no Waza*); contest experience; and continuation of *Katame Waza* ability with use in contest. Use of Judo terminology.

Sankyu (3 Kyu): Continuation of study with ability to demonstrate *San-Kyo* (3rd Principle of *Go Kyo no Waza*). Ability to develop *Nage Waza* on left and right sides per student's choice. Introduction to *Kansetsu Waza* under supervised practice only; additional contesting to point of being a major part of training; *Katame Waza* ability to a point of application with confidence in contest. Should understand Judo rationale to point of being able to discuss or teach junior Judo trainees, but such teaching under supervision of Yudansha. Terminology to a fluent degree.

Nikyu (2 Kyu): Yon-Kyo (4th Principle of *Go Kyo no Waza*) proficiency and continuation of development of favorite technique *(Nage Waza)*; practice of left and right *Nage Waza*. Development of *Katame Waza* so that complete fluency exists in categories of *Osae* and *Shime Waza. Kansetsu Waza* applied in practice under Yudansha supervision. Teaching abilities must begin to develop at this stage and should be encouraged under Yudansha supervision. The spirit of Judo must be developed. Contest successes and extensive contest work. Fluency with Judo terminology. Introduction to *Uke* for formal *Nage* no *Kata*.

Ikkyu (1 Kyu): Continuation of junior rank requirements with practice of *Go Kyo* (5th Principle of *Go Kyo no Waza)* to a reasonable degree of proficiency. *Katame Waza* should include ability to fluently use all categories with *Kansetsu* restricted to practice only as directed by Yudansha. Teaching responsibility must be assumed at this level with complete knowledge of conducting formal class practice. Should be conversant with rationale of Kodokan Judo and have some supervised referee and judgment of match training. Completely conversant with common Judo terminology. Introduction to *Tori* for formal *Nage no Kata*.

SHIAI LINE-UP FORM

WASHINGTON JUDO CLUB

<u>DAN</u> BELT DIVISION

(line up)

<u>ALL</u> TEAM   Date <u>1 September 1957</u>

	Full Name	Rank	Club	Age	Ht.	AAU Number
1.	ANDERSON, John	Nidan	Baltimore			
2.	TAKEMORI, James	Nidan	Washington			
3.						
4.	QUINTON, Ed.	Shodan	Boston			
5.	WATRIN, Tom	Shodan	Boston			
6.	COOK, R.	Shodan	New Brunswick, N. J.			
7.	SALES, S. E.	Shodan	Baltimore			
8.	KNIGHT, R. R.	Shodan	Andrews			
9.	TAKEMORI, Edwin	Shodan	Washington			
10.	TYNER, Richard	Shodan	Washington			
11.	BUSHEY	Shodan	Bolling			
12.	LOMAS, Charlie	Shodan	Washington			
13.						
14.						
15.						

SHIAI RESULTS FORM

SHUFU JUDO YUDANSHAKAI

ADMIN FORM 10: Shiai Results

3, 4, 5, 6 Kyu ___ Belt Division

Date _1 September 1957_

Individual ___ Shiai

Ippon	○
Waza Ari	△
Hikiwake	×
Yuseigachi	Y
Hansokumake	H
Fushen-sho	F

REFEREE _Lomas_ ___ Sho DAN ___ TIME STARTED ___

JUDGES ___ DAN ___ TIME FINISHED ___

___ DAN ___ BOUT TIME LIMIT _3 minutes_

KOHAKU SHIAI ___ POINT SYSTEM _×_ ROUND _1st_ ___

	RED			RESULTS		WHITE		
	Name	Rank	Club			Club	Rank	Name
1.	Cribben	5	Boston	Kesa	○	Wash.	4	Hamlin
2.	Cook	5	New Bruns.	○ Ushirogoshi		Wash.	5	Gunlock
3.	Seidel	6	Balt.	×		Wash.	4	Davis
4.								
5.	Garner	4	ARDC	△ Sasae △ Sasae		Wash.	4	Wheeler
6.	Bonacci	4	Wash.	○ Osoto		Balt.	3	Widdows
7.								
8.	Mendez	3	Balt.	○ Yokoshiho		Boston	3	Oliver
9.	Keaton	3	Balt.	Tateshiho	○	Wash.	3	Bush
10.								
11.								
12.								

CHAMPION ___ 2nd ___ 3rd ___

Glossary

ANZA 安坐 An informal manner of sitting in which the legs are folded and the body rests on the buttocks. Used for long extended periods of sitting or by injured trainees.

ASHIHARAI 足払 A foot or leg technique which employs the sweeping action of the leg to apply the body's power in throwing an opponent.

ASHI WAZA 足技 Category of throwing techniques which employ the foot or leg.

ATO NO SEN 後の先 More commonly referred to as Go no Sen, which see.

AWASE WAZA 合せ技 Complete victory obtained by scoring two different incomplete techniques which are added together for the score.

AYUMI ASHI 歩み足 A method of normal walking movement in which the feet move alternately, one ahead of the other.

BEIKOKU 米国 Referring to the U. S. A.

BUTSUKARI 打つかり Judo training method of repetitively applying form of throwing action to opponent without necessarily completing the technique. (see Uchikomi)

CHIKARA 力 Power or strength. Used to refer to excessive strength employed in Judo techniques.

DAN 段 Degree or grade in reference to the Judo rank system.

DEASHIHARAI 出足払い Advanced Foot Sweep. Throwing technique of the leg category. The first technique in the Go Kyo no Waza.

DERU-PON 出るポン To score a point against your opponent as he comes forward at beginning of bout.

DOJO 道場 Exercise hall or gymnasium for the practice of various martial arts of Japan.

FUSEGI 防ぎ Defense.

FUSEN-SHO 不戦勝 Term used in officiating Judo matches indicating a default match.

GAKE 掛 Hooking action.

GAKU 額 Framed picture or writing.

GARI 刈 Reaping action.

GASSHUKU 合宿 Training camp. Boarding out.

GETA 下駄 A form of wooden shoe which is held on the foot by a cord between the big toe and the second toe.

GODO 剛道 Expression connoting "strength way."

GO KYO NO KAISETSU 五教の解説 The explanation of the Five Principles of Technique, the categorized Judo throwing techniques used as a basis of teaching Kodokan Judo. (see below)

GO KYO NO WAZA 五教の技 The Five Principles of Technique or categorized Judo throwing techniques used as a basis of teaching Kodokan Judo. (see above)

GO NIN GAKE 五人掛 Five man "take-down" or "one against five." A test of skill which pits one Judoka against 5 successive opponents.

GO NO SEN 後の先 A form of competitive initiative by which you start defensive action at the instant the opponent's attack is being made.

309

GOSHINHO 護身法 Methods of self-defense. A prearranged formal exercise at Kodokan. (Woman's Division)

GOSHINJITSU 護身術 Technique of self-defense. A pre-arranged formal exercise at Kodokan. (Men's Division)

GYAKU 逆 Opposite or reverse action. Commonly refers to Kansetsu Waza, which see.

HAIRIKATA 入り方 Method of entry into throwing, grappling, or striking technique.

HANDO NO KUZUSHI 反動の崩し Breaking of opponent's balance by his reaction to a preparatory diversionary attack launched by yourself in the opposite direction to the intended technique.

HANSOKUMAKE 反則負け Violation of rules in Judo contest.

HANEGOSHI 跳腰 Spring Hip. Throwing technique of the waist category. The fifth technique of the third Kyo in the Go Kyo no Waza.

HANTEI 判定 Verbal command used by Referee to signal Judges to indicate their choice of winner of Judo match.

HAPPO NO KUZUSHI 八方の崩し Eight directions of unbalance.

HARAI 払い Sweeping action.

HARAIGOSHI 払腰 Sweeping Loin. A throwing technique of the waist category. The seventh technique of the second Kyo in the Go Kyo no Waza.

HARAITSURIKOMIASHI 払釣込足 Sweeping Drawing Ankle. A throwing technique of the leg category. The sixth technique of the third Kyo in the Go Kyo no Waza.

HENKA 変化 Variation or modification of the basic style.

HIDARI JIGOTAI 左自護体 Left Defensive Posture.

HIDARI SHIZENTAI 左自然体 Left Natural Posture.

HIKIWAKE 引分 A draw in the judgment of a Judo match.

HIZAGURUMA 膝車 Kneel Wheel. A throwing technique of the leg category. The second technique of the First Kyo in the Go Kyo no Waza.

IPPON SEOINAGE 一本背負投 Shoulder throw. A form of throwing technique of the hand category. The eighth technique of the First Kyo in the Go Kyo no Waza.

IPPON SHOBU 一本勝負 Match decided on the basis of one point.

ITAMI WAKE 痛み分け Term used in officiating Judo matches indicating a loss by injury which made it unable for a contestant to continue.

JIGOHONTAI 自護本体 Basic Defensive Posture.

JIKAN 時間 Term used by Referee to indicate "time out."

JOSEKI 上席 Upper place or side in Dojo which in proper Dojo etiquette is reserved for senior Judoka.

JOZA 上座 Upper seat or seat of honor in Dojo which in proper Dojo etiquette is reserved for senior Judoka. A (see Kamiza) substitute term not commonly used.

JU 柔 Japanese ideogram connoting the idea of adaptability, flexibility; suppleness of mind and body. More commonly translated to mean "gentleness."

JUDO 柔道 Usually refers to the system of Jigoro Kano labeled Kodokan Judo which is a system of training mind and body for efficient daily use.

JUDOGI 柔道着 Traditional costume worn by Judo exponents, consisting of jacket, trousers, and belt.

JUDOKA 柔道家 Judo expert. Today commonly connoted to imply any practitioner of Judo.

JUNBI UNDO 準備運動 Exercises of a "warm-up" nature.

JU NIN GAKE 十人掛 Ten man "take-down" or "one against ten." A test of skill which pits one Judoka against 10 successive opponents.

JU NO KATA 柔の形 A prearranged symmetrical exercise called Forms of Gentleness. Depicts principles of Judo as applied to self-defense.

KACHINUKI SHIAI 勝ち抜き試合 A form of Kohaku Shiai (which see) in which the winner continues to compete until drawn out or defeated.

KAIKYU SHIAI 階級試合 A type of contest which pits contestants of like rank together.

KAESHI 返し Overturning or countering of opponent's offensive action.

KAKARIGEIKO 掛り稽古 A training method in Randori to develop endurance which requires the performer to take on consecutive opponents within a time limit.

KAKE 掛 Execution stage of a throwing technique.

KAMIZA 上座 Upper Seat. Seat of honor which in proper Dojo etiquette is reserved for senior Judoka.

KANGEIKO 寒稽古 Special winter training of a vigorous nature for an extended period of consecutive days during the coldest time of the year.

KANSETSU WAZA 関節技 The category of grappling which treats of joint locking or dislocation techniques as applied to the bones and joints of the body.

KATA 形(型) Prearranged, symmetrical formal exercise. Descriptive of various fundamentals. Highly ceremonial.

KATACHI 形 Refers to "form only." Applied in training which requires only basic movement without full effect.

KATAME NO KATA 固めの形 A prearranged symmetrical exercise called Forms of Grappling. Depicts principles of ground techniques.

KATAME WAZA 固め技 Grappling techniques in general.

KEGA 怪我 Injury.

KEIKO 稽古 Practice.

KENSHUSEI 研修生 Research student specially selected for advanced study.

KESAGATAME 袈裟固 In ground techniques, a holding or immobilization technique.

KIAI 気合 A shout or cry used in coordination with a severe exertion to execute a technique. May be used for psychological or physical purposes.

KIHON RENSHU 基本練習 Fundamental practice of basic elements necessary to establish technique.

KODANSHA 高段者 High grade Black Belt holder of Kodokan, 5 Dan or above.

KODOKAN 講道館 Mother school of Judo founded by Jigoro Kano in 1882 in Tokyo.

KOHAKU SHIAI 紅白試合 A form of contest which brings together two teams, one designated "Red" and the other, "White." Identified by a red or by a white ribbon, respectively, worn tied around the belt line of each teammate.

KOHO UKEMI 後方受身 Rear Falling Method using shock dispersion to avoid injury.

KOKORO-E 心得 Attitude of mind in sincere understanding and appreciation of values.

KOSHIKI NO KATA 古式の形 A prearranged symmetrical exercise called Forms of Antique. Depicts principles of Judo.

KOSHINAGE 腰投げ Various types of hip or waist techniques used in throwing.

KOSHIWAZA 腰技 Category of throwing techniques employing principally the waist or hip.

KOSOTOGAKE 小外掛 Minor Outer Hooking. A throwing technique of the leg or foot category. The first technique of the third Kyo of the Go Kyo no Waza.

KOSOTOGARI 小外刈 Minor Outer Reaping. A throwing technique of the leg or foot category. The first technique of the second Kyo in the Go Kyo no Waza.

KOTEN SHIAI 高点試合 A form of competition requiring no teams and useful in individual evaluations.

KOUCHIGARI 小内刈 Minor Inner Reaping. A throwing technique of the leg or foot category. The second technique of the second Kyo in the Go Kyo no Waza.

KO WAZA 小技 Minor or small technique requiring a slight amount of body movement.

KUMIKATA 組み方 Methods of grasping the opponent.

KUZUSHI 崩し State of unbalance from which stability cannot be regained.

KYOSHI NO KAMAE 据姿の構え Kneeling posture.

KYU 級 Ungraded student who has not yet attained Black Belt status. Ranks of "class" rather than "grade." See Mudansha.

MACHI DOJO 町道場 Small independent Dojo outside central school. Private Dojo.

MAITTA 参った Expression used by defeated Judo exponents indicating "I'm beaten." Victor must respect this verbal signal by terminating any offensive action being applied.

MAKIKOMI 巻込み Winding action.

MATE 待て Verbal command used by Referee to indicate no further action permitted by contestants.

MIGI JIGOTAI 右自護体 Right Defensive Posture.

MIGI SHIZENTAI 右自然体 Right Natural Posture.

MO SUKOSHI もう少し Referee term implying "a little more" is necessary to make a score.

MUDANSHA 無段者 Student who is ungraded or has not yet obtained the degree of Black Belt. A Kyu or rank of "class."

NAFUDAKAKE 名札掛け Name board used in Dojo to show names and seniority of members.

NAGE NO KATA 投の形 A prearranged symmetrical exercise called Forms of throwing. Depicts principles of throwing techniques.

NAGE WAZA 投技 Throwing techniques in general.

NE WAZA 寝技 Techniques, both of throwing and grappling, performed from a lying or semi-reclining position.

NIHON SHOBU 二本勝負 Match decided on the basis of two points.

NOGAREKATA 逃れ方 Methods of escape.

OBI 帯 Belt. Refers to part of Judo costume which denotes rank of Judo exponent.

OKURIASHIHARAI 送り足払い Sweeping Ankle. A throwing technique of the leg or foot category. The fifth technique of the second Kyo in the Go Kyo no Waza.

OSAEKOMI 抑え込み Term used by Referee to indicate an immobilization is in effect.

OSAEKOMI TOKETA 抑み込み解けた Referee's term used to indicate the breaking of an immobilization.

OSAEKOMI WAZA 抑え込み技 Category of grappling which treats of holding or immobilizations of the body. Basic category of grappling.

OSOTOGARI 大外刈 Major Outer Reaping. A throwing technique of the leg or foot category. The fifth technique of the first Kyo in the Go Kyo no Waza.

OUCHIGARI 大内刈 Major Inner Reaping. A throwing technique of the leg or foot category. The seventh technique of the first Kyo in the Go Kyo no Waza.

O WAZA 大技 Major or large technique requiring a large movement of the body.

RANDORI 乱取り Method of Judo practice which makes use of "free exercise" in which opponents attack and defend in accordance with specific rules and spirit.

REIGISAHO 礼儀作法 Dojo etiquette or "mat manners."

RENMEI 連盟 Federation.

RENRAKU 連絡 Connecting or combination techniques.

RENRAKU HENKA WAZA 連絡変化技 Connection-Variation techniques.

RENSHU 練習 Practice.

RENZOKU 連続 Continuous techniques.

RITSUREI 立礼 Formal salutation requiring a standing bow or salute.

RYU 流 School.

SANKAKU 三角 Triangle. Used in reference to "figure 4" action of legs to hold opponent.

SASAETSURIKOMIASHI 支釣込足 Propping-drawing Ankle. A throwing technique of the leg or foot category. The third technique of the first Kyo in the Go Kyo no Waza.

SEIRYOKU ZENYO KOKUMIN TAIIKU 精力善用国民体育 A prearranged symmetrical exercise called Forms of National Physical Education. Based on the Principle of Maximum Efficiency.

SEIZA 正座 Kneeling seated posture used in formal Dojo etiquette.

SEN 先 Initiative in applying mental power, technical skill and physical strength to gain advantage over the opponent.

SEN-SEN NO SEN 先先の先 Highest form of initiative by which mental power, technical skill and physical power are applied to gain advantage over the opponent before he can institute an attack.

SEOINAGE 背負い投げ Shoulder throw. A throwing technique of the hand category. The eighth technique of the first Kyo in the Go Kyo no Waza.

SHIAI 試合 Contest. Competitive matches in tournament.

SHIAIJO 試合場 Contest area.

SHIME WAZA 締め技 Category of grappling which treats of choking the neck or body.

SHIMOSEKI 下席 Lower side or place in proper Dojo etiquette at which students assemble.

SHIMOZA 下座 Lower seat in Dojo at which students assemble.

SHINKYU SHIAI 進級試合 A form of Judo promotional contest for Kyu or Mudansha.

SHINTAI 進退 Body movement of a linear variety.

SHISEI 姿勢 Posture or stance.

SHIZENHONTAI 自然本体 Basic Natural Posture of Judo.

SHOCHUGEIKO 暑中稽古 Special summer training of a vigorous nature for an extended period of consecutive days during the hottest time of the year.

SHUMATSU UNDO 終末運動 Exercises used to close or finish the training session. "Cooling-off" exercises.

SOATARI SHIAI 総当り試合 "Round-robin" tournament.

SOKUHO UKEMI 側方受身 Side Falling Method using shock dispersion to avoid injury.

SONOTA その他 Miscellaneous.

SOTAI RENSHU 総体練習 Partner practice. Practice of couples together.

SUKASHI すかし Evasive action applied against opponent's attack.

SUTEGEIKO 捨て稽古 A method of training in throwing by which no regard for the "point" is held.

TACHI WAZA 立ち技 Techniques applied in a standing or upright position.

TAIKO 太鼓 Ceremonial drum used to call training and other sessions to order.

TAIOTOSHI 体落し Body Drop. A throwing technique of the hand category. The sixth technique of the second Kyo in the Go Kyo no Waza.

TAISABAKI 体捌き Body movement of a turning nature.

TAISHO 大将 Team captain.

TAISO 体操 Calisthenics.

TANDOKU RENSHU 単独練習 Solo practice. Practice by oneself.

TANI OTOSHI 谷落し Valley Drop. A throwing technique of the sacrifice category (side). The second technique of the fourth Kyo in the Go Kyo no Waza.

TATAMI 畳 Traditional Japanese rice mats used for various martial arts practice.

TAWARA 俵 A rice bale.

TENTORI SHIAI 点取り試合 A form of competition based on "man to man" or direct elimination procedures.

TE WAZA 手技 Throwing techniques of the hand category in general.

TOKUI WAZA 得意技 Favorite or "pet" technique.

TOMOENAGE 巴投げ High Circle Throw. A throwing technique of the sacrifice category (back). The seventh technique of the third Kyo in the Go Kyo no Waza.

TORI 取り The active partner who performs the technique intended.

TSUBAMEGAESHI 燕返し Swallow (bird) Counter. A counter-throwing technique of the leg or foot category. Not classified in the Go Kyo no Waza.

TSUGI ASHI 継ぎ足 A method of walking in which one foot "follows" the other, never passing it.

TSUKINAMI SHIAI 月次試合 Monthly Dojo contest.

TSUKURI 作り Preparatory action by tori against uke in order to effect a technique. A fitting or blending action induced by tori while uke is in a state of unbalance.

TSURIKOMI 釣込み Lift-pull action applied to opponent to disturb his balance.

TSURIKOMIGOSHI 釣込腰 Lift-pull Loins. A throwing technique of the waist category. The fourth technique of the second Kyo in the Go Kyo no Waza.

UCHIKOMI 打ち込み Judo training method of repetitively applying throwing action to opponent without necessarily completing actual technique. (see Butsukari)

UCHIMATA 内股 Inner Thigh. A throwing technique of the leg or foot category. The eighth technique of the second Kyo in the Go Kyo no Waza.

UKE 受 Passive partner or partner who receives the intended action of the technique employed.

UKEMI 受身 Methods of falling to the ground utilizing shock dispersion to avoid injury.

USHIROGOSHI 後腰 Rear Loins. A throwing technique of the waist category. The fifth technique of the fifth Kyo in the Go Kyo no Waza.

UTSURIGOSHI 移り腰 Changing Hip. A throwing technique of the waist category. The fifth technique of the fourth Kyo in the Go Kyo no Waza.

UWAGI 上着 Jacket

WAZA 技 Technique

WAZA-ARI 技あり A Referee term used to imply that some technique exists (usually 80% or more) but not to the extent of warranting a full point or Ippon. Scores as a half-point.

WAZA ARI AWASETE IPPON 技有り合わせて一本 Verbal command used by Referee to indicate completion of scoring one point by adding incomplete techniques.

YAKUSOKUGEIKO 約束稽古 A training method which is a prearranged practice of free exercise in which partners offer little or no resistance to the attacks of the other.

YOTEN 要点 Key point.

YUDANSHA 有段者 Degree holder or Black Belt. One of Dan rank. Significant of various levels of expert.

YUDANSHAKAI (JUDO) 有段者会 Association of Black Belt holders chartered and recognized as administrators of Judo in the name of the Kodokan.

YUSEIGACHI 優勢勝ち Referee's term implying a victory by superiority. A decision in favor of the contestant displaying the best Judo.

ZANSHIN 漸進 A state of alertness with regard to continuing attack against controlled or defeated opponent if necessary.

ZAREI 座礼 Formal salutation requiring a kneeling bow or salute.

ZA-ZEN 座禅 kneeling motionless in concentrated thought with the object of introspection in search of the truth.

ZEN 禅 The Japanese interpretation of Chinese Buddhism in various forms which is an intricate religious philosophy.

ZENPO KAITEN UKEMI 前方回転受身 Forward tumbling (rolling or somersault) falling method using shock dispersion to avoid injury.

ZENPO UKEMI 前方受身 Forward falling method using shock dispersion injury.

ZUBON ズボン Trousers

Bibliography

Selected Readings

CAPEN, E. K., "The Effect of Systematic Weight Training on Power, Strength, and Endurance," *Research Quarterly,* 21:83, 1950.

CHUI, E., "The Effect of Systematic Weight Training on Athletic Power," *Research Quarterly,* 21:188, 1950.

KARPOVITCH, P. V., "Incidence of Injuries in Weight Lifting," *Journal of Physical Education,* 48:81, 1951.

MASLEY, J. W., "Weight Training in Relation to Strength, Speed, and Coordination," *Research Quarterly,* 24:308–315, 1953.

WILKINS, B. M., "The Effect of Weight Training on Speed of Movement," *Research Quarterly,* 23:361–369, 1952.

ZORBAS, WILLIAM S. and KARPOVITCH, P. V., "The Effect of Weight Lifting Upon the Speed of Muscular Contractions," *Research Quarterly,* 22:148, 1951.

McCLOY, C. H., *"Weight Training for Athletes,"* Strength & Health p. 8 July, 1955.

MURRAY, JIM, *Weight Lifting and Progressive Physical Training,* New York: A. S. Barnes & Company, 1954.

MURRAY, JIM & KARPOVITCH, P. V., *Weight Training in Athletics,* Englewood Cliffs, New Jersey: Prentice-Hall, Inc., 1956.

KARPOVITCH, P. V., *Physiology of Muscular Activity*, Saunders, 5th edition, 1959.

CURETON, T. K., *Physical Fitness of Champion Athletes*, Urbana, University of Illinois Press, 1951, p. 286–313.

KESSLER, H. H., "The Determination of Physical Fitness," *Journal Of the American Medical Association*, 115:1951, (Nov. 9, 1940).

BILL, D. B., "The Economy of Muscular Exercise," *Physiological Reviews*, 16:278, (April, 1936).

DUPAIN, G. Z., "Specific Diets and Athletic Performance," *The Research Quarterly*, 10:33–40, (Dec. 1939).

JONES, HARDIN, "It's the Blood Flow," *Time*, (Oct. 20, 1952)

HOFFMAN, BOB, *Better Athletes Through Weight Training*, York, Pennsylvania, 1960.

HINES, L. E. and PARKER, R. J., "Effect of Ascorbic Acid on Capillary Fragility," *Proc. of the Institute of Medicine of Chicago*, 17:356, 1949.

Index

INCLINE TRAINING, 219

INJURIES: anesthetizing of, 75; minor, 74; causes of, 74; ear, 76; elimination of, 73; excuses and, 74; frequency of, 73; kinds of, 73–76; protectional devices against, 73–76

INOKUMA, ISAO, 14, 23, 26, 74, 85, 116, 140, 146, 153, 176, 189–190, 197, 202, 206, 218, 269

INSTRUCTION, 45–46, 48

INSTRUCTOR (see Instructor Advice)

INSTRUCTOR ADVICE, for class orientation, 49; for class sessions, 49; for competition, 53; for teaching methods, 49; for the Dojo, 53; for the local Yudanshakai, 52–54; for Dojo organization, 53; for procedure, 50; for judging individual's achievement, 52; for student evaluation, 49, 52; for national recognition, 54; for preparing instruction, 50–51; for safety precautions, 53–54; for self evaluation, 49–50, 52; for techniques of instruction, 51–52

INTERNATIONAL JUDO FEDERATION, 100, 285

IOWA STATE UNIVERSTY, 118

IPPON SEOINAGE, 136, 142, 187

IPPON SHOBU, 103

ISHIKAWA, TAKAHIKO, 23, 85, 139–140, 163

ITO, H., 22

ITO, KAZUO, 86

ITO, S., 22

IWATA, H., 24

JAPANESE JUDO CHAMPIONS, attainments of 137–138; beginning age of, 139–143; base of study of, 139–143; intense training of, 46–47, 139–143; average age of, 139–143; job source of, 139–143; ranks of, 139–143; use of weight training by, 140; height and weight of, 139–143; favorite techniques of, 141–142; synthesis of, 142

JBBF (see Judo Black Belt Federation of U.S.A.)

JENSEN, JACKIE, 116

JIGOHONTAI, 77

JIKAN, 294

JOHANSON, INGEMAR, 116

JOHNSON, RAFER, 116

JOINT LOCKING TECHNIQUES, 92, 137

JONES, DR. HARDIN, 121

JONES, STAN, 116

JOSEKI, 65–69

JOZA, 65

JU, 20

JUDGES, 104–113, 293–294

JUDO: age in relation to practice of 71–72; building endurance for, 44–45, 86, 97, 101–103, 117–118, 120–122, 129–130; building speed for, 44–45, 122; building strength for, 44–45, 120–122, 203–221; building techniques for, 44–45; contest emphasis for, 43–44, 97–98; coordination for, 38–40; costume for, 55, 59, 291–292; educational process, 19, 43–44, 99, 125–126, 129; force used in, 38–40; fundamentals in, 76–79; gentleness in, 20–23; improving performance of, 46; international status of, 19, 100; Japanese champions in, 23, 137–143; Japanese terms in, 28; Kodokan emblem uses in, 72; myths about, 20–23; objectives and purposes of, 43–45; physical principle of, 20–23; practice area for, 56–61; programs for training in, 43–53, 125–130; rank attainment in, 49, 52, 54, 289–290; school area for, 56; skill in, 38–40, 44–45; speed in 35, 44–45; strength in, 20–25, 120–122; a study and practice of, 43–44, 46, 48, 50–51, 125–126; supply expenditures for, 53; timing in, 38–40, 89–90; training triad for, 43; weight training and, 115–123

JUDO BLACK BELT FEDERATION OF THE U.S.A., 19, 52, 286

JUDO INSTITUTE OF MARYLAND, 14

JUDO TRAINING PROGRAMS, for beginner, 127; for camping out, 129–130; with endurance emphasis, 129; with grappling emphasis, 128; for heavy training, 126; for minimum time, 127; for pre-arranged form emphasis, 128–129; for throwing emphasis, 127

JUDOGI, 55, 59, 93–94, 298

JUDOKA, 24, 142

JUNBI UNDO, 27, 126, 147–175

JU NIN GAKE, 85

JU NO KATA, 69

KACHINUKI SHIAI, 102–103, 110–113

KAESHI WAZA, 89

KAIKYU SHIAI, 103

KAKARIGEIKO, 86

KAMINAGA, AKIO, 23, 140

KAMIZA, 58, 65–69

KANEMITSU, Y., 24, 77

KANGEIKO, 86

KANO, RISEI, 18

KANO, JIGORO, 18–22, 43–44, 121

KANSETSU WAZA, 92, 137

KARPOVITCH, DR. PETER, 120

KATO, M., 42

KATACHI, 129

KATAME NO KATA, 69, 87–88

KATAME WAZA, 86–92, 128, 137, 177 191–192

KATA, M., 42

KATO, SHUZO, 24

KAWAKAMI, M., 24, 99

KAWAMURA, T., 12 3

KEGA, 73–76

KELLY, JACK JR., 116

KENSHUSEI, 14, 114, 138

KERR, GEORGE, 123, 189

KESAGATAME, 137, 248

KIAI, 40–41

KIHON RENSHU, 76